Praise for *Reading the Psalms Theologically* from scholars and ministry leaders around the world

"This is a volume begging to be written for some time now, for it is an issue
and left vacant even while the Psalms have continued to be a so
itual comfort to many readers. Up to this point, very l
how the five books appearing in the Psalms form an inte
Howard and Schmutzer have brought together their ow
this problem, along with an outstanding group of colleag
understanding on this topic. I commend this book to all wh salms
over the years but have found little help thus far on the sub hat really unifies
the message and theology found in these 150 psalms."

—**WALTER C. KAISER JR., president emeritus, Gordon-Conwell Theological Seminary**

"*Reading the Psalms Theologically* is a gift to the church. Its superb essays mostly treat the psalms as a loaf of bread, not as slices. The contributors share a high view of inspiration, carefully researched their topic, exalt Christ, and argue their thesis cogently, albeit I might not necessarily agree with every single essay in all respects."

—**BRUCE K. WALTKE, professor emeritus, Regent College / Knox Theological Seminary**

"This holistic and theological exploration of Israel's praise and laments will not disappoint. Its penetrating analysis boldly challenges common assumptions while demonstrating the abiding relevance of this ancient material in today's world. Whatever one's interest in the Psalter or biblical theology, this is a volume well worth adding to our library and reading more than just the once."

—**PAUL R. WILLIAMSON, Moore Theological College (Australia)**

"A stimulating collection of relevant research on the Psalter marks this volume. Meticulously researched, globally engaged, and current in scholarship, this volume will provoke, stretch, and challenge. Warmly recommended!"

—**HEATH A. THOMAS, Oklahoma Baptist University**

"Exegetically rigorous, theologically informed, pastorally applied—these essays bring readers up to date with the latest moves in Psalms' scholarship while also demonstrating the potential such work has to open up both individual psalms and the Psalter itself for theological reflection and pastoral application. An essential read for anyone studying the Psalms today."

—**DAVID G. FIRTH, Trinity College Bristol / University of the Free State**

"*Reading the Psalms Theologically* includes a host of solid, theologically rich essays that will stir the soul and supply insight into the Psalter's message and lasting significance. Especially rewarding are those studies that consider the place of the Messiah and the nations in the book and that revel in the Psalter's portrait of divine presence and sovereignty. This collection progresses scholarship and serves the church, and I am delighted these studies are now available."

—**JASON S. DEROUCHIE, Midwestern Baptist Theological Seminary**

"Here is state-of-the-art Psalms scholarship! The scope of this volume is impressive, covering 'macro' questions of Psalter shape, important themes, and 'micro' matters relating to individual psalms. ... The reader should not expect to agree with every thesis but should not fail to be stimulated in essay after essay."

—**JAMES HELY HUTCHINSON, Institut Biblique de Bruxelles**

"A splendid collection of essays by senior, mid-career, and junior scholars from seven different countries. The essays display some of the exciting research currently being done on the Psalter, viewing the psalms from a theological perspective and showcasing quality academic scholarship with relevance to ministers and the life of the church. I highly recommend this superb volume."

—**PAUL R. RAABE, Grand Canyon University**

"This collection of essays, each focused on the formation of psalms and the Psalter, brings together contributors both familiar and new. ... The pitch—for ministers, students and lay leaders—is just right, as the pastoral implications of psalmody are sustained throughout."

—**SUSAN GILLINGHAM, professor emerita, University of Oxford**

"A tremendously helpful volume in understanding contemporary approaches to the book of Psalms. The recognition of a coherent structure and themes to the book of Psalms is one of the most important advances in understanding the book (and individual psalms), but the insights of these explorations have not always been readily accessible to non-scholars. This volume presents the latest developments in psalms study in a way that is accessible for pastors, students, and interested laypeople. ... I highly recommend this book for anyone who wants to better appreciate and more effectively utilize the psalms in growing in their relationship with God."

—**PETER T. VOGT, Bethel Seminary**

"*Reading the Psalms Theologically* presents a collection of scholarly studies that adds a significant, sometimes underappreciated dimension to our understanding of the Psalter—namely, its varied poetically expressed teachings about the great God to whom we pray. ... This team of distinguished scholars has provided us with a cornucopia of resources that will instruct and inspire all lovers of the Psalter. The target readership is specified as 'pastors, students, and well-motivated laypeople.' I wish to add another worthy group to this list: all Scripture translators and consultants throughout the world, who will also profit much from this multifaceted exposition."

—**ERNST R. WENDLAND, Stellenbosch University**

"This sizable collection of essays is theologically robust, interacts with an impressive breadth of past and present research, and tackles challenging hermeneutical questions with aplomb. The essays are exemplary in their careful evaluation of existing consensuses, critical yet irenic engagement with scholars across the globe, and attention to Scripture's coherence and enduring relevance. A collection that should be both read and emulated!"

—**DANIEL TIMMER, Puritan Reformed Theological Seminary / Faculté de théologie évangélique (Montreal)**

"An impressive volume that shines light upon the biblical-theological import of the Psalter's arrangement and its themes. Many readers will be grateful for the chance to get up to speed on scholarship but most of all for the opportunity to savor more theological riches through these careful studies on the Psalms."

—**ANDREW T. ABERNETHY, Wheaton College**

"The editors and their diverse writing team deserve commendation and thanks for producing this volume, which makes an important contribution to our understanding of the Psalter. ... The collection deserves the careful attention of those who love the Psalms and are committed to proclaiming them to the church."

—**ROBERT B. CHISHOLM, JR., Dallas Theological Seminary**

"Howard and Schmutzer have brought together an impressive list of contributors to address the need for genuine theological readings of the Psalter. They have left us in their debt by defending and illustrating a thoroughly canonical and mostly synchronic approach to the Psalms. Each contributor approaches and interprets the text in a way that has been missing in many circles and will be a great benefit for every reader of the Psalms as Scripture."

—**BILL T. ARNOLD, Asbury Theological Seminary**

"The book convincingly upholds the view that the Psalter should be read as a coherent and unified book ... without losing sight of the unique contribution of each individual psalm. ... Seasoned scholars as well as committed readers of the Psalms will find this book intellectually stimulating and spiritually rewarding, yet full of insights and encouragement for the Christian life."

—**YACOUBA SANON, Alliance Theological Seminary, Côte d'Ivoire**

"The editors should be congratulated with yet another academic contribution to psalms research. This book belongs to the study room, university library, classroom, and research desk of all theological scholars and students."

—**DIRK J. HUMAN, University of Pretoria**

"Howard and Schmutzer have teamed up again to provide us with a rich volume that not only brings us up to date with recent trends in reading the Psalter as a book but also gives extensive attention to pressing issues such as suffering, lament, the nations, and God's nature and character. Everyone from professors and theological students to pastors, teachers, and those who simply love the Psalms will find this book to be a great help."

—**KEVIN CHEN, Christian Witness Theological Seminary**

"*Reading the Psalms Theologically* ranges widely across the Psalter in perceptive ways that will stimulate scholarship and faith. The contributors show us how to grasp firmly both the 'forest' of the whole Psalter's structure as well as the 'trees' of individual psalms, units, and themes. What is more, each essay comes from the perspective of committed Christian faith, which will awaken a greater appetite for the marvelous God of the Psalms."

—**JERRY HWANG, Singapore Bible College**

"While the Psalms deserve careful academic study, such an approach cannot plumb the depth and breadth of human experiences and emotions that prompted their writing and that are touched by their reading. This is literature to be lived in order to be learned, so a purposefully theological approach such as is presented here—in contrast to a strictly analytical one—is totally appropriate. The wide representation of gender, denomination, and theological background of the contributors is to be lauded, as is the range of topics within Psalms studies."

—DAVID W. BAKER, Ashland Theological Seminary

"With essays that dig deeply into the shape, metaphors, themes, and intertextuality of the Psalter, this book is an important contribution to Psalms scholarship that will be felt for years to come. Personally, it will be an invaluable resource in my Psalms classes, helping us to understand how the theology of Israel's ancient worshiping community has and should inform our theology as Christians."

—ELIZABETH H. P. BACKFISH, William Jessup University

"In recent decades, studies of the book of Psalms have taken on an integrative emphasis: viewing individual psalms in their own right and also as part of a coherent whole. This facilitates a biblical theological approach to the book. This volume, written from a conservative evangelical perspective, and including contributions from leading scholars, is a useful and helpful addition to that biblical theological approach. Articles are well-researched and offer insightful and stimulating discussion of the structure of the Psalter and possible overarching theological emphases, of key theological themes within the book, and also of the theological significance of individual psalms within the Psalter and within their wider Old and New Testament context."

—ROBIN ROUTLEDGE, Mattersey Hall (England)

"*Reading the Psalms Theologically* presents a multifaceted view of the theology of the book of Psalms, ranging from the metanarrative of the book to treatments of individual psalms and groups of psalms. The volume will prove to be especially useful to masters and doctoral students and to pastors and laypersons who are serious students of the Psalter."

—NANCY L. DECLAISSÉ-WALFORD, professor emerita, Mercer University School of Theology

"Librarians, scholars, advanced students of the Psalms, and those interested in the connection of the Psalms to the life of the church and its ministry, will find much help in this collection of essays. Congratulations to the contributors, editors, and publishers for giving us all such a fine volume!"

—W. H. BELLINGER, JR., professor emeritus, Baylor University

"The psalms not only give voice to the joys and sorrows of human experience, they provide instruction on a vast array of theological issues. *Reading the Psalms Theologically* guides pastors and scholars in exploring the Psalter's expansive landscape. ... I heartily recommend this volume for anyone desiring a close examination of some of the most significant theological topics in the psalms."

—JIM JORDAN, Training Leaders International

"Recent study of the Psalter has increasingly highlighted the design of this biblical book, seeing in its present shape a coherent theological message. This volume not only reviews this recent trend, but advances it, providing key trajectories that will surely impact the interpretation and appropriation of the Psalter for years to come."

—MARK J. BODA, McMaster Divinity College

"The book of Psalms is the doxological heart of the Christian Bible, and the contributors to this volume have written faithfully in light of this fundamental conviction. Their approach is canonical, redemptive-historical, biblical-theological, practical, and pastoral. ... There are many treasures to be mined from the essays contained in this book."

—MILES V. VAN PELT, Reformed Theological Seminary (Jackson)

"*Reading the Psalms Theologically* offers a rich foray into contemporary psalms scholarship, inviting readers to consider new proposals concerning the shape and shaping of the Psalter while also giving robust attention to the central theological claims that appear throughout the book. The editors and contributors are to be congratulated for the careful scholarship reflected in these accessible and learned essays."

—W. DENNIS TUCKER, George W. Truett Theological Seminary

"I commend this volume to Psalms scholars, and academics and ministers with a passion for reading and engaging with theological readings of the Bible."

—JOHN A. COOK, Asbury Theological Seminary

"The latest on reading the Psalms canonically. Examples of doing biblical theology on the Psalms. Pastoral reflections on the book of Psalms. *Reading the Psalms Theologically* has all three. ... This book provides an example of what it means to read and interpret the psalms theologically, scholarly, and pastorally."

—FEDERICO G. VILLANUEVA, Langham Partnership

"An engaging collection of essays on wide-ranging subjects that orient readers in current trends in Psalms study and provide an entrée into the theology of the Psalter as a whole. ... This volume offers a wealth of stimulating studies and keen insights that will whet the reader's appetite to delve ever deeper into the Psalter's theology and witness to Christ."

—ADAM HENSLEY, Australian Lutheran College, University of Divinity

"*Reading the Psalms Theologically* rests on the conviction that [the psalms] form as a coherent whole. Anyone who has prayed the psalms sequentially over any length of time—like the monastics, of course—will have intuited this to some extent. But what Howard and Schmutzer provide through this fine collection of essays is a theological, not to mention canonical, articulation of that intuition. Themes emerge in the Psalter that are rich in meaning and spiritual intent. ... What this book provides, without ever reneging on scholarly integrity, is an unmistakably dominical rendering of the Psalter. As you read in these pages about the paradox of suffering, messianic promise, as well as eschatological hope for the nations—themes that recur through all 150 psalms—you too may find your heart burning within you."

—IAN STACKHOUSE, senior pastor, Guildford Baptist Church (United Kingdom)

"It is encouraging to see the interest that the book of Psalms has had in the last twenty years, and this book should encourage the study of the book of Psalms."

—WILLEM A. VANGEMEREN, professor emeritus, Trinity Evangelical Divinity School

"For the past four decades, interest in the literary and theological shape of the Psalter has dominated Psalms research. This volume insightfully summarizes and analyzes this scholarship and offers fresh perspectives from some of the leading scholars in the field. The introductory essay by David Howard and Michael Snearly alone is worth the cost of the book."

—JEROME F. D. CREACH, Pittsburgh Theological Seminary

"You will enjoy and benefit from reading *Reading the Psalms Theologically*, whether you are new to the study of Psalms as a canonical whole or a seasoned scholar. A good range of articles from a good range of contributors makes this volume a valuable resource."

—MARK D. FUTATO, SR., Reformed Theological Seminary (Orlando)

"Those who long to read the book of Psalms as a book—reading individual psalms in their literary context and then enriching their theology through reading psalms together in a manner that is appropriate rather than naïve—such readers will find much help in [this volume]."

—JOHN C. BECKMAN, Bethlehem College and Seminary

"This is a good resource for any pastoral ministry providing not just sermon material but also valuable insights into dealing with the sort of everyday issues that both the readers of the Psalms and people today face. Students will find it a helpful foundation for further study. Motivated lay people will discover new ways to understand the development and message of the Psalter in a way that looks back on Israel's history and forward to the New Testament. A wide range of scholarly expertise is represented, but the contributors share the conviction that the book of Psalms is not simply a random collection of Hebrew poetic texts but an organized book with overarching themes and theological instruction that is still relevant."

—JAMES KEOWN, adjunct faculty, Union Theological College Belfast

"*Reading the Psalms Theologically* takes a refreshingly deep dive into the Psalter. Such study, as Howard and Schmutzer note, highlights the theological patterns and perennial applicability of the Psalms to the lives of God's people. This volume's rigor and depth provide pastors with essential insights for preaching, teaching, and counseling."

—CHRIS CASTALDO, lead pastor, New Covenant Church (Naperville, Illinois)

""This volume has much to offer to expositors of Scripture for preaching and teaching. Moreover, the authors have a high regard for Scripture as the authoritative word of God, which sings through every chapter in the collection. The book is intellectually enriching as it is pastorally faithful."

—JOSHUA M. PHILPOT, pastor for worship and administration, Founders Baptist Church, Spring, Texas

READING *the* PSALMS THEOLOGICALLY

READING *the* PSALMS THEOLOGICALLY

EDITED BY

DAVID M. HOWARD JR.

ANDREW J. SCHMUTZER

STUDIES IN SCRIPTURE & BIBLICAL THEOLOGY

Reading the Psalms Theologically
Studies in Scripture and Biblical Theology

Lexham Academic, an imprint of Lexham Press
1313 Commercial St., Bellingham, WA 98225
LexhamPress.com

Print ISBN 9781683596523
Digital ISBN 9781683596530
Library of Congress Control Number 2022947472

Lexham Editorial: Derek R. Brown, Allisyn Ma, David Bomar, Allie Boman
Cover Design: Brittany Schrock
Typesetting: Mandi Newell

To Walter C. Kaiser Jr. and Bruce K. Waltke
Wise, godly, and brilliant men,
each a mentor, colleague, and friend.

—David Howard

To Robert B. Chisholm Jr. and Richard E. Averbeck
Creative and dedicated Hebrew teachers,
faithfully "declaring His power to the next generation."

—Andrew Schmutzer

Contents

Abbreviations

AB	Anchor Bible
ABD	*Anchor Bible Dictionary*
AcBib	Academia Biblica
ACCS	Ancient Christian Commentary on Scripture
AcT	*Acta Theologica*
AIL	Ancient Israel and Its Literature
ANEM	Ancient Near East Monographs
ANF	*Ante-Nicene Fathers*
AOTC	Abingdon Old Testament Commentaries
BBB	Bonner biblische Beiträge
BBR	*Bulletin for Biblical Research*
BCOTWP	Baker Commentary on the Old Testament Wisdom and Psalms
BECNT	Baker Exegetical Commentary on the New Testament
BHS	*Biblia Hebraica Stuttgartensia*
Bib	*Biblica*
BZAW	Beihefte zur Zeitschrift für die alttestamentliche Wissenschaft
CBQ	*Catholic Biblical Quarterly*
CBQMS	Catholic Biblical Quarterly Monograph Series
CC	Continental Commentary
ChrLit	*Christianity and Literature*
CTQ	*Concordia Theological Quarterly*
CurBR	*Currents in Biblical Research*
DDD	*Dictionary of Deities and Demons in the Bible*
ECC	Eerdmans Critical Commentary
ET	English Translation
FAT	Forschungen zum Alten Testament
FRLANT	Forschungen zur Religion und Literatur des Alten und Neuen Testaments

HALOT	*The Hebrew and Aramaic Lexicon of the Old Testament*
HBM	Hebrew Bible Monographs
HBT	*Horizons in Biblical Theology*
HS	*Hebrew Studies*
HSM	Harvard Semitic Monographs
HTR	*Harvard Theological Review*
HUCA	*Hebrew Union College Annual*
IBS	*Irish Biblical Studies*
ICC	International Critical Commentary
JBL	*Journal of Biblical Literature*
JETS	*Journal of the Evangelical Theological Society*
JNSL	*Journal of Northwest Semitic Languages*
JQR	*Jewish Quarterly Review*
JSNT	*Journal for the Study of the New Testament*
JSOT	*Journal for the Study of the Old Testament*
JSOTSup	Journal for the Study of the Old Testament Supplement Series
JSS	*Journal of Semitic Studies*
KHC	Kurzer Hand-Commentar zum Alten Testament
LHBOTS	The Library of Hebrew Bible/Old Testament Studies
LXX	Septuagint
MT	Masoretic Text
NAC	New American Commentary
NIBCOT	New International Biblical Commentary on the Old Testament
NICNT	New International Commentary on the New Testament
NICOT	New International Commentary on the Old Testament
NIDOTTE	*New International Dictionary of Old Testament Theology and Exegesis*
NIVAC	New International Version Application Commentary
OBO	Orbis Biblicus et Orientalis
ÖBS	Österreichische biblische Studien
OBT	Overtures to Biblical Theology
OTE	*Old Testament Essays*
OTL	Old Testament Library
OTS	Old Testament Studies
PBM	Paternoster Biblical Monographs
Presb	*Presbyterion*
PRSt	*Perspectives in Religious Studies*

RB	*Revue biblique*
RBL	*Review of Biblical Literature*
RevExp	*Review and Expositor*
SBB	Stuttgarter biblische Beiträge
SBL	Society of Biblical Literature
SBLDS	Society of Biblical Literature Dissertation Series
SCS	Septuagint and Cognate Studies
SEÅ	*Svensk exegetisk årsbok*
SJOT	*Scandinavian Journal of the Old Testament*
StBibLit	Studies in Biblical Literature
STDJ	Studies on the Texts of the Desert of Judah
StudBib	*Studia Biblica*
SubBi	Subsidia Biblica
SVT	Supplements to Vestus Testamentum
TDOT	*Theological Dictionary of the Old Testament*
TJ	*Trinity Journal*
TOTC	Tyndale Old Testament Commentaries
TynBul	*Tyndale Bulletin*
VT	*Vestus Testamentum*
VTSup	Supplements to Vestus Testamentum
WBC	Word Biblical Commentary
WTJ	*Westminster Theological Journal*
WUNT	Wissenschaftliche Untersuchungen zum Neuen Testament
ZAW	*Zeitschrift für die alttestamentliche Wissenschaft*

Preface

Despite the never-ending stream of books on the Psalter, there is still a need for strong theological studies of the Psalms. Simple word studies or witty sermons are popular in many circles. Yet there is a growing hunger for theological studies, especially rich integrative forays into these ancient Hebrew poems.

The vision for this project grew out of a passion for a more biblical-theological reading of the Psalms, yet an approach that was broadly integrative. We are interested in a foundational theological method that respects etymology, a sensitivity to literary techniques, a curiosity for Israelite faith, and a willingness to explore pastoral concerns. We want to dig into the whole loaf rather than just a slice of the Psalter.

A core value of theological analysis is its applicability to contemporary issues in life, be they famines, pandemics, social unrest, creation care, crises of faith, oppressed people, or the persecution of the saints—hardly foreign issues in the Psalms! Clearly, the Psalter is still relevant. Esteem for the Psalms also works from the opposite direction, coming from suffering itself. The life of Claus Westermann (1909–2000) holds a gritty story that illustrates this well. Living in Germany during Hitler's rise to power, and the outbreak of World War II, Westermann served as a translator on the Russian front. Later taken prisoner in a Russian prisoner-of-war camp, he wrote,

> There were times when you could not understand God anymore. You had to speak against God. Then we saw that this was what really happens in the Psalms. ... In Russian prison camp one time we stood in a circle to have a worship service. One of us was asked to pray. He read Psalm 103. We were standing with our heads bowed, stooped over. But afterward we thought, "That's not the way to praise God? Such a psalm has to be spoken with joy, your head raised, your body erect!"

> In that experience we learned the difference between real praise and our notion of prayer. Then we began my dissertation, writing on a little board, sometimes trading bread for paper. It was then that we discovered that the psalms of the Old Testament really come out of human experience.[1]

This helps explain why Westermann believed experience and exegesis must be connected. It also explains the topic of his dissertation, "The Praise of God in the Psalms" (Zurich, 1949). Wanting to help the laity understand the Scriptures, Westermann later wrote, "These psalms were actually supposed to express the varied suffering of many dissimilar people. We ought never therefore recognize only a single individual behind one of these psalms but always a long succession of people who have prayed."[2] The Psalms not only capture such pathos, but they also help redeem our own stories. Our lives find a ready and transforming home in the Psalter.

This volume follows on our previous volume, *The Psalms: Language for All Seasons of the Soul* (Chicago: Moody, 2013). In this volume, we have chosen contributors with a commitment to write with a biblical-theological perspective and an eye to ministers and the life of the church. Among our nineteen contributors, there are senior, midcareer, and junior scholars from seven different countries represented. Writing and compiling this text during the Covid-19 pandemic was not easy. We thank our contributors for pressing through this obstacle and bringing first-rate scholarship to the book.

The volume begins with an essay surveying recent currents in canonical/editorial criticism (i.e., holistic readings of the Psalter). Five essays follow that show this method at work. Following this are five essays that explore themes in lament and suffering. Then, three essays investigate topics related to the nations and the gods. Finally, four essays explore divine presence and sovereignty. We hope these eighteen essays will make a significant contribution to Lexham's Studies in Scripture and Biblical Theology (SSBT) series. We are very thankful that Lexham chose to work with us, seeing the

1. Comments by Claus Westermann at the *Sprunt Lectures* (Union Theological Seminary in Virginia, February 1, 1977). Existentially powerful in Westermann's story, Psalm 103 contains the words, "The Lord works righteousness and justice for all the oppressed. … He remembers that we are dust" (Ps 103:6, 14b NIV).

2. Claus Westermann, *Handbook to the Old Testament*, trans. Robert H. Boyd (Minneapolis: Augsburg, 1967), 218.

project through to the end, with special thanks to Derek Brown, the project's editor, and his team.

It is our sincere desire that readers of all stations will find their faith renewed and theology enriched by the wisdom and love of the Psalms in the studies offered here.

David M. Howard Jr. and Andrew J. Schmutzer
Fourth Week of Easter, 2021

1

Reading the Psalter as a Unified Book: Recent Trends

David M. Howard Jr. and Michael K. Snearly

In this essay, we survey developments in Psalms studies in the area of the "shape and shaping" of the book of Psalms, beginning with the groundbreaking work of Gerald Wilson in 1985, though our major focus is works since 2000. We trace the two major trajectories of interpretation, one that sees primarily a "wisdom" or "democratizing" focus in the book's final form and one that sees primarily a "royal" or "messianic" focus. We then deal with the "canonical" question as it relates to Qumran, review various skeptics' concerns, and address some hermeneutical questions arising from holistic readings of the book of Psalms. We conclude by showing some of the benefits of such readings.

Previously, David Howard has published state-of-the-field surveys of Psalms studies focusing on the period since 1970.[1] Since then, several other surveys have appeared, the best of which are by Kenneth Kuntz, many of the essays in *The Oxford Handbook of the Psalms*, and Beat Weber's extensive bibliography.[2]

---

1. David M. Howard Jr., "Recent Trends in Psalms Study," in *The Face of Old Testament Studies: A Survey of Contemporary Approaches*, ed. D. W. Baker and B. T. Arnold (Grand Rapids: Baker Academic, 1999), 329–68; David M. Howard Jr., "The Psalms and Current Study," in *Interpreting the Psalms: Issues and Approaches*, ed. D. Firth and P. Johnston (Downers Grove, IL: InterVarsity, 2005), 23–40.

2. J. Kenneth Kuntz, "Continuing the Engagement: Psalms Research Since the Early 1990s," *CurBR* 10 (2012): 321–78; William P. Brown, ed., *The Oxford Handbook of the Psalms* (Oxford: Oxford University Press, 2014); Beat Weber, "BiblioPss1990ff.: Bibliography of Psalms

In the present essay, however, we survey the narrower question of the "shape and shaping" of the Psalter, which has been the most active avenue of research in the past several decades.[3] This approach reads individual psalms as independent texts, but it also proceeds to interpret them in light of surrounding psalms, whether consecutive or parts of smaller or larger collections. Ultimately, the approach attempts to discern the Psalter's overall, unified message. This has significant implications for our reading of the book of Psalms, which we will try to elucidate in our conclusion. Our focus here will primarily be on works since 2000.

1985–2000

The publication in 1985 of Gerald Wilson's *The Editing of the Hebrew Psalter* launched this new avenue of research.[4] Although there was a long history of similar approaches before Wilson, none were as ambitious and systematic as Wilson's.[5] In his work, Wilson laid out a careful methodological foundation for examining a collection of psalms as a "book," in that he traced other examples of hymnic collections from the ancient Near East: the Sumerian Temple Hymn Collection and Catalogues of Hymnic Incipits as well as the Qumran Psalms manuscripts. He then proceeded to analyze the biblical Psalter as a unified "book," with running themes; he paid special attention to patterns in the superscriptions and other indicators of editorial shaping. He saw Psalm 1 as the introduction to the book and Psalms 146–150 as its conclusion. Early on, the royal figure of "David"[6] predominates, whereas

---

and the Psalter since 1990," Update 67 (V.2022): https://www.academia.edu/5910732/BiblioPss1990ff_Bibliography_of_Psalms_and_the_Psalter_since_1990.

3. For surveys since 2000, see Marvin E. Tate, "Rethinking the Nature of the Psalter," in *Psalms 1–50*, ed. P. C. Craigie, WBC 19, rev. ed. (Nashville: Nelson, 2004), 438–72; Nancy L. deClaissé-Walford, ed., *The Shape and Shaping of the Book of Psalms: The Current State of Scholarship*, AIL 20 (Atlanta: Society of Biblical Literature, 2014); Brown, *Oxford Handbook of the Psalms*; Adam D. Hensley, *Covenant Relationships and the Editing of the Hebrew Psalter*, LHBOTS 666 (New York: T&T Clark, 2018), 6–34; and Gert T. M. Prinsloo, "Reading the Masoretic Psalter as a Book: Editorial Trends and Redactional Trajectories," *CurBR* 19 (2021): 145–77.

4. Gerald Henry Wilson, *The Editing of the Hebrew Psalter*, SBLDS 76 (Chico, CA: Scholars Press, 1985).

5. A very useful historical review of rabbinical and precritical scholarship is found in David C. Mitchell, *The Message of the Psalter: An Eschatological Programme in the Book of Psalms*, JSOTSup 252 (Sheffield: Sheffield Academic, 1997), 15–65; see now also Steffen Jenkins, "The Antiquity of Psalter Shape Efforts," *TynBul* 71 (2020), 161–80.

6. When we refer to "David" (in quotes) in this essay, we mean any of the following at different times: (1) the historical David (who we believe was a real historical figure), (2) any of the Davidic successor kings, (3) "David" as a symbol of the Davidic covenant and its continuing

after Psalm 89 (the end of Book III), the focus on the royal "David" recedes, replaced by a focus on Yahweh's kingship and "David" the weak, humble "Everyman." So, in the end, the Psalter's message is that all individuals are called to "dependence on YHWH" and "obedience to his Law."[7]

Wilson's work was the catalyst for understanding the Psalter not simply as a random collection of individual psalms but as a unified collection with overarching theme(s). Since then, Psalms scholars have devoted much attention to such an approach. Significant works in English before 2000 include the programmatic essays in Clinton McCann's *The Shape and Shaping of the Psalter* and books by Jerome Creach, Nancy deClaissé-Walford, David Mitchell, and David Howard.[8] These all tended to focus synchronically on the Psalter's final form. In Europe, especially Germany, attention was also being given to the Psalter's shaping, but the focus was more diachronic, concentrating on the history of proposed redactions before the final form. Significant works from this period include books by Matthias Millard, Klaus Koenen, and Gunild Brunert, and works of Erich Zenger.[9]

---

promises, (4) "David" as a literary figure within the psalms or their superscriptions, or (5) this literary "David" as an organizing figure in smaller collections of the Psalter's final form.

7. Wilson, *Editing*, 227. In an important early essay building upon Wilson's work, Walter Brueggemann argued that Psalms 1 and 150 open and close the Psalter by emphasizing simple obedience and praise, respectively. In between, however, the very real struggles of life are indicated by the laments and even the hymns (typified by Pss 25 and 103, respectively). He argued that a critical turning point in the Psalter is found at Psalm 73, which encompasses both suffering and hope. Thus, the pure, unmitigated praise urged at the end of the Psalter (Ps 150) is now informed by individuals' and communities' struggles and experiences of God's covenantal love (*hesed*). See Brueggemann, "Bounded by Obedience and Praise: The Psalms as Canon," *JSOT* 50 (1991): 63–92.

8. J. Clinton McCann Jr., ed., *The Shape and Shaping of the Psalter*, JSOTSup 159 (Sheffield: JSOT Press, 1993); Jerome F. Creach, *The Choice of Yahweh as Refuge in the Editing of the Psalter*, JSOTSup 217 (Sheffield: Sheffield Academic, 1996); Nancy L. deClaissé-Walford, *Reading from the Beginning: The Shaping of the Hebrew Psalter* (Macon, GA: Mercer University Press, 1997); Mitchell, *Message of the Psalter*; David M. Howard Jr., *The Structure of Psalms 93–100*, Biblical and Judaic Studies 5 (Winona Lake, IN: Eisenbrauns, 1997). These (and Wilson's work) are all reviewed in Howard, "Recent Trends," 332–42.

9. Matthias Millard, *Die Komposition des Psalters. Ein formgeschichtlicher Ansatz*, FAT 9 (Tübingen: Mohr Siebeck, 1994); Klaus Koenen, *Jahwe wird kommen, zu herrschen über die Erde: Ps 90–110 als Komposition*, BBB 101 (Weinheim: Beltz Athenäum, 1995); Gunild Brunert, *Psalm 102 im Kontext des Vierten Psalmenbuches*, SBB 30 (Stuttgart: Katholisches Bibelwerk, 1996). These are also reviewed in Howard, "Recent Trends," 332–42. For Zenger, see discussion below and corresponding notes.

2000–2022

Introduction

The trickle of books and essays launched by Wilson's work has turned into a torrent since 2000. This is now the dominant subject of research in Psalms studies (though other avenues continue to flourish as well). Hundreds of essays and articles, and dozens of books and dissertations, have been devoted to studying the "shape and shaping" of the Psalter. Two significant collections of essays in the 2000s, edited by Peter Flint and Patrick Miller (*The Book of Psalms: Composition and Reception*)[10] and Erich Zenger (*The Composition of the Book of Psalms*),[11] illustrate this: the former consists of twenty-eight essays, with at least seven on the topic of "The Psalter as Book," while the latter—only five years later—consists of forty-five essays, well over half on the same topic, broadly speaking. A new term, "editorial criticism," has even come into use.[12]

Most scholars have followed Wilson in his basic analysis of the Psalter's main structures and trajectories, with agreement that it should be read as a true "book" with a literary context—that is, that adjoining psalms correspond to one another, that smaller collections within the Psalter are meaningful parts of the larger structure, and that a storyline unfolds throughout the book.

Where agreement begins to break down, however, concerns the nature of that storyline, and it centers around the role of "David." For Wilson and most who have followed him, the Psalter came together in two stages: first, Psalms 1–89 and then Psalms 90–150. Psalm 1 functions as the introduction to the entire Psalter, emphasizing wisdom and Torah. Psalm 89 is pivotal, in that here the Davidic covenant is viewed as "broken, failed."[13] The rest of the Psalter attempts to deal with this "failure," focusing on Yahweh's (not David's) eternal kingship and the importance of Torah obedience. Wilson saw a "final wisdom frame" that "had the last word" over an earlier "royal

10. Peter W. Flint and Patrick D. Miller Jr., eds., *The Book of Psalms: Composition and Reception*, SVT 99 (Leiden: Brill, 2005).

11. Erich Zenger, ed., *The Composition of the Book of Psalms*, Bibliotheca, Ephemeridum Theologicarum Louvaniensium 238 (Leuven: Peeters, 2010).

12. Jamie A. Grant, "Editorial Criticism," in *Dictionary of the Old Testament: Wisdom, Poetry & Writings*, ed. Tremper Longman and Peter Enns (Downers Grove, IL: InterVarsity, 2008), 149–56.

13. Wilson, *Editing*, 213.

covenant frame" that had emphasized the (failed) Davidic covenant.[14] We might call this a "wisdom" or "democratizing" perspective.

Wilson's analysis has set the agenda for further discussions of the Psalter's final shape and message; the book-length treatments of the entire Psalter by Millard, Creach, and deClaissé-Walford mentioned above tend to follow Wilson in this understanding, as have many of the works since 2000 (see below). (We should note that Wilson, in two final essays before his death in 2005, moderated his position somewhat, allowing for the importance of Ps 2 as a companion psalm of some sort to Ps 1, for example, and thus allowing for some sort of a "messianic" understanding in the Psalter.[15])

However, a growing number of studies have pushed back against the idea of a "failed" Davidic covenant and have emphasized instead the persistence of the figure of "David" through to the very end of the book, including a vision for a future "David" (or "Messiah"). For these scholars, Psalms 1 and 2 function *together* as the Psalter's introduction, emphasizing wisdom and Torah obedience (Ps 1) and Yahweh's (the Divine King's) decree establishing the anointed Davidic king (*mashiach*, "messiah") on Mount Zion (Ps 2). "David" returns as an important figure after Psalm 89, especially in Psalms 101, 110, 132, 138–145. We might call this a "royal" or "messianic" perspective, and this would bring the Psalter's message into line with much of the rest of the Hebrew Bible (and of the New Testament). Before 2000, David Mitchell's view was the most prominent treatment in this regard.[16]

We turn now to trace studies in both of these directions.[17]

Wisdom/Democratizing Approaches

Following Wilson's lead, many scholars argue that all the roles, actions, and functions attributed to the royal figure in the Psalms ultimately are applied

14. Gerald H. Wilson, "Shaping the Psalter: A Consideration of Editorial Linkage in the Book of Psalms," in *Shape and Shaping*, ed. McCann, 72–92.

15. Gerald H. Wilson, "King, Messiah, and the Reign of God: Revisiting the Royal Psalms and the Shape of the Psalter," in Flint and Miller, eds., *Book of Psalms*, 391–406; Gerald H. Wilson, "The Structure of the Psalter," in Firth and Johnston, eds., *Interpreting the Psalms*, 229–46.

16. Mitchell, *Message of the Psalter* (reviewed briefly below).

17. John Crutchfield has argued that studies from these two perspectives have tended to be mutually exclusive: John C. Crutchfield, "The Redactional Agenda of the Book of Psalms," *HUCA* 74 (2003): 21–47. We do not claim this. We note, for example, that studies emphasizing the royal/messianic perspective often note the central role that wisdom and Torah were to play in the life of the king. In addition, worship (a third overarching theme, according to Crutchfield) includes psalms from both perspectives. Crutchfield does make a contribution by explicitly pointing out these overlaps, which often are ignored.

to the people of God at large. God's kingdom will be ushered in by his people, not by a single, specific person (Messiah). Such a wisdom or democratizing perspective is signaled at the outset by the wisdom in Psalm 1 and at the end by the kingship of Yahweh in Psalm 145. The "David" found in the latter parts of the Psalter (especially Pss 138–144) is seen as weak, dependent on Yahweh the Great King, and his future is nonexistent or else absorbed into Yahweh's kingship.

Erich Zenger has been one of the most influential scholars exploring the shaping and message of the Psalter in numerous essays and commentaries.[18] He sees it as a well-ordered and well-planned collection in its final form. In a final essay before his death, he surveys the literature and lays out the case for interpreting both individual psalms (*Psalmenexegese*) as well as the larger book of Psalms (*Psalterexegese*).[19] For Zenger, the Psalter did not have a liturgical or religious *Sitz im Leben* originally, but it was intended to function as a "literary sanctuary" of sorts (*Heiligtum*), where the one praying enters into Israel's liturgy by means of his prayer for the deliverance of Israel and the world, and Yahweh's kingship over both of these is exalted.[20] In the end, the Davidic figure is democratized as "Everyman."[21]

Egbert Ballhorn, a student of Hossfeld, argues that the end of the Psalter witnesses to the democratization of the Davidic promises.[22] He sees an inextricable relationship between Books IV and V such that they cannot and should not be separated with respect to their composition and message. He connects Psalms 105–107 together as a unit and argues that they link the two books (IV and V) together rather than separate them. By the end of the book, then, "David" is no longer a key figure in the Psalms.

---

18. Entrée into Zenger's work in English may be had via his "New Approaches to the Study of the Psalter," *Proceedings of the Irish Biblical Association* 17 (1994): 37–54; Zenger, "The Composition and Theology of the Fifth Book of Psalms 107–145," *JSOT* 80 (1998): 77–102; and his collaborations with Frank-Lothar Hossfeld: *Psalms 51–100* and *Psalms 101–150*, Hermeneia (Minneapolis: Augsburg Fortress, 2005, 2011).

19. Erich Zenger, "Psalmenexegese und Psalterexegese: Eine Forschungsskizze," in Zenger, ed., *Composition*, 17–65. We might note that this is reminiscent of Bruce K. Waltke's early call for "A Canonical Process Approach to the Psalms," in *Tradition and Testament*, ed. John S. Feinberg and Paul D.Feinberg (Chicago: Moody, 1981), 3–18.

20. Erich Zenger, "Der Psalter als Buch: Beobachtungen zu seiner Enstehung, Komposition und Funktion," in *Der Psalter in Judentum und Christentum*, ed. Erich Zenger, Herders Biblische Studien 18 (Freiburg: Herder, 1998), 1–57.

21. Zenger, "Composition and Theology," 98–99.

22. Egbert Ballhorn, *Zum Telos des Psalters: Der Textzusammenhang des Vierten und Fünften Psalmenbuches (Ps 90–150)*, BBB 138 (Berlin: Philo, 2004). See also Ballhorn, "The Psalter as a Book: Genre as Key to Its Theology," in *The Psalter as Witness: Theology, Poetry, and Genre*, ed. W. D. Tucker Jr. and W. H. Bellinger Jr. (Waco, TX: Baylor University Press, 2017), 155–69.

Marko Marttila argues essentially the same point in his book on "collective reinterpretation."[23] He explores the redactional development of the Psalter and how its development may have been influenced by the community editing it. Marttila argues that, ultimately, the (postexilic) community edited the Psalter for its own purposes, and thus the Psalter is not about "David" or even the "I" figure that appears in the psalms. Another example of this kind of editing can be seen in the "Great Psalms Scroll" from Qumran (11QPs[a]), which displays a different editorial arrangement of psalms that presumably better fit the needs of the Qumran community.[24]

Bernard Gosse focuses his study of the Psalter's structure on the use of the term *mashiach* ("Messiah") throughout the book (Pss 2:2; 18:51 [Eng 50]; 20:7 [Eng 6]; 28:8; 84:10 [Eng 9]; 89:39, 52 [Eng 38, 51]; 105:15; 132:10, 17).[25] He sees a development in the use of the word: early on, it refers to the royal Davidic scion (i.e., the classic messianic figure). Starting with the Elohistic Psalter (Pss 42–83), however, the term takes on a more religious nuance, transforming the hope of the people of God from a person (king) to temple worship more generally.

Robert Wallace's work mostly follows in the footsteps of Wilson and deClaissé-Walford, and he accepts Wilson's thesis of an overarching wisdom frame that relegates the royal/messianic frame to secondary status.[26] In Book IV, Wallace sees a Mosaic frame (with Wilson), but goes beyond this to say that "Moses can be read as the unifying character throughout Book IV."[27] He sees "David" and the kingship in Psalms 101–103 as subordinated to "Moses" and Torah (he speaks of "Davidic sanction of Moses's primacy"[28]), and Psalms 104–106 echoing the Mosaic "voice" of Psalms 90–92. Interestingly, in his 2014 essay, he proposes an "already but not yet" quality for Book V, where the Davidic prospects resurface in a "desire for, but not yet fully realized, Davidic coregency with God."[29] This brings Wallace into

23. Marko Marttila, *Collective Reinterpretation in the Psalms*, FAT 2/13 (Tübingen: Mohr Siebeck, 2006).

24. See below, under "Qumran and the Biblical Psalter."

25. Bernard Gosse, *L'espérance messianique davidique et la structuration du psautier* (Paris: Gabalda, 2015). (Gosse's references are to Hebrew verse numbering ; English verse numbers are bracketed. Elsewhere in this essay, we follow English versification for simplicity.)

26. Robert E. Wallace, "Gerald Wilson and the Characterization of David in Book 5 of the Psalter," in *Shape and Shaping*, ed. deClaissé-Walford, 193–208; see esp. 193.

27. Robert E. Wallace, *The Narrative Effect of Book IV of the Hebrew Psalter*, StBibLit 112 (New York: Lang, 2007), 93.

28. Wallace, *Narrative Effect*, 92.

29. Wallace, "Gerald Wilson and the Characterization of David," 205.

much closer harmony with many of the works indicated under the royal/ messianic rubric below.

Dennis Tucker analyzes Book V from an altogether different perspective: with the Persian (Achaemenid) empire as a backdrop.[30] For him, the final form came together in this period, and therefore any and all references to nations, foreign powers, and more, refer to the Persian Empire; thus, even Psalm 137, which specifically mentions Babylon, he sees as a stand-in for Persia.[31] For Tucker, the flip side to "deconstructing power" is "constructing" Yahweh's power, so he emphasizes Yahweh's kingship over all human powers. Though he does not engage in the debate about the Davidic line in the Psalms, presumably he would see an emphasis on it as antithetical to the emphasis on Yahweh's kingship.

Christine Jones deals with the Asaph psalms (50, 73–83).[32] Her thesis is that "the Psalms of Asaph as a collection guide the reader through the turmoil experienced by the people as a result of the exile."[33] Many of the Psalter's themes are challenged here, "including the promise of the Davidic monarchy, God's sovereignty, God's *hesed*, and the fate of the righteous,"[34] but Jones sees evidence that these psalms provide a way for the faithful to go forward. Since she explicitly follows Wilson and McCann, she too does not see much hope for the Davidic monarchy after Book III, except as reinterpreted or democratized.

Three shorter works in the above vein deserve mention here. Nancy deClaissé-Walford has written extensively on these topics, and in her essay on the metanarrative of the Psalter, she traces a storyline throughout the book.[35] For her, "The story of the shaping of the Psalter is the story of the shaping of survival. ... [It] gave the people a new rationale for existence, a new statement of national identity. With God as sovereign, the people could survive as a distinctly identifiable entity within the vast empires that governed them—Persian, Greek, and Roman."[36] For her, David's role is explained

30. W. Dennis Tucker Jr., *Constructing and Deconstructing Power in Psalms 107–150*, AIL 19 (Atlanta: Society of Biblical Literature, 2014).

31. Tucker, *Constructing*, 119–24.

32. Christine Danette Brown Jones, "The Psalms of Asaph: A Study of the Function of a Psalm Collection" (PhD diss., Baylor University, 2009). See also Jones, "The Message of the Asaphite Collection and Its Role in the Psalter," in deClaissé-Walford, ed., *Shape and Shaping*, 71–85.

33. Jones, "Psalms of Asaph," 2.

34. Jones, "Psalms of Asaph,"196.

35. Nancy L. deClaissé-Walford, "The Meta-Narrative of the Psalter," in Brown, ed., *Oxford Handbook of the Psalms*, 363–76.

36. deClaissé-Walford, "Meta-Narrative," 374–75.

in this way: "David, the great king, acknowledges God as king [in Psalm 145] and calls on Israel and all creation to join with him in celebration."[37]

Gregory Goswell has recently defended Wilson against his critics. He states, "We have sought to defend Wilson's sequential reading of the Hebrew Psalter, which gives it a distinctly non-messianic cast."[38] Among other things, he attempts to explain away the significance of Davidic psalms—especially 110 and 132—after the supposed "failure" of the Davidic covenant in Psalm 89. Nevertheless (and somewhat ironically), he concludes that "it is proper for the Christian to find Jesus in the Psalter. ... Jesus is to be identified with the Divine King who helps people in their distress, the apocalyptic human figure exalted by God in Ps. 110:1, and the promised 'David' who models humble dependence on God."[39] We agree with this latter statement, but it is difficult to see how Goswell reconciles his two assertions.

Susan Gillingham's interests are predominantly in reception history of biblical texts, and concerning the Psalter, she sees the Levitical singers as the ones responsible for compiling its final form in the postexilic era.[40] She sees seven lines of evidence supporting this:

> [1] Their particular Davidic interests, [2] their interests in Moses and the Law, [3] their concerns to teach and preach through music and song, [4] their emphasis on singing above sacrifice, [5] their identification with the poor and needy, [6] their affirmation of God's promises for Zion linked to the traditions of both Creation and the Exodus, and [7] their interest in the voice of prophecy alongside the human voices of prayer—all these interests merge and meld in the various collections in the five books of the Psalter. I can think of no more likely candidates for the complex compilation process of the Psalter than the Levitical singers.[41]

She does not see the psalms as messianic in any way, except as imposed at the latest stage: they "were certainly not written as Messianic

37. deClaissé-Walford, "Meta-Narrative," 374.

38. Gregory Goswell, "The Non-Messianic Psalter of Gerald H. Wilson," *VT* 66 (2016): 524–41; repr. in Andrew T. Abernethy and Gregory Goswell, *God's Messiah in the Old Testament: Expectations of a Coming King* (Grand Rapids: Baker Academic, 2020), 193.

39. Goswell, "Non-Messianic Psalter," 196.

40. Susan Gillingham, "The Levitical Singers and the Compilation of the Psalter," in *Trägerkreise in den Psalmen*, ed. F.-L. Hossfeld et al., BBB 178 (Göttingen: Bonn University Press, 2017), 35–59.

41. Gillingham, "Levitical Singers," 55–56.

compositions. … [It] is possible to talk about the Messiah in the Psalms—not as a theological agenda arising out of the psalms themselves, but as one which has been imposed on them."[42] Nevertheless, her brief for a postexilic vision that kept the idea of "David" alive comports with the positive picture of "David" found in 1–2 Chronicles, for example. This comports with a point David Howard has made,

> We should remember that another biblical work that is indisputably postexilic … is 1–2 Chronicles, a work that is overwhelmingly positive about the Davidic kingship. Thus, just because Judah had experienced exile does not mean that it had abandoned all hope in the promises and benefits of the Davidic Covenant.[43]

Thus, Gillingham's work, which does not treat Psalms "messianically," might occupy a mediating position between the two trajectories, since she agrees that the Levites kept the idea of "David" alive.[44]

Roland Meynet's commentary on Book V is unique because he specifically focuses on the composition of the fifth book of Psalms as a whole more than the individual psalms therein.[45] He has a more "rhetorical" approach, as he has written extensively on that topic.[46] His analysis of Book V yields a chiastic structure that centers around Psalm 119, thus making Psalm 119 the key to understanding the rest of the book. While not explicitly committed to a certain narrative storyline of the Psalms, we deduce from his commentary that Meynet understands that the Psalter is intended to provide wisdom for the people of God, with little emphasis on the royal/messianic perspective.

42. Susan Gillingham, "The Messiah in the Psalms: A Question of Reception History and the Psalter," in *King and Messiah in Israel and the Ancient Near East*, ed. John Day, JSOTSup 270 (Sheffield: Sheffield Academic, 1998), 237.

43. Howard, *Structure*, 205.

44. Her conjecture about the Levites' role in the final compilation of the Psalter is just that: conjecture. But it does show how the figure of "David" permeates the Psalter, as it does in 1–2 Chronicles.

45. Roland Meynet, *Le Psautier. Cinquième Livre (Ps 107–150)*, Rhetorica Biblica et Semitica 12 (Leuven: Peeters, 2017). He has also published commentaries on Books I, III, and IV: *Le Psautier. Premier Livre (Ps 1–41)*, Rhetorica Biblica et Semitica 16 (Leuven: Peeters, 2018); *Le Psautier. Troisième Livre (Ps 73–89)*, Rhetorica Biblica et Semitica 19 (Leuven: Peeters, 2019); *Le Psautier. Quatrième Livre (Ps 90–106)*, Rhetorica Biblica et Semitica 23 (Leuven: Peeters, 2020).

46. E.g., Roland Meynet, *Treatise on Biblical Rhetoric*, International Studies in the History of Rhetoric 3 (Leiden: Brill, 2012).

Royal/Messianic Approaches

The other main trajectory of editorial-critical analysis sees David—and, by extension, the anointed Davidic king—as the central figure, along with Yahweh himself, of the book from beginning to end. Book-length treatments of the Psalter's overall message by David Mitchell, Jamie Grant, Palmer Robertson, Adam Hensley, and Peter Ho deserve special mention here.

David Mitchell's was the first full-blown counter to Wilson's "non-Davidic" work.[47] He proposed his own interpretation: that the Psalter is to be interpreted eschatologically and that the Davidic kingship, far from being downplayed and viewed as "failed" in the Psalter, forms the basis for the eschatological hope in a messianic figure found throughout the collection. He states that "the messianic theme is central to the purpose of the collection,"[48] and that the Psalter

> was designed by its redactors as a purposefully ordered arrangement of lyrics with an eschatological message. This message ... consists of a predicted sequence of eschatological events. These include Israel in exile, the appearing of a messianic superhero, the ingathering of Israel, the attack of the nations, the hero's suffering, the scattering of Israel in the wilderness, their ingathering and further imperilment, the appearance of a superhero from the heavens to rescue them, the establishment of his *malkut* [kingship] from Zion, the prosperity of Israel and the homage of the nations.[49]

Mitchell faults Wilson and others for reading the Psalter historically (tying it in specifically with Israel's preexilic, exilic, and postexilic situations) rather than eschatologically, whereby the vision looks far beyond these historical periods.[50]

Jamie Grant argues that the psalms are organized around the royal statutes found in Deuteronomy 17:14–20 and that the juxtaposition of royal psalms next to the three Torah psalms (Pss 1, 19, 119) was instrumental in

47. Mitchell, *Message of the Psalter*.

48. Mitchell, *Message of the Psalter*, 87.

49. Mitchell, *Message of the Psalter*, 15. See also his essay in this volume.

50. See also his "Lord, Remember David: G. H. Wilson and the Message of the Psalter," *VT* 56 (2006): 526–48, where he further critiques Wilson and argues that the kingship of Yahweh and the Messiah are not mutually exclusive.

shaping the Psalter: Psalms 1–2, 18–21, and 118–119.[51] For him, Torah, kingship, and democratization are inseparable in the book: the king is to be like the ideal in Deuteronomy (not like the historical kings), keeping Torah and not lifting himself above his "brothers" (Deut 17:20). The king as exemplar is to model what the people should aspire to. But against many who see "David" as dismissed by the end of the Psalter, Grant argues that the *idea* of an ideal, royal figure ("David") is present in the Psalter's final form, an idea that finds its ultimate expression in "Jesus the King."[52]

Another book-length treatment that attempts to tell the unified "story" of the Psalter is Palmer Robertson's.[53] For him, the essence of each of the Psalter's five books can be captured by five words: Confrontation, Communication, Devastation, Maturation, and Consummation. He states that "from a redemptive-historical perspective, the Lord's covenant with David provides the essential theological framework for understanding the Psalms."[54] He also stresses Jamie Grant's point about the significance of three Torah psalms included alongside three messianic psalms, revealing pivotal points in the Psalter.[55] The climax of the historical-redemptive "covenant chorale" in the Psalter focuses on the dual promises to David of *dynasty* and *dwelling place*, both expressed in the term "house" (*bayit*) in 2 Samuel 7:11, 13. Thus, Robertson is situated firmly in the royal/messianic tradition.

Whereas much of the focus we've been discussing has been on the Psalter's editors' view of the Davidic covenant—failed or still important—Adam Hensley has helpfully added to the discussion a focus on how this covenant relates to the earlier Abrahamic and Mosaic covenants.[56] Hensley argues that "the Psalter's editors viewed the Abrahamic, Mosaic, and Davidic covenants as a theological unity and anticipated their common fulfillment through a future Davidic successor."[57] He asserts that Book IV "royalizes" the Abrahamic and Davidic covenant themes, "especially through the small

51. Jamie A. Grant, *The King as Exemplar: The Function of Deuteronomy's Kingship Law in the Shaping of the Book of Psalms*, AcBib 17 (Atlanta: Society of Biblical Literature, 2004).

52. Grant, *King as Exemplar*, 295.

53. O. Palmer Robertson, *The Flow of the Psalter: Discovering Their Structure and Theology* (Phillipsburg, NJ: P&R, 2015).

54. Robertson, *Flow*, 14.

55. Robertson, *Flow*, 15–16.

56. Adam D. Hensley, *Covenant Relationships and the Editing of the Hebrew Psalter*, LHBOTS 666 (New York: T&T Clark, 2018).

57. Hensley, *Covenant Relationships*, 9.

Davidic group of psalms in Pss 101–103."[58] He proposes "an essential coherence and continuity between these covenants that centers on the awaited king."[59]

Peter Ho's recent book is an ambitious project to explain the *how* and the *why* of the Psalter's macrostructure and message (in some ways reminiscent of physicists' attempts to formulate a "unified field theory" or "Theory of Everything," one that explains everything in the universe).[60] He identifies thirty-two organizational principles behind the Psalter's shape and message, thirteen formal and nineteen tacit. Formal indicators include such things as book divisions, prologue (Pss 1–2), epilogue (Pss 146–150), superscriptions, and postscript (Ps 72:20); tacit indicators include leitmotifs in the prologue (Yahweh and the Davidic/messianic kingship; Zion temple; Yahweh's Torah and Torah-fidelity), genre motifs, concatenation, messianic and eschatological perspective (Pss 101–103 and 108–110), and more.[61] He sees three sections in the Psalter: Books I, II–III, and IV–V, each with four subgroups, and he unpacks each of these, including all of their relationships with each other. The Psalter is to be read in at least three dimensions: linearly, concentrically, and intertextually.[62]

Ho's is a complex analysis, not easily followed in its many figures and charts, but it leads to important conclusions that must be taken into account in future research; indeed, even his all-encompassing methodology must influence future work.[63] His conclusions are noteworthy, grounded as they are in his exhaustive methodology:

> The logic of the MT-150 is a reception of the Davidic covenant wrapped in the clothing of Hebrew poetry. The primary leitmotifs of the Psalter, found in the Prologue (Pss 1–2), [are] an interweaved ternion of Kingship, Zion and Torah-piousness. ... The macrostructural logic of the Psalter is thus an unfurling and relecture of the Davidic covenant (in 2 Sam 7 and other texts). It is a search for blessedness, made possible under a larger trans-temporal reality that traces the

---

58. Note that here, Hensley reads Psalms 101–103 in almost exactly the opposite way that Wallace does (see above).

59. Hensley, *Covenant Relationships*, 10.

60. Peter C. W. Ho, *The Design of the Psalter: A Macrostructural Analysis* (Eugene, OR: Pickwick, 2019); see also his "The Shape of Davidic Psalms as Messianic," *JETS* 62 (2019): 515–31.

61. Ho, *Design*, 35–37.

62. Ho, *Design*, 333.

63. His essay in this volume provides a simpler synopsis of his work.

> establishment, fall and "re-establishment" of the Davidic promises via an ideal anointed king. The posture hitherto of the *chasidim* ["the faithful"] is that of trusting prayer and patience because of YHWH's unfailing חסד ["faithful/covenant love"].[64]

It should be clear that Ho's work embraces and reaffirms most of the royal/messianic works reviewed immediately above; indeed, it does the same for most of the small-scale works immediately below. As such, it stands as an indispensable work, largely persuasive in its main contours, and cannot be ignored going forward.

Beyond such whole-Psalter treatments above, studies devoted to sections of the Psalter are increasing in number. Because of the debate over how Books IV and V (Pss 90–150) "answer" the crises seen in Book III, it seems the greatest interest focuses on those two books, including the conclusion to the Psalter, Psalms 146–150, though studies of the earlier books are still to be found.

Robert Cole has written two detailed monographs—one on Psalms 1–2 and one on Book III (Pss 73–89)—in both of which the royal/messianic perspective governs throughout.[65] For Cole, the introduction to the Psalter (Pss 1–2), and thus the rest of the book, is about the co-kingship of Yahweh and his Messiah; he sees the righteous man of Psalm 1 as the "anointed one" (or Messiah) of Psalm 2. In Book III, Cole sees the royal/messianic perspective permeating throughout, in contrast to most studies, which see a despairing note throughout most of the book, culminating in the "failed" Davidic covenant of Psalm 89. For example, he sees the people of Psalms 87–88 and the Davidic figure of Psalm 89 as "alive and joyful in 89."[66] The answer to the delay in fulfillment of the Davidic covenant is to be found in Psalms 90 and following. Cole's exhaustive cataloguing of every possible repetition—thematic, lexical, even phonetic—without controlling for more and less significant ones leaves his work open to criticism,[67] but the general import of his argument nevertheless holds.

64. Ho, *Design*, 337.

65. Robert L. Cole, *Psalms 1–2: A Gateway to the Psalter*, HBM 37 (Sheffield: Sheffield Phoenix, 2013); and Cole, *The Shape and Message of Book III (Psalms 73–89)*, JSOTSup 307 (Sheffield: Sheffield Academic, 2000).

66. Cole, *Shape*, 230.

67. See Michael K. Snearly, *The Return of the King: Messianic Expectation in Book V of the Psalter*, LHBOTS 624 (New York: T&T Clark, 2016), 19 and n. 32; Stephen J. Smith, *The Conflict between Faith and Experience, and the Shape of the Psalms 73–83*, LHBOTS 723 (London: T&T Clark, 2022), 26, 27–28, 64–65.

Another study in Book I is that of Andrew Witt, who sees "David" (and the "Davidic voice") as part of the Psalter's animating dynamic. He understands "David" in Psalms 3–14 to be the ideal and representative figure whose persona we can trace throughout the Psalter. This figure also points us ahead typologically to the establishment of a just kingdom in fulfillment of the Davidic covenant.[68]

Immediately following this minicorpus is the chiastically arranged section of Psalms 15–24, which Carissa Quinn studied at the "micro-level." A student of David Howard, she examined all the significant lexical and thematic links, developing a much more sophisticated system than he had to determine significant versus incidental links throughout. Her conclusion fits in the same trajectory we are laying out here:

> The collection exhibits movement toward the consummation of YHWH's kingdom, with the deliverance of the faithful Davidic king being the turning point in the collection. This message is significant because it defines the messianic expectation in terms of the suffering and deliverance of the Davidic king and the ingathering of all nations into the kingdom of YHWH as the result. ... That this collection and its storyline were preserved through a time when there was no human king creates the expectation of a future king, beyond the time of David or the early Israelite kings.[69]

Stephen Smith analyzes the Asaph psalms (73–83) against the background of not simply the exile but more specifically the destruction of Jerusalem and the temple. He sees a sustained note of faith *throughout* these psalms, despite the preponderance of laments (or "psalms of despair") here:

> the study has revealed a sustained concern to *strengthen* [the] foundations [of faith, i.e. "psalms of hope,"] which appeared to be crumbling under the weight of one of the most disorienting crises in ancient Israel's National history. The collection's shape resolves this crisis for the reader/singer in a consistent way throughout: its two major units encourage resolute commitment to "the God of Israel's faith"—ultimately the doctrine "God is good to Israel" (73:1)—in the face of

68. Andrew Carl Witt, *A Voice without End: The Role of David in Psalms 3–14*, Journal of Theological Interpretation Supplements 20 (University Park, PA: Eisenbrauns, 2021).

69. Carissa M. Quinn Richards, "The King and the Kingdom: The Message of Psalms 15–24" (PhD diss., Golden Gate Baptist Theological Seminary, 2015), 253. Forthcoming, Lexham Academic.

> circumstances that appeared to severely undermine this Divine profile. … The overarching theological message that emerges is that God is good to Israel—despite conflicting evidence.[70]

Further, he states that "these so-called 'laments' … do not represent faith's failure but its high point."[71]

Much more interest seems to be focused on Books IV and V. Here, works by Michael McKelvey, David Gundersen, Ian Vaillancourt, Michael Snearly, James Todd, and Jill Firth deserve mention.

Michael McKelvey focuses on the message of Book IV of the Psalter, arguing that it was formed "as a response to the theological crisis of the exile and the fall of the Davidic monarchy in Book III, especially Psalm 89."[72] He identifies three "voices" in Book IV: Moses, King Yahweh, and David. The voices "appear to speak to the post-exilic audience with a particular message: The LORD reigns; he always has and always will."[73] Yahweh's promise to David "will be fulfilled by a messianic, Davidic king who will institute YHWH's eschatological, transnational kingdom and will reign in the ideal manner of divine kingship."[74]

In a similar vein, David Gundersen argues that Book IV "sustains the hope that God will keep his promises to David by restoring Israel with a king from David's line."[75] Thus, Moses (Ps 90) emerges to intercede with God on behalf of the unfulfilled Davidic covenant (Ps 89). Because Yahweh still reigns (Pss 93–100), he will uphold this covenant, demonstrated in the royal Davidic Psalm 101, "a central psalm sustaining Davidic hope in Book IV."[76] David's prayer in Psalm 102 then echoes Moses's intercession in Psalm 90, and David is forgiven and restored in Psalm 103, showing that the Davidic covenant has not "failed."

Ian Vaillancourt also attempts to discern the development of a storyline within the Psalter.[77] He demonstrates that Wilson's hypothesis—that the

70. Smith, *Conflict between Faith and Experience*, 185. See also Stephen John Smith, "The Shape and Message of Psalms 73–78," *CBQ* 83 (2021): 20–39

71. Stephen John Smith, *Conflict between Faith and Experience*, 68.

72. Michael G. McKelvey, *Moses, David and the High Kingship of Yahweh: A Canonical Study of Book IV of the Psalter*, Gorgias Biblical Studies 55 (Piscataway, NJ: Gorgias, 2014), 325.

73. McKelvey, *Moses, David*, 326.

74. McKelvey, *Moses, David*, 326.

75. David Alexander Gundersen, "Davidic Hope in Book IV of the Psalter" (PhD diss., The Southern Baptist Theological Seminary, 2015), 240. See also his essay in this volume.

76. Gundersen, "Davidic Hope," 264.

77. Ian J. Vaillancourt, *The Multifaceted Saviour of Psalms 110 and 118: A Canonical Exegesis*, HBM 86 (Sheffield: Sheffield Phoenix, 2019); see also his "Formed in the Crucible of Messianic Angst:

royal/messianic figure of the early portion of the Psalms is transformed into simply a collective hope—cannot be sustained by the actual evidence of Book V. Looking at the first portion of Book V, Psalms 107–118 in general and Psalms 110 and 118 specifically, Vaillancourt argues that the role of the royal/messianic figure, or what he prefers to call a "figure of salvation," is actually expanded rather than minimized, having multiple offices (e.g., priest, king). He too is situated in this royal/messianic tradition.

Michael Snearly, a student of Howard, builds on his mentor's emphasis on key-word links, showing how this phenomenon can be grounded in the broader fields of text linguistics and poetics.[78] Snearly's work seeks to provide a more objective footing for editorial criticism and to demonstrate how larger blocks of text can be analyzed. He uses Book V as his example text, where he sees a renewed emphasis on the messianic promises made to David based on the editorial arrangement. His title, *Return of the King*, refers both to the "return" of the literary "David" in Book V and to the very real messianic expectations expressed therein.

James Todd's work on Psalms 135–137 reinforces the work of Snearly and others on Book V, in that he sees these psalms forming a clear link between the preceding (Pss 120–134) and following (Pss 138–145) collections, and that "David" is integral to all three.[79] Even though these psalms do not refer to "David" by name, Todd builds off the clear emphases on "David" in Psalms 132 and 144, along with numerous lexical and other links between Psalms 135–137 and these other collections, to show that "the ultimate hope at the end of the Psalter rests upon Yahweh's future establishment of the Davidic Covenant."[80]

In a similar vein to Snearly, Jill Firth has noted how "David" has been "re-presented" in Book V of the Psalter, arguing that "the suffering of David is foregrounded in Psalms 140–143, but David is not down-played (contra Wilson) or disempowered (contra Tucker, Hossfeld and Zenger), showing continuity with Books I–III in royalty, international warfare and dependence on God. *Relecture* of Psalm 18 in Psalms 140–143 revisits God's past

The Eschatological Shape of the Hebrew Psalter's Final Form," *Scottish Bulletin of Evangelical Theology* 31 (2013): 127–44.

78. Michael K. Snearly, *Return of the King*.

79. James M. Todd III, *Remember, O Yahweh: The Poetry and Context of Psalms 135–137* (Eugene, OR: Wipf & Stock, 2015).

80. Todd, *Remember, O Yahweh*, 129.

rescue of David as a ground for confidence for the future fulfilment of the Davidic promises."[81]

Italy has emerged as an influential locus of editorial-critical analysis under the direction of Gianni Barbiero and his students.[82] On the topic of messianism in the Psalter, Barbiero takes the position that there is nothing contradictory between the reign of Yahweh and the reign of the Messiah. For example, he sees a strong messianic emphasis in Psalms 144–145.[83] He also writes:

> So now to the question so central in the psalter of the king-messiah. It is true that in books IV and V the messianic figure has particular characteristics (on the one hand it is not called my *melek* ["king"], on the other it has a priestly dimension, cf. Ps 110). Ps 149, which is in structural correspondence with Ps 2 is a collective psalm, which transposes the role of the messiah to the *saddiqim-'anawim* ["the godly and the humble"]. … But the individual character of the messiah remains: undoubtedly the royal psalms of the IV–V book (Ps 101; 110; 132; 144) have an individual character. Ps 144 is emblematic in this regard, which together with Ps 145 concludes the fifth book and the psalter.[84]

Stefan Attard, a student of Barbiero, examines Book II (Pss 42–72) in depth, outlining a coherent flow of thought in the book, where the Korahite (Pss 42–49) and Davidic (Pss 51/52–71/72) collections, reflecting a backdrop of exile, have more in common than most scholars have noted, and where Psalms 50–51 function as a hinge between the two.[85] Thus, he can speak of a "Davidisation" of Book II, but this "David" is the penitent (and persecuted) king, starting in Psalm 51 and extending through the end of the book.[86] He states that "the intertwining of the theme of the poor with that of the Exile

81. Gillian Claire Firth, "The Re-Presentation of David in Psalms 140–143" (PhD diss., Australian College of Theology, 2016), iii. See also her essay in this volume.

82. See especially Gianni Barbiero, *Il regno di JHWH e del suo Messia: Salmi scelti dal primo libro del Salterio*, *StudBib* 7 (Rome: Città Nuova, 2009); Barbiero, *Perché, o Dio, ci hai rigettati? Salmi scelti dal secondo e terzo libro del Salteri*, Analecta Biblica 6 (Rome: Gregorian & Biblical Press, 2016).

83. Gianni Barbiero, "Messianismus und Theokratie: Die Verbindung der Psalmen 144 und 145 und ihre Bedeutung für die Komposition des Psalters," *OTE* 27 (2014): 41–52.

84. Barbiero, personal communication to Snearly, July 25, 2020 (Snearly translation).

85. Stefan M. Attard, *The Implications of Davidic Repentance: A Synchronic Analysis of Book 2 of the Psalter (Psalms 42–72)*, Analecta Biblica Dissertationes 212 (Rome: Gregorian & Biblical Press, 2016).

86. Attard, *Implications*, 358–61.

in [Book II] allows the poor to interpret their life experiences as a reflection of the exilic persecution to which David's own life corresponded."[87] He speaks of the "restoration of Zion in the Davidic Ps 51 and 69," showing that "Zion theology" was "a highly Davidic concern"[88] and that "the reinstallation of the Jerusalem cult (Ps 51) is supplemented by a *messianic* perspective."[89] In the end, then, Attard sees a future for the Davidic monarchy, centered around Zion, "where the messianic king would exercise dominion," thus moving beyond the individual, historical David to "David," the symbol of the eternal Davidic covenant.[90]

So Kun Ahn, another Barbiero student, argues a similar position in her dissertation on Psalms 146–150.[91] Her goal is to demonstrate (1) that Psalms 146–150 are a cohesive textual unit and (2) that they function as the conclusion of the Psalter. Her work examines the ways that these psalms interact with one another, seeing them as a fitting final summary to the Psalter. She concludes that "in books I–III the (messianic) idea is highlighted by placing the royal psalms at the end of each book: Psalms 2, 72, and 89 show that the king outlined here is subordinated to the sovereignty of God. In Books IV-V, however, the psalms of King YHWH are grouped together, while the royal psalms are scattered in the composition, as witnesses of messianic hope."[92]

Jerome Skinner's work focuses on the thirteen Davidic historical superscriptions with a threefold emphasis: (1) the historical David and his situation, (2) hope for future generations, based on David's life, and (3) all of these ultimately messianic. He writes, "For NT writers, the life of David was seen as typological in the final form of the [Hebrew Bible], and the portrayal of his life was the springboard from which Israel's awaited King was understood."[93] His is not an editorial-critical work per se, but it nevertheless dovetails well with the works above.

---

87. Attard, *Implications*, 460. Here, Attard's "David" is the historical David who was persecuted by enemies, allowing an identification between him and the poor.

88. Attard, *Implications*, 462.

89. Attard, *Implications*, 463; emphasis Attard.

90. Attard, *Implications*, 464.

91. So Kun Ahn, "I Salmi 146–150 come conclusione del Salterio" (PhD diss., Pontifical Biblical Institute, 2008).

92. Ahn, "I Salmi 146–150," 280 (Snearly translation).

93. Jerome L. Skinner, "The Historical Superscriptions of Davidic Psalms: An Exegetical, Intertextual, and Methodological Analysis" (PhD diss., Andrews University Seventh-Day Adventist Theological Seminary, 2016), 370.

Finally, we might note that David Howard has also argued for the importance of the royal/messianic perspective in the Psalter,[94] and, additionally, that Psalms 1–2 together constitute the Psalter's introduction, thus highlighting the Psalter's dual focus on Yahweh's supreme kingship and the Davidic king's role in that, contra the Wilson-McCann hypothesis that Psalm 1 functions as a stand-alone introduction.[95] Furthermore, he has attempted a whole-Psalter analysis focusing on this interplay between divine and human kingship.[96]

Royal/Messianic Perspectives in Light of Traditional Christian Interpretation

Traditional Christian interpretation over the centuries saw the Psalms almost exclusively through the lens of the Messiah. Precritical commentators such as Spurgeon, Hengstenberg, Delitzsch, and Alexander followed in this tradition.[97] Most of the works reviewed in the previous section do not superimpose this lens on the texts in this way, but certain strands of contemporary evangelical scholarship do tend in this direction.

Note, for example, the Reformed scholar Richard Belcher's comment: "All the Psalms, either directly or indirectly, relate to the person and/or work of Christ."[98] See also Bruce Waltke's understanding that the words of the psalmists were ultimately the words of Christ, which was fully developed and defended by his student Jerry Shepherd.[99]

Such approaches remind one of Augustine's comment that "Christ meets and refreshes me everywhere in those Books [referring to the Psalms],

94. David M. Howard Jr., "The Case for Kingship in the Old Testament Narrative Books and the Psalms," *TJ* 9 (1988): 19–35, esp. 33–35.

95. Howard, "Wisdom and Royalist/Zion Traditions in the Psalter," in *Structure*, 200–207; and Howard, "The Proto-MT Psalter, the King, and Psalms 1 and 2: A Response to Klaus Seybold," in *Jewish and Christian Approaches to the Psalms: Conflict and Convergence*, ed. Susan Gillingham (Oxford: Oxford University Press, 2012), 182–89.

96. Howard, "Divine and Human Kingship as Organizing Motifs in the Psalter," in *The Psalms: Language for All Seasons of the Soul*, ed. Andrew Schmutzer and David Howard (Chicago: Moody, 2013), 197–207; and Howard, "Introduction to Psalms," in *NIV Biblical Theology Study Bible*, ed. D. A. Carson (Grand Rapids: Zondervan, 2018), 868–76.

97. See Howard, *Structure*, 3–4 for details.

98. Richard P. Belcher Jr., *The Messiah and the Psalms: Preaching Christ from All the Psalms* (Fearn, Scotland: Christian Focus Publications, 2006), 195.

99. Waltke, "A Canonical Process Approach"; Jerry Eugene Shepherd, "The Book of Psalms as the Book of Christ: The Application of the Christo-Canonical Method to the Book of Psalms" (PhD diss., Westminster Theological Seminary, 1995).

everywhere in those Scriptures."[100] Or Francis of Assisi's "Christ first, Christ last, Christ all and in all," referring to the gospel, though also characteristic of much of traditional Christian interpretation.[101]

From a very different theological perspective, evangelical dispensational scholars tend to see many psalms—or even the Psalter as a whole—as messianic. The *Moody Handbook of Messianic Prophecy*, for example, includes twenty essays on messianism in the Psalms.[102] The Messiah is not only present in Psalm 2 and other royal psalms, but he is also the "man" in Psalm 1.[103] Even so-called "imprecatory psalms" (such as Ps 69) are considered laments of the Messiah himself.[104]

QUMRAN AND THE BIBLICAL PSALTER

The discovery in the 1940s and 1950s of at least thirty-nine psalms manuscripts in the caves at Qumran and nearby has given rise to new questions about the formation of the Psalter. The most important of these manuscripts is the so-called Psalms Scroll (11QPs[a]) discovered in Cave 11 and published by James Sanders.[105] It contains portions of some thirty-nine psalms from the biblical Psalter, as well as several others from outside the Psalter. Its order is radically different from the present canonical order evidenced in all other manuscript traditions. In addition, many other discoveries have fleshed out a picture of a canonical development of the Psalter whereby the first three books (Pss 1–89) appear to have reached a fixed order and arrangement at Qumran much earlier than Books IV and V (Pss 90–150).

Thus, Sanders, Wilson, Flint, and others have argued that 11QPs[a] (more recently called 11Q5) represented a rival "canonical" Psalter to the traditional Masoretic Text Psalter and that, as such, the MT Psalter was in flux until at least the end of the first century AD.[106] These arguments of Wilson and oth-

100. Augustine, *Against Faustus the Manichaean* 12.27; quoted in Michael Cameron, *Christ Meets Me Everywhere: Augustine's Early Figurative Exegesis*, Oxford Studies in Historical Theology (Oxford: Oxford University Press, 2012), vi.

101. Quoted in Donald P. Hustad, "Music and the Church's Outreach," *RevExp* 69 (1972): 178.

102. Michael Rydelnik and Edwin Blum, eds., *The Moody Handbook of Messianic Prophecy: Studies and Expositions of the Messiah in the Old Testament* (Chicago: Moody, 2019). For our purposes here, see especially Cole, "Compositional Unity," 451–56, and Postell, "Messianism in the Psalms," 457–75. See also Postell's essay in this volume.

103. Robert L. Cole, "Psalms 1–2: The Divine Son of God," in *Moody Handbook*, 477–91; and Cole, Psalms 1–2: A Gateway.

104. Randall L. McKinion, "Psalm 69: The Lament of the Messiah," in *Moody Handbook*, 591–603.

105. James A. Sanders, *The Dead Sea Psalms Scroll* (Ithaca, NY: Cornell University, 1967).

106. Wilson, *Editing*, 63–92; and Wilson, "The Qumran Psalms Scroll (11QPs[a]) and the Canonical Psalter: Comparison of Editorial Shaping," *CBQ* 59 (1997): 448–64; see also Sanders,

ers have mostly been accepted as the prevailing view,[107] despite alternative opinions expressed by earlier scholars such as Shemaryahu Talmon, Moshe Goshen-Gottstein, and Patrick Skehan.[108] Similar reservations were expressed in the 1990s by such scholars as Menahem Haran, Roger Beckwith, David Mitchell, and Heinz-Josef Fabry, who argued that 11QPs[a] was never understood to be canonical, and that the radical divergences in order plus the inclusion of noncanonical psalms are due to liturgical reasons and not to a separate canonical tradition.[109]

Several recent challenges have been mounted to the Sanders-Wilson-Flint-Ulrich hypothesis concerning 11QPs[a] and the MT Psalter. Adam Hensley has reviewed previous arguments and added his own, concluding that "the relationship of Qumran MSS to the canonical Psalter as Wilson and Flint interpret it remains highly speculative, and others more convincingly explain them as liturgically inspired arrangements that presuppose an existing MT Psalter."[110]

Another challenge is by David Willgren, whose work is reviewed below. Suffice it to say here that his observations about the fluid nature of so many Qumran texts and his challenge to the "Qumran Psalms Hypothesis" of Wilson and others also undermine that hypothesis and render the possibility of a single proto-MT text still to be a viability (even if Willgren himself does not see such a text).

Klaus Seybold has defended the idea of a proto-MT Psalter that preserved the mainstream Jerusalem tradition.[111] At the very least, we can affirm that Seybold's work calls into question the hypothesis that the biblical Psalter was not closed until the late first century AD. Perhaps one strand at Qumran—one group of texts presented most clearly by 11QPs[a]—was not

---

Psalms Scroll; Peter W. Flint, *The Dead Sea Psalms Scrolls and the Book of Psalms*, STDJ 17 (Leiden: Brill, 1997); and many publications since.

107. The most recent discussion in this direction of which we are aware is by Eugene Ulrich; see his discussion of 11QPs[a] in Ulrich, *The Dead Sea Scrolls and the Developmental Composition of the Bible*, SVT 169 (Leiden: Brill, 2015), 194–99. He too sees 11QPs[a] as "a variant edition of the Psalter" (page 199).

108. Wilson, *Editing*, 73–88.

109. Menahem Haran, "11QPs[a] and the Canonical Book of Psalms," in *Minhah le-Nahum*, ed. Marc Brettler and Michael Fishbane, Nahum M. Sarna Festschrift, JSOTSup 153 (Sheffield: JSOT Press, 1993), 193–201; Roger Beckwith, "The Early History of the Psalter," *TynBul* 46 (1995): 1–28; Mitchell, *Message of the Psalter*, 21–26, esp. 22–23; Heinz-Josef Fabry, "Der Psalter in Qumran," in Zenger, ed., *Der Psalter in Judentum und Christentum*, 137–63.

110. Hensley, *Covenant Relationships*, 39.

111. Klaus Seybold, "The Psalter as a Book," in Gillingham, ed., *Jewish and Christian Approaches*, 168–81; and Howard's response: "The Proto-MT Psalter," 182–89.

fixed as "canonical" until that time. But Seybold succeeds, in our estimation, in reminding us that there was a separate, normative tradition, centered at Jerusalem, dating much earlier—as far back as the third century BC, perhaps—which helps to explain the LXX and the MT, as well as other traditions at Qumran. An analogy here would be the fact that the book of Esther is not found at Qumran, whereas it has been clearly understood as authoritative and canonical in mainstream Jewish (Masoretic) tradition.

Similarly, Erich Zenger:

> The Psalms roll, 11QPs[a], is not a witness to a second "canonical" form of the Psalter alongside that of the MT/LXX but is "a creative continuation of part of the proto-masoretic Psalter (Ps 101–150*). ... In terms of its textual form, 11QPs[a] reveals itself as a Qumran product, as independent, unique, and as a whole *sub*ordinate to the MT forms of the text."[112]

Most recently, Drew Longacre has echoed such perspectives: "many scholars [have previously argued that] the 11Q5 [=11QPs[a]] psalter was directly dependent on the full MT psalter as a secondary composition, and further recent detailed textual studies have led to a near consensus that the 11Q5 psalter is actually dependent on a psalter very similar to the MT psalter."[113]

We are thus convinced that 11QPs[a] was a thoroughly Qumran product, likely for liturgical use, but arising from a proto-MT Psalter. However, we also stress the following point: Even if we were to grant Sanders's and the others' position for the sake of argument, the legitimacy nonetheless remains of studying a text such as the MT, which at the very least represents a legitimate and old canonical tradition, one that certainly reflects the official Pharisaic canon of the turn of the Christian era (following Seybold).

As Sid Z. Leiman wrote many years ago,

> Precisely because of the sectarian nature of the Qumran community, scholars must bear in mind that the content and development of a

112. Erich Zenger (with Frank-Lothar Hossfeld), *Psalms 3: A Commentary on Psalms 101–150*, Hermeneia (Minneapolis: Fortress, 2011), 607, quoting from Ulrich Dahmen, *Psalmen- und Psalterrezeption im Frühjudentum: Rekonstruktion, Textbestand, Struktur und Pragmatik der Psalmenrolle 11QPsa aus Qumran*, STDJ 49 (Leiden: Brill, 2003), 313.

113. Drew Longacre, "The 11Q5 Psalter as a Scribal Project: Standing at the Nexus of Textual Development, Editorial Processes, and Manuscript Production," *ZAW* 134 (2022), 3–4 [full essay, 1–27].

sectarian canon probably has little or no bearing on the content and development of other sectarian (or normative) canons.[114]

SKEPTICS

To be sure, there have been skeptics concerning editorial criticism who do not see any intentional arrangement in the Psalter. These include Roland Murphy, John Goldingay, Norman Whybray, Tremper Longman, and Erhard Gerstenberger;[115] critiques of all of these have already been made by Snearly[116] and we do not address them here.

A more recent challenge has come from Hermann Spieckermann.[117] His is a straightforward effort to reverse the recent trend of editorial criticism entirely. His essay is "a plea for ending the hunt for the message inscribed into the final shaping of the Psalter. … The psalms are waiting to be appreciated as textual individuals and each psalm as part of its special position in a manageable cluster of texts."[118] This final comment is curious, since individual psalms have never lacked for attention as "textual individuals."

Perhaps the most significant recent challenges have focused on the evidence of physical manuscripts, not only from Qumran, but also the LXX and medieval Hebrew manuscripts. These include works by David Willgren, Alma Brodersen, Eva Mroczek, Mika Pajunen, and William Yarchin.

Pride of place among these belongs to David Willgren, who has challenged the very notion of an intentionally ordered Psalter. In his 2016 dissertation,[119] Willgren argues that the Psalter is an "anthology," which he defines

114. Sid Z. Leiman, *The Canonization of Hebrew Scripture: The Talmudic and Midrashic Evidence*, Transactions of the Connecticut Academy of Arts and Sciences 47 (Hamden, CT: Archon, 1976), 34.

115. Roland E. Murphy, "Reflections on Canonical Interpretation of the Psalms," in McCann, ed., *Shape and Shaping of the Psalter*, 21–28; John Goldingay, *Psalms 1* (Grand Rapids: Baker Academic, 2006), 36; and Goldingay, *Psalms 3* (2008), 11–12; Norman Whybray, *Reading the Psalms as a Book*, JSOTSup 223 (Sheffield: Sheffield Academic, 1996); Tremper Longman III, "The Messiah: Explorations in the Law and the Writings," in *The Messiah in the Old and New Testaments*, ed. Stanley E. Porter (Grand Rapids: Eerdmans, 2007), 23–24; Erhard S. Gerstenberger, "Der Psalter als Buch und als Sammlung," in *Neue Wege der Psalmenforschung: Für Walter Beyerlin*, ed. Klaus Seybold and Erich Zenger, Herders Biblische Studien 1 (Freiburg: Herder, 1994), 3–13. See also, more recently, Longman's comments in *Psalms*, TOTC 15–16 (Downers Grove, IL: IVP Academic, 2014), 33–36.

116. Snearly, *Return of the King*, 10–17.

117. Hermann Spieckermann, "From the Psalter Back to the Psalms: Observations and Suggestions," *ZAW* 132 (2020): 1–22.

118. Spieckermann, "From the Psalter," 21.

119. David Willgren, *Like a Garden of Flowers: A Study of the Formation of the "Book" of Psalms* (Lund: Lund University Press, 2016). It was slightly revised as *The Formation of the "Book" of*

as "a compilation of independent texts, actively selected and organized in relation to some present needs."[120] For him, the contents of the anthology are mostly random and can be reorganized at any time. Whatever patterns that might be seen in the Psalter are mostly coincidental and owe their existence to the dynamics of the time periods during which the various redactions of the "book" took place. He speaks of the Psalter as a "*garden* of flowers," where one can stroll through it, enjoying different parts (none of which would be organically connected to other parts), as opposed to a "*garland* of flowers";[121] the latter is "a created entity—a sum of its parts—that remains incomplete if not arranged together."[122] As such, Willgren's approach is robustly diachronic, not synchronic, situating itself in the European approaches mentioned above.

In a more recent essay, Willgren critiques the tendencies of editorial/canonical criticism to focus on a so-called final product (in other words, the MT as preserved in the Leningrad Codex of AD 1008), working backward to (presumed) smaller, earlier collections; these are too "teleological."[123] Instead of "variants" from the presumed proto-MT, Willgren prefers the language of "variance" (borrowed from the New Philology), meaning that the many differences among texts are themselves the "primary characteristic" of text transmission: "Rather than as deviations from a fixed text, variance was seen as integral to the transmission process,"[124] implying that throughout the transmission process, the idea of a "fixed" text was not important. For Willgren, then, to ask about such a fixed text is simply to ask an improper question.

Willgren's is an important and sustained challenge to most of the work reviewed above. Here we can offer only the following brief critiques.[125] First, Willgren pays scant attention to the actual MT "book" of Psalms, focused as he is on shifting extrabiblical collections at Qumran and elsewhere. In doing

---

Psalms: Reconsidering the Transmission and Canonization of Psalmody in Light of Material Culture and the Poetics of Anthologies, FAT 2/88 (Tübingen: Mohr Siebeck, 2016).

120. Willgren, *Garden*, 26.

121. Willgren, *Garden*, 28–29.

122. As Michael G. McKelvey puts it (review of Willgren, *WTJ* 79 [2017]: 162).

123. David Willgren, "A Teleological Fallacy in Psalms Studies? Decentralizing the 'Masoretic' Psalms Sequence in the Formation of the 'Book' of Psalms," in "Quellen und Intertextualität. Methodische Überlegungen zum Psalterende," in *Intertextualität und die Entstehung des Psalters*, ed. Alma Brodersen, Fredericke Neumann, and David Willgren, FAT II/114 (Tübingen: Mohr Siebeck, 2020), 33–50.

124. Willgren, "Teleological Fallacy," 36.

125. A more extended analysis and critique is offered by Smith, *Conflict between Faith and Experience*, 6–8.

so, he ignores three decades' worth of work on the MT Psalter; while there remains much disagreement both methodologically and content-wise, general consensus *has* developed around the major trajectories in the Psalter, at least in the dual tracks outlined above.

Second, he asserts that "paratextual" indicators[126] in the book, such as the superscriptions, the doxologies concluding the Psalter's "books," the place and function of Psalms 1 and 2 as introductions to the book, or the *hallelujah* psalms ending the book (Pss 146–150) were simply products of different redactions, meaning very little in the Psalter's final form.[127] However, in addition to the work of three-plus decades on precisely such paratexts, we can also observe that the Bible itself includes at least two anthologies that also include paratextual indicators: Proverbs and Song of Songs (to say nothing of many prophetic books).

Third, Willgren deprecates seeing repeated words and phrases as having any editorial significance, saying that "recurring language is an intrinsic feature to poetry."[128] Here he creates somewhat of a straw figure: Not every repetition or pattern should be seen as significant, something that sometimes overeager editorial critics do not seem to be aware of; criteria for distinguishing between significant and insignificant repetitions must be developed. Howard has attempted to do this in early works,[129] and his method has been refined and advanced by several of his students, including Snearly[130] and especially Carissa Quinn.[131]

Fourth, his metaphors of a "garden" and a "garland" are too simplistic. The latter implies a rigid string, consecutively ordered, as if the entire Psalter consists solely of concatenated psalms. Indeed, proponents of the editorial-critical approach might argue that a "garden" is more like what they see in the Psalter: small strings of consecutively ordered psalms interrupted by small (or large) collections, some of which might be chiastic

126. These are roughly what Wilson called "explicit" and "tacit" indicators (of editorial activity). For Willgren's definition of paratexts, see *Garden*, 51–60.

127. Willgren, *Garden*, chaps. 8–12 (pages 133–289); tellingly, he titles this section "In Search of the *Artificial*" (emphasis added).

128. Willgren, *Garden*, 159.

129. Howard, *Structure*, 98–102; and Howard, "A Contextual Reading of Psalms 90–94," in McCann, ed., *Shape and Shaping of the Psalter*, 114–17, esp. 117; and Howard, "Psalm 94 among the Kingship of YHWH Psalms," *CBQ* 61 (1999): 667–85, esp. 671–72 and n. 11.

130. Snearly, *Return of the King*, 51–53, and in more detail, "The Return of the King: An Editorial-Critical Analysis of Psalms 107–150" (PhD diss., Golden Gate Baptist Theological Seminary, 2012), 83–87.

131. Richards, "The King and the Kingdom," 59–86.

(e.g., Pss 15–24), not linear. The variegated collections one encounters in the Psalter fit very well with Willgren's "garden," one in which the different parts do indeed complement each other, with paratextual signposts leading readers through it, yielding meaningful trajectories of themes (or an overall theme).[132]

Alma Brodersen too is a skeptic.[133] After considering Psalms 146–150 in the MT, the Dead Sea Scrolls, and the LXX—which she sees as parallel texts, none dependent on the other—she concludes that "Psalms 146–150 are originally separate texts. They were not originally written to end or frame the Psalter as a unit. ... Psalms 146–150 do not refer to one another or Psalms 1–2 at all and share almost no reference texts."[134] Hers is a robustly diachronic approach: she criticizes "Synchronic Psalms Exegesis" as ignoring "the ancient origins of the texts."[135] But synchronic exegesis does not *claim* to be able to discern things like dates, *Sitz im Leben*, and more—all very subjective matters, as witnessed by the wide variety of proposals for such matters among commentators. Rather, it focuses on the evidence of the written 150-psalm Psalter available to us today.[136] Thus, her assertions that there are no links among most of Psalms 146–150 ignores extensive work that *has* been done and that *does* show many links, regardless of questions of original composition.[137] In this respect, her approach is very much like Willgren's emphasis on "variance."

Eva Mroczek and Mika Pajunen are also influential voices arguing that there was no concept of a recognizable "book" of Psalms in the Qumran period. Mroczek states that "close attention to the Qumran psalms manuscripts reveals little evidence for the primacy of the book of Psalms—or in

---

132. For further critique, see the reviews by Benjamin J. Noonan, *BBR* 27 (2017): 253–55; Marco Pavan, *Biblica* 99 (2018): 124–27; and especially Michael G. McKelvey, *WTJ* 79 (2017): 161–63; Ho, *The Design of the Psalter*, 58–61, and Ho, *Journal for the Evangelical Study of the Old Testament* 6 (2020): 73–76. On the other hand, Erhard Gerstenberger has a very positive review in *RBL*, January 2018, https://www.sblcentral.org/home/bookDetails/11966?search=Willgren%20formation%20psalms&type=0.

133. Alma Brodersen, *The End of the Psalter: Psalms 146–150 in the Masoretic Text, the Dead Sea Scrolls, and the Septuagint*, BZAW 505 (Berlin: Walter de Gruyter, 2017); see, further, Brodersen, "Quellen und Intertextualität. Methodische Überlegungen zum Psalterende," in Brodersen, Neumann, and Willgren, eds., *Intertextualität*, 7–31.

134. Brodersen, *End of the Psalter*, 270.

135. Brodersen, *End of the Psalter*, 3.

136. On the issues relating to *which* versions of the Psalter should be studied, see our comments below on William Yarchin's work.

137. For example, So Kun Ahn, "I Salmi 146–150," and Michael Snearly, *Return of the King*, 171–84.

fact, for its very existence as a unified collection."[138] Similarly, Pajunen: "the [Qumran] manuscript statistics cannot be used as evidence for the influence of a particular *book* of psalms, and furthermore that there probably was no fixed authoritative book of psalms during this period."[139] We learned of these works too late for our own extended critique in this essay, but we note Longacre's comment: "Recognition of the proto-MT and 11Q5 psalters as substantial, well-defined, influential, and closely related collections would invalidate the argument of Eva Mroczek...that there was no conceptual category of a determinate 'book of Psalms' in the Second Temple period."[140]

William Yarchin has mounted a challenge from a different direction. He has amassed an extensive database of "over 400 medieval Hebrew manuscripts ... 200 manuscripts from the Cairo Geniza, and all of the relevant incunabula."[141] The *content* and *order* of these do not differ from the traditional 150 psalms known to us today as the "biblical" (or "Masoretic") Psalter, but the *configuration* of these varies widely. So, for example, in the Leningrad Codex, which forms the basis for most modern English translations, Psalms 114 and 115 are presented as one psalm, so that the Leningrad Codex contains only 149 psalms. Examples such as this are myriad across the hundreds of manuscripts that Yarchin has surveyed; to sample just a few examples from Book IV: Psalms 92 and 93, 94 and 95, 96 and 97, 98 and 99, and 103 and 104 are all presented as one psalm, not two, and Psalm 118 is presented as two psalms (118:1–4/118:5–29), not one.[142]

---

138. Eva Mroczek, *The Literary Imagination in Jewish Antiquity* (Oxford: Oxford University Press, 2016), 26.

139. Mika S. Pajunen, "Perspectives on the Existence of a Particular Authoritative Book of Psalms in the Late Second Temple Period," *JSOT* 39 (2014), 139 [full essay, pages 139-63]. See also his essays, "Textual Plurality of Scripture in the Dead Sea Scrolls and Theories of Textual Transmission," *Biblische Notizen* 186 (2020), 7–28; and "Glocal, Local, or Group Specific? Origins of Some Particular Scribal and Interpretive Practices in the Qumran Scrolls," *Scriptures in the Making: Texts and Their Transmission in Late Second Temple Judaism*, eds. Raimo Hakola, Jessi Orpana, Paavo Huotari, Contributions to Biblical Exegesis & Theology 109 (Leuven: Peeters, 2022), 33–56.

140. Longacre, "11Q5 Psalter as a Scribal Product," 4n11.

141. William Yarchin, "Is There an Authoritative Shape for the Hebrew Book of Psalms? Profiling the Manuscripts of the Hebrew Psalter," *RB* 122 (2015): 359. See also William Yarchin, "Why the Future of Canonical Hebrew Psalter Exegesis Includes Abandoning Its Own Premise," in Gianni Barbiero, Marco Pavan, and Johannes Schnocks, eds., *The Formation of the Hebrew Psalter: The Book of Psalms between Ancient Versions, Material Transmission and Canonical Exegesis*, FAT 151 (Tübingen: Mohr Siebeck, 2021), 119–38. Note: *The Cairo Geniza* was a treasure-trove of Jewish manuscripts discovered in the mid-eighteenth century in a synagogue in Egypt. See Paul Kahle, *The Cairo Geniza*, 2nd ed. (Oxford: Blackwell, 1959); "Geniza Lab: Princeton University," https://genizalab.princeton.edu. "Incunabula" were early printed books.

142. Yarchin, "Future of Canonical Hebrew Psalter Exegesis."

In all, Yarchin finds "more than 150 different psalms-configurations" among the Hebrew manuscripts, only one of which corresponds to what we know as the "biblical" Psalter.[143] Among these, he documents manuscripts with as few as 143 psalms and as many as 154 psalms. We should emphasize that all of these have the same content *and order*—those in the 150-psalm Bible familiar to us—the only difference being in how the psalms are divided or combined.[144]

Yarchin's challenge is that the "received" 150-psalm Psalter has no more priority than the dozens of different configurations found in the manuscripts he has surveyed. He envisions future Psalms studies analyzing any and all of the different configurations, seeing hundreds of new "psalms" available for study, as multiple psalms are joined together into the new groupings noted above. As such, editorial criticism as currently practiced will have to give way to an almost endless number of psalms combinations and groupings.

Like Willgren's, Yarchin's work presents a direct and important challenge to traditional editorial criticism. We offer several responses here.

First, unlike some of the Qumran manuscripts, which contain psalms not found in the traditional biblical Psalter, Yarchin's manuscripts all preserve the content of that traditional Psalter in its traditional order. Thus, his discussion is different from discussions of Qumran Psalms materials. So even though Yarchin sees endless possibilities in the different psalms configurations, it nevertheless is the case that the general *flow* of the Psalter's themes remains unchanged.

Second, Yarchin specifically excludes the LXX from his discussion.[145] While this is understandable, given his parameters limited to Hebrew manuscripts, it is an unfortunate exclusion, because the LXX testimony is that there was already in the third century BC an ordered collection that is essentially the same as the 150-psalm Psalter we now know. The title to Psalm 151 is especially instructive: "This psalm is ascribed to David as his own composition [though it is outside the number (of the one hundred fifty)], after he had fought in single combat with Goliath" (RSV). The LXX thus stands out against Yarchin's work.

Third, it is telling that the most common configuration in Yarchin's database is the TR-150, with 84 psalters representing 21 percent of the total.[146] No other configuration comes close to this. Yarchin acknowledges that "TR-150

143. Yarchin, "Is There an Authoritative Shape," 362.
144. Yarchin, "Is There an Authoritative Shape," 360–61.
145. Yarchin, "Is There an Authoritative Shape," 357.
146. Yarchin, "Is There an Authoritative Shape," 360, 362–63.

is the most widely *attested* Hebrew Psalter-configuration," but he then goes on to assert (rather curiously) that "it was by no means the most widely *used* configuration."[147] He mentions "the full range of manuscript evidence" that points away from this, but he does not explain how this is so. On the face of it, the TR-150 appears to be rooted in something earlier than the medieval Hebrew manuscripts.

Fourth, Yarchin asserts that scholars should now begin treating such groupings as Psalms 9 and 10, 42 and 43, 70 and 71, 90 and 91, 114 and 115, and dozens more as single, discrete compositions. In fact, commentaries have routinely noted similarities among many such groupings, while still treating each psalm individually. Yarchin also ignores the hundreds of form-critical, rhetorical, and poetic studies that have shown well-structured, coherent psalms throughout the Psalter.

To take one pairing that Yarchin mentions as an example (Pss 94 and 95), Howard has analyzed these two psalms as discrete psalms, showing their internal structure and coherence.[148] He also has shown significant connections between them, arguing that Psalm 94 fits well among the kingship of Yahweh psalms, even though it is not one of them, form-critically.[149] And yet, despite the significant lexemes and motifs that bind them together, it is difficult to see them as a single, coherent psalm, contra Yarchin.

Two recent critiques of the above skeptical approaches (which have come to our attention too late for significant interaction) are by Marco Pavan and Peter C. W. Ho.[150] Ho's conclusion mirrors our own: "While differences are seen in the arrangement of psalms in DSS psalters, minor deviations in the superscriptions of the LXX psalters, and paratextual fluidity in medieval psalters, it is hard to qualify such differences as the same kind of editorial changes seen in the formational period of the Hebrew Psalter. Such differences can be explained as historical receptions rather than bona fide compositional diversity."

147. Yarchin, "Is There an Authoritative Shape," 363.

148. Howard, *Structure*, 43–61.

149. Howard, *Structure*, 119–22, 129–31; and Howard, "Psalm 94 among the Kingship of YHWH Psalms," 667–85.

150. Marco Pavan, "The Psalter as a Book? A Critical Evaluation of the Recent Research on the Psalter," in *The Formation of the Hebrew Psalter: The Book of Psalms between Ancient Versions, Material Transmission and Canonical Exegesis*, ed. Marco Pavan, Gianni Barbiero, and Johannes Schnocks, FAT I 151 (Tübingen: Mohr Siebeck, 2021), 11–82; Peter C. W. Ho, "Can an Integrative Reading of the Masoretic Psalter Stand in the Presence of Variants Discovered Around Qumran with a Different Canonical Order?" in *Holistic Readings on the Psalms and the Twelve*, ed. Matthew Ayars and Peter C. W. Ho. Forthcoming.

HERMENEUTICAL ISSUES

Certain hermeneutical questions sometimes arise among readers for whom such "canonical" approaches as outlined above are new. Traditionally, most readers have approached the Psalter atomistically, looking only at individual psalms, assuming that they are included in the work in random fashion. The idea of a unified collection is new to them. Here we address two of these questions.

What is the relationship between a psalm's original meaning (as a stand-alone psalm) and its meaning in context alongside other psalms or in the final collection?

Many scholars use such terms as "reinterpreting" or "re-presenting" individual psalms when they are considered in the context of smaller or larger collections in the Psalter, often indicating that the psalm's original meaning is thereby changed. We do not understand meaning in the Psalter in this way. Rather, we maintain that a psalm's essential meaning does *not* change as it is considered in context with other psalms, in the final Psalter, or even as quoted in the New Testament. We can certainly speak of a psalm's meaning being progressively "unfolded" or "illuminated" as it is considered in its surrounding literary context (*Sitz im Text*)—its original meaning perhaps presented only *in nuce*, "in seed form," and revealed more fully later.

To take the example of Psalm 1, we understand the original reference to the "blessed" one to be anyone who follows in the way of Yahweh's Torah (1:1–2). However, when juxtaposed with Psalm 2, with its references to the Davidic king (2:6–7), we are reminded of the description of the godly king in Deuteronomy 17:18–20, which is echoed almost word for word in Psalm 1:2; in this way, we can see the faithful Davidic king in Psalm 2 as the exemplar of the blessed one of Psalm 1, both succeeding by reading and meditating on God's word. The king is not to be "above his brothers" (Deut 17:20), and so we can see the meaning of the blessed one as "Everyman" in Psalm 1 now being attached to the king, who is to be one *of* the people and also their representative. Then, when we read further in the Psalter and see the figure of "David" predominating, we can understand the message in Psalm 1 with even more clarity.

Or, to take Psalm 2, we understand it to refer initially to the historical promises to David as detailed in 2 Samuel 7. David was Yahweh's "anointed one" (Ps 2:2; see also 1 Sam 16:12–13; 2 Sam 5:3), and his offspring would be called Yahweh's "son" (Ps 2:7; see also 2 Sam 7:14). But the Davidic promises were also intended for his descendants (2 Sam 7:14–16) and Yahweh's kingdom was entrusted into the hand of David's sons (2 Chr 13:5). So, Psalm 2 should be understood as referring not simply to David, the individual, but to "David" as represented by any of his royal descendants (imperfect as many of them were). The prophets foretold the coming of Israel's redeemer as the greater descendant of David (e.g., Isa 9:7; 16:5; 22:22; Jer 23:5; 33:15; Hos 3:5). The New Testament then presents Jesus, the "Messiah" (or "anointed one") as this greater "David" (John 7:42; Acts 13:23; 2 Tim 2:8), thus unpacking a further aspect of the meaning of Psalm 2. All of these senses of "David" are simply extensions of the original meaning of Psalm 2.[151]

How does the idea of the Psalter coming together in stages relate to the concept of divine inspiration of Scripture?

We understand the entire Bible to be "God-breathed" (or "inspired by God"), as Paul puts it in 2 Timothy 3:16, and so another question arises in a collection such as the Psalter as to where, exactly, the locus of inspiration is to be found—in other words, what stage(s) of a text that came together over time is/are inspired? Only the original writing? Only the final form? Something in between?

We affirm that the Spirit inspired the writing of the very words of individual psalms when they were originally written. We base this on Jesus's words in Matthew 22:41–45 (NIV), where he states that David, "speaking by the Spirit," uttered the words from Psalm 110:1. That is, when Psalm 110 was first written, this was done through the inspiration of the Holy Spirit.

But we also affirm that the Spirit superintended the process that finally resulted in the collection that we call "the book of Psalms." We base this on several factors:

1. Jesus taught the two disciples on the road to Emmaus about "*everything* … that is written about me in the Law of Moses, the Prophets, and the Psalms" (Luke 24:44 NIV; emphasis added). The word "everything" (*panta*) presumably refers to the entire book of Psalms, that is, its final form, just as it does the entire "Law of Moses" and "the Prophets."
2. Concerning the Pentateuch, among those who hold to (essential) Mosaic authorship, as we do, there is virtually unanimous agreement that Moses himself did not compose the chapter about his

151. We follow here the hermeneutic of Bruce Waltke in his "A Canonical Process Approach to the Psalms" and, from a different perspective, Walter C. Kaiser Jr., *The Uses of the Old Testament in the New* (Chicago: Moody, 1985), especially chapters 2 and 7 (on Pss 16 and 40, respectively).

own death and burial (Deut 34). Thus, their understanding of divine inspiration must include the inspiration of this later addition (and perhaps others) to the main "book of Moses." Likewise for the final form of the Psalter, including such later editorial indicators as Psalm 72:20—"This concludes the prayers of David son of Jesse" (NIV)—attached to a psalm attributed to Solomon.

3. In most of the prophetic books, the words that the prophets spoke in the streets of Jerusalem and elsewhere were done under divine authority ("Thus says the Lord"), but many of their oracles were spoken over many years and were collected—by the prophets themselves or by later disciples, all under divine inspiration—into the final, written form of the canonical books at a later time than when they were originally spoken. Again, so too for the book of Psalms.

CONCLUSION: SO WHAT?

Much of this volume's target audience consists of pastors, students, and well-motivated laypeople. All the authors in this work are concerned, ultimately, with speaking to God's people, the church, and so a legitimate question of our essay might certainly be: So what? What is to be gained from reading the Psalter as we have outlined above?

We believe that there is much merit in understanding the book of Psalms not simply as a random collection of unrelated psalms, but also as an organized, unified "book" that has an overarching message, to which the individual psalms and smaller psalm collections contribute.

Since the 150 psalms were collected intentionally in the final, biblical Psalter, there is much merit in looking at them in their "literary context," much like we do in other books of the Bible. For example, in the book of Isaiah, we do not simply read each prophetic oracle on its own, but we read them in relation to other oracles, all of them ultimately contributing to the book's overall message. The same is true with the book of Psalms.

At the simplest level, then, one can profit from considering links in adjacent psalms, reflecting on such truths as these (to cite only a few of many dozens of examples):

- The ways of the righteous versus the wicked in Psalms 1 and 2 (individual level in Ps 1 and national level in Ps 2)
- How Yahweh's "holy hill" (Zion) is emphasized in Psalms 2:6 and 3:4

- Confidence in Yahweh's protection as the psalmist lies down, sleeps, and awakes: Psalm 3 as a "morning" psalm and Psalm 4 for the evening (Pss 3:5 and 4:8)
- The nature of true sacrifice in Psalms 50 and 51 (psalms of Asaph and of David)
- How the national crisis in Psalm 89 is "answered" in Psalm 90 and following psalms
- How Israel's history is told in Psalm 105 from God's gracious and forgiving perspective and in Psalm 106 from his angry and vengeful perspective.

Or, one can consider larger structures, such as Psalms 15–24, where the outer psalms (15 and 24) echo each other, bracketing the section, and then each successive "pair" (Psalms 16 and 23, 17 and 22, 18 and 20/21) echoes each other and forms a concentric "ring" around Psalm 19 at the center, which focuses on God's word in creation and in his Torah.

Or, at another level, one can profit by considering the key psalms at the "seams" of the Psalter, including the royal/messianic psalms in Psalms 2, 72, 89, and 144, or the bracketing of the entire Psalter with psalms affirming both the human kingship of David and the divine kingship of Yahweh in Psalm 2 and then again in Psalms 144–145. Or one can enter into the final crescendo of praise closing the Psalter in Psalms 146–150, ending in the most purely praise-oriented psalm in the entire book (Ps 150); here it is as if the editors of the Psalter are saying, "It's all been said and done; all that remains is to praise God!"

Reading the Psalter in this way brings its message into harmony with the rest of the Old Testament, which consistently has a forward-looking bent. The Abrahamic, Mosaic, and Davidic covenants all point ahead to the ultimate covenant, the new one, ushered in by the true "David," Jesus the Christ (or Messiah). To deny the lasting significance of the Old Testament covenants is to impoverish one's reading of the Psalms and, indeed, one's own life of faith.

Such a reading also helps provide insight into how the writers of the New Testament understood these psalms. The writer of Hebrews, for instance, makes the case in chapter 1 that the Son/Messiah is superior to the angels by using references from the Psalter almost exclusively. In Acts 4, the two texts used as the basis for two separate messages about Jesus are both from the Psalms (Book V and Book I, respectively). It reminds us of when Jesus, on the road to Emmaus after his resurrection, reminded the two unnamed disciples, "This is what I told you while I was still with you: Everything must be fulfilled that is written about me in the Law of Moses, the Prophets and the Psalms" (Luke 24:44 NIV).

While we are convinced that the Psalter speaks of an eternal dimension to the Davidic kingship and the Davidic promises, we also believe that the church can learn much from what we have described above as "wisdom/democratizing" perspectives. These perspectives tend to emphasize "David" as humble, poor and needy, dependent on Yahweh, and that certainly is true of all human kings (see Deut 17:14–20, esp. vv. 18–20). The king's dependence on Torah, on reading God's word, is certainly apropos today, as are the king's concerns for integrity and the poor and needy in such passages as Psalms 69:32–33, 140:12, or all of 101. When the king speaks of his own plight, he himself is among the "poor and needy," for example, in Psalms 35–41. The principles of godly leadership laid out for the king in Deuteronomy 17 are echoed for a leader like Joshua (Josh 1:6–9), for Ezra (Ezra 7:6, 10), and for anyone (Ps 1)—all of which are instructive in today's world.

Therefore, in the end we joyfully affirm with David in Psalm 145:1, "I will exalt you, my God the King; I will praise your name for ever and ever" (NIV); with the final psalmist, "Let everything that has breath praise the Lord" (Ps 150:6 NIV) *Hallelujah!*; and with the voices of all of creation, "To him who sits on the throne and to the Lamb be blessing and honor and glory and might forever and ever!" (Rev 5:13 ESV).[152]

---

152. Special thanks are due to several people for their help in producing this essay: (1) Librarians Sandra Oslund of Bethel University and Barbara Winters of Bethlehem College and Seminary (BCS) for above-the-call-of-duty service in giving access to their libraries in the midst of the Covid pandemic; (2) Josh Bremerman, David Howard's TA at BCS, for innumerable works tracked down online; (3) John Piper, Howard's colleague at BCS, for suggestions on some hermeneutical questions to address; (4) William Yarchin for permission to include a forthcoming essay of his; and (5) the following colleagues for suggestions on works for inclusion here: Nancy de-Claissé-Walford, Jason DeRouchie, Sue Gillingham, Jamie Grant, Jim Hamilton, Peter Ho, Philip Johnston, Clint McCann, and Stephen Smith.

2

The Macrostructural Design and Logic of the Psalter: An Unfurling of the Davidic Covenant

Peter C. W. Ho

The search for a principle to unite the 150 psalms has gone on for more than seventeen centuries. Although renewed efforts in this search from the 1980s have yielded important results, Psalms scholarship has yet to reach a consensus. Crystalized from my larger work, The Design of the Psalter: A Macrostructural Analysis, *this chapter is an important step toward that consensus. It explores how the entire Psalter is designed, explains why it is coherent as a whole, and opens up a new paradigm to understand the Psalms.*

As early as the third to fourth century, Hippolytus of Rome had struggled to understand the logic behind the arrangement of the Psalter. He argued that numerical-symbolic reasons, rather than historical, were behind the arrangement of the Psalter.[1] Sixteen centuries later, the English scholar Thomas Boys argued that the arrangement of the Psalms is based on poetic structuring via parallelisms.[2] Although the search for the logic of the Psalter has taken center stage in Psalms scholarship since Gerald Wilson's

1. Alexander Roberts, James Donaldson, and A. Cleveland Coxe, eds., *ANF* 5 (New York: Scribner's Sons, 1919), 200; additional references to Hippolytus's works (in original and English) can be found in Craig A. Blaising and Carmen S. Hardin, *Psalms 1–50*, ACCS 7 (Downers Grove, IL: InterVarsity Press, 2004), 188, 411.

2. Thomas Boys, *A Key to the Book of Psalms* (London: Seeley and Son, 1825), 54.

seminal work in 1985,[3] three decades later, Marvin Sweeney surmised that "no one has yet successfully explained the rationale behind [the Psalter's] arrangement."[4]

This impasse, in my view, is due to a confounding of factors. We have come to a point where the growth in the scholarship has generated a mammoth of methods and conclusions demanding consolidation. Unfortunately, such consolidation remains wanting. While there is a growing number of studies on a unit of adjacent psalms, there are comparatively fewer studies that look at the Psalter as a whole.[5] Conclusions reached on one part of the Psalms often orbit independently about a different part of the Psalter. Moreover, the fragmentary approach of form criticism remains entrenched in Psalms scholarship. Emerging studies of textual variants in medieval Hebrew manuscripts and the Qumran Psalters further complicate the issue.[6]

Notwithstanding such difficulties, this essay seeks a furtherance to the seminal questions of how the Psalter is a coherent whole, and *why*. In brief, I argue that: (1) the book of Psalms has a macrostructural integrity that is shaped by different literary techniques requiring a multimethodological approach to understand it holistically; (2) there is a coherent macrostructural shape to the Masoretic Psalter, and the Psalter can be divided into three parallel sections (Books I, II–III, and IV–V) with four groups each; (3) the logic that underlies the shape of the Psalter is the

---

3. Gerald H. Wilson, *The Editing of the Hebrew Psalter*, SBLDS 76 (Chico, CA: Scholars Press, 1985).

4. Marvin A. Sweeney, "Form and Eschatology in the Book of the Twelve Prophets," in *The Book of Twelve & The New Form Criticism*, ed. Mark J. Boda et al., ANEM 10 (Atlanta: SBL Press, 2015), 160.

5. An early article in 1991 by John Walton has raised the possibility of an organizational logic for the whole Psalter. His methodology rests primarily on semantics (or "content") and historical parallels to the books of 1–2 Samuel. Walton's use of the metaphor of "cantata" is a catch-all phrase that means different psalms written over different times are put together coherently. Unfortunately, his methodology locks him in, and he is unable to articulate a coherence to the entire sequence of the Psalter. He recognizes this limitation at various points in his article; for instance, on Psalms 46–48, Walton admits that "there is an intriguing lacuna in the correlation that I am uncertain how to explain. The next event in the narrative of Samuel is the Davidic covenant in 2 Samuel 7. There is no correlating psalm here in book 2. That fact represents either a serious and perhaps mortal blow to the theory or could perhaps be explained by the observation that the whole cantata is about the covenant, *so all of the appropriate psalms addressing it are used at other key junctures. Whatever solution might be suggested would play a significant role in confirming or refuting any hypothesis*." Emphasis mine. John H. Walton, "Psalms: A Cantata about the Davidic Covenant," *JETS* 34.1 (1991): 26, 30.

6. William Yarchin, "Were the Psalms Collections at Qumran True Psalters?," *JBL* 134.4 (2015): 775–89.

metanarrative of God's people, seen under the expression of the Davidic covenant. The finer details of my proposals are found in *The Design of the Psalter: A Macrostructural Analysis.*[7]

We begin by asking a methodological question. How should we approach the Psalms? What is the nature of the Psalms as Hebrew poetry? In Figure 2.1 below, I summarize three hermeneutical perspectives in approaching the Psalms.

Figure 2.1 – Three Hermeneutical Perspectives to Interpreting the Psalms

(1) INDIVIDUAL: HOW DIFFERENT TECHNIQUES WORK TOGETHER	(2) INTRATEXTUAL: HOW DIFFERENT COLLECTIONS COHERE INTO LARGER UNITS	(3) INTERTEXTUAL: HOW THE DAVIDIC NARRATIVES RELATE TO THE PSALMS
• Up to the single psalm • How different poetic techniques, form, and meaning correlate at the poem level (if at all) • Precision of interpretation increases when various approaches align • *Proposal: Employ poetic, semantic, and linguistic approaches to the text and see if, and how, they cohere*	• Up to the level of the book(s) of the Psalter • How the techniques work beyond the single psalm • Key techniques include: the use of prologue, superscriptions, concentric and linear readings • *Proposal: The use of central motifs helps us see three sections with four groups each across entire Psalter*	• Davidic references (at least 50%) assume knowledge of the Historical books • Key themes: Torah, kingship, Zion, prayer in affliction • Metanarrative linked by central motifs suggests: establishment, fall, and reestablishment of a Davidic king and Zion • *Proposal: Unfurling of the Davidic Covenant*

In the study of biblical Hebrew poetry, scholars have traditionally focused on systematizing literary features such as parallelisms, colometry,[8] and meter—a field of study known as poetics.[9] Linguistic analysis of po-

7. Peter C. W. Ho, *The Design of the Psalter: A Macrostructural Analysis* (Eugene, OR: Wipf & Stock, 2019).

8. The division of biblical Hebrew poem into their clauses (or colon).

9. Wilfred G. E. Watson, *Classical Hebrew Poetry: A Guide to Its Techniques*, JSOTSup 26 (Sheffield: JSOT Press, 1984); Luis Alonso Schökel, *A Manual of Hebrew Poetics*, SubBi 11 (Rome: Editrice

etic discourses, however, has developed more recently.[10] While the latter is usually limited to the sentence,[11] literary analyses do not have such limitations. As such, conclusions from these two approaches are very different. Because the book of Psalms, as a whole, has a multifaceted expression, multimethodological explorations (e.g., poetic, semantic, linguistic, prosodic approaches) are necessary to capture its full-orbed meaning. The precision of interpretation increases when various approaches align in their conclusions.

Next, the macrostructure of the entire Psalter is only elucidated via distinct collections of psalms, just as distinct strophes and stanzas elucidate the structure of an individual psalm. This assumes some sort of organization across the boundaries of psalms, a phenomenon already recognized (e.g., the twin psalms 111 and 112, 135 and 136). We have terms like "strophes" and "stanzas" to help us identify larger poetic units within a single poem, but we currently have no agreed terminology to identify groups of psalms. For the purposes of our analysis we will now define a nomenclature of eight compositional units of psalms, graded from the single psalm to the entire Psalter: (1) psalm; (2) pair or twin psalm; (3) subcollection; (4) collection/subgroup; (5) group; (6) book(s) of the psalms; (7) section (Books I, II–III, and IV–V); (8) Psalter.[12]

I have found that there are many different techniques at work in the shaping of the Psalter.[13] Important techniques of shaping include the use of superscriptions, repetitions, genre characterizations, *inclusios*, chiasmi, and even the canonical history of Israel. For instance, consider how Psalms 1–2 are a pair of psalms that begin the Psalter. The unity of Psalms 1–2 have

---

pontificio Istituto biblico, 1988).

10. See especially Michael O'Connor, *Hebrew Verse Structure* (Winona Lake, IN: Eisenbrauns, 1980); Ernst R. Wendland, *Discourse Perspectives on Hebrew Poetry in the Scriptures* (New York: United Bible Societies, 1994); Nicholas P. Lunn, *Word-Order Variation in Biblical Hebrew Poetry: Differentiating Pragmatics and Poetics*, PBM (Eugene, OR: Wipf & Stock, 2006).

11. Matthew Ian Ayars, *The Shape of Hebrew Poetry: Exploring the Discourse Function of Linguistic Parallelism in the Egyptian Hallel* (Leiden: Brill, 2019), 14.

12. Of these, only the subcollection, collection, group, and section require further elaboration. A subcollection includes several adjacent psalms usually with a common superscription, common theme, or motif (e.g., *mikhtam* in the superscription of the Davidic psalms 56–60). A collection/subgroup of psalms is made up of two or more subcollections and can be defined by a common superscription (e.g., psalms of David, psalms of Korah). A group is a major unit of several collections.

13. Ho, *Design of the Psalter*, 35–37.

been well noted and debated.[14] But something more is at work beyond mere semantic parallels. Consider Figure 2.2 below.

Figure 2.2 – Structural Divisions, Parallels, and Contrasts of Psalms 1 and 2

PSALM 1:1–2, STROPHE I	**PSALM 2:1–3, STROPHE I**
The "ways" of the "blessed man" The essence of his "way" = Torah piety	The "ways" of the kings and nations The essence of their "way" = against Yahweh and his anointed
PSALM 1:3, STROPHE II (CENTER) Attributes of the "blessed man" Located at the heavenly "Zion" Center word = "that blessed man"	**PSALM 2:4–9, STROPHES II–III (CENTER)** Attributes of the "anointed king" Located at Zion Center word = "my [Yahweh's] son"
PSALM 1:4–6, STROPHE III Outcome of both the wicked and the righteous Judgment before the righteous Ends with the wicked perishing	**PSALM 2:10–12, STROPHE IV** Outcome of both the kings and judges of the earth Destruction before the Son Ends with the blessed under Yahweh's refuge

The structural-semantic parallels between Psalms 1 and 2 are striking. Both psalms can be seen as a triptych (an image across three panels hinged together), having concentric and linear dimensions. The linear dimension traces the *way* and corresponding *outcome* of the righteous and wicked through each psalm. Concentricity of the psalms highlights the blessed state of the righteous man in the paradisiacal garden (Ps 1) and the triumphant messianic king at Zion (Ps 2). Together, they carry the leitmotifs of Torah-piousness, kingship, and Zion, which are seen strategically across the Psalter.

The third hermeneutical perspective to the book of Psalms is to consider its theological thrust. Prima facie, it assumes that the reader is familiar

14. Robert L. Cole, *Psalms 1–2: Gateway to the Psalter*, HBM 37 (Sheffield: Sheffield Phoenix, 2013); Jesper Høgenhaven, "The Opening of the Psalter: A Study in Jewish Theology," *SJOT* 15.2 (2001): 169–80.

with the Davidic narratives. The Psalter's preoccupation with Torah, kingship, and Zion parallels important eschatological texts elsewhere (Mic 2:12–13; 4:3–4; Isa 11:1–9). Since Israel maintained a covenantal relationship with Yahweh through the sacrificial system, the destruction of the temple would have created a seismic theological conundrum, especially in light of the Davidic covenant in 2 Samuel 7. It is necessary, therefore, to explore if and how the Psalter expresses such theological struggle poetically. Putting on these hermeneutical lenses from the outset, I'll now present a proposal of the Psalter's superstructure.

BOOK I (PSS 3–41)

Book I, as a whole, has been studied by a number of scholars. An important structural proposal views Psalms 1–2 as the prologue, followed by a four-part division (Pss 3–14; 15–24; 25–34; 35–41).[15] I have adopted and modified such a structure by Gianni Barbiero (Fig. 2.3),[16] with the following explanation.

Barbiero observes a combination of different literary techniques at work in the final shape of Book I. He sees, for instance, the use of alternating Day (D)/Night (N) psalms, and alternating external-hostility (EH)/personal-distress (PD) psalms, linking Psalms 3–14 (Group 1).[17] And they are either communal (CL) or individual laments (IL). He argues that Psalms 3–7, as a unit, has an orientation toward Zion. In contrast, in Psalms 10–14, Yahweh looks outward from Zion. At the center, Psalms 8 and 9 focus on Yahweh's kingship and judgment.

In Psalms 15–24, 25–34, and 35–41 (Groups 2, 3, 4), the genre character of individual psalms forms a chiasmus in each group. For instance, Group 2 is framed by entrance liturgies (Pss 15, 24) and Group 3 is framed by acrostic psalms having common motifs of the poor and justice (Pss 25, 34). At the center of these three groups, there are emphases on Yahweh's kingship, the Torah, and the Zion temple.[18] The last group (35–41) highlights a different motif at the center (supplication), which we will discuss subsequently.

---

15. J. Clinton McCann Jr., "Reading from the Beginning (Again): The Shape of Book I of the Psalter," in *Diachronic and Synchronic*, ed. Joel S. Burnett, W. H. Bellinger, and W. Dennis Tucker Jr. (New York: T&T Clark, 2007), 129–42.

16. Gianni Barbiero, *Das erste Psalmenbuch als Einheit: eine synchrone Analyse von Psalm 1–41*, ÖBS 16 (Frankfurt: Peter Lang, 1999). My modifications are primarily in Psalms 35–41. I also arrived at a different central emphasis for each of the four groups.

17. See Psalms 3:6, 8; 4:5, 9; 5:4; 6:7; 7:7; 8:4; 9:20; 10:12; 11:2; 12:6; 13:4; 14:2, 5. All references are in MT unless otherwise stated.

18. Psalms 18–21 are framed with *inclusios*. Psalms 18–19 begin and end with Yahweh/my God as "my rock" (both have "rock" with a first-person suffix); Psalm 20 is framed by a call to

Figure 2.3 – Gianni Barbiero's Structure of Book I with Modifications

Psalm	1	2	3	4	5	6	7	8	9	10	11	12	13	14	15	16	17	18	19
Superscription	Tr	Kg	Lament							Lament					EL				
Shape of collection *Genre classification and special SS notations*			D	N	D	N	D			D	N	D	N	D		Cf			
			EH	PD	EH	PD	EH	N	D	CL	IL	CL	IL	CL			L		
																		Kg	
																			Tr
			Kingship & judgment																
			Supplication					H	Thk	Supplication								Cosmic &	
			To Zion					YHWH Kg		Away from Zion									
			Group 1 (12 psalms)												**Group 2**				
Group motif			**Lament** Reign of man												**Torah** Reign of messianic king				

Abbreviations

- **Cf** confidence psalm
- **CL** communal lament
- **D** day psalm
- **EH** external hostilities
- **EL** entrance liturgy
- **H** hymn
- **IL** individual lament
- **Kg** kingship

20	21	22	23	24	25	26	27	28	29	30	31	32	33	34	35	36	37	38	39	40	41
				EL	Individual lament						Thanksgiving hymn				Sup						Sup
			Cf		PJ									PJ		H				Thk	
		L				W					W						Sap		Sap		
Kg	Thk								Kg	Thk								Sup			

Psalms 20–24	Psalms 25–34			Psalms 35–41
Torah praise	**Kingship & temple hymns**			**A memorial**
	To temple	Yhwh Kg	From Zion	
(10 psalms)	**Group 3** (10 psalms)			**Group 4** (7 psalms)
				Lament The servant of Yhwh
Torah Reign of messianic king	**Yhwh-kingship, Zion** Reign of Yhwh			

L lament

N night psalm

PD personal distress

PJ motif of the poor and justice

Sap sapiential

Sup supplication

Thk thanksgiving hymn

Tr Torah

W motif of the wicked

An important technique in shaping a unit of psalms is the use of superscriptions. Consider the superscriptions of Psalms 3–7. Functioning as frames, Psalms 3 and 7 are the only two with historical superscriptions and fronted by the phrase, "of David." In contrast, the superscriptions of Psalms 4–6 consist of musical notations fronted by the phrase "to the choirmaster." This is presented visually below:

A: Of David > historical superscript concerning Absalom (Ps 3)
B: To the choirmaster > stringed instrument (Ps 4)
C: To the choirmaster > with the flutes (Ps 5)
B': To the choirmaster > stringed instrument, eight-stringed lyre (Ps 6)
A': Of David > historical superscript concerning Cush (Ps 7)

In brief, Book I can be delineated into four main groups. The motifs emphasized at the center of the first three groups are: kingship, Torah, and the temple. Key structuring techniques include: (1) concentric (chiastic) arrangements of psalms; (2) structural emphases of the motifs of Yahweh's kingship, Torah, temple, and supplication; (3) use of superscriptions as structuring devices; and (4) orientation vis-à-vis Zion.

BOOKS II–III (PSS 42–89)

Superscription is also a key technique used to bind Books II–III together.[19] Across these two books, the superscriptions form a chiastic Korahite-Asaphite-Davidic-Asaphite-Korahite arrangement (see Pss 42–49; 50; 51–72; 73–83; 84–89). Furthermore, the Elohistic Psalter stretches from Psalms 42 to 83, binding Books II–III together.[20] More convincing is the parallel genre

Yahweh to "answer"; Psalm 21 begins and ends with the phrase "in your strength" (this form occurs only four times in the Hebrew Bible, and it is found twice in Psalm 21). These *inclusios* are not found in the rest of the psalms of the group. Likewise, Psalms 29–30 make special references to Yahweh's judgment and the temple (esp. 30:1, the only superscription associated with the temple).

19. M. D. Goulder, "The Social Setting of Book II of the Psalter," in *The Book of Psalms: Composition and Reception*, ed. Peter W. Flint and Patrick D. Miller, SVT 99 (Leiden: Brill, 2004), 349–67; and Goulder, *The Prayers of David (Psalms 51–72): Studies in the Psalter*, II, JSOTSup 102 (Sheffield: JSOT Press, 1990).

20. Frank-Lothar Hossfeld and Erich Zenger, "The So-Called Elohistic Psalter: A New Solution for an Old Problem," in *A God So Near: Essays on Old Testament Theology in Honor of Patrick D. Miller*, ed. Brent A. Strawn and Nancy Bowen (Winona Lake, IN: Eisenbrauns, 2003), 35–51; Joel S. Burnett, "Forty-Two Songs for Elohim: An Ancient Near Eastern Organizing Principle in the Shaping of the Elohistic Psalter," *JSOT* 31 (2006): 81–101.

order of the Korahite and Asaphite psalms. Consider the parallel Korahite subgroups in Figure 2.4 below.[21]

Figure 2.4 - Parallel Genre Structures between the Two Korahite Subgroups

KORAHITE SUBGROUP I Psalms 42–49 (Secondary Superscription)	GENRE CATEGORY	KORAHITE SUBGROUP II Psalms 84–89 (Secondary Superscription)
42–43 (maskil)	Individual Lament	84 (Korahite)
44 (maskil)	Communal Lament	85 (Korahite)
45 (love song)	**Kingship**	**86 (prayer)**
46–48 (Korahite)	Divine Response (Yahweh's kingship)	87 (song)
49 (Korahite)	Individual Lament	88, 89 (song, maskil)

In the center column, notice that the Korahite psalms (Subgroups I and II) begin and end with laments. At the center are kingship (in bold) and divine-response psalms. Within each of the subgroups, we also see secondary superscriptions taking a shape corresponding to the genre characterization of the subgroup (words in the parentheses). So, for Psalms 42–44, the word *maskil* is placed before the "Korahite" reference in the superscription. Psalms 46–49 do not have *maskil* in the superscription. At the center, Psalm 45 has a superscription with a unique reference to "love song." This phenomenon is repeated in the second Korahite subgroup. References of Korahite and "song" respectively surround the center, Psalm 86, which in turn, contains a unique reference to "prayer." This suggests that Psalm 86 is not randomly placed.

21. Susan Gillingham, "The Zion Tradition and the Editing of the Hebrew Psalter," in *Temple and Worship in Biblical Israel*, ed. John Day, Oxford Old Testament Seminar (London: T&T Clark, 2005), 308–41 (323).

Strikingly, the above phenomenon is also found in the Asaphite subgroups (Fig. 2.5), suggesting intentionality.

Figure 2.5 - Parallel Genre Structures between the Two Asaphite Subgroups

ASAPHITE SUBGROUP I Psalms 50, 73–77 (Secondary Superscription)	GENRE CATEGORY	ASAPHITE SUBGROUP II Psalms 78–83 (Secondary Superscription)
50, 73 (Asaphite)	Didactic/Sapiential	78 (maskil)
74 (maskil)	Communal Lament	79–80 (Asaphite)
75–76 (song)	**Divine Response**	**81–82 (Asaphite)**
77 (Asaphite)	Lament	83 (song)

Like the Korahite subgroups, the Asaphite subgroups have parallel genre structures. Here, they begin with didactic psalms and end with laments. At the center, we observe psalms that depict the destruction of Jerusalem (Pss 74; 79–80). No other psalm in the entire Psalter depicts the ruins of Jerusalem with such vividness. Such depictions demand Yahweh's response (75–76 and 81–82). The Asaphite subgroups also have secondary superscriptions arranged in corresponding shapes. In Figure 2.5, Psalms 50, 73, and 77 have an Asaphite secondary superscription framing Subgroup I. But this arrangement is remarkably reversed in the Asaphite Subgroup II, where the Asaphite secondary superscription is found within the frames instead. Such consistency is unlikely to be merely coincidental.

Figure 2.6 illustrates how Books II–III form a single unit. Note the four main groups in Books II–III: Korahite Subgroup I (42–49), Davidic psalms (51–72),[22] Asaphite Group (73–83), and Korahite Subgroup II (84–89). In the

22. I consider Psalms 51–71 as a unit of the Davidic Group. Although Psalms 66, 67, and 71 do not have the Davidic superscription, note that Psalms 66 and 67 are part of a collection with the superscript "a song" (Pss 65–68) and are all part of the thanksgiving genre. This means the editor(s) wants us to see them as a unit. Psalm 71 can be seen as a pair with Psalm 70 (see also Pss 9–10; 32–33; 42–43). Note that Psalm 71 mirrors 51 as a petition psalm. Psalm 72 has a Solomonic superscription and stands out like the Asaph psalm, Psalm 50.

rows designated "Superscription" and "Structural Shape of Collection," I summarized each psalm's superscription and genre. Secondary superscriptions are also added above or under the boxes. For instance, Psalms 56–60 are Davidic psalms and marked as "D" or "Dh." "Dh" are superscriptions ascribed to David and containing additional historical information. In terms of genre, Psalms 56–60 are characterized as petition/trust, having *mikhtam* as secondary reference in the superscription.

The entire Davidic Group (51–71) is framed by petition and lament psalms on both ends (51–55, 68–71). At the center, we see a series of trust (56–60), confidence (61–64), and thanksgiving (65–68) psalms. Like the Korahite and Asaphite subgroups, we observe similar macroshaping techniques at work in this Davidic Group. The concentration of historical superscriptions (51–52; 54; 56–57; 59–60; 63) work in tandem with the content of the psalms to picture a David who is deeply afflicted and praying. These imageries of a broken David reflect his downfall after his sin with Bathsheba as seen in the historical books. More specifically, the placement of Psalm 51, with its reference to Nathan's judgment, is not random. Placed at the head of this group, it shows us subsequent psalms that highlight David's afflictions as the outworking of God's judgment. This entire unit concludes with Psalms 71–72 depicting David's concluding years and the transition to Solomon's kingship (71:18; 72:1, 20).[23]

This brokenness of the human Davidic king is paired with the brokenness of the Zion temple depicted in the Asaphite psalms (esp. Pss 74, 79). From a macrostructural point of view, the two major groups at the center of Books II–III (Pss 51–72 and 73–83) highlight the fall of human kingship and the Zion temple respectively.

In brief, Books II–III consist of four groups, forming the second major section of the Psalter. While Book I highlights the establishment of the human king, Torah, and Zion temple, Books II–III highlight the reverse: a Davidic king who lacked Torah piety, leading to a broken kingship and Zion temple. There is a striking consistency in the use of shaping techniques. Structural units are consistently concentric. At the center of these units, we often find psalms of kingship. Also striking is the presence of a solitary psalm at the center of the last group of both sections (Pss 38, 86), depicting an afflicted Davidic king in prayer.

23. Peter C. W. Ho, "The Shape of Davidic Psalms as Messianic," *JETS* 62 (2019): 515–31. Psalm 71 does not have a Davidic superscription, but pairs closely with Psalm 70 and mirrors Psalm 51.

Figure 2.6 – Macrostructure of Books II–III of the Psalter

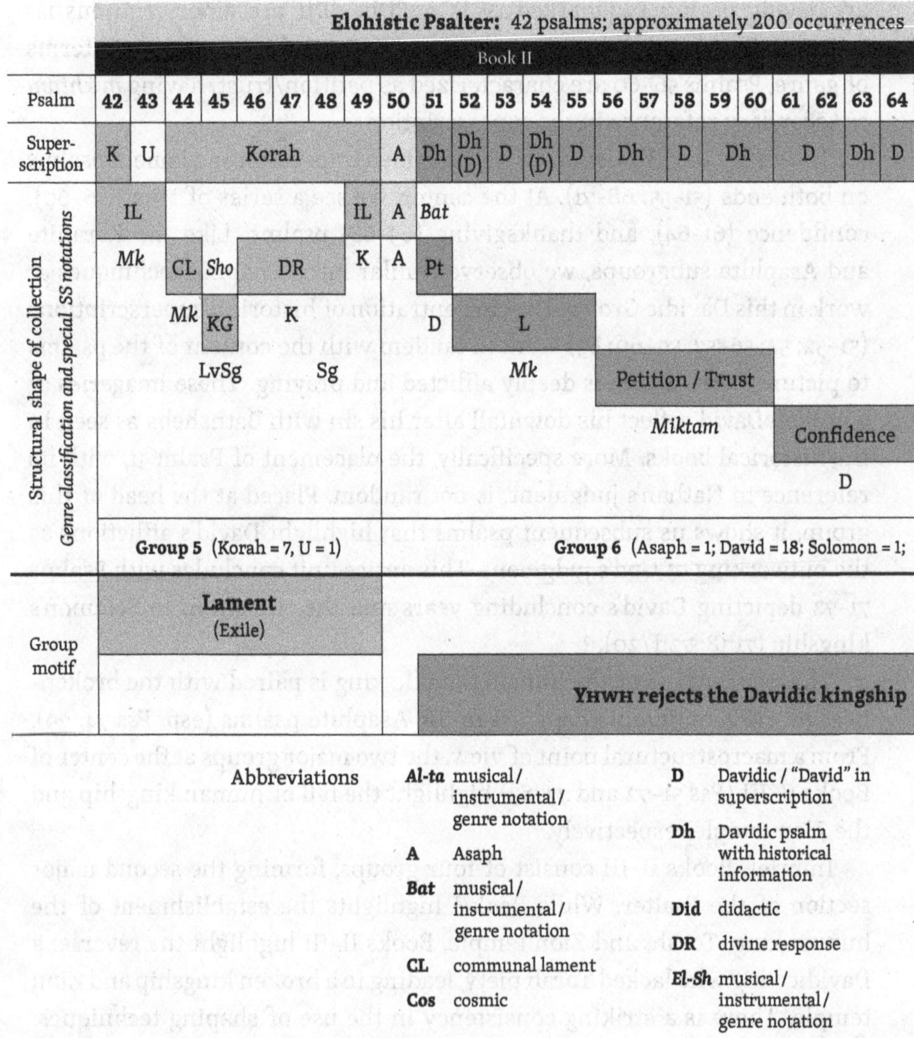

Elohistic Psalter: 42 psalms; approximately 200 occurrences
Book II
Psalm
42 43 44 45 46 47 48 49 50 51 52 53 54 55 56 57 58 59 60 61 62 63 64
Super-scription
K U Korah A Dh Dh (D) D Dh (D) D Dh D Dh D Dh D
Structural shape of collection
Genre classification and special SS notations
IL
IL A Bat
Mk
CL Sho DR K A Pt
Mk KG K D L
LvSg Sg Mk
Petition / Trust
Miktam
Confidence
D
Group 5 (Korah = 7, U = 1)
Group 6 (Asaph = 1; David = 18; Solomon = 1;
Group motif
Lament
(Exile)
YHWH rejects the Davidic kingship
Abbreviations
Al-ta musical / instrumental / genre notation
A Asaph
Bat musical / instrumental / genre notation
CL communal lament
Cos cosmic
D Davidic / "David" in superscription
Dh Davidic psalm with historical information
Did didactic
DR divine response
El-Sh musical / instrumental / genre notation

of "Elohim" and 44 occurrences of "YHWH"

								Book III																
65	**66**	**67**	**68**	**69**	**70**	**71**	**72**	**73**	**74**	**75**	**76**	**77**	**78**	**79**	**80**	**81**	**82**	**83**	**84**	**85**	**86**	**87**	**88**	**89**
D	Ps	Sg	Davidic			U	Sol	Asaph											K		D	K		E
							Sol	Did				*Jed*	Did	*El-Sh*					IL				IL	IL
					Mem	Pt		A	CL	*Al-ta*		IL	*Mk*	CL		*Git*		IL	K	CL		DR	Sg	*Mk*
				L		U			*Mk*	DR		A		A		DR		Sg		K	Kg	Sg		
Thanksgiving				D						Sg						A					Pry			
	Sg																							
Untitled =1; Others =2)								**Group 7** (Asaph = 11)											**Group 8** (K + E = 5; D = 1)					
																			Lament (Kingship, Covenant)					
because of sin								**YHWH rejects the Temple because of sin**																

E	Ethan	**L**	lament	**Pt**	petition
Git	musical/ instrumental/ genre notation	**LvSg**	love song	**Sg**	song
IL	individual lament	**Mem**	"a memorial"	***Sho***	musical/ instrumental/ genre notation
Jed	musical/ instrumental/ genre notation	***Mk***	musical/ instrumental/ genre notation	**Sol**	Solomon
K	Korah	***mlk***	YHWH Malak psalm	**U**	untitled
Kg	kingship	**Pry**	prayer		
		Ps	psalm		

BOOKS IV–V (PSS 90–150)

Books IV and V of the Psalter have been well researched.[24] They are often studied independently from each other and separate from Books I–III.[25] Book V is more problematic; besides being the longest, it has the most variegated superscription types, resisting simple groupings by superscription. We posit that Books IV and V, while distinct from each other, form a unit consisting of four major groups. When these two books are seen as a single entity, many structural difficulties of Book V are also resolved. We will highlight some salient arguments pertinent to our analysis.[26]

First, note that Psalms 104–106 at the end of Book IV function like "hinge psalms," linking the end of Book IV to the beginning of Book V. Together, four adjacent psalms, 104–107, are interlocked by formulaic phrases across the common seam of the books. Three adjacent psalms, 104–106, end with the formulaic *hallelujah*; but Psalms 105–107 begin with the formulaic "give thanks."[27] All four psalms (104–107) are similar in length (averaging forty-three verses per psalm) and genre, in contrast to the Davidic psalms around them.

Figure 2.7 – Chapter Length and the Unity of Psalms 104–107

	PSALM	NUMBER OF VERSES	TOTAL VERSES	AVERAGE
DAVIDIC	101 102 103	8 29 22	59	19.7
DOXOLOGICAL SUPERSCRIPTION	104 105 106 (Book IV) 107 (Book V)	35 45 48 43	171	42.8
DAVIDIC	108 109 110	14 31 7	52	17.3

24. Jerome F. D. Creach, "The Shape of Book Four of the Psalter and the Shape of Second Isaiah," *JSOT* 80 (1998): 63–76; Michael G. McKelvey, *Moses, David and the High Kingship of Yahweh: A Canonical Study of Book IV of the Psalter* (Piscataway, NJ: Gorgias, 2013).

25. Egbert Ballhorn, *Zum Telos des Psalters: Der Textzusammenhang des Vierten und Fünften Psalmenbuches (Ps 90–150)*, BBB 138 (Berlin: Philo, 2004), 382.

26. For details, see Ho, *Design of the Psalter*, 102–33.

27. See Psalms 104:35; 105:45; 106:48; 105:1; 106:1; 107:1.

But the clearest reason why Psalms 104–107 are a unit is the continuous metanarrative of the canonical history of God's people across them, traced from God's creation (104); to Israel's nationhood and exodus (105); to her idolatry, leading to her captivity and oppression by foreign nations (106). Psalm 107 begins with descriptions of Israel's redemption and ingathering from four corners of the lands (107:2).

Figure 2.8 and Figure 2.9 (see the following pages) illustrate my proposal for these two books. Rows are drawn with increasing generalization. The row "Superscript" characterizes each psalm's superscription. The row below it ("Occurrences") provides a visualization of important words that are repeated in each psalm. For instance, in Figure 2.9, Psalm 135 contains five occurrences of the root *HLL* (praise), and four occurrences of *BRK* (bless). This visualization allows us to easily see that Psalm 134 (with two occurrences of *BRK*), and Psalm 136 (with four occurrences of *HD*), are a unit of three psalms that stand out in the immediate horizon with their emphases of blessing, praise, and thanksgiving. But notice also that these emphases also occur in Psalms 104–107 with the same sequence (Fig. 2.8).

These parallels are not coincidental as both Psalms 104–107 and 135–137 trace the canonical story of God's people from creation, to exile, to hopes of ingathering and restoration. Figure 2.10 summarizes seven motifs along this canonical story with parallel references from these two sets of psalms.

Once these parallels between Psalms 104–107 and 135–137 are seen, further structural parallels between the larger units of Psalms 104–119 and 135–150 can be recognized. Consider Figure 2.8 and Figure 2.9 again. Each of these units has a Davidic subgroup at the center (108–110; 138–145) and concludes with Hallel psalms (111–119; 146–150).[28] Interestingly, these two subgroups of Hallel psalms are framed by acrostics and alphabetical compositions.[29] Both have the most sustained recurrences of the root *HLL* in the *piel* imperative, and only these two subgroups sustain the motif of Torah in Book V.[30] Finally, both these subgroups trace the motifs of the praise of Yahweh, God's creation (111:1–7; 115:15; 146:6), deliverance

28. As Psalm 119 is a complete acrostic, it is the complete praise of the Torah, which parallels Psalm 150, an exhaustive praise of Yahweh.

29. Psalms 111–112 and 119 are clearly acrostic psalms. Psalms 145 and 150, framing the final Hallel, are alphabetic acrostics and an alphabetical composition respectively. Anthony R. Ceresko, "Endings and Beginnings: Alphabetic Thinking and the Shaping of Psalms 106 and 150," *CBQ* 68.1 (2006): 32–46 (esp. 42–44).

30. Words like "precepts," "commandment," "utterance," and "judgment" are found almost exclusively in these two places.

Figure 2.8 – A Proposal for the Macrostructure of Books IV-V, Part 1 (Pss 90–119)

	Book IV													
Psalm	**90**	**91**	**92**	**93**	**94**	**95**	**96**	**97**	**98**	**99**	**100**	**101**	**102**	**103**
Superscription	M	U	Ps	*mlk*		U		*mlk*	Ps	*mlk*	Thk	D	Aff	D
Occurences of certain words or formulaic phrases							*BRK*	*HD*		M	*BRK* *HD*			M *BRK* *BRK* *BRK*
Shape of collections	Sup	Trust	Thk Sg	Yhwh Malak								P D	Sup D	Thk D
Shape of groups	Group 9													
	Mosaic Moses sings (Deut 32); the ideal "righteous one"; brink of entry											**Davidic** David sings; the ideal afflicted king in Zion		
	Take refuge in Yhwh's house			**Yhwh's kingship in Zion**								Live righteously in Yhwh's house		
Structual central motif (Books IV–V)	**Yhwh's cosmic kingship; judgment from Zion**													
	The "righteous" walking right in the Torah (90–92) > Yhwh's kingship (93–100) > A Davidic king that walks right (100–103) > Time of blessings begins (101)													

Abbreviations

Aff psalm of affliction

Ash "blessed"

BRK *piel* imperative masculine plural of *brk* ("bless")

brk *piel* imperative feminine singular of *brk*

D Davidic/"David" in superscription

Dir For the choir director

			Book V												
104	105	106	107	108	109	110	111	112	113	114	115	116	117	118	119
brk	HD	*HLL*	HD		D			*HLL*			U		*HLL*	HD	*Ash*
HLL	*HLL*	HD							*HLL*		*HLL*	*HLL*	*HLL*	HD	
	M	M							*HLL*						
		M							*HLL*						
		M													
		HLL													
brk	HD	*HLL*	HD	Plea		DR	Torah		*HLL*						Tr
	HLL			Sg	L	D			Theocentric			Universal			
					Dir, D										

Group 10

Canonical history		Praise of YHWH
Canonical history Creation to exile; brink of entry		Praise of YHWH Creation to exile; enter gates of Zion at Ps 118; end with Torah praise; acrostic
	YHWH establishes afflicted, Davidic king in Zion	

A victorious messianic king; Torah glorified

Alphabetical psalm (103) > Canonical history (104–107) > Victorious David (108–110) > Acrostic (111–112) > Hallelujah (113–117) > "Righteous" enter earthly Zion (118) > Acrostic, perfect praise of Torah (119); righteous David at the Zion-Temple

DR divine response
HD *hiphil* imperative of *ydh*
HLL Hallelujah (*piel* imperative)
L lament
M Moses
mlk YHWH Malak psalm
P praise
Ps psalm
Sg song
Sup supplication
Thk thanksgiving
U untitled

Figure 2.9 – A Proposal for the Macrostructure of Books IV–V, Part 2 (Pss 120–150)

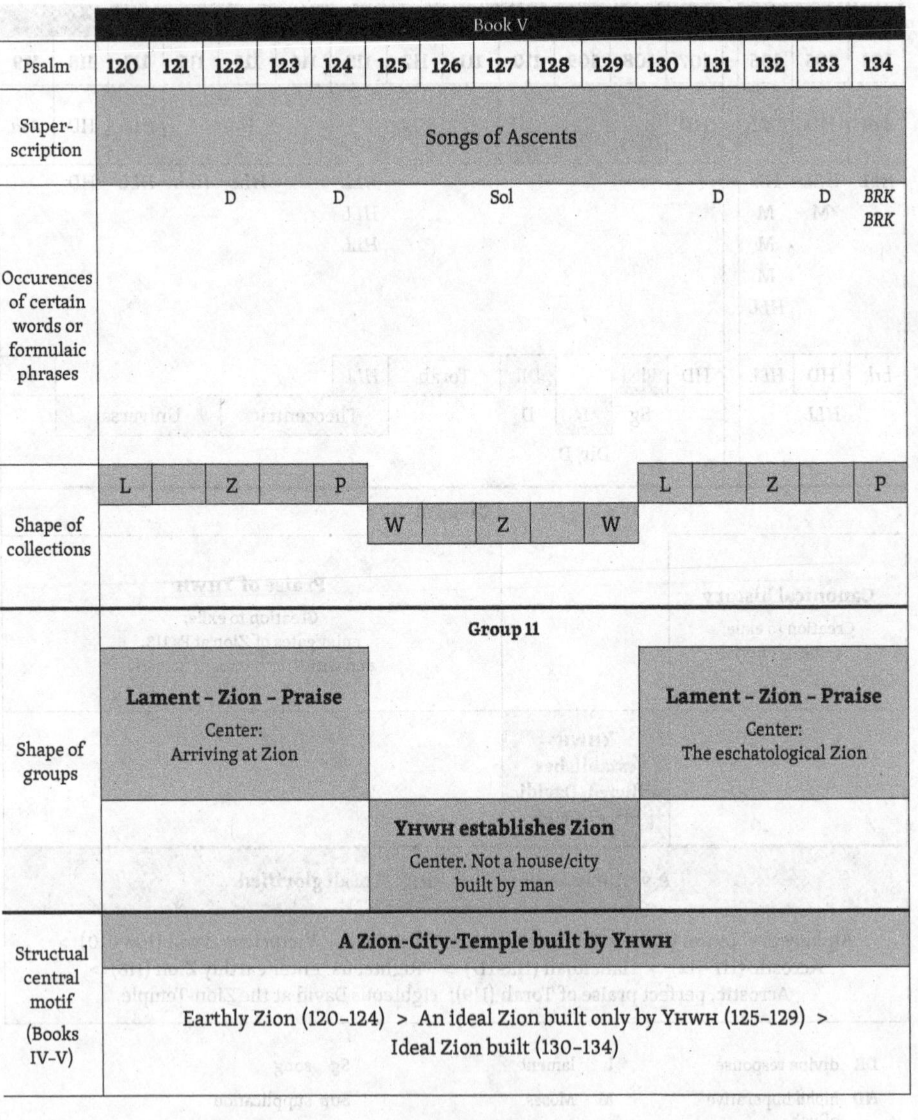

Book V
Psalm
120
121
122
123
124
125
126
127
128
129
130
131
132
133
134
Super-scription
Songs of Ascents
Occurences of certain words or formulaic phrases
D
D
Sol
D
D
BRK
BRK
Shape of collections
L
Z
P
W
Z
W
L
Z
P
Group 11
Shape of groups
Lament – Zion – Praise
Center: Arriving at Zion
Lament – Zion – Praise
Center: The eschatological Zion
YHWH establishes Zion
Center. Not a house/city built by man
Structual central motif (Books IV–V)
A Zion-City-Temple built by YHWH
Earthly Zion (120–124) > An ideal Zion built only by YHWH (125–129) > Ideal Zion built (130–134)

Abbreviations

BRK *piel* imperative masculine plural of *brk* ("bless")

Chas *Chasidim*

Cos cosmic

D Davidic/"David" in superscription

Dir for the choir director

HD *hiphil* imperative of *ydh*

HLL Hallelujah (*piel* imperative)

Book V															
135	**136**	**137**	**138**	**139**	**140**	**141**	**142**	**143**	**144**	**145**	**146**	**147**	**148**	**149**	**150**
HLL	*HD*	U	Davidic				h	Davidic			*HLL*	*HLL*	*HLL*	*HLL*	*HLL*
HLL	*HD*										*HLL*	*HLL*	*HLL*	*HLL*	*HLL*
HLL	*HD*											*HLL*			*HLL*
HLL	*HD*											*HLL*			*HLL*
BRK												*HLL*			*HLL*
BRK												*HLL*			*HLL*
BRK												*HLL*			*HLL*
BRK												*HLL*			*HLL*
HLL												*HLL*			*HLL*
												HLL			*HLL*
															HLL
															HLL
Great Hallel		Jns	Kg							Kg	Ind	W		W	Uni
				Med	Individual lament				P			Isr		*Chas*	
			D	Dir	Dir	D	*Msk*	D	D	P			Cos + *Chas*		

Group 12

Canonical history Creation to exile		**Praise of Yhwh** Creation to restored Zion; people in Zion Ps 149; end with praise of Yhwh; alphabetic
Praise in house of God	**Supplication**	Praise in house of God

Supplication of afflicted David

Praise in God's House and back into exile (135–137) > Alphabetic (138) >
Davidic (138–145) > Acrostic (145) >
Praise; creation to Zion; righteous Israel in Zion (148–150) >
Perfect praise of Yhwh; alphabetic (150)

h	historical superscrption	**Kg**	kingship	**U**	untitled
Ind	individual psalm	**L**	lament	**Uni**	universal
Isr	Israel in focus	**Med**	meditative	**W**	motif of the wicked
Jns	Janus psalm	***Msk***	*Maskil*	**Z**	motif of Zion
		P	praise		

of God's people (114:1–2; 146:7–9; 147:2), and entry into Zion (118:20; 147:2, 12–13; 149:2).

Figure 2.10 - Parallel Trajectories from Creation to Exile in Psalms 104–107 and 135–137

PSALMS 104–107	COMMON MOTIFS IN THE TRAJECTORY	PSALMS 135–137
104:2–32	Yahweh's creation and providence	135:6–7; 136:4–9
105:6–24	Yahweh's choosing and forming a people	135:4
105:25–43	Yahweh's deliverance of Israel from Egypt	135:8–9
105:44	Yahweh's giving of the land to Israel	135:9–12
106:6–7, 19–22, 35–39	Israel's persistent idolatry	135:14–18
106:41–47	Yahweh's giving up of Israel to the Babylonian exile	137:1–4

Moving now to Psalms 90–103 and 120–134 (in Figs. 2.8 and 2.9), note how Psalms 90–103 can be seen as a unit with three collections. The Yahweh reigns psalms (93–100)[31] are framed by three Mosaic (90–92)[32] and Davidic (101–103) psalms respectively. Psalms 90–103 as a whole is framed by a series of motifs occurring, stunningly, in reverse order:

A Reference to "Moses" (90:1)

B Yahweh's everlasting and universal nature (90:1–2)

C Fleeting nature of humankind (90:5–6)

D Yahweh consumes humankind in anger because of sins and iniquities (90:7–8)

---

31. David M. Howard Jr., *The Structure of Psalms 93–100*, Biblical and Judaic Studies 5 (Winona Lake, IN: Eisenbrauns, 1997).

32. Psalms 90–92 can be seen as a Mosaic triptych. Psalms 90–92 are sapiential in tone, emphasizing the motifs of living righteously before God and dwelling in him. The motif of dwelling in 90:1 is sustained at the beginning of Ps 91, where one "dwells in the secret place of Elyon" (cf. 91:9). This imagery is also presented in 92:13–16. The common arboreal motifs, secure dwelling in God's house for the "righteous," and connections to Exodus 23:20 and Leviticus 26:8 (cf. Ps 91:7, 11) bind them together. See also McKelvey, *Moses, David and the High Kingship of Yahweh*, 85–90.

A′ Reference to "Moses" (103:7)
D′ Yahweh removes humankind's transgressions; not angry (103:8–9, 12)
C′ Fleeting nature of humankind (103:15–16)
B′ Yahweh's everlasting and universal nature (103:17–19)

This fits well with our earlier discussion that Psalms 104–106 are linked to Psalm 107. The final group left for comment is the Songs of Ascents (Pss 120–134; Fig. 2.11, p. 58), which as a whole, has a three-part structure and a movement toward the ideal eschatological city.[33]

The first five psalms (120–124) could depict a journey to the earthly gates of Jerusalem.[34] But the Jerusalem city presented at the structural center (122:5–7) is not ideal. In contrast, Psalm 127, at the center of the next five psalms, envisions a blissful society built by God's own hands. And Psalm 132,[35] at the center of the third set of five psalms, depicts a time in postexilic Zion when a Davidic king will sprout (132:17–18). In short, Psalms 122, 127, and 132, centrally located in the three separate units of the Songs of Ascents, form a triptych for Zion. Its final pane shows a renewed and ideal Zion city ruled by a righteous, divine, Solomonic-messianic figure (127:1; 132:11–12).

We are now able to summarize the entire superstructure of the book of Psalms. The last rows in Figures 2.3, 2.6, 2.8, and 2.9 identify the structural central motifs of the twelve groups of psalms. When these central motifs are placed side by side, a strikingly coherent structure emerges. Figure 2.12 (p. 59) illustrates the superstructure of the Psalter based on the central motifs of the twelve major groups of psalms in three major sections (Books I, II–III, IV–V).

---

33. Michael Rohde, "Observations on the Songs of Ascents: A Discussion about the So-Called Zion-Theology of Psalms 120–134," *Baptistic Theologies* 1.2 (2009): 24–42 (esp. 25); Frank-Lothar Hossfeld and Erich Zenger, *Psalms 3: A Commentary on Psalms 101–150*, Hermeneia (Minneapolis: Fortress, 2011), 394.

34. From "Meshech" and "Kedar" in Psalm 120, to the "hills" in Psalm 121, to "House of Yahweh in Jerusalem" in Psalm 122.

35. Psalms 122 and 132 are the two psalms in the entire Psalter with the highest number of "Zion/temple markers"; Gillingham, "Zion Tradition," 313–14.

Figure 2.11 – Central Motifs and Structure of the Songs of Ascent

<table>
<tr><td>Psalm</td><td>120</td><td>121</td><td>122</td><td>123</td><td>124</td><td>125</td><td>126</td><td>127</td><td>128</td><td>129</td><td>130</td><td>131</td><td>132</td><td>133</td><td>134</td></tr>
<tr><td>Superscription</td><td></td><td></td><td>D</td><td></td><td>D</td><td></td><td></td><td>Sol</td><td></td><td></td><td></td><td>D</td><td></td><td>D</td><td></td></tr>
<tr><td rowspan="2">Shape of collections</td><td colspan="5">Subgroup 1</td><td colspan="5">Subgroup 2</td><td colspan="5">Subgroup 3</td></tr>
<tr><td colspan="5">L   Zion   P
Central motif</td><td colspan="5">W   Zion   W
Central motif</td><td colspan="5">L   Zion   P
Central motif</td></tr>
<tr><td rowspan="2">Occurrences of YHWH</td><td colspan="4">12x YHWH</td><td colspan="3">12x YHWH</td><td colspan="5">12x YHWH</td><td colspan="3">12x YHWH</td></tr>
<tr><td></td><td></td><td>1x YHWH</td><td></td><td></td><td></td><td></td><td>3x YHWH</td><td></td><td></td><td></td><td>1x YHWH</td><td></td><td></td><td></td></tr>
<tr><td rowspan="2">Shape of subgroups</td><td colspan="5">Lament – Zion – Praise
Center = earthly Zion</td><td colspan="5"></td><td colspan="5">Lament – Zion – Praise
Center = eschatological Zion</td></tr>
<tr><td colspan="5"></td><td colspan="5">YHWH establishes Zion
Center = Not a house/city built by man</td><td colspan="5"></td></tr>
<tr><td rowspan="2">Central motif of Group 11</td><td colspan="15">A Zion-City-Temple built by YHWH</td></tr>
<tr><td colspan="15">Earthly Zion (120-124) > An Ideal Zion built only by YHWH (125-129) > Ideal Zion built (130-134)</td></tr>
</table>

Abbreviations

D	"David" in superscription	**Sol**	"Solomon" in superscription
L	lament	**W**	motif of the wicked
P	praise psalm		

Figure 2.12 - Central Motifs of All 12 Groups in the 3 Sections of the Masoretic Psalter

SECTION 1

BOOK I: ESTABLISHMENT OF THE DAVIDIC KINGSHIP AND ZION				
1–2	3–14	15–24	25–34	35–41
Prologue	YHWH's cosmic kingship; judgment from Zion	Victorious messianic King; Torah glorified	Dedication: historical Zion-temple; YHWH's kingship	Supplication of afflicted David

GROUP 1 2 3 4

SECTION 2

BOOK II: FALL OF THE DAVIDIC KINGSHIP		BOOK III: FALL OF THE ZION-TEMPLE	
42–49	50–72	73–83	84–89
Messianic King and his bride	Fall of Davidic kingship (and YHWH's response)	Fall of Zion-temple (and YHWH's judgment)	Supplication of afflicted David

GROUP 5 6 7 8

SECTION 3

BOOK IV: KINGSHIP OF YHWH AND IDEAL DAVID	BOOK V: ESTABLISHMENT OF THE IDEAL KINGSHIP AND ZION-CITY		
90–103	104–119	120–134	135–150
YHWH's cosmic kingship; judgment from Zion	Victorious messianic King; Torah glorified	Restoration; eschatoloical Zion-temple; divine-messianic kingship	Supplication of afflicted David

GROUP 5 6 7 8

The first groups of every section (Groups 1, 5, 9) are consistently focused on Yahweh's or the Messiah's kingship. The last groups of every section (Groups 4, 8, 12) are consistently focused on a supplicating, afflicted Davidic figure.[36] Central motifs of the two groups at the center develop a metanarrative across the three sections. First, note the establishment of Davidic

36. To be specific, note that Psalms 38, 86, and 138–145 all depict a praying afflicted Davidic figure centralized in the last Davidic groups.

kingship and the dedication of the temple at Zion (Groups 2, 3). This is followed by the fall of Davidic kingship and Zion (Groups 5, 6). But the Psalter ends with the reestablishment of an ideal Davidic king and Zion temple (Groups 10, 11). In this way, the central motifs trace the establishment, fall, and reestablishment of the Davidic kingship and Zion temple. The consistent motif of a supplicating, afflicted Davidic figure in the fourth group of all three sections suggests a persistent presence of afflictions and distresses, counterbalanced by the persistent restatement of Yahweh's kingship in the first group of all three sections.

This storyline of the Psalter is not developed from successively arranged psalms, rather, it is visible only under a larger schema as the central motifs are laid out. This centralized view is not dissimilar to what we know about chiasmus occurring at the psalm level. We just need to view this across a number of consecutive psalms. A further summary of these observations is shown in Figure 2.13 below.

Figure 2.13 – Concentric and Linear Structures of the Group Central Motifs

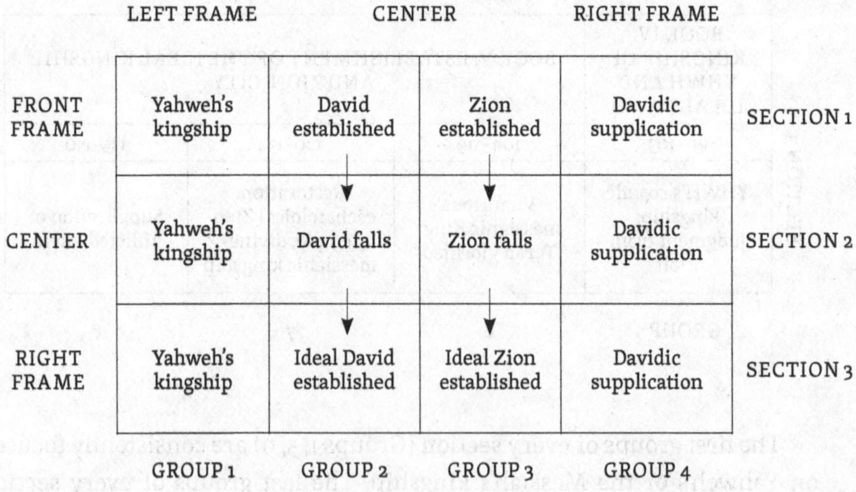

LEFT FRAME
CENTER
RIGHT FRAME
FRONT FRAME
Yahweh's kingship
David established
Zion established
Davidic supplication
SECTION 1
CENTER
Yahweh's kingship
David falls
Zion falls
Davidic supplication
SECTION 2
RIGHT FRAME
Yahweh's kingship
Ideal David established
Ideal Zion established
Davidic supplication
SECTION 3
GROUP 1
GROUP 2
GROUP 3
GROUP 4

THE SHAPE OF THE DAVIDIC PSALMS

The macrostructural proposal above is remarkably collaborated by an independent investigation of all psalms ascribed to David.[37] Like the five books of the Psalter, the Davidic psalms can be divided into five collections.[38] Figure 2.14 below captures the key contours across the five Davidic Collections (DCs).

Figure 2.14 - Characterization of the Five Davidic Collections (DC) in the Psalter

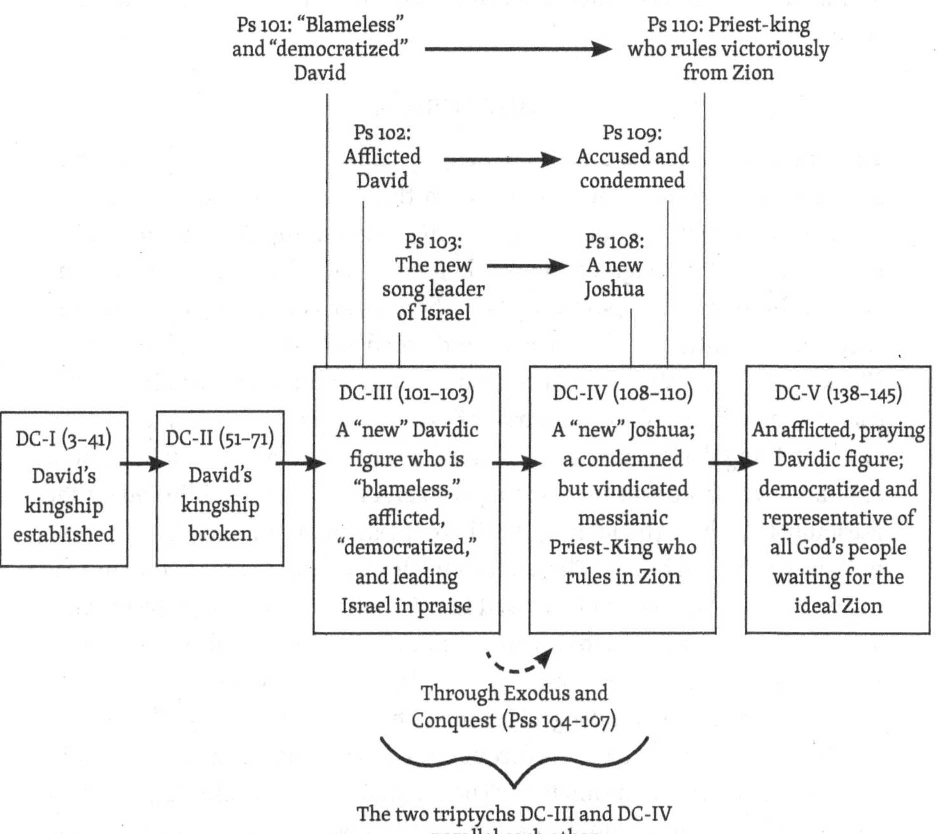

37. Ho, "Shape of Davidic Psalms as Messianic."

38. Scholars do not agree with the number of Davidic Collections. See Christoph Buysch, *Der Letzte Davidpsalter: Interpretation, Komposition Und Funktion Der Psalmengruppe Ps 138–145*, SBB 63 (Stuttgart: Katholisches Bibelwerk, 2010), 15; Hossfeld and Zenger, *Psalms 3*, 524; Gordon Wenham, *Psalms as Torah: Reading Biblical Song Ethically* (Grand Rapids: Baker Academic, 2012), 48.

Note how DCs-III and IV identify an ideal victorious Davidic figure. These five DCs unfurl a crystallized form of the messianic hopes of the Davidic covenant (2 Sam 7). Again, they tell the story of the establishment (DC-I), fall (DC-II), and more specifically, the reestablishment (DC-III–IV) of an ideal Davidic king who will usher in a new era at the end times (144–145 in DC-V). Interestingly, this new David- and Joshua-like figure arising in Psalms 101–103 and 108–110 is also afflicted. The last DC (138–145), however, depicts a period of prayer and waiting for the people of God (the democratized Davidic figure). At the end, this Davidic king hands over his kingship to Yahweh in the last Davidic psalm (145), just before the final hallelujah psalms.

CONCLUSION

The search for a principle to unite the 150 psalms has gone on for more than seventeen centuries. Renewed efforts in this search since the 1980s have yielded important results, though Psalms scholarship has yet to reach a consensus on the design of the whole Psalter. This chapter seeks furtherance to the seminal questions of how the Psalter is a coherent whole, and why. Structurally, the Psalter can be divided into three parallel sections (Books I, II–III, IV–V) and each section has four groups arranged concentrically. When the motifs at the center of every group are viewed synchronically, a striking design appears—a metanarrative tracing the establishment and fall of the *historical* Davidic kingship and Zion temple, followed by the reestablishment of the ideal (yet afflicted) Davidic figure and Zion temple built by God's own hands. The underlying logic of the Psalter is the unfurling of the Davidic covenant, weaved into God's larger purposes for his chosen people from creation to consummation. This understanding has at least three major implications. First, every psalm will need to be reread in light of this superstructure and logic. Second, other poetic texts (e.g., the Book of the Twelve) could be revisited through the lens of macrostructuring techniques gleaned from our analysis. The technique of chiasmus is more pervasive and more intricate in the Psalms than we have previously known. Scholarship's claim that there is an inadequate structure or no structure at all need not be sustained when we learn to see the Psalter's design with this proposal. Finally, the Psalter's message in this new light will have to be reviewed against other early interpretations (e.g., the Qumran Psalter and the New Testament).

3

David's Biblical Theology and Typology in the Psalms: Authorial Intent and Patterns of the Seed of Promise

James M. Hamilton Jr.

This essay argues that the biblical authors operated from a shared worldview, that the individual psalms are indeed connected with each other and intended to be read together, that the primary background for interpreting the Psalter is earlier Scripture, and that these starting points allow us to understand David to present himself in the Psalms as a type of the One to come. Reading the Psalter this way flows organically into the interpretation—and claims of fulfillment—found in the New Testament.

INTRODUCTION[1]

Could David have understood himself as a type of the future king from his line? For him to have held such a position, what biblical-theological understanding of earlier Scripture would have been required? If the New Testament quotes the Psalms as having been written by David and

1. An earlier version of this material was presented in the invited session of the Psalms and Hebrew Poetry Section at the national meeting of the Evangelical Theological Society on November 21, 2019. My thanks to the Steering Committee for the invitation, and to David Gundersen, Josh Philpot, Sam Emadi, and Mitch Chase who read this essay and offered invaluable feedback.

typologically fulfilled in Jesus (e.g., Ps 41:9 in John 13:18[2]), is it conceivable that these conclusions are exegetically valid because they are the interpretations intended by David the human author?

In this essay I seek a sympathetic reading of David's biblical theology, one that takes as a working hypothesis the idea that David understood himself as a prefiguring type of the future king God promised to raise up from his line of descent (see 2 Sam 7:12–14; Acts 2:30–31). Through careful attention to Psalm 8 and its immediate context, I seek to show the validity of the interpretation of the Psalms seen in the New Testament.

The demonstration of my case involves a number of ideas, not all of which can be defended in this brief essay: first, that we have access to what David thought in the psalms that he wrote, which entails understanding the superscriptions to attribute authorship.[3] Second, we would have to conclude that David had access to as much Scripture as had been written at the time he lived,[4] and that in those Scriptures he saw patterns of events that matched things that happened to him. Third, in the Psalms David meant to present himself as an installment in these patterns, expecting them to be repeated and fulfilled in the life of the seed of promise. Fourth, we would have to assume that David's worldview was built from that earlier Scripture to which he had access. Fifth, and related to the foregoing, would be the idea that the biblical authors had a coherent worldview—that they were all in basic agreement with one another.[5]

---

2. Raymond E. Brown notes, "The rabbis understood this passage in Ps xli 10(9) to refer to Ahithophel's conspiracy with Absalom against David (II Sam xv 12)." Raymond E. Brown, *The Gospel According to John*, AB (Garden City, NY: Doubleday, 1970), 554. The rabbis are correct: David refers back to his own experience of betrayal, but in my view David does so expecting his experience to be fulfilled in the life of the seed God promised to him (2 Sam 7:12). See James M. Hamilton, "John," in *John–Acts*, vol. 9, ESV Expository Commentary, ed. Iain M. Duguid, James M. Hamilton Jr., and Jay Sklar (Wheaton, IL: Crossway, 2019), 221.

3. The superscriptions were understood to ascribe authorship in the Old Testament itself (2 Sam 22:1; 23:1; 2 Chron 29:30), in the New Testament (e.g., Mark 12:35–37 and parallels), and in the Talmud (*b. Bathra 14b*). For discussion, see §4, and esp. §4.1, in James M. Hamilton, "Introduction," in *Psalms*, 2 vols., Evangelical Biblical Theology Commentary (Bellingham, WA: Lexham, 2021), 25–52.

4. I take the view that the Pentateuch, for example, was written by Moses (e.g., Deut 31:24; Josh 23:6; Neh 8:1; Luke 2:22), and that Moses really did lead Israel out of Egypt in 1446 BC (1 Kgs 6:1). It seems to me that Joshua 24:26 indicates that Joshua wrote the book that bears his name, and the book of Judges appears to have been written by David's time, ca. 1000 BC (cf. Jdg 1:21 and 2 Sam 5:6).

5. For my attempt to show that all the biblical authors agreed on the same big idea, the gravitational center, at the heart of their worldview, see James M. Hamilton, *God's Glory in Salvation through Judgment: A Biblical Theology* (Wheaton, IL: Crossway, 2010).

The first section of this essay briefly discusses the shared worldview out of which the biblical authors operated. My goal is to trace the contours of the interpretive perspective the biblical authors, including David, employed as they interpreted earlier Scripture and their own experience.[6] The second and third sections of this study will use Psalm 8 to illustrate two points: the interconnectedness of the Psalter and how that affects interpretation of individual psalms, and the importance of understanding earlier Scripture as the most significant ideological background against which the Psalms must be understood. The fourth section of this essay will then consider indications that David presents himself in the Psalms as a type of the one to come.

A SHARED WORLDVIEW

God created the world as good, but the man and woman were tempted into rebellion by the serpent, bringing death and judgment into God's creation (Gen 1:1–3:13). This judgment puts enmity between the seed of the woman and the seed of the serpent, reproductive difficulty and conflict between man and woman, and, with a curse on the ground, banishment from the garden and the presence of God (3:14–24). With the judgment, however, comes the promise that the seed of the woman will bruise the serpent's head (3:15).[7] The Genesis 3:15 promise is elaborated upon in the blessing of Abraham (Gen 12:1–3) and Judah (Gen 49:8–12), and those blessings are reinforced (e.g., in Num 23–24) and interpreted and expanded in the promises made to David (2 Sam 7).[8]

The promises provoke the hope that the seed of the woman will arise as the king from David's line, seed of Judah, seed of Abraham. He will triumph over the serpent, defeating the one who brought sin and death into the world and renewing God's reign in God's world. As a result, the effects of sin and death will be banished from God's world: the dead will be raised;

---

6. See the descriptions of the goal of biblical theology in Stephen G. Dempster, *Dominion and Dynasty: A Biblical Theology of the Hebrew Bible*, New Studies in Biblical Theology (Downers Grove, IL: InterVarsity, 2003), 36; and Thomas R. Schreiner, *Paul, Apostle of God's Glory in Christ: A Pauline Theology*, 2nd ed. (Downers Grove, IL: InterVarsity, 2020), 1. Also helpful is Brian Rosner's definition of biblical theology in "Biblical Theology," in *New Dictionary of Biblical Theology*, ed. T. Desmond Alexander, Brian S. Rosner, and D. A. Carson (Downers Grove, IL: InterVarsity, 2000), 10. See further James M. Hamilton, *What Is Biblical Theology?* (Wheaton, IL: Crossway, 2014).

7. See Walter Wifall, "Gen 3:15—A Protevangelium?," *CBQ* 36 (1974): 361–65; and James M. Hamilton, "The Skull Crushing Seed of the Woman: Inner-Biblical Interpretation of Genesis 3:15," *The Southern Baptist Journal of Theology* 10.2 (2006): 30–54.

8. James M. Hamilton, "The Seed of the Woman and the Blessing of Abraham," *TynBul* 58 (2007): 253–73.

hearts will be changed to sin no more; and the curse on the land will be purged with blessing renewed.

The promises God makes also shape the interpretive expectations of those who embrace them. In a forthcoming book on typology, I hope to demonstrate that God's promises shape the interpretive patterns the biblical authors see in historical events, resulting in their presentation of key people, events, and institutions as prefiguring, foreshadowing types of things to come.

Having quoted Psalm 69:9, Paul told the Romans that "whatever was written in former days was written for our instruction, that through endurance and through the encouragement of the Scriptures we might have hope" (Rom 15:4, ESV).[9] The Psalms were intended to do exactly what Paul describes in Romans 15:4, and they particularly accomplish this function when we see three things about the Psalter: first, that the psalms are all interconnected resulting in the conclusion that the whole book is to be read together; second, that worldview considerations demand that earlier Scripture be seen as the primary backdrop of the Psalter; and third, that David *understood himself* as a type of the one to come and spoke of his own experience as such.

INTERCONNECTEDNESS

To illustrate the Psalter's interconnectedness, we will examine the way that interconnectedness influences the interpretation of Psalm 8. Before looking at how Psalm 8 flows right out of Psalms 1–7, however, let us first consider an alternative perspective.

In the 2014 New International Commentary on the Old Testament (NICOT) volume on Psalms, Rolf A. Jacobson wrote the commentary on Psalm 8.[10] He reads the psalm as pertaining to humanity in general rather than to either David himself or the future king from his line. This can be seen from Jacobson's rendering of Psalm 8:4 (MT 8:5), "What are human beings that you remember them? Or mortal persons that you attend them?" In keeping with this rendering, Jacobson summarizes the psalm with the words,

9. Scripture quotations are taken from the English Standard Version (ESV), unless otherwise noted.

10. Nancy deClaissé-Walford, Rolf A. Jacobson, and Beth LaNeel Tanner, *The Book of Psalms*, NICOT (Grand Rapids: Eerdmans, 2014), 120–28.

> The first stanza starts with a focus on the *glory* of God in creation and ends with a question about the value of humanity. The second stanza answers this question by affirming that God has crowned humanity with *glory* and ends with a discussion of the various creatures over whom humans have been given responsibility.[11]

To approach Psalm 8 in this way is to fail to read the psalm in light of *both* its superscription *and* its context in the Psalter.

Robert Cole has decisively shown that Psalms 1 and 2 are the "gateway to the Psalter."[12] That is to say, Psalms 1 and 2 introduce the whole Psalter. Together they set the scene, the characters, the conflict, and promise the plot's resolution. Psalm 1 celebrates the blessed man who delights in the Torah and rejects the counsel, way, and seat of wicked sinners who scoff at God. Psalm 2 further identifies these enemies as those who plot against Yahweh and his anointed king, the Messiah. Psalm 2 poetically reformulates the 2 Samuel 7 promises to David, warning anyone who persists in rebellion that their doom is certain. An *ashrey* (אשרי) *inclusio* surrounds the two psalms—the first opening with this term, the second closing with it: "Blessed is the man" (1:1), and "blessed are all who take refuge in him" (2:12).

Psalm 3 continues in this vein.[13] The raging of the nations against Yahweh and his anointed in 2:1–3 is illustrated by Absalom's revolt against David in Psalm 3 (superscription [MT 3:1]). Yahweh's Psalm 2 decree (2:6–9), including his setting of his King on Zion, his "holy hill," announced in 2:6, forms the basis for David's pleas in Psalm 3—pleas that Yahweh answers from his "holy hill" in 3:4 (MT 3:5).

The "vain words" David's enemies love in 4:2 (MT 4:3) recall the way "the peoples plot in vain" in 2:1. Yahweh's setting apart of the man of his lovingkindness (חסיד) in 4:3 (MT 4:4) refers to Yahweh's decree concerning his king in 2:6–9, and in both Psalms 3 and 4 David speaks of how he lies down to sleep in safety because of Yahweh's promise to him (3:5; 4:8 [MT 3:6; 4:9]).

Psalm 5 references the "morning" (2x in 5:3 [MT 5:4]), which strongly links it to the *lying down* and *sleeping* in Psalms 3 and 4. David complains of the "lies" of his enemies in both 4:2 and 5:6 (MT 4:3; 5:7), and his reference to the "holy temple" in 5:7 recalls the "holy hill" of 2:6 and 3:4 (MT 5:8; 3:5). The

11. deClaissé-Walford, Jacobson, and Tanner, *Book of Psalms*, 120.

12. Robert L. Cole, *Psalms 1–2: Gateway to the Psalter* (Sheffield: Sheffield Phoenix, 2013).

13. The following is only a sampling of the connections between Psalms 3, 4, 5, 6, 7, and 8. For my own attempt to document the connections in a more comprehensive way, see the "Context" discussions of these psalms in Hamilton, *Psalms*.

rejoicing of those who take "refuge" in Yahweh in 5:11 (MT 5:12) flows out of the blessing on those who take "refuge" in Yahweh's Messiah in 2:12, while the assertion that Yahweh blesses "the righteous" in 5:12 (MT 5:13) reminds us that Yahweh knows the way of "the righteous" in 1:6, that his blessing is on his people in 3:8 (MT 3:9), and that he lifts up his countenance on his people in 4:6 (MT 4:7; cf. Num 6:24–26).

When David asks Yahweh not to rebuke him in his "wrath" in 6:1 (MT 6:2), he employs the same term used to reference the "wrath" visited on the enemies in 2:5 and 2:12. Similarly, when he asks not to be "disciplined" in 6:1 (MT 6:2) he employs the term rendered "be warned" in the phrase, "be warned, O rulers of the earth" in 2:10 (יסר), and along the same lines, when David speaks of his soul as "troubled" in 6:2, 3, and 10 (בהל MT 6:3, 4, 11), he uses the same term rendered "terrify" in 2:5. In Psalm 6 David seems to be crying out to Yahweh not to treat him the way Psalm 2 says Yahweh treats his enemies. Also connecting Psalms 5 and 6 is the phrase "workers of evil" in 5:5 and 6:8 (MT 5:6 and 6:9, unfortunately the ESV renders the first "evildoers" and the second "workers of evil," but the same Hebrew phrase appears in the two verses).

Repeated words and phrases continue in Psalm 7, where in 7:1 (MT 7:2) David takes "refuge" in God, reinforcing the same idea from 5:11 (MT 5:12) and 2:12. When David says "save me" in 7:1b he repeats what he said, "save me," in 6:4 (MT 7:2; 6:5). He refers to his "soul" in 7:2 (MT 7:3) as he had in 6:3–4 (MT 6:4–5). The "enemy" mentioned in 7:5 is referenced by the same term from 6:10 (MT 7:6; 6:11). The glory in 7:5 was likewise mentioned in 3:3 and 4:2 (MT 3:4; 4:3) and anticipates 8:5.

All this resonance in terminology indicates that the subjects introduced in Psalms 1 and 2 continue to be the topics under discussion in Psalms 3, 4, 5, 6, and 7. When we get to Psalm 8, the connectedness continues. Here I present the list of lexical points of contact between Psalm 8 and its neighbors from my commentary on Psalms:

8:1, 9 (MT 8:2, 10) "how majestic is your name"
5:11 (MT 5:12) "the ones who love your name"
7:17 (MT 7:18) "the name of Yahweh Most High"
9:2 (MT 9:3) "your name, O Most High"

8:1 (MT 8:2) "in all the earth"
2:8 "ends of the earth"
8:2 (MT 8:3) "you established strength" (יסדת)
2:2 "rulers gather together" (נוסדו from יסד)

8:2 (MT 8:3) "your adversaries"
3:1; 6:7; 7:4, 6; 10:4 (MT 3:2; 6:8; 7:5, 7; 10:5) "adversary(ies)"

8:2 (MT 8:3) "the hater"
3:7; 6:10; 7:5; 9:3, 6 (MT 3:8; 6:11; 7:6; 9:4, 7) those who hate

8:3 (MT 8:4) "your heavens"
2:4 "the one who sits in the heavens"

8:3 (MT 8:4) "which you made ready" (כוננתה)
7:9, 12, 13; 9:7; 10:17 (MT 7:10, 13, 14; 9:8) make ready (forms of כון)

8:4 (MT 8:5) "man" (אנוש)
9:19, 20; 10:18 (MT 9:20, 21) "man" (אנוש)

8:4 (MT 8:5) "you remember him"
6:5; 9:6, 12 (MT 6:6; 9:7, 13) remembrance/remember

8:4 (MT 8:5) "son of man (Adam)"
80:17 (MT 80:18) "son of man (Adam)"
cf. 144:3; 146:3

8:5 (MT 8:6) "glory"
3:3; 4:2; 7:5 (MT 3:4; 4:3; 7:6) "glory"

8:5 (MT 8:6) "you crowned him" (תעטרהו)
5:12 (MT 5:13) "you surround him" (תעטרנו)

8:6 (MT 8:7) "you put" (שתה)
3:6; 9:20 (MT 3:7; 9:21) "set"
See also: 8:4 (MT 8:5) "son of Adam"—with "Seth's" name, שת

As I have written in my commentary:

> This list of verbal and thematic links between Psalm 8 and surrounding Psalms shows that Psalm 8 was intended to be read not in isolation but in sequence, not as making abstract statements about humanity in general but as continuing the flow of thought that began with the blessed man in Psalm 1, identified him as the Lord's anointed king in

> Zion in Psalm 2, then traced his Davidic difficulties with the wicked haters who rebelled against him in Psalms 3–7.[14]

Along with the interconnectedness of the Psalter, I contend that the worldview of the biblical authors demands that we read the Psalms primarily against the backdrop of earlier Scripture.

THE PSALMS AND EARLIER SCRIPTURE

In the same way that the intellectual milieu of the romantic poets provides the context in which their poetry can be more deeply understood, the thought-world founded by Moses and built upon by the Prophets receives the finishing touches provided by the Writings. The symbolic universe in which the songs of the psalmists reverberate is that of earlier Scripture. To summarize briefly: God made the world good; humanity sinned; and God's promises indicate that he will overcome sin and its consequences, namely death, and restore the world to achieve the purposes he initiated at creation. These promises begin with the word to the serpent about the seed of the woman (Gen 3:15), flower into the blessing of Abraham (12:1–3), ripen into the blessing of Judah (49:8–12), and come into full fruit with the 2 Samuel 7 covenant promises made to David. The hope heralded in the Psalms is the hope for the kingdom of God that comes when David's seed sits on the everlasting throne.

Yahweh revealed himself as the one God who made heaven and earth, the sea and the dry land, and Moses taught the people Yahweh chose for himself. In the Torah, Moses also teaches Israel a typological understanding of how God has acted for Israel in the past and how he will save them in the future.[15]

Once again, I want to interact with Rolf Jacobson's reading of Psalm 8 to clarify what I am trying to say here. Just as Jacobson does not read Psalm 8 in the flow of thought stemming from Psalms 1 and 2, he also does not read particular statements in Psalm 8 against the thought-world of earlier Scripture.

The ESV renders Psalm 8:2 (MT 8:3) as follows:

---

14. Hamilton, *Psalms 1–72*, 147.

15. See my essay, "The Exodus in Biblical Theology," in *The Law, The Prophets, and the Writings: Studies in Evangelical Old Testament Hermeneutics in Honor of Duane A. Garrett*, ed. Andrew M. King, William R. Osborne, and Joshua M. Philpot (Nashville: Broadman & Holman, 2021), 77–91.

Out of the mouth of babies and infants,
you have established strength because of your foes,
to still the enemy and the avenger.

Jacobson's comments run as follows:

> The creation motif of the psalm thoroughly permeates this stanza, as vv. 1b and 3 indicate. But v. 2bc may also reflect the creation motif, as Nahum Sarna has argued [citing Sarna, *On the Book of Psalms*, 53–61]. The *enemy and avenger* in v. 2c are best explained as a reference to the foes that God overcomes in the process of creation. As is well known, the mythic concept of creation as a conflict was commonly held among Israel's neighbors. Within the Old Testament, vestiges of this mythic idea are found. In Ps. 74:13–14a, 16–17, for example, ... it is particularly enlightening that both Psalms 8 and 74 refer to God's *might* ([transliterating Hebrew עֹז]; cf. Isa. 51:9; Ps. 89:11). The term is part of the vocabulary of the creation conflict myth, lending support to the view that the phrase *you have established might because of your foes, to put an end to enemy and avenger* is another reference to the act of creation.[16]

It is true that Israel's neighbors commonly held to "the mythic concept of creation as a conflict," but this position is foreign to the account in Genesis. The claim that the texts Jacobson references, Psalms 74 and 89 and Isaiah 51, attest to this creation conflict would seem to reflect a failure to distinguish between different worldviews.

There is no conflict in Genesis 1 and 2, but conflict is introduced in Genesis 3:15. I would argue, and have in my commentary, that Psalms 74 and 89 (and Isa 51) are interpreting the crossing of the Red Sea as a crushing of the serpent's head—anticipatory fulfillments of Genesis 3:15. With Genesis 3:15 dealing with the seed of the woman, the Lord establishing strength by means of babies and infants would seem to fit in that context as well. In fact, the term rendered "enemy" (אויב) is related to the term rendered "enmity" in Genesis 3:15 (איבה). To capture the connection between the enemies who are at enmity, I have rendered Psalm 8:2 (MT 8:3),

From the mouth of babes and sucklings you established strength,
because of your adversaries,
to cause the one at enmity and the avenger to cease.

16. deClaissé-Walford, Jacobson, and Tanner, *Psalms*, 123–24.

It is not only the lexical connection between "enmity" and "the one at enmity" that ties Psalm 8:2 (MT 8:3) to Genesis 3:15. There is also the fact that God's adversary is spoken of in the singular. The Psalms regularly acknowledge that God has many enemies, as can be seen in 2:1–3. The singular enemy referenced in Psalm 8:2 (MT 8:3) could be the primal Enemy, the one who instigated the others, whose downfall will mean their end.

Understanding the singular enemy as the serpent of Genesis 3 would explain how God has established strength to silence him through babies. The prohibition on eating of the tree in Genesis 2:17 warned that death would result. The man and woman transgressed and ate, and then in a vain attempt to avoid the death penalty, tried to hide from God (3:8). When God began speaking words of judgment over the serpent, he stated that the seed of the woman would bruise his head (3:14–15).

The statement that they would have seed who would oppose the serpent revealed that the man and woman would not die immediately, giving them hope for ongoing life and the bearing of children, and the statement that the seed would bruise the head of the serpent revealed that their seed would punish God's enemy.

The Bible locates the conflict in which Yahweh engages not in creation but in redemption. Jacobson's reading, then, has displaced the biblical conflict background for the one assumed in the alternative worldview held by Israel's idolatrous neighbors.

In Psalm 8 David no doubt reflects on creation, but his reflections are not limited to Genesis 1 and continue into Genesis 3. David might even allude to both Genesis 1 and Genesis 15 in Psalm 8:3 (MT 8:4) when he speaks of *looking* at Yahweh's *heavens*, the work of his fingers, the moon and the stars. The Genesis 1 overtones are obvious. Might there be an allusion as well to Abraham saying that Yahweh had given him no seed in Genesis 15:3, in response to which Yahweh takes him outside and tells him to look at the heavens and number the stars in 15:5?

And that brings us to David's famous and much-contested statement in Psalm 8:4 (MT 8:5), which Jacobson renders,

> What are human beings that you remember them?
> Or mortal persons that you attend them?

Jacobson footnotes this line, and in the footnote he states, "The Hebrew reads, lit.: 'What is man that you remember him? The son of man that you attend him?' The above translation reflects a desire to use inclusive language."[17]

In his explanation of his rendering, Jacobson has imported a concern from our culture—for inclusive language—into an ancient text whose author does not seem to have shared that concern. Jacobson's introduction of the concern for inclusive language also shifts the language from singulars to plurals. Those plurals refer to humanity in general but consider the import of the *singulars* used by the author of Psalm 8. In my literal rendering of the Psalter, I translated Psalm 8:4 (MT 8:5) as follows:

> What is man [*Enosh*] that you remember him,
> the son of Adam that you visit him?

The first instance of "man" in the opening question, "What is man," renders the Hebrew term אנוש, which is also the name of Seth's son in Genesis 5:6. It appears that just as אדם, the name of the first man, came to be used to refer to man in general, so the name אנוש, son of the son of Adam, came to be used to refer to man in general, as seen in the plural form of "man" (איש), אנשים (men, from אנש).

Psalm 8 is poetry. Poetry is often intentionally allusive. In the questions he poses in this verse, David has alluded to the first three generations in the line of descent of the seed of the woman—Adam, Seth, and Enosh—and he has done so in reverse order: third-generation Enosh, second-generation son of Adam, and then in that reference we hear of first-generation Adam himself. The reference to the line of descent of the seed of the woman so carefully traced in Genesis (see the genealogies in Gen 5 and 11) would fit nicely with the understanding of the "babies and infants" in Psalm 8:2 (MT 8:3) proposed above.

Jacobson's transformation of David's singulars into plurals negates connections not only to earlier Scripture—the overtones of Genesis just discussed—but also to later Scripture. For instance, in Daniel 7, the kingdoms are presented as beasts. At the end of Psalm 8, the son of man exercises Adamic dominion (Gen 1:28) over the beasts. In Daniel 7, the dominion of the beasts is taken away and given to one like a "son of man."[18] Jacobson's translation, however, ignores any possible connection to the son of man in

---

17. deClaissé-Walford, Jacobson, and Tanner, *Psalms*, 121 and 121n10.

18. Jean Daniélou, *From Shadows to Reality: Studies in the Biblical Typology of the Fathers*, trans. Wulstan Hibberd (London: Burns and Oates, 1960), 15, writes, "Psalm 8 is apparently the link between Genesis and Daniel, showing us, as it does, a son of man who should reign over creation and particularly the animal world."

Daniel 7, to say nothing of the connection to the son of man in the Gospels and in Hebrews 2.

The larger point I am making here is that earlier Scripture is the most important backdrop for understanding the Psalms. The Torah of Moses was intended to have a shaping influence on Israel's worldview, and those who wrote Scripture understood themselves to be operating in that worldview. The fact that the believing community recognized these writings as Scripture indicates that the authors' self-understanding was validated by others who embraced, promoted, and protected that Mosaic worldview.

My interaction with Jacobson's commentary on Psalm 8 also indicates that if earlier Scripture is not treated as the primary background against which the Psalms are to be interpreted, some other background will inevitably prove determinative. Jacobson's comments on Psalm 8:2 (MT 8:3) treat ancient Near Eastern myths about the gods engaging in conflict at creation as the primary background for understanding that verse, and his translation of Psalm 8:4 (MT 8:5) allows our own cultural context and its concern for inclusive language to eclipse not only concerns arising from what David wrote and from David's cultural context but also concerns for connections David sought to make with earlier Scripture and for connections later biblical authors sought to make with what David wrote.

If Psalm 8 is read without regard for its superscription that ascribes authorship to David, without regard for its relationships with the psalms that precede and follow it in the Psalter, and if the ancient Near Eastern worldview is allowed to eclipse the biblical worldview, then Psalm 8 can be taken to endorse ancient Near Eastern myths as it refers to humanity in general, with nothing much to say about the coming Messiah.

But if we read Psalm 8 in its literary context, understanding it in continuity with Psalms 1–2 and 3–7 and 9–41 and so forth, then in Psalm 8 we can see David contemplating his own new-Adam role as one who is to exercise the dominion God has given to him (see especially Gen 1:26, 28 and Ps 8:6–8 [MT 8:7–9]). Moreover, David understands the purpose of his dominion to be the extension of Yahweh's glory, and he understands that dominion to be in conflict with the way "the enemy and the avenger" seeks to establish his own dominion through the kings of the nations who set themselves against Yahweh and his anointed (Ps 2:1–3).

David understands that God chooses the weak things of the world, things like babies and infants, to shame the strong, and David understands that God made a promise about the seed of the woman, whose descent can be traced down from Adam through Seth and Enosh to Abraham and Judah and Boaz to Jesse. Standing in that line of descent, David knows that God keeps his promises, those made in words of judgment over the serpent (Gen 3:15) and those made to the likes of Abraham (12:1–3), Judah (49:8–12), and David himself (2 Sam 7:8–17). The man who wrote Psalm 8, after all, also wrote Psalm 110.

TYPOLOGY

My contention in this section is that David's understanding of both God's promises and the patterns of earlier Scripture led him to present himself in the Psalms as a type of the one to come. That is to say, David consciously and intentionally speaks of his own experience, and yet he means to present himself as a type, a foreshadowing prefigurement of the seed from his line whose throne God promised to establish forever (2 Sam 7:12–14).

The book of Samuel may not have been written until after David's death, but David received the word of Yahweh from Nathan the prophet as narrated in 2 Samuel 7. As Luke presents Peter proclaiming on the day of Pentecost, David was a prophet who knew "that God had sworn with an oath to ... set one of his descendants on his throne" (Acts 2:30). Acts 4:25 also reveals that David wrote Psalm 2 "by the Holy Spirit."

With these pieces of information in mind (Davidic authorship of Ps 2, prophetic status, and knowledge of the 2 Sam 7 promises), consider the poetic reformulation of 2 Samuel 7:14 in Psalm 2:7. The promise of new-Adam,[19] representative-Israelite sonship[20] in 2 Samuel 7:14 reads:

> I will be to him a father, and he shall be to me a son.

David's poetic reformulation in Psalm 2:7, where it would appear David himself is the speaker, reads:

> The Lord said to me, "You are my Son; today I have begotten you."

19. Genesis 5:1–3 implies that Adam is God's son, since Adam's son Seth is described as being in his image and likeness (5:3) as Adam was in God's (1:26–27; 5:1). If Seth in Adam's image is Adam's son, then Adam in God's image is what Genesis 5 implies and Luke 3:38 asserts: "the son of Enos, the son of Seth, the son of Adam, the son of God."

20. Adam is presented as God's son, and then Yahweh declares the nation of Israel to be a new-Adam son of God when he identifies Israel as his son in Exodus 4:22–23.

At the risk of belaboring the point, let me put 2 Samuel 7:14 and Psalm 2:7 right next to each other:

> 2 Samuel 7:14, "I will be to him a father, and he shall be to me a son."
>
> Psalm 2:7, "The LORD said to me, 'You are my son; today I have begotten you.' "

Here David places himself, the speaker of the psalm, in the role of the promised seed. God made the promise about the seed in 2 Samuel 7, and David speaks as the recipient of the promise in Psalm 2. Just to be clear: the promise in 2 Samuel 7 pertains to David's seed, the one who would descend from his line, but David speaks about himself as the recipient of the promise in Psalm 2, speaking, as it were, as though he himself were the seed.[21] Such a move would fit with the idea that David means to present the difficulties he faces from his adversaries, beginning in Psalms 3–7, as illustrations of the Psalm 2:1–3 nations raging against Yahweh and his anointed.

The Psalms display a thorough knowledge of earlier Scripture. One result of being a prophet led by the Holy Spirit would be the Holy Spirit ensuring that David correctly discerned what earlier biblical authors sought to communicate. Thus, David would have seen the historical correspondences and points of escalation that Moses built into the narratives about Joseph and himself.[22] David would have seen that Joseph was identified as God's choice to reign, then rejected by his kinsmen, then exalted as "an anticipatory fulfillment of the blessing of Abraham" who overcame the enmity between himself and the seed of the serpent who had sold him into slavery.[23]

David would have seen the same pattern of events in the life of Moses, who was identified as beautiful and unexpectedly delivered, only to be rejected by his kinsmen before being used by the Lord to overcome the seed of the serpent at the exodus from Egypt.

And David, reflecting on his own experience, would have seen that after he was identified as the one to be king by the anointing of Samuel, his own

21. See Jonathan Edwards, *The Works of Jonathan Edwards: Religious Affections*, ed. John E. Smith (New Haven: Yale University Press, 2009), 109: David "in many of the Psalms, speaks in the name of Christ, as personating him."

22. See further James M. Hamilton, "Was Joseph a Type of the Messiah? Tracing the Typological Identification between Joseph, David, and Jesus," *The Southern Baptist Journal of Theology* 12 (2008): 52–77.

23. Samuel Cyrus Emadi, "Covenant, Typology, and the Story of Joseph: A Literary-Canonical Examination of Genesis 37–50" (PhD diss., The Southern Baptist Theological Seminary, 2016).

kinsmen rejected him and sought to kill him, but through all he was delivered, eventually reigning over Israel and Judah and crushing the head of the seed of the serpent when the smooth stone found its mark.

With each installment in these historical correspondences, their significance escalates. As the Spirit prompted David rightly to interpret what he saw in the narratives about Joseph and Moses and in his own experiences, I contend the Spirit enabled David to foresee that the seed promised to him would have similar experiences of being identified as God's chosen one, rejected by his kinsmen, persecuted even unto death, only to be raised up as he crushed the serpent's head and redeemed his people.

This understanding would explain how Luke can present Peter introducing his quotation of Psalm 16—a quotation in which David will speak in the first-person singular of himself and his own experience—with the words, "For David says concerning him ..." (Acts 2:25). Peter says that David speaks concerning *him*, Jesus, but Peter presents David speaking of *himself* ("I," "me," "my"). By speaking of himself, conscious that his own experience typified that of the one to come, David spoke "concerning *him*."

This approach—the view that David spoke of his own experience consciously intending to present himself as a type of the one to come—would also explain how in Psalm 18 David speaks of Yahweh's deliverance of him from the hand of Saul and all his enemies using exodus (Ps 18:7–17 [MT 18:8–18]) and conquest (18:37–42 [MT 18:38–43]) imagery before concluding in 18:50 (MT 18:51),

> Great salvation he brings to his king,
> and shows steadfast love to his anointed,
> to David and his offspring [seed] forever.

David essentially says that his own experience corresponds to the exodus pattern, and in the psalm's final verse, he indicates that this pattern will be repeated in the life of the seed of promise, the one who will bring to typological fulfillment everything written "in the Law of Moses and the Prophets and the Psalms" (Luke 24:44).

CONCLUSION

David presented himself as a type of the one to come in the Psalms. He had seen patterns in the lives of Joseph and Moses that he recognized in his own life, and in Psalm 18 David even presents the way Yahweh delivered him with imagery and terms meant to recall what Yahweh did at the exodus from Egypt (see esp. Ps 18:7–17 [MT 18:8–18]). David presents himself as an installment in the patterns seen in the lives of Joseph and Moses and at the exodus, and I contend that he does this expecting these patterns to be repeated and fulfilled in the life of his descendant (see Ps 18:50 [MT 18:51]). I have tried to demonstrate these claims in this study by showing how David engages earlier Scripture in Psalm 8 and by seeking to show how the interconnectedness of the Psalms puts Psalm 8 into a wider field of meaning that begins in Psalms 1 and 2 and develops across the whole of the Psalter.

If we read the Psalms in light of their superscriptions, against their intended primary backdrop (earlier Scripture), and if we read them in their immediate context (pervasively interconnected with one another), we will see author-intended points of historical correspondence and escalation between people, events, and institutions, which is to say, we will see the way the psalmists themselves have understood the types in earlier Scripture and make further installments in typological patterns by means of their poetry. The best poetry, after all, points beyond itself to life, to big truths, and to ultimate hopes. This is what David and the psalmists do as they sing their lives in light of the past and in anticipation of the future.

4

A Story in the Psalms? Narrative Structure at the "Seams" of the Psalter's Five Books

David "Gunner" Gundersen

The Psalter is organized into five books, and the psalms at the beginning and end of each book have been called "seams." These seam psalms advance a narrative trajectory tracing the promise of the Davidic covenant in Israel's history and hopes. This trajectory reflects one of the organizing principles of the Psalter's arrangement.

Four decades ago, Gerald Wilson began arguing that the Psalms are intentionally arranged.[1] One of his key observations was that royal psalms mark the "seams" of the Psalter's first three books (Pss 2, 72, 89).[2] The Psalms are organized into five total books, and a "seam psalm" is one placed at the beginning or end of a book. According to Wilson, these royal seam psalms display a thematic sequence that advances a theological agenda.[3] John Walton

1. Jewish and Christian authors, ancient and modern, have hinted at or explored the mystery of the Psalter's structure. But Wilson's insights launched the intense scholarly explorations of the past four decades (Gerald H. Wilson, *The Editing of the Hebrew Psalter*, SBLDS 76 [Chico, CA: Scholars Press, 1985]). In contrast, Goldingay writes, "Understanding the order belongs to God alone" (John Goldingay, *Psalms 1-41*, BCOTWP [Grand Rapids: Baker Academic, 2006], 37).
2. Gerald H. Wilson, "The Use of Royal Psalms at the 'Seams' of the Hebrew Psalter," *JSOT* 35 (1986): 85–94.
3. Wilson, "Use of Royal Psalms at the 'Seams,' " 87–88.

similarly argues that "the progression of the seam psalms" is vital for identifying the "editorial agenda" in the Psalter.[4]

In this essay, I propose that most of the Psalter's seam psalms work together to advance a loose narrative trajectory, thereby revealing part of the organizing principle and theological message of the book of Psalms.[5] When taken together, these seam psalms uphold a developing story tracing the promise of the Davidic covenant in Israel's history and hopes (Pss 1–2, 71–73, 88–91, 104–107, 145, 146–150).

This narrative impulse does not unfold in lockstep chronological fashion in the Psalter, nor is it the exclusive organizing principle for the Psalms. For example, Peter Ho argues convincingly that the canonical form of the Psalter is arranged with several overarching editorial methods: a linear trajectory, concentric groupings of psalms, and rich resonance with other Old Testament texts and themes, especially the David narratives in 1–2 Samuel. Ho wisely recognizes that these editorial methods and features are complementary rather than contradictory, producing a cohesive structure and message that "unfurls" the Davidic covenant.[6] My own harmonious suggestion is that most of the seam psalms are pillars bearing significant structural weight in the Psalter, helping to uphold its overall message.

Is it valid to evaluate these "seams" and seek to discern an organized agenda and message in the Psalms? I believe so, for at least three reasons. First, the doxologies that close each book make clear that the canonical Psalter is intentionally organized into five books. Second, the initial two psalms clearly set a theological agenda developed throughout the rest of the Psalms.[7] Third, there are striking psalms at the seams, such as one of two

4. John H. Walton, "Psalms: A Cantata about the Davidic Covenant," *JETS* 34 (1991): 23. Of course, scholars take many different views on whether the Psalms are intentionally arranged, the extent of their potential arrangement, and the message (if discernible) of the book as a whole.

5. I say "most" because the seam between Books I and II does not stand out like the others for reasons addressed below.

6. Peter C. W. Ho, *The Design of the Psalter: A Macrostructural Analysis* (Eugene, OR: Pickwick, 2019), 331–38.

7. Scholars debate whether Psalms 1–2 or Psalm 1 alone introduces the Psalter. Gillingham surveys the field in Susan Gillingham, *A Journey of Two Psalms: The Reception of Psalms 1 and 2 in Jewish and Christian Tradition* (Oxford: Oxford University Press, 2013), 261–98. In English, the most exhaustive treatment of links between Psalms 1 and 2 is found in Robert L. Cole, *Psalms 1–2: Gateway to the Psalter*, HBM (Sheffield: Sheffield Phoenix, 2012), 46–141. On the other hand, Willis argues that Psalm 1 is a single entity in John T. Willis, "Psalm 1—An Entity," *ZAW* 91

Solomonic appearances (Ps 72), a devastating and lengthy reflection on the Davidic covenant (Ps 89), the only Mosaic psalm (Ps 90), a series of long historical hymns crossing from Book IV into Book V (Pss 104–107), and the unique fivefold doxology closing Book V (Pss 146–150). The five-book division, the first two psalms, and the striking nature of many seam psalms encourage this investigation.

When we survey the seam psalms together, what kind of loose narrative flow emerges? Psalms 1–2 set the messianic agenda with a portrait of the ideal Israelite (Ps 1) followed by God's enthronement promise to his anointed "son" (Ps 2).[8] Books I–II portray the life, sufferings, and deliverances of David. Book II ends with an elderly David (Ps 71) as the Davidic promises are transferred to his royal son Solomon (Ps 72). Hopes are dashed in Psalm 73 as Book III begins, and Book III ends in darkness: an individual lament (Ps 88) joined with a confused dirge about the apparent failure of the Davidic promises (Ps 89). Moses then opens Book IV by interceding for the covenant-breaking people (Ps 90). Book IV walks the exilic wilderness and concludes with a hymnic history of the nation (Pss 105–106) marked by an exilic prayer for regathering (Ps 106:47). This prayer for regathering is answered at the beginning of Book V (Ps 107:3). Book V then ends with Davidic worship for Yahweh's rich mercy, his covenant-keeping faithfulness, and his eternal kingdom (Ps 145). The Psalter concludes with a five-psalm doxology as the storyline crescendos with global, eschatological praise (Pss 146–150).

THE AGENDA: PSALMS 1–2

Psalms 1–2 form the "gateway" to the Psalter.[9] These untitled pillars welcome worshipers into the Psalms with two complementary portraits. In

---

(1979): 381–401. Kraus believes that "Psalm 2 originally was counted as Psalm 1, for Psalm 1 was considered a preamble." He appeals to a variant reading of Acts 13:33 where Psalm 2 is cited as the first psalm (Hans-Joachim Kraus, *Psalms 1–59*, trans. H. C. Oswald [Minneapolis: Fortress, 1993], 125). See also David M. Howard Jr., "The Proto-MT Psalter, the King, and Psalms 1 and 2: A Response to Klaus Seybold," in *Jewish and Christian Approaches to the Psalter: Conflict and Convergence*, ed. Susan Gillingham (Oxford: Oxford University Press, 2012), 182–89; and Howard, "Divine and Human Kingship as Organizing Motifs in the Psalter," in *The Psalms: Language for All Seasons of the Soul*, ed. Andrew J. Schmutzer and David M. Howard Jr. (Chicago: Moody, 2013), 200n8. Here I am not arguing that Psalms 1–2 should be read as a single psalm but that together they introduce and foreshadow the message of the Psalter.

8. Scripture quotations, including individual words, are taken from the English Standard Version (ESV) unless noted otherwise.

9. Cole, *Psalms 1–2*. See also Patrick D. Miller, "The Beginning of the Psalter," in *Shape and Shaping of the Psalter*, ed. J. Clinton McCann Jr., JSOTSup Series 159 (Sheffield: Sheffield Academic, 1993), 83–92.

Psalm 1, a blessed man exemplifies the ideal reader (and king), choosing the way of wisdom and flourishing in submission to God's law. In Psalm 2, God preappoints his messianic "son" to rule from Zion over the very nations in mutiny against him. Together these psalms set a conflict-filled trajectory toward a messianic future where the rule of an anointed Davidide embodies and enacts the reign of God.

Verbal and thematic links create much of the resonance between this introductory pair. For example, the "beatitudinal envelope"[10] marked by the repeated makarism "blessed" (אשרי, Pss 1:1; 2:12) wraps divine favor around the man who submits to God's law and takes refuge in his anointed king. In addition, this Joshua-like man "meditates" (יהגה, 1:2) on Yahweh's law, while the rebellious nations "plot" (יהגו, 2:1) against Yahweh's anointed. The scoffers have a "seat" (מושב, 1:1) in which this righteous man refuses to "sit" (ישב, 1:1), while the wicked "set themselves" (יתיצבו, 2:2) against Yahweh who "sits" (יושב, 2:4) in the heavens.[11] The "way" of the wicked (דרך, 1:1) is alien to the righteous and leads to death (דרך, 1:6; 2:12), but the "way" of the righteous (דרך, 1:6) is favored by Yahweh. Thus the "way of the wicked will perish" (ודרך רשעים תאבד, 1:6) like the uprising kings who will "perish in the way" (תאבדו דרך, 2:12). Finally, the Torah-saturated man is an Edenic tree that "gives" its fruit (יתן, 1:3) as Yahweh promises to "give" the nations (ואתנה, 2:8) as his Messiah's inheritance.[12]

10. Cole, *Psalms 1–2*, 30.

11. The root יצב (Ps 2:2) rhymes with the root ישב (Pss 1:1; 2:4) so that the mutinous earthly kings are taking their temporary stand against the one who sits permanently in the heavens.

12. This paragraph is adapted from David Gundersen, "Davidic Hope in Book IV of the Psalter" (PhD diss., The Southern Baptist Theological Seminary, 2015), 52. The ESV translates the verb נתן as "yields." See Cole, *Psalms 1–2*, 46–141, for a detailed study of the relationship between this pair of psalms.

Figure 4.1 - Select Word-Links between Psalms 1 and 2

VERSE	MASORETIC TEXT	ENGLISH
1:1	אשרי	blessed
2:12	אשרי	blessed
1:2	יהגה	meditates
2:1	יהגו	plot
1:1	במושב	in the seat
1:1	ישב	sits
2:4	יושב	he who sits
2:2	יתיצבו	set themselves
1:6	תאבד	(it) will perish
2:12	תאבדו	you perish
1:1	בדרך	in the way
1:6	דרך	the way
1:6	דרך	the way
2:12	דרך	in the way
1:3	יתן	yields
2:8	אתנה	I will give

Both psalms incorporate big-picture time elements, forecasting a chronological sweep of history that looks toward the far horizon. Psalm 1 anticipates eschatological judgment and vindication: the righteous will stand and the wicked will be swept away (1:5–6). Psalm 2 then sets a trajectory that is at once royal, messianic, global, and eschatological. Yet there is a dark spirit of insurrection seen in the psalm's international uprising (2:1–3, 9), projecting the conflict that scars the rest of the Psalter.

Psalm 3, then, is no surprise. "Many" are rising against God's anointed king (3:1, 2, 6). Yet the superscription names David's son Absalom rather than the kings of foreign nations. Thus, even those closest to the Messiah—Israelites and even Davidides—are seen to join the rebellion against God's chosen king. Yet David is confident in God's protection and salvation (3:3–8).

If the Psalter displays a cohesive message, and if Psalms 1–2 are indeed gateway pillars engraved with central themes, we should not be surprised to see these same themes developed, expanded, conflicted, and resolved as the Psalter tells its grand story.

BETWEEN BOOKS I AND II: PSALMS 39, 41, AND 42–43

According to Palmer Robertson, Book I depicts "confrontation" between the Messiah and his enemies. Absalom headlines Psalm 3, and Book I closes with David betrayed by a close confidante (Ps 41:9).[13] Thus Book I is bracketed by betrayal. The covenant king is chased even by those whose loyalty he most ought to possess—a dear son (Ps 3) and a "close friend" (41:9).

David is afflicted throughout Book I. In fact, two particular psalms near the end of the book are heavily death oriented (Pss 39, 41). Of course, the entire Psalter is shrouded with suffering, despair, affliction, and near-death experiences. But these final psalms of Book I express the extremes of David's sufferings, using chronological end-of-life language.

In Psalm 39, David measures his days and finds himself "fleeting" (39:4). His lifetime is "a few handbreadths," "as nothing," a "mere breath," and a "shadow" (39:5). This core theme is established through repetition: the psalm closes with this vision of mankind as a "breath" (39:11), making David a "sojourner" and a "guest" passing through life quickly like his ancestors (39:12). He senses that he is about to "depart" and be "no more" (39:13).

In Psalm 41, though God mercifully "restore[s] him to full health" (41:3), we find a "sickbed" and "illness." David's enemies eagerly await his death: "When will he die, and his name perish?" (41:5). "A deadly thing is poured out on him" (41:8a). "He will not rise again from where he lies" (41:8b). "They imagine the worst for me," David says (41:7). Yet David still closes the psalm with confidence in God (41:11–12).

Although the threat of death is clear near the end of Book I, the seam between Books I and II does not stand out like other seams. Walton suggests that "Psalm 41 is the weakest conclusion of any of the five books."[14] Wilson, while highlighting the royal psalms at the seams of Books I–III (Pss 2, 72, 89), notices this weaker link in Psalm 41 and attempts an explanation:

> It is clear that Ps. 41, which concludes the first book, is not normally identified as one of the "royal" psalms. While this psalm is traditionally associated with David (see the superscript), and some still attempt

13. O. Palmer Robertson, *The Flow of the Psalms: Discovering Their Structure and Theology* (Phillipsburg, NJ: P&R, 2015), 83. Robertson argues that Book II maintains this conflict but that Book II also stresses communication between God's chosen king and the nations.

14. Walton, "A Cantata about the Davidic Covenant," 25.

> to connect it with events in the life of the king when he "was ill and his enemies tried to overthrow him," it evidences no distinctly "kingly" theme which would set it apart from other prayers for healing.
>
> Perhaps a better explanation for the absence of a royal psalm at the end of Book One is to recognize that the redactional movement to combine Books One and Two into a single Davidic collection (a movement marked by the postscript in Ps. 72.20, "The prayers of David son of Jesse are ended") had already taken place when these royal psalms were set in their present positions. As a result, we are left with two major blocks of material (Pss 2–72, 73–89) which are marked at their "seams" by royal psalms.[15]

In the canonical Psalter, Books I and II are heavily Davidic. They depict the life and sufferings of David, whose prayers and patterns foreshadow the Messiah. Therefore, the seams between these books play less of a role in advancing a broad narrative movement. In contrast, later seam psalms will mirror major shifts in Israel's history (Pss 72, 89, 90, 106, 107). Yet there are still ripples of forward movement between Books I and II: Book I winds down with a vulnerable David still confident that God will establish him (Pss 39, 41); the Korahite series opening Book II (Pss 42–49) sets a tone of stability since David assigned them to worship at the settled tabernacle (1 Chr 6:31, 37);[16] despair is met with hope in the shared refrain of Psalms 42–43 (42:5, 11; 43:5); and the second half of these Korahite songs presents a royal psalm (Ps 45) and visions of subdued nations and a restored Zion (Pss 46–49). As Book II begins, it seems that David is gaining stability.

BETWEEN BOOKS II AND III: PSALMS 71–73

Psalms 71, 72, and 73 seem to move from David's old age (Ps 71) to Solomon's kingdom (Ps 72) to the devastating breakdown that followed (Ps 73).[17] Near the end of Book I, David appeared near death (Pss 39, 41). Now near the end of Book II, he is an elderly man (Ps 71). These similar endings to Books I and II illustrate the serious challenges to the Davidic promises. It also signals

15. Wilson, "Use of Royal Psalms at the 'Seams,'" 87–88.

16. James M. Hamilton Jr., *Psalms Volume I: Psalms 1-72*, Evangelical Biblical Theology Commentary (Bellingham, WA: Lexham Academic, 2021), 432, 448.

17. Psalm 71 is untitled but reflects a Davidic hue due to its heavily Davidic context (Pss 51–71) as well as the book-closing doxology appearing after Psalm 72: "The prayers of David, the son of Jesse, are ended" (72:20).

that the Davidic promises will be ultimately fulfilled in the future, with David's descendant(s).

Age terminology fills Psalm 71, setting a nostalgic mood. Walton explains the possible significance:

> Psalm 71 is very appropriately placed because that is at the end of the section dealing with David's reign and David speaks twice in the psalm about being "old and gray." David's age is hardly the thematic center of the psalm, but this element could have been significant enough to influence the placement.[18]

Figure 4.2 – Age Terminology in Psalm 71

v. 5	from my youth	מנעורי
v. 6	from before my birth	מבטן
v. 6	took me from my mother's womb	ממעי אמי אתה גוזי
v. 9	Do not cast me off in the time of old age	אל־תשליכני לעת זקנה
v. 17	from my youth	מנעורי
v. 18	even to old age and gray hairs	וגם עד־זקנה ושׂיבה
v. 18	another generation	לדור

David's aging condition in Psalm 71 raises the question of royal succession. The appearance of Solomon in the superscription of Psalm 72 suggests an answer.[19] Psalm 72 seems to function as a prayer-promise by David for his heir Solomon, or a prayer-wish by Solomon for his own kingship, since Solomon is the first royal son to inherit the Davidic throne and covenant promises.[20] Even if the ל-prefixed superscription reflects Solomonic authorship ("by Solomon" rather than "for" or "to" or "about" Solomon"), Psalm 72 still functions as a prayer for the Davidic descendant(s). The postscript at the end of Book II, "The prayers of David, the son of Jesse, are ended" (72:20), "functions to underscore the message that the reign of the

18. Walton, "Cantata about the Davidic Covenant," 24.

19. Many canonical interpreters recognize this succession movement from David to Solomon in Psalm 72: Wilson, *Editing*, 211; Michael Barber, *Singing in the Reign: The Psalms and the Liturgy of God's Kingdom* (Steubenville, OH: Emmaus Road, 2001), 104–5; Mark D. Futato, *Interpreting the Psalms: An Exegetical Handbook*, Handbooks for Old Testament Exegesis (Grand Rapids: Kregel, 2007), 82–84; Howard N. Wallace, *Psalms*, Readings: A New Biblical Commentary (Sheffield: Sheffield Phoenix, 2009), 119, 122.

20. The imperfect verbs throughout Psalm 72 can function as future-oriented promises ("he will") or jussives expressing prayers ("may he"). The ambiguity seems deliberate.

human king in the Davidic Psalter of Book II has come to an end and that hope no longer lies in David's kingship but in his posterity's."[21] Elements of the psalm overlap with the Solomonic account in Kings, such as the "gold of Sheba" presented to the king (Ps 72:15; 1 Kgs 10:10).[22]

Psalm 72 anticipates the fulfillment of Psalm 2. The "ends of the earth" promised to God's anointed king in 2:8 appear in 72:8. Worldwide dominion, homage, tribute, and gifts are given to him (72:8–11; 2:8, 11–12). The kings of earth bow before him (72:9, 11; 2:11). Strikingly, in both psalms this king is called a "son" (בן, 72:1; 2:7), as God promised David in 2 Samuel 7:14.

Psalm 72 reaches further back into the story, as well. The Abrahamic promises come to fruition through the Davidic king. The people dwell in their own "land" (72:16) of "mountains" and "hills" (72:3). Descendants multiply like the grass in the fields (72:16). All the families on earth find their blessing in this royal son's reign: "May people be blessed in him, all nations call him blessed" (72:17).

The transition to Psalm 73, then, is a theological, emotional, and narratival whiplash. Psalm 72 glides on the clouds of hope while Psalm 73 crashes into the desert of reality. In Psalm 72, the righteous flourish and prosper under the envisioned reign of God's anointed Davidic king. But in Psalm 73, the "arrogant" and the "wicked" enjoy prosperity (73:3), upending Israel's hopes. The wicked in 73:9 seem aligned with the wicked nations in Psalm 2 as they array themselves against the God enthroned in the heavens: "They set their mouths against the heavens, and their tongue struts through the earth" (73:9).[23]

Psalms 72–73 form a disillusioning mixture of covenant and conflict. This mixture marks Book III as a whole. The seventeen psalms of Book III capture Israel moving into exile as the temple is razed and the king cast down. McCann argues that Book III presents a rhythmic cycle of hope and lament, as Israel hopes in God amidst their coming exile while also lamenting the destruction caused by their sin.[24]

---

21. Ho, *Design of the Psalter*, 97.

22. For the rich connections between Psalm 72 and Solomon in 1 Kings 1–10, see Sidney Greidanus, *Preaching Christ from Psalms: Foundations for Expository Sermons in the Christian Year* (Grand Rapids: Eerdmans, 2016), 95.

23. Cole provides an extensive rundown of connections among the psalms of Book III, including the seam at Psalms 72–73 (Robert L. Cole, *The Shape and Message of Book III* [Psalms 73–89], JSOTSup Series 307 [Sheffield: Sheffield Academic, 2000]).

24. J. Clinton McCann Jr., "Books I–III and the Editorial Purpose of the Psalter," in McCann, ed., *Shape and Shaping of the Psalter*, 97.

BETWEEN BOOKS III AND IV: PSALMS 88–90

Twin Ezrahite psalms close Book III: Heman's (Ps 88) and Ethan's (Ps 89).[25] Both are titled משכיל (*maskil*). Psalm 88 is known for its hopeless lament, Psalm 89 for its covenant catastrophe. The fate of individual (Ps 88) and community (Ps 89) are bound in the juxtaposition of these two psalms. Further, king and people are intertwined as the people crumble along with the Davidic throne (Ps 89).

> Psalm 89, with its lament over God's "faithlessness" toward his own great promises, can be read as an intensification of Psalm 88. Both psalms utter an intense cry for the saving "steadfast love/graciousness" and "faithfulness" of God (88:12 and 89:2–3, 9, 15, 25, 29, 34, 50).[26]

Book III has already mourned the fall of the temple (73:17; 74:3–8; 79:1; 84:2–5, 10). Now it mourns the fall of the king (89:39–52). McCann suggests that the cycle of lament and hope in Book III is meant to cultivate hope in the shadow of exile even before Books IV–V.[27] But 89:1–38, which McCann charts as a ray of hope, serves mainly as a rhetorical rise setting up the covenantal collapse of 89:39–52. The epic recounting of the Davidic promises in 89:1–38 only makes the dissonance unbearable when the king is cast down (89:39), the crown defiled (89:40), and the covenant (apparently) renounced (89:40). Psalm 89:1–38 does instill hope, but the structure and progression of Psalm 89 deliberately creates a mystifying covenantal contradiction.

The stakes are high: "The Davidic monarchy … is reckoned to be not simply a political achievement (which it was) but a strategy of YHWH's governance of the world whereby the Davidic king is YHWH's regent to maintain order and justice in creation."[28] The fall of God's king, therefore, not only

---

25. Ethan the Ezrahite and Heman appear in 1 Kings 4:31 (MT 5:11), listed as sages whom Solomon surpassed: "For he was wiser than all other men, wiser than *Ethan the Ezrahite, and Heman*, Calcol, and Darda, the sons of Mahol, and his fame was in all the surrounding nations" (emphasis added).

26. Frank-Lothar Hossfeld and Erich Zenger, *Psalms 2: A Commentary on Psalms 51–100*, trans. L. M. Maloney, Hermeneia (Minneapolis: Fortress, 2005), 397.

27. McCann, "Books I–III and the Editorial Purpose of the Psalter," 97. Beth Tanner observes that these psalms "fluctuate between songs of praise and prayers for help" (Nancy deClaissé-Walford, Rolf A. Jacobson, and Beth LaNeel Tanner, *The Book of Psalms*, NICOT [Grand Rapids: Eerdmans, 2014], 583).

28. Walter Brueggemann and W. H. Bellinger Jr., *Psalms*, New Cambridge Bible Commentary (New York: Cambridge University Press, 2014), 385.

disturbs his people but disorders the world.[29] The world of the Psalter, too, is overturned if God fails to keep his promises to David. The sheer internal dissonance in Psalm 89, especially considering the promises of Psalms 2 and 72, demands a response.[30]

In response, Moses dramatically enters the Psalter as Book IV begins with Psalm 90. With prophetic authority as a "man of God," Moses voices a confessionary intercession for rebellious Israel now suffering God's wrath. In the narrative flow of the Psalter, Moses is imagined reformulating his successful supplication from Sinai, pleading that Yahweh "turn" and "relent" rather than abandon his Davidic king and people whose future is just as precarious as that infamous golden calf-generation. If you were part of a sinning Israelite community facing divine judgment, fearful that God might not keep his covenant promises, who would you want praying for your people? Moses's intercessory track record in the Pentateuch makes him the perfect intermediary in the wake of Psalm 89, where the Davidic covenant has apparently collapsed. Thus Psalm 90 responds to Psalm 89 by continuing and complementing the complaint over the fall of the Davidic throne, but now adding a confession of sin (90:7–11) and a historic covenant intercessor (Moses). Therefore Psalm 90 is perfectly placed to carry forward the narrative flow of the seam psalms.

29. This sense that cosmic order is maintained through the reign of Yahweh's representative helps explain the necessity and message of the "Yahweh reigns" series (יהוה מלך, Pss 93–100). When the Davidic reign ceased, divine rule was questioned.

30. The section above is borrowed heavily from Gundersen, "Davidic Hope in Book IV," 59–61.

Figure 4.3 – Exodus 32:12–14 in Psalm 90:13–16

PASSAGE	LEXICAL CONNECTIONS	
Ex 32:12	"Turn"	שוב
Ps 90:13	"(Re)turn"	שובה
Ex 32:12	"relent"	הנחם
Ex 32:14	"relented"	נחם
Ps 90:13	"Have pity"	הנחם
Ex 32:12	"with evil intent"	ברעה
Ex 32:12	"disaster"	הרעה
Ex 32:14	"disaster"	הרעה
Ps 90:15	"evil"	רעה
Ex 32:13	"your servants"	עבדיך
Ps 90:13	"your servants"	עבדיך
Ps 90:16	"your servants"	עבדיך

BETWEEN BOOKS IV AND V: PSALMS 104–106, 107

The inordinate number of references to Moses in Book IV (7x: 90:1; 99:6; 103:7; 105:26; 106:16, 23, 32), the consistent wilderness language, and the explicit links to the Pentateuch cast an exilic hue over the book. But despite Israel's new exile, Yahweh still reigns (Pss 93, 95–99), a Davidide will rule (Pss 101–103), and a Davidic figure waits in the wings (Ps 101).

Book IV begins with a Mosaic intercession (Ps 90) and divine response (Pss 91–92). Yahweh still reigns despite all appearances (יהוה מלך, "Yahweh reigns," Pss 93–100), and his reign leads to the reappearance and restoration of David and the nation (Pss 101–103). With king and people restored (Ps 103), the reordered creation rejoices (Ps 104), and Book IV closes with a hymnic series recounting Israel's history up to the exile (Pss 104–106).

Psalms 101–103 form a Davidic triad, with the untitled Psalm 102 displaying Davidic shadow due to its placement between two Davidic psalms (Pss 101 and 103). Psalms 103 and 104 are united by their shared incipit and closing, "Bless the Lord, O my soul," along with hook-words between them (e.g., "his messengers" [מלאכיו] in 103:20 and 104:4). Psalm 104 is a janus psalm, facing both ways as it caps the Davidic series (101–103) and begins a hymnic history series (104–106). Psalms 104, 105, and 106 retell Israel's history: creation (104), Abraham through the exodus (105), and the exodus through the exile (106).

Psalm 106 closes Book IV by tracing the history of Israel's rebellion. It ends in striking fashion. Prior to the book-closing doxology (106:48), the final line pleads with God to save his people and gather them in from the nations so that they might praise him (106:47). Thus Psalm 106 reflects Israel's exilic captivity, and Book IV as a whole ends with a note of anticipation: "Save us, O Lord our God, and gather us from among the nations, that we may give thanks to your holy name and glory in your praise" (Ps 106:47).

How will God respond to this plea from his people? Psalm 107 begins Book V as a tightly structured hymn praising Yahweh for his redemption.

Figure 4.4 - Outline of Psalm 107

vv. 1–3	*Yahweh faithfully redeems his people*
vv. 4–9	Example 1: desert wanderers led home
vv. 10–16	Example 2: miserable captives freed
vv. 17–22	Example 3: foolish sinners delivered
vv. 23–32	Example 4: storm-tossed merchants rescued
vv. 33–42	Summary of Yahweh's goodness
v. 43	*Invitation to reflect*

The introduction to Psalm 107 (107:1–3) celebrates a new exodus as God's people are "gathered in from the lands, from the east and from the west, from the north and from the south" (107:3). The unmistakable hook between Psalms 106 and 107 is the prayer in 106:47 answered in 107:3:

Save us, O Lord our God,
  and *gather us* [קבץ] *from among the nations,*
that we may *give thanks* [ידה] to your holy name
  and glory in your praise (Ps 106:47, emphasis added).

Oh *give thanks* [ידה] to the Lord, for he is good,
  for his steadfast love endures forever!
Let the redeemed of the Lord say so,
  whom he has redeemed from trouble
and *gathered in* [קבץ] *from the lands,*
  from the east and from the west,
  from the north and from the south (Ps 107:1–3, emphasis added).

The fourfold ingathering from the north, south, east, and west (107:3) matches Israel's scattering "among the nations" (106:47). This fourfold ingathering also introduces the fourfold metaphor of redemption throughout the psalm (107:4–32). Thus Book V begins with a celebratory return from exile suggesting the restoration of the nation.

Overall, there is a sweeping movement from the end of Book III (Ps 89) to the beginning of Book V (Ps 107). Psalm 89 ended Book III with a desperate plea for God to remember his covenant with David. Book IV indicates that God is still a covenant-keeping God as Moses immediately echoes his famous intercessory prayer from the Pentateuch: "Turn from your burning anger and relent [נחם] from this disaster against your people" (Exod 32:12). Then in 106:45–46, as Book IV ends, we find a covenant-keeping bookend with 90:13 as God again hears his people's plea.

> For their sake he remembered his covenant,
>   and relented [נחם] according to the abundance of his steadfast love.
> He caused them to be pitied
>   by all those who held them captive.

This covenant faithfulness of God leads the psalmist to conclude Psalm 106 with a prayer for regathering (106:47), and this prayer for regathering is answered by the comprehensive redemption of Yahweh in Psalm 107. Once again, we find seam psalms advancing a broad narrative movement in the Psalter.

THE CRESCENDO: PSALMS 145, 146–150

Book IV opened with a seam psalm recounting how God has regathered the scattered Israelites (Ps 107). David reappears with a Davidic series (Pss 108–110) followed by a series exulting in God's new exodus (Pss 111–118). Psalm 119 stands as a magnificent pillar in Book V, lauding God's law, and the Psalms of Ascents (Pss 120–134) center on building a "house" (Ps 127).[31] Three untitled psalms celebrate Yahweh's covenant faithfulness (Pss 135–136) before remembering the bitter Babylonian captivity (Ps 137). Book V proper then

31. Robertson points out the "pinnacle" position of Psalm 127 in the Psalms of Ascents (*Flow of the Psalms*, 232). The term "house" likely holds a double meaning—God must be the rebuilder of both Israel's dynastic house (royal line) and religious house (temple) as they return from exile. This double meaning mirrors the wordplay with "house" found in the initial Davidic promises in 2 Samuel 7.

closes with another Davidic series (Pss 138–145), followed by a fivefold doxology (Pss 146–150).

If the five books of the Psalter indeed carry a cohesive message reflecting the narrative development of the Davidic covenant promises, how would we expect its final book to end? Prior to the fivefold doxology (Pss 146–150), the final regular psalm (Ps 145) presents a Davidic voice extolling God (145:1–3) for his omnigenerational faithfulness (145:4–7). David echoes God's self-revelation to Moses as a covenant-keeping God (Ps 145:8; Exod 34:6) and declares that God's kingdom is everlasting (145:11–13). His might has been shown in mercy (145:14–20), so that worldwide praise is rightly his (145:10, 21). In many ways, Psalm 145 summarizes the Psalter's message.

Books I, II, III, and IV each close with a brief doxology. These four doxologies mark off the first four books of the Psalter. Book V is followed by an amplified doxology in the form of five full psalms (146–150). Each begins and ends with the same invitation: "Praise the Lord!" (הללו־יה). This crescendo not only ties together the doxological theme running through the seams of the Psalter but gathers several threads running through the Psalter as a whole.

Based on the four clear doxologies concluding the first four books, Psalm 145 seems to conclude with its own doxology prior to the five-psalm doxology that crescendos the entire Psalter. In other words, it seems that Book V has its own mini-doxology (145:21) before the supersized doxology that concludes the Psalter as a whole (Pss 146–150).

The apparent doxology to Book V (145:21) is a personal word, departing slightly from the typical formula. It has certain unique characteristics, such as a first-person reference ("my mouth," פי) and the term "flesh" (בשׂר). But it still shares four specific elements with the other four doxologies—the term "bless" (ברך), the name of Yahweh, a universal summons to worship, and a doubled expression ("forever and ever," לעולם ועד). Because there is a clear break between the final Davidic series (Pss 138–145) and the untitled five-psalm doxology (Pss 146–150), and because there is a pattern of doxologies closing each of the first four books, it seems that Psalm 145:21 should be read as the doxology closing Book V.[32]

Figure 4.5 – Repeated Elements in the Psalter's Doxologies

ELEMENT	BOOKS
"bless(ed)"	I–V
"Yahweh"/"name"	I–V
doubled expression	I–V
"amen"	I–IV
"God of Israel"	I, II, IV
universal scope	II, IV, V

Figure 4.6 – Doxologies in the Psalter

BOOK I	41:13	Blessed be the LORD, the God of Israel, from everlasting to everlasting!
BOOK II	72:18–19	Blessed be the LORD, the God of Israel, who alone does wondrous things. Blessed be his glorious name forever; may the whole earth be filled with his glory! Amen and Amen!
BOOK III	89:52	Blessed be the LORD forever! Amen and Amen.
BOOK IV	106:48	Blessed be the LORD, the God of Israel, from everlasting to everlasting! And let all the people say, "Amen!" Praise the Lord!
BOOK V	145:21	My mouth will speak the praise of the LORD, and let all flesh bless his holy name forever and ever.
BOOKS I–V	146–150	FIVE FULL PSALMS: HALLELUJAH!

The doxological rivers in Psalms 41, 72, 89, 106, and 145 flow into the dancing ocean of 146–150. The promise-prayers asking that "the whole earth be filled with his glory" (72:19) and that "all flesh bless his holy name" (145:21) are fulfilled in the universal symphony of every-creature praise in 146–150.

32. See also Howard, "Divine and Human Kingship," 199, and Ho, *Design of the Psalter*, 73.

Thus, even the doxological seams are finally bound together in a full tapestry as all creation rises to rejoice. The universal dominion promised in Psalm 2, anticipated in 72, and unfulfilled in 89, is now fulfilled in the divine imagination of the Psalter.

CONCLUSION

The Psalter seems to tell a story—moving from lament to praise, from affliction to celebration, from David son of Jesse to the branch rising from his roots. I suggest that the narrative flow evident within the seam psalms is one piece of suggestive evidence that this forward movement is the Psalter's intention. The messianic hope is a narrative hope, weighed down with all the tension and beauty of a storytelling chronology.

What then is the Psalter? The Psalter is a carefully crafted postexilic anthology with a narrative structure reflecting Israel's historical hope for the restoration of the Davidic kingdom whose establishment would consummate the purposes and promises embedded in God's covenants with Abraham, Israel, and David.[33]

33. This is my adapted summary of Barber's view from *Singing in the Reign*, 35, 57, 59, 81, 85–86, 133, 137. Barber also emphasizes a divine covenant with Adam.

5

Does the Book of Psalms Present a Divine Messiah?

Seth D. Postell

In this essay, the messianism of the Psalter is considered in light of the literary structure of the book of Psalms as a whole. By looking at several of the key psalms, this essay highlights a consistent conflation of the human and the divine identities of the Messiah. The Davidic king is the quintessential human being who fulfills the creation mandate on the one hand, and a divine figure worthy of worship on the other. The exegetical and theological conclusions about the Messiah's dual identity in the Psalter is supported by a close comparison of the messianism in the book of Daniel.

INTRODUCTION

Though the deity of Jesus is a firm pillar of faith well supported by the New Testament authors, the fact that the New Testament teaches the deity of Jesus does not allow us to automatically assume that the Old Testament predicts a divine Messiah. In this essay, we want to answer the following question: Does the book of Psalms present a divine Messiah? Though the New Testament authors quoted and/or alluded to the book of Psalms in their affirmation of the deity of Jesus,[1] I want to look at the grammatical-historical evidence in the book of Psalms itself.

1. See, for example, Ephesians 4:8–10 (a citation of Ps 68:18); Hebrews 1:8–12 (a quotation of Ps 102:26–28). In both cases, these psalms in their original context refer to God, and Paul and the author of Hebrews apply them to Jesus.

In this article, I will argue that the book of Psalms does, in fact, present a divine Messiah. I hope to bolster my thesis by comparing the "Christology" of the Psalter with another postexilic book, the book of Daniel, and the concept of Messiah found there. Although Jesus recognized a relationship between David's Lord in Psalm 110:1 and the Son of Man in Daniel 7:13 (see Matt 26:64; Mark 14:62; Luke 22:69)[2] and was also accused of blasphemy for applying these verses to himself,[3] I am unaware of other studies that have highlighted the extent to which the Psalter's messianic vision overlaps with Daniel's. In this essay, I hope to show that Jesus's conflation of Psalm 110:1 and Daniel 7:13 is not by loose association. Instead, it is based on the recognition that both books share a virtually identical expectation of a human Messiah who partakes of the divine identity.

THE MESSIANISM OF THE PSALTER

The compositional unity and the messianic vision of the Psalter has been thoroughly discussed and well-defended elsewhere[4] and is, therefore, as-

2. "But Jesus said, 'I am. And you will see the son of man sitting on the right hand of power. And coming with the clouds of the heavens' "(Mark 14:62). This translation is my own; all translations of the Bible in this essay are my own unless stated otherwise. I will also be using the versification in the Masoretic Text of the Hebrew Bible, which at times differs from the English translations, particularly in the book of Psalms. On the importance of Psalm 110:1 for New Testament Christology, see Richard Bauckham, "The Power and the Glory: The Rendering of Psalm 110:1 in Mark 14:62," in *From Creation to New Creation: Biblical Theology and Exegesis*, ed. Benjamin L. Gladd and Daniel M. Gurtner (Peabody, MA: Hendrickson, 2013), 83–101.

3. According to Bauckham, in "*Power and the Glory*," 96, Jesus's reference to God as "the power" in the context of other Jewish literature emphasizes God's enthroned presence, thereby highlighting his participation in God's sovereign rule.

4. For a defense of the compositional unity of the Psalter, see Brevard S. Childs, *Introduction to the Old Testament as Scripture*, 1st American ed. (Philadelphia: Fortress Press, 1979); Robert L. Cole, "Psalms 1 and 2: The Psalter's Introduction," in *The Psalms: Language for All Seasons of the Soul*, ed. Andrew J. Schmutzer and David M. Howard Jr. (Chicago: Moody, 2013), 183–96; Robert L. Cole, "Compositional Unity in the Five Books of the Psalms: A Canonical Approach," in *The Moody Handbook of Messianic Prophecy: Studies and Expositions of the Messiah in the Old Testament*, ed. Michael Rydelnik and Edwin Blum (Chicago: Moody, 2019), 451–56; David M. Howard Jr., "Divine and Human Kingship as Organizing Motifs in the Psalter," in Schmutzer and Howard, *The Psalms: Language for All Seasons of the Soul*, 197–208; David C. Mitchell, *The Message of the Psalter: An Eschatological Programme in the Books of Psalms*, JSOTSup 252 (Sheffield: Sheffield Academic Press, 1997); David C. Mitchell, "Lord, Remember David: G. H. Wilson and the Message of the Psalter," *VT* 56, no. 4 (2006): 526–48; Seth D. Postell, "A Literary, Compositional, and Intertextual Analysis of Psalm 45," *Bibliotheca Sacra* 176.702 (2019): 573–89; Seth D. Postell, "Messianism in the Psalms," in Rydelnik and Blum, *The Moody Handbook of Messianic Prophecy*, 457–75; Postell, "Psalm 16: The Resurrected Messiah," in *The Moody Handbook of Messianic Prophecy*, 513–27; Michael K. Snearly, "The Return of the King:

sumed in this essay. The book as a whole has a sevenfold structure, with each of the books ending with a doxology of praise.[5]

The sevenfold structure is as follows:

Introduction (Pss 1–2)

Book I (Pss 3–41)

Book II (Pss 42–72)

Book III (Pss 73–89)

Book IV (Pss 90–106)

Book V (Pss 107–145)

Concluding Doxology of the Psalter (Pss 146–150)[6]

Cole, in a number of publications, has demonstrated the compositional unity of Psalms 1–2 based on extensive lexical, thematic, phonetic, and poetic connections.[7] Not only are these psalms highlighted by their placement at the head of the Psalter, but also by their lack of superscriptions.[8] These psalms are also bound by an *inclusio* that pronounces a blessing upon the man in the first verse of Psalm 1 and those who trust in him in the last verse of Psalm 2 (Ps 1:1; 2:12).

Cole and Howard have also noted the function and strategic importance of these psalms for the theological message of the Psalter as a whole.[9] Analogous in function to the introduction of Genesis, which also lacks the superscription "these are the generations" (Gen 1:1–2:3),[10] these two psalms introduce the key themes of the book of Psalms. A central theme that

---

Book V as a Witness to Messianic Hope in the Psalter," in Schmutzer and Howard, *The Psalms: Language for All Seasons of the Soul*, 209–18.

5. Psalms 41:14; 72:18–20; 89:53; 106:48; 146–150.

6. Howard, "Divine and Human Kingship," 202.

7. Robert L. Cole, "An Integrated Reading of Psalms 1 and 2," *JSOT* 26.4 (2002): 75–88; Cole, "Psalms 1 and 2: The Psalter's Introduction"; Robert L. Cole, *Psalms 1–2: Gateway to the Psalter*, HBM 37 (Sheffield: Sheffield Phoenix Press, 2013); Robert L. Cole, "Psalms 1–2: The Divine Son of God," in Rydelnik and Blum, *The Moody Handbook of Messianic Prophecy*, 477–90; see also, Howard, "Divine and Human Kingship," 200.

8. Howard, "Divine and Human Kingship," 200, notes the addition of superscriptions in the Old Greek (OG) to all but the first two psalms, suggesting that early on these psalms were regarded as the introduction to the book.

9. Cole, *Gateway to the Psalter*; Howard, "Divine and Human Kingship."

10. The rest of Genesis is divided into ten *tōlĕdōṯ* sections (Gen 2:4; 5:1; 6:9; 10:1; 11:10, 27; 25:12, 19; 36:1, 9 [Esau's *tōlĕdōṯ* is repeated twice]; 37:2), the fact of which strongly highlights the strategic literary importance of Genesis 1:1–2:3 as the introduction to the book.

appears elsewhere in the macrostructure of the book is a king who is identified in Psalm 2 as the Messiah (*māšiaḥ*) and the son of the Lord (Ps 2:2, 7). The identification of the king as the Lord's son is almost certainly an allusion to God's promise to David in 2 Samuel 7:14. This thesis is strongly supported by the literary seams of the Psalter[11] as well as other royal psalms[12] that frequently refer to the Davidic covenant.

The description of this king in Psalms 1–2 as one who perfectly fulfills the Torah of the king (see Deut 17:14–20; Pss 1:2; 19:8–15 [ET 7–14]; 119) and rules as God's vice-regent over the earth appears in the seams of the book (Ps 45:7, 17; 72:8, 11; 89:25-27), suggesting that the postexilic composer of the Psalter identified this king as the Messiah. Two things stand out in the description of this king that will be quite relevant for our discussion of the book of Daniel. First, the rule of this king is portrayed as a fulfillment of the creation mandate (compare Ps 8:5–9 with Gen 1:26–28).[13] Second, clear boundaries marking the distinction between the divine identity and the human identity of this king are frequently blurred in these psalms.

THE MESSIAH'S RULE AND THE CREATION MANDATE

The two introductory psalms (Pss 1–2) are followed by a cluster of lament psalms (Pss 3–7),[14] the first and last of which reference Absalom's rebellion against King David in their superscriptions. The superscription of Psalm 3:1 makes this quite obvious: "A Psalm of David. When he fled from before Absalom his son." Psalm 7 seemingly refers to the end of Absalom's rebellion by virtue of the superscription: "A *Shiggaion* of David. Which David sang to the LORD concerning the words of Cush, the Benjaminite." The reference to Cush in the superscription in light of the earlier reference to Absalom in Psalm 3:1 suggests that Cush is "Cushi" who told David that Absalom and all who "rose up against"[15] David were dead (2 Sam 18:31–32). Thus, the opening cluster of lament psalms in Psalms 3–7 casts the persecution of David and

11. See Psalms 72 and 89, both of which represent the last psalms in their respective books. See Mitchell, "Lord, Remember David," and Gerald H. Wilson, "The Use of Royal Psalms at the 'Seams' of the Hebrew Psalter," *JSOT* 35 (1986): 85–94.

12. See Psalms 18:51; 132:11–18.

13. Solomon's reign in 1 Kings 1–11 is also described as a fulfillment of the creation mandate. See L. Alonso-Schökel, "Motivos Sapienciales y de Alianza en Gn 2–3," *Bib* 43.3 (1962): 302–3, and Seth D. Postell, *Adam as Israel: Genesis 1–3 as the Introduction to the Torah and the Tanakh* (Eugene, OR: Pickwick, 2011), 131–33.

14. Gianni Barbiero, *Das erste Psalmenbuch als Einheit: eine synchrone Analyse von Psalm 1–41*, ÖBS 16 (Frankfurt: Peter Lang, 1999), 721.

15. A key phrase that opens this group of Psalms (Ps 3:2).

his historical deliverance from the hand of Absalom as a prophetic picture of the persecution of the Messiah (Pss 3:2; 4:3; 5:6; 6:8–9; 7:3, 5–7)[16] as well as his future victories over the rebellious rulers in Psalm 2.

Given the carefully designed web of shared lexemes and thematic parallels linking Psalms 1–8, it appears entirely justified to identify the son of man in Psalm 8:5 as the Lord's Son in Psalm 2 (Ps 2:2, 12; cf. Ps 89:27–28). Support for identifying the son of man as the Son of the Lord in Psalm 2 is the description of the son of man's unparalleled rule in Psalm 8 (Ps 2:8–9). Josh Mathews makes a good case for an intentional parallel between "the works of God's fingers" (Ps 8:4) and "the works of God's hands" (Ps 8:7), suggesting that the rule of the son of man is not a generic description of humanity's exercise of the creation mandate, but a specific exercise of messianic rule over the entire realm of creation (the heavens and the earth).[17] God has literally put the entire universe under the son of man's feet (Ps 8:5; 89:27–28; 110:1). The rule of the son of man is described in terms of creation's three realms listed in the creation mandate (Gen 1:26–30): the earth, the heavens, and the sea (Ps 8:8–9). As was originally intended at creation, the son of man will rule over the ravenous beasts (Ps 7:3; see also 10:9; 17:12; 22:14, 22; Isa 11:1–9; 65:25).

The portrayal of the rule of a Davidic king as a fulfillment of the creation mandate is not limited to Psalm 8. According to Psalm 2, the Messiah's rule will extend to the ends of the earth (Ps 2:8). The same phrase is used to describe the Messiah's reign in another structurally significant psalm. Psalm 72 not only serves as the final psalm in Book II but it is ascribed to King Solomon (Ps 72:1). In Psalm 72:8, we read: "And may he rule from sea to sea, and from the river to the ends of the earth." Not only does this verse appear in another well-known messianic prophecy (Zech 9:10), but it also uses a word for "rule" that appears in the creation mandate: *rādh* (רדה).

> And God said, "let us make humankind in our image according to our likeness, and let them rule [*rādh*] the fish of the sea, and the flying creatures of the sky, and the beasts and over all the earth and over every creeping thing which creeps upon the earth. …" And God blessed them and God said to them, "Bear fruit and multiply and fill the earth and conquer it. And rule [*rādh*] the fish of the sea and the

16. Of interest, the enemies are portrayed as ravenous lions (Ps 7:3; see also 10:9; 17:12; 22:14, 22), beasts over whom the son of man is supposed to rule.

17. Josh Mathews, "Psalm 8: The Messianic Son of Adam," in Rydelnik and Blum, *The Moody Handbook of Messianic Prophecy*, 508.

> flying creatures of the sky and over every animal which creeps upon the land." (Gen 1:26, 28)

Given the superscription linking Psalm 72 with King Solomon, it comes as no surprise that this same verb is used to describe Solomon's reign: "And he was ruler [*rādh*] over everything beyond the river, from Tiphsah and to Gaza, over all the kings beyond the river, and he had peace in every direction around him" (1 Kgs 5:4 [ET 4:24]). Several words in this passage are repeated in the description of the Messiah's reign in Psalm 72: rule (*rādh*; Ps 72:8), river (Ps 72:8; cf. 1 Kgs 5:1 [ET 4:21]), peace (Ps 72:3, 7; likely a play on words with Solomon's name in 72:1 [*shalom* and *Shlomo*]). The description of a reign over a vast territory bounded by rivers, both in Psalm 72 (also Ps 89:26) and in 1 Kings 5:4 (cf. 1 Kgs 5:1), may in fact be an allusion to Adam's original rule from Eden whence the paradisiacal rivers flowed (Gen 2:10–14). The likelihood of this connection is further strengthened when we consider the description of Solomon in 1 Kings 5:13 as one who had knowledge of the trees (עצים), the beasts (בהמה), the flying creatures (עוף), the creeping things (רמש), and the fish (דגים), all of which are categories unmistakably tied to the creation mandate: trees (Gen 1:29; 2:9, 16), beasts (Gen 1:26; 2:20), flying creatures (Gen 1:26, 28, 30; 2:19–20), creeping things (Gen 1:26, 28, 30), and fish (Gen 1:26, 28).[18] These creation-mandate categories are also repeated in Psalm 8:8–9.

Thus, we can see that Psalms 2, 8, and 72 (all key psalms in the structure of the book) describe the messianic King as the quintessential son of man, an individual king, whose rule will be characterized by the mandate given to mankind in the beginning. The Messiah in the book of Psalms is most clearly, quintessentially, a son of Adam, and a human being in the image of God.

THE CONFLATION OF THE LORD AND HIS MESSIAH IN THE PSALTER

As has been noted by many scholars, any attempt to understand the theological intentions of the book of Psalms must begin with a thorough analysis of

---

18. For a discussion of these, and other parallels between Genesis 1–3 and 1 Kings 1–11, see Postell, *Adam as Israel*, 132–33. Further support for a messianism tied to the fulfillment of the creation mandate may be found in Isaiah 11 and 65, where the Messiah's rule is described as the reestablishment of peace between humanity and the animal world—every animal except one, the serpent (Isa 65:25).

the psalms in the seams of the macrostructure of the Psalter.[19] The psalms in the seams of the Psalter focus on an exalted king whose rule is predicated upon the faithfulness of God to fulfill his promises to the house of David (Pss 2:7; 45:7–8;[20] 72:17;[21] 89:27–29; 110:1–2[22]). The identity of the exalted king and the Lord is consistently conflated in these psalms.

Psalm 2

Not only do Psalms 1–2 serve as the introduction to the Psalter,[23] but they are also very closely related. Robert Cole provides an impressive list of lexical links between Psalms 1–2, the presence of which encourages an integrated reading of one psalm in light of the other and also points to a strategic conflation of divine identity between the Lord and his Son.[24] The blessed man of Psalm 1:1 is identified as the Son (בר) of the Lord in Psalm 2 who becomes a source of blessing for all who trust in him (Ps 2:12).

The character pairing in the macrostructure of Psalm 2 further reinforces this conflation of divine identity. The Lord and his Messiah act in tandem throughout the entire psalm. In verses 1–3, the wicked conspire against the Lord and his Messiah, with the intent of casting off *their* [the Lord and his Messiah's] bonds and *their* [the Lord and his Messiah's] fetters. The warning at the conclusion of the psalm (2:10–12) calls the kings and the rulers of the earth to reconcile with the Lord and his Messiah whom they have mutually offended (2:10–12). This character pairing also shows up in 2:4–9, where we see the joint response of the Lord and his Messiah to this earthly rebellion. The distinction of "persons"—Lord and Messiah—is evident in the dialogue between the Lord and his Son in verses 6–9.

Although a distinction of persons is not as clear in Psalm 2:4–5, the consistent character pairing throughout the remainder of the psalm suggests

19. Cole, "Psalms 1 and 2: The Psalter's Introduction"; Mitchell, "Lord, Remember David"; Postell, "Messianism in the Psalms"; Snearly, "Return of the King"; Gerald H. Wilson, *The Editing of the Hebrew Psalter*, SBLDS 76 (Chico, CA: Scholars Press, 1985); and Wilson, "The Use of Royal Psalms at the 'Seams' of the Hebrew Psalter."

20. Psalm 45 stands in a prominent location in the opening of Book II. See Postell, "A Literary, Compositional, and Intertextual Analysis of Psalm 45."

21. The reference to the exalted name of the Messiah is most likely an allusion to God's promise to make David's name great (2 Sam 7:9).

22. The relationship between Psalms 2 and 110 and its importance to the structure of the Psalter have been well noted and well defended by others; see Cole, "An Integrated Reading of Psalms 1 and 2."

23. Howard, "Divine and Human Kingship," 202–3.

24. Cole, "Psalms 1–2: The Divine Son of God," 83–84.

that the first and second cola of each of these verses represent two distinct entities as well: the Lord and his Messiah.

Figure - 5.1

THE LORD	HIS MESSIAH
He who sits in heaven laughs (2:4a)	*'ădōnāy* ["the Lord"] mocks them (2:4b)
He speaks to them in his anger (2:5a)	and in his fury, he terrifies them (2:5b)

This distinction of persons in 2:5a–b seems likely because of the *waw* ("and") in 2:5b and also because of the reference to the anger/fury in both cola: "He speaks to them in his anger (2:5a); and in his fury he terrifies them (2:5b)." This dual reference to anger in this verse corresponds to the two offended persons at the end of the psalm (Ps 2:11–12). And though the anger of the Lord is implied in Psalm 2:11, it is specifically referenced with respect to the Son in Psalm 2:12.

Though the distinction of persons in 2:4a–b is less clear in the Masoretic Text (MT), this is the obvious reading of the LXX and Syriac, which include a *waw* in 2:4b: "*And* the Lord [*kai ho kyrios*] mocks them." The replacement of *'ădōnāy* with the Tetragrammaton (the four Hebrew letters, YHWH, used for the name of God) in some Masoretic manuscripts and targums belie a secondary scribal attempt to avoid the somewhat awkward use of *'ădōnāy* in the second colon. It also disrupts the poetic structure of the psalm, where the divine name appears only once in each of the psalm's three stanzas.[25] The use of *'ădōnāy* in 2:4b is most likely the author's way of distinguishing this figure from Yahweh.[26]

It is crucial to note in the plot of Psalm 2 that the rebellious rulers are not only called to serve Yahweh (2:11) but also to "kiss the Son" and to "put their trust in him" (2:12). This pronouncement of blessing on those who trust in the Son is remarkable when one considers that this verb with the *bet* preposition "to trust in" (חסה ב-) is used exclusively of a human response to the deity in the book of Psalms (Pss 5:12; 16:1; 18:3, 31; 25:20; 31:20; 34:9, 23; 37:40;

---

25. Yahweh's name is mentioned once in the rebellion against the Lord and his Messiah (2:1–3; cf. v. 2), once in the response of the Lord and his Messiah to the rebellion (2:4–9; cf. v. 7), and once in the call for the rebels to be reconciled with the Lord and his Messiah (2:10–12; cf. v. 11).

26. Although the Tetragrammaton is also used by the targum in 2:4b, it is not used to merge the figure of 2:4a with the figure of 2:4b, but rather to distinguish the two figures. Yahweh is clearly not the subject of the second colon; rather, it is the *mymr'* (the Word of Yahweh) who is laughing alongside the one who is seated in heaven.

61:5; 64:11). This identification of the Messiah in 2:4b as *ʾᵃdōnāy* seated with Yahweh in heaven (2:4a) in whom the nations must put their trust conflates the divine identity of Yahweh with his Son.

Psalm 45

Psalm 45 serves a strategic function, not only as part of the introductory collection[27] of Psalms at the opening of Book II (Pss 42–49), but also as a bridge between the divine absence in Psalms 42–44 and the divine presence in Psalms 46–49 within this collection.[28] In Psalm 45, the king is addressed directly as God, *ʾᵉlōhîm* (Ps 45:7). His defeat of the enemies on the battlefield (Ps 45:4–6) and his enthronement in the palace (Ps 45:7–10) turn the cries of divine abandonment and distance (Pss 42:4, 10–11; 43:2; 44:10, 24) into a glorious celebration of God's presence with the armies of Israel and with his chosen city (Ps 46:2, 6, 8, 12). The messianic King is presented in Psalm 45 as "God with us," who loves his people like a royal bridegroom who loves his bride (Ps 45:11–17).

There are several ways in which we see the conflation of God and the Messiah in this remarkable psalm. First, the king bears an identity that is distinct from God (Ps 45:2, 6, 10, 12, 14–16), yet is also identified as God. The divine identity of the king is established not only by a direct statement (Ps 45:7), but also by virtue of the function of Psalm 45 in a compositional reading of this group of Sons of Korah psalms. There are numerous lexical and thematic links of the juxtaposing psalms in this collection. Everywhere the word "king" (singular) is mentioned in this collection it refers exclusively to God (Pss 44:5; 47:3, 7–8; 48:3, 5) followed by the sole exception of Psalm 45. The Sons of Korah make it clear that God is king. The explicit identification of the king as God in Psalm 45 can hardly be accidental within its broader context.

Second, the king of Psalm 45 receives the same kind of adoration as the divine king in the surrounding psalms of the Sons of Korah, an adoration that would appear idolatrous were it not for the divine identification of this king in Psalm 45:7. Several verses in the juxtaposing psalms of the Sons of Korah extol and worship God the king:

27. Psalms 42–49 are psalms of the Sons of Korah.

28. For a thorough literary analysis of Psalm 45 in the context of Psalms 42–49, see Postell, "A Literary, Compositional, and Intertextual Analysis of Psalm 45."

> You are my God King, O God, command salvation for Jacob. (Ps 44:5)
>
> For Yahweh the Most High is feared, a great king over the whole earth. (Ps 47:3)
>
> Sing to God, sing; sing to our king, sing. For the king over the earth is God, sing a maskil. God reigns over the nations, God sits upon his holy throne. (Ps 47:7–9; see also 48:3)

The adoration of the divine king in the psalms of the Sons of Korah is consistent with the worship of God we see throughout the Psalter as a whole.

Psalm 110

Structurally, the opening collection of psalms in Book V is remarkably similar to the opening collection of psalms in Book II. In both collections, messianic psalms serve as a bridge (Pss 45; 110) from pleas for deliverance (Pss 42–44; 107–109) to praise for deliverance (Pss 46–49; 111–113).[29] In Psalms 45 and 110, moreover, the Messiah is given names of divine exaltation: *ᵉlōhim* (Ps 45:7); *ʾᵃdōni* (Ps 110:1). Although the MT does not use *ʾᵃdōni* (אדני) in such a way as to refer exclusively to the deity, it is crucial to note that the consonantal text leaves open the possibility that the two figures in Psalm 110, Yahweh (יהוה) and *ʾᵃdōni* (אדני) allude to the same two figures in Psalm 2: Yahweh (Ps 2:2) and *ʾᵃdōnāy* (Ps 2:4b).[30] The likelihood of this connection is bolstered by the repeated language in Psalms 2:7 and 110:3, where the consonantal text is identical: ילדתיך.[31] Cole highlights other shared language: both psalms refer to אדני who is seated (Ps 2:4; 110:1) and ruling from Zion (Ps 2:6; 110:2).[32] The reference to "my holy mount" (הר קדשי) in Psalm 2:6 is quite similar to "holy array" (הדרי קדש) in Psalm 110:3.[33]

---

29. Michael A. Rydelnik, "Psalm 110: The Messiah as Eternal King Priest," in Rydelnik and Blum, *The Moody Handbook of Messianic Prophecy*, 678.

30. As is well noted by Rydelnik, "Psalm 110: The Messiah as Eternal King Priest," 679, "It would be mistaken, therefore, to base the entire interpretation of the psalm (i.e. where the addressee is human or divine) solely on a single Hebrew vowel."

31. The linkage is explicit in the LXX: *ἐγὼ σήμερον γεγέννηκά σε* (Ps 2:7); *ἐκ γαστρὸς πρὸ ἑωσφόρου ἐξεγέννησά σε* (Ps 110:3).

32. Cole, "An Integrated Reading of Psalms 1 and 2," 84.

33. Cole, "An Integrated Reading of Psalms 1 and 2," 84.

Additional support for reading אדני in Psalm 110:1 as *ᵃdōnāy* (divine) rather than *ʾᵃdōni* comes by way of the reference to *ᵃdōnāy* in Psalm 110:5. Rydelnik provides compelling arguments for identifying *ᵃdōnāy* in Psalm 110:5 as the messianic ruler of 110:1.[34] First, he notes that all other third-person references in the third and final stanza of this psalm refer to the messianic King (110:5–7), the fact of which is particularly clear in verse 7, where the third-person reference to drinking from a brook or lifting up the head hardly seems appropriate language for Yahweh.[35] Second, the reference to *ᵃdōnāy* at the right hand of Yahweh is an unmistakable allusion to the first verse of the psalm, where the Lord is called to sit at the right hand of Yahweh.[36] Syntactically and thematically, therefore, it makes the most sense to identify both references to אדני in the psalm as one and the same person, sitting at the right of Yahweh. Given the consistent conflation of the Lord and his Messiah in the other messianic psalms we have looked at, the blurring of the lines between Yahweh and the Messiah in verse 5 appears to be part of a consistent compositional strategy in the book of Psalms.[37]

THE PARALLEL "CHRISTOLOGY" OF DANIEL: SON OF MAN, SON OF GOD

Thus far, we have seen how the Psalter presents the Messiah as the quintessential son of man whose rule fulfills the creation mandate on the one hand (Pss 8:5; 45:3), and as a divine figure who is worthy of praise and adoration on the other (Pss 45:18; 72:17). In this final section, I hope to strengthen my exegetical and theological conclusions by looking at the messianism of the book of Daniel, another postexilic composition. For our purposes, it is essential to notice how Daniel's portrayal of the Messiah is incredibly similar to the portrayal of the Messiah in the Psalter.

34. Rydelnik, "Psalm 110: The Messiah as Eternal King Priest," 683–84.

35. On the difficulties with verse 7, see Frank-Lothar Hossfeld and Erich Zenger, *Psalms 3: A Commentary on Psalms 101–150*, trans. Linda M. Maloney, vol. 19C, Hermeneia, ed. Klaus Baltzer (Minneapolis: Fortress Press, 2011), 150–51, and Allen P. Ross, *A Commentary on the Psalms: Volume 3 (90–150)*, vol. 3, Kregel Exegetical Library (Grand Rapids: Kregel Academic, 2016), 357.

36. The reference to the wrath (*ʾappô*) of the divine Messiah against the kings (Ps 110:5) may also be a textual link to Psalm 2:10, 12.

37. Mitchell, *The Message of the Psalter*, 262.

The Son of Man in Daniel

In a recent dissertation, Daewoong Kim makes a compelling case for extensive literary allusions to Genesis in Daniel.[38] In addition to the numerous cases in which Daniel is cast as a "second Joseph" in the court of a foreign king,[39] the book of Daniel contains several allusions to the primeval history of Genesis (Gen 1–11). The reference to "the land of Shinar" in Daniel 1:2 is striking when one considers that the phrase appears only four times in all of Scripture (Gen 10:10; 11:2; Zech 5:11; Dan 1:2), and seemingly draws a parallel between Nebuchadnezzar and Nimrod, the first mighty king of Babylon (see Gen 10:8–12).[40] The reference to "good gold" in Daniel 2:32 is reminiscent of the "good gold" in the land of Havilah (Gen 2:11), and Nebuchadnezzar's rule is clearly described, at least in a twisted sort of way, as a fulfillment of the creation mandate as described in both versions of the creation account.[41]

Figure 5.2

"You O King are the king of kings to whom the God of Heaven has given the kingdom, the power, the might, and the glory. And he has given into your hand all the sons of men who dwell, the animals of the field, and the birds of the sky; and he has given you rule over all of them. You are the head of gold." (Dan 2:37–38; see also 2:39)	"And God blessed them, and God said to them, be fertile and multiply and fill the earth and conquer it. And rule over the fish of the sea and the birds of the sky and over every living animal that creeps on the earth." (Gen 1:28)	"And YHWH God formed from the ground every animal of the field and every bird of the sky, and he caused them to come to the man to see what he would call them. And everything which the man called a living creature, that was its name. And the man named all the cattle and the birds of the sky and all the animals of the field." (Gen 2:19–20)

38. Daewoong Kim, "Biblical Interpretation in the Book of Daniel: Literary Allusions in Daniel to Genesis and Ezekiel" (PhD diss., Rice University, 2013).

39. Compare Daniel 1:10 with Genesis 40:6; Daniel 1:15 with Genesis 41:2, 18; Daniel 1:20 with Genesis 41:24. Note also the parallels between the story of Nebuchadnezzar's dream and Daniel's interpretation with Pharaoh's dream and Joseph's interpretation (compare Dan 2:3 with Gen 41:8; Dan 2:1, 3 with Gen 40:8; 41:8, 15).

40. Kim, "Biblical Interpretation in the Book of Daniel," 52–74.

41. Kim, "Biblical Interpretation in the Book of Daniel," 149.

Given these clear allusions to the creation mandate, it can hardly be coincidental that the rule of the stone is described as a mountain that will "fill the whole earth" (Dan 2:35; cf. Gen 1:28; 9:1).[42] In other words, the creation mandate will be given back to the "stone"[43] who will establish the kingdom of God (Dan 2:44–45; cf. 2:48).

Daniel's victory over the wild lions in chapter 6 (Dan 6:8, 13, 17, 20–21, 23, 25, 28) sets the stage for the Messiah's victory over the four wild beasts in Daniel's vision in 7:3–8, 13–14. Of interest is the identification of the Messiah as one "like a son of man" in Daniel 7:13. Given the allusions to the creation mandate in the earlier chapters, it makes perfect sense to identify the Messiah as one like a son of man who overcomes the four beasts (Dan 7:13) in fulfillment of God's design for creation. Daniel's depiction of the Messiah as a quintessential son of man who conquers the beastly kingdoms to rule over creation fits hand in hand with the description of the messianic reign in the book of Psalms.[44]

The Divine Messiah in Daniel

The book of Daniel not only presents the Messiah as one who fulfills the creation mandate but also as one who partakes in the divine identity. Daniel's vision of the one like the son of man is striking. Daniel sees a vision of one like a son of man coming on the clouds, clearly parallel to the stone that was not cut by human hands (Dan 7:13; cf. 2:34, 45).[45] The one like the son of man is given authority by the Ancient of Days, and all the peoples, nations, and languages worship/serve (*plḥ*) him (Dan 7:14). The reference to the "peoples, nations, and languages" calls to mind the universal gathering in Daniel 3 of nations to worship Nebuchadnezzar's image (Dan 3:4, 7, 31). Daniel 7 provides the ultimate triumph of God's kingdom over the kingdoms of the earth and the establishment of true worship for all nations.

---

42. For similar thoughts on Genesis 9:1, see Kim, "Biblical Interpretation in the Book of Daniel," 54.
43. Could the Messiah-stone in Daniel be an allusion to the Messiah-stone in Psalm 118:22? There, the rejected stone becomes the very block upon which the entire temple holds together.
44. Although never published, John Sailhamer put forth the idea in a class lecture that the phrase "kiss the Son" (*naššᵉqû-ḇar*) in Psalm 2:12 and "son of man" (*ḇar ʾᵉnāš*) in Daniel 7:13 may be an intentional play on words.
45. The stone (*ʾeḇen*) may have intentionally been chosen because of its similarity to the Hebrew word for "son" (*bēn*).

And here we are confronted with the obvious conflation of identity between the Ancient of Days and the one like a son of man.[46] With the establishment of God's eternal kingdom, all peoples, tribes, and languages worship the son of man, the Messiah (Dan 7:14), something that appears to fly in the face of the clear theological message of Daniel 3 and 6. How can these nations worship something (Nebuchadnezzar's image in chapter 3) or someone (King Darius in chapter 6) other than the God of heaven? The answer must be that the one like the son of man in Daniel represents a divine figure.

In light of Daniel 3 and 6, worship is an action that is rendered by the people of Israel to the God of Israel, and it is the theological vision set forth by the author of Daniel for all the peoples of the earth. The exclusive worship of the God of Israel is so important that all four of the heroes of the book are willing to die rather than to worship anything or anyone other than the true God. It is unthinkable, therefore, to interpret Daniel 7:14 with respect to the nations worshiping the people of Israel.[47] Thus, we must interpret the one like a son of man as a figure who is somehow distinct from God and yet mysteriously included in the identity of the One True God. Daniel's presentation of the Messiah, a quintessential son of man who shares in the identity of the One True God is remarkably similar to the depiction of the Messiah in the book of Psalms, particularly in the seams of the book. This parallel presentation, furthermore, suggests that a belief in a fully human and divine Messiah is grounded in the theological intentions of these postexilic authors. The book of Psalms, like the book of Daniel, presents a divine Messiah.

CONCLUSION

In this essay, we sought to answer the question: Does the book of Psalms present a divine Messiah? The messianism of the Psalter was considered in light of its literary structure, along with the dual presentation of the Messiah as both a human figure who fulfills the creation mandate as well as a divine figure whose identity is consistently conflated with the Lord, who is worshiped by Israel and the nations. By looking at Psalms 2, 8, 45, 72, and 110 we see a king whose reign fulfills God's original purposes for

---

46. The Ancient of Days and the son of man are not merely conflated in the Old Greek; they are completely equated: "I was observing in a vision of the night and behold, upon the clouds of heaven like a son of man coming, and like the Ancient of Days was passing by" (Dan 7:13 OG; so also Rev 1:13–14).

47. Contra Kim, "Biblical Interpretation in the Book of Daniel," 214–19.

humanity—a quintessential son of man. At the same time, we encountered a king who is called Lord (אדני) and God (אלהים), whose actions and attributes are divine, a king in whom Israel and the nations trust, to whom the authors write love songs, one who is praised forever, and who is seated with Yahweh in heaven.

We then looked at the book of Daniel, another postexilic composition, which likewise presents a vision of a son of man (stone) who brings to obedience all the beastly kingdoms of the earth and rules in Adam's stead. The book of Daniel tells the story of four Hebrews from the exile who would rather die than worship/serve (*plḥ*) a false deity, and whose wholehearted commitment to serve God alone culminates in the vision of all peoples, nations, and languages worshiping/serving the one like the son of man. The messianism of Daniel is so similar to the Psalter that one can claim with a high degree of confidence that Jesus's conflation of the vision of the son of man (Dan 7:13–14) with the Lord seated at the right hand of power (Ps 110:1) draws together two sides of a single theological presentation of a divine Messiah who is the quintessential Son of Man.

The New Testament's authors have accurately appealed to the book of Psalms to establish the divine identity of the Messiah. Our apologetic for the divine Messiah, therefore, is not merely based on the creative exegesis of the early Jewish believers in Jesus, but deeply grounded in the grammatical-historical meaning of the books upon which they base their claims.

6

The Suffering Servant in Book V of the Psalter

Jill Firth

The concept of "servant" is consistent across the Psalter, connoting status, dependence, or loyalty, and a righteous, royal, suffering servant is depicted in the portrayal of David and of the "I" of the ledavid *("of David": לדוד) psalms. After examining the vocabulary of "serving" and "servants" in the Psalter, I consider all occurrences of the noun* עבד *(servant, servants) in Books I–IV (Pss 1–106) and Book V (Pss 107–150), and examine any changes in relation to David, kingship, and suffering in Book V.*

"Thus it is written, that the Messiah is to suffer," says Luke (Luke 24:46).[1] However, some scholars have seen Luke's scriptural suffering Messiah as "an early Christian invention or oxymoron."[2] New Testament researchers have turned to the Psalter to seek a background to Jesus's suffering, convinced, like Joshua Jipp, that "it is in the psalms that one consistently finds the sufferings of King David," who is "the righteous royal sufferer par excellence."[3] Meanwhile, some Old Testament scholars have questioned the

1. Scripture quotations are from the NRSV, unless otherwise noted, but Hebrew numbering is used for Psalms.

2. Joshua W. Jipp, "Luke's Scriptural Suffering Messiah: A Search for Precedent, a Search for Identity," *CBQ* 72 (2010): 256.

3. Jipp, "Suffering Messiah," 256–57, 259. See also, Stephen P. Ahearne-Kroll, "Psalms in the New Testament," in *The Oxford Handbook of the Psalms*, ed. William P. Brown (Oxford: Oxford University Press, 2014), 272; Margaret Daly-Denton, "Early Christian Writers as Jewish Readers: The New Testament Reception of the Psalms," *The Review of Rabbinic Judaism* 11 (2008): 184–85; Peter Doble, "Luke 24.26, 44—Songs of God's Servant: David and His Psalms in Luke-Acts," *JSNT*

relationship between David and kingship in Book V of the Psalter. Gerald Wilson has proposed that, after Psalm 89, David is no longer a king, but only a servant. Frank-Lothar Hossfeld and Erich Zenger have suggested "changing ideas about the king," and Dennis Tucker argues that in Psalm 144, the royal theme is "diminished."[4]

This study is in four parts. First, I lay groundwork on "serving" and "servants" in the Psalter, drawing on the taxonomy of Edward Bridge.[5] In the second and third sections, I consider all occurrences of the noun עבד (servant, servants) in Books I–IV (Pss 1–106) and Book V (Pss 107–150), in relation to David, kingship, and suffering. Finally, I examine any changes in presentation of David at the end of the Psalter, utilizing Amy Cottrill's analysis of the language of powerlessness in lament psalms.[6] I argue that the concept of "servant" is consistent across the Psalter, connoting status, dependence, or loyalty, and that a righteous, royal, suffering servant is depicted in the portrayal of David and of the "I" of the *ledavid* ("of" David: לדוד) psalms.[7]

"SERVING" AND "SERVANTS" IN THE PSALTER

Verb and Noun

The lexeme עבד occurs as both the verb "to serve" and as the noun "servant" in the Psalter. The verb עבד (to serve) has two main meanings in the Psalter: subjection as a vassal to an overlord, and worship to a deity. The verb עבד occurs eight times in Books I–IV, where it is always plural. Two references to nations and rulers serving the Davidic king are related to the conceptual domain vassal-overlord (Pss 18:44; 72:11). Six references to people serving

---

28 (2006): 269; Richard B. Hays, *Echoes of Scripture in the Gospels* (Waco, TX: Baylor University Press, 2016), 86–87, 159–62, 230–37, 324–29.

4. Gerald H. Wilson, "King, Messiah, and the Reign of God: Revisiting the Royal Psalms and the Shape of the Psalter," in *The Book of Psalms: Composition and Reception*, ed. Peter W. Flint and Patrick D. Miller Jr. (Leiden: Brill, 2005), 401–5; Frank-Lothar Hossfeld and Erich Zenger, *Psalms 3: A Commentary on Psalms 101–150*, Hermeneia, ed. Klaus Baltzer, trans. Linda M. Maloney (Minneapolis: Fortress, 2011), 589–90; W. Dennis Tucker Jr., *Constructing and Deconstructing Power in Psalms 107–150* (Atlanta: SBL Press, 2014), 134, 182–83.

5. Edward J. Bridge, "Loyalty, Dependency and Status with YHWH: The Use of *'bd* in the Psalms," *VT* 59 (2009): 360–78.

6. Amy C. Cottrill, *Language, Power, and Identity in the Lament Psalms of the Individual*, LHBOTS 493 (New York: T&T Clark, 2008).

7. I use *ledavid* as a designation for psalms with the title לדוד (which can be translated "of" David, "to" David, or "for" David), without engaging the debate about Davidic authorship.

Yahweh (Pss 2:11; 22:32; 100:2; 102:23), or idols (Pss 97:7; 106:37), may evoke the domains both of vassal-overlord and of worship.[8] As a verb, עבד does not occur in Book V.

The noun עבד (servant) is found fifty-six times in the Psalter, occurring in each of the five books in both the singular (עבד) and the plural (עבדים). In the Psalter, as in the Old Testament as a whole, עבד can refer to vassals, courtiers, temple staff, prophets, personal attendants, workers, or slaves.[9] The noun can indicate status, deference, or loyalty, and "your servant" can be a circumlocution for "I."[10]

Status, Deference, Loyalty, and Suffering

In the Old Testament, status is indicated by the terms עבד יהוה (servant of Yahweh), עבדי (my servant), and עבדו (his servant). "Servant of Yahweh" is applied to Moses (Deut 34:5) and Joshua (Josh 24:29), and God also uses the honorific and relational term עבדי (my servant) for significant leaders including Abraham (Gen 26:24), Caleb (Num 14:24), David (e.g., 2 Sam 3:18, 1 Kgs 11:13; 2 Kgs 20:6), Isaiah (Isa 20:3), Job (Job 1:8), Isaiah's "servant" (Isa 42:1), Israel (Isa 41:8), Jacob (Isa 44:1–2), Nebuchadrezzar (Jer 25:9), and Zerubbabel (Hag 2:23). Leaders named as עבדו (his servant) include Moses (Exod 14:31), David (1 Kgs 8:66), Elijah (2 Kgs 10:10), and Jonah (2 Kgs 14:25). In the Psalter, David is twice called "servant of Yahweh" (עבד יהוה, Pss 18:1; 36:1), and "my servant David" (דוד עבדי, Ps 89:4, 21), and is named "his servant David" (דוד עבדו, Ps 144:10) in comparable honor to Abraham and Moses (Ps 105:6, 26, 42). The servant is sometimes "chosen" (בחר, Pss 78:70; 89:4; 105:6, 26) or "found" (מצא, Ps 89:21).[11]

"Servant" language was used to indicate deference or loyalty in the ancient Near East, as in a prayer to Marduk: "Do not destroy the servant who is your handiwork."[12] The affirmation "I am your servant" (אני עבדך, Pss 116:16; 119:125; 143:12) can be a statement of loyalty, as exemplified by the use of the phrase by Hushai (2 Sam 15:34), Elijah (1 Kgs 18:36), and Ahaz (2 Kgs 16:7).

In the Old Testament, עבדך (your servant) is used as a circumlocution for "I" in speaking to other people (Gen 32:5; 1 Sam 17:32), and to God (e.g., by

8. Bridge, "Loyalty," 363–64.

9. Edward J. Bridge, "The Metaphoric Use of Slave Terms in the Hebrew Bible," *BBR* 23 (2013): 14–27.

10. Bridge, "Loyalty," 369–70, 373–77.

11. Emile Nicole, "בחר," *NIDOTTE* 1:640.

12. Anna Elise Zernecke, "Mesopotamian Parallels to the Psalms," in Brown, *The Oxford Handbook of the Psalms*, 36.

Abraham, Gen 19:19; Moses, Exod 4:10; Samuel, 1 Sam 3:9). This is consistent with ancient Near Eastern practice, as can be seen in the Lachish letters, where the writer uses עבדך (your servant) as a term of deference, addressing his superior as אדני (my lord).[13] In the Psalter, עבדך (your servant) is frequently (twenty-six times) a substitute for the personal pronoun "I," especially in the *ledavid* psalms (e.g., Pss 19:12; 69:18; 86:2; 143:2), and Psalm 119, where it typically indicates deference to Yahweh. The plural עבדיך (your servants) can be a circumlocution for "we" (e.g., Pss 79:10; 89:51; 90:13, 16).[14]

In the Psalter, most suffering concerns danger and persecution from enemies, and rejection and betrayal by friends. The New Testament picture of the suffering of the servant uses Isaiah and Zechariah along with the Psalms.[15]

I now turn to the use of "servant" (עבד) and "servants" (עבדים) in Books I–V, considering status, dependence, and loyalty in relation to David, kingship, and suffering.

THE "SERVANT" AND THE "SERVANTS" IN BOOKS I–IV

Books I–III (Pss 1–89)

The first occurrence of the noun "servant" in the Psalter indicates David's status, when he is named as "David, the servant of Yahweh" in the *ledavid* heading of Psalm 18:1 (לעבד יהוה לדוד). In this psalm, David is described as "his king" (מלכו), and "his anointed" (משיחו), and God's חסד (steadfast love) is affirmed also to David's "descendants forever" (לזרעו עד־עולם, Ps 18:51). Psalm 18 is David's thanksgiving for deliverance from all his enemies, who hated him, were too mighty for him (Ps 18:18), and, like cords of death and Sheol, encircled him (אפפוני חבלי־מות, Ps 18:5). The *ledavid* heading of Psalm 36 also names David, "the servant of Yahweh" (לעבד יהוה לדוד, Ps 36:1), in a psalm where the "I" describes danger from the deceit of the wicked.

David's status is affirmed in Psalms 78 and 89 in Book III. In Psalm 78:70 ("of" Asaph), "his servant David" (דוד עבדו) is chosen (יבחר) and brought to

13. Edward J. Bridge, "Polite Language in the Lachish Letters," *VT* 60 (2010): 524–25.

14. Bridge, "Loyalty," 366–70. In some manuscripts, Psalm 89:51 has the singular form, "your servant" (עבדך), see *BHS* footnote, and Marvin E. Tate, *Psalms 51–100*, WBC 20 (Nashville: Nelson, 1990), 412n51b.

15. Michael R. Stead, "Suffering Servant, Suffering David, and Stricken Shepherd," in *Christ Died for Our Sins: Essays on the Atonement*, ed. Michael R. Stead (Barton, ACT: Barton Books, 2013), 62, proposes a fusion of the Psalter's suffering king with Isaiah's suffering servant (Isa 40–55) and Zechariah's stricken shepherd (Zech 9–14).

be a shepherd of God's people. In Psalm 89 ("of" Ethan), David is named by God as "my servant David" (דוד עבדי, Ps 89:4, 21), "my chosen one" (בחירי, Ps 89:4), and "one chosen from the people" (בחור מעם, Ps 89:20). God found "my servant David" (דוד עבדי, Ps 89:21) and anointed him (משחתיו, Ps 89:21) as a sign of favor and royal covenant. While his crown (a synecdoche for kingship) is in the dust, and he is covered in shame (Ps 89:38–45), the suffering Davidic descendant is still described as "your servant" (עבדך, Ps 89:40), paralleled with "your anointed" (משיחך, Ps 89:39). Like Psalm 18, Psalm 89 has a significant collocation of David, the Davidic descendant, "anointed," kingship, "servant," and suffering.

In Books I–III, the "I" of the *ledavid* psalms eight times uses the self-designation "your servant" (עבדך) to indicate dependence: in Book I (Pss 19:12, 14; 27:9; 31:17); Book II (Ps 69:18); and Book III (Ps 86:2, 4, 16).[16] "Your servant" occurs in the presence of the insolent (Pss 19:14; 86:14), adversaries (Pss 27:9; 69:18), danger (Pss 27:9; 86:2), nets laid for him (Ps 31:5), and shame, insults, and dishonor (Pss 31:17; 69:18). In Books I–III, the circumlocution "your servant" is used only by the "I" of the *ledavid* Psalms, and perhaps by the suffering Davidic descendant in Psalm 89:40.[17]

In Books I–III, using plural nouns, the nation or the faithful are related to Yahweh as "his servants" (עבדיו, Pss 34:23; 69:37 2x), where God's trustworthiness is affirmed in the context of the afflictions of the righteous (see Ps 34:19), and enemies, insults, and dishonor (see Ps 69:5, 8, 20). In a plea for help in the context of the destruction of Jerusalem, Psalm 79 ("of" Asaph) calls for vengeance for the blood of "your servants" (עבדיך, Ps 79:2, 10). In Psalm 89 ("of" Ethan) Yahweh's speedy action is requested as enemies taunt "your servants" (Ps 89:51).

Book IV (Pss 90–106)

In Book IV, status and relationship with Yahweh are affirmed in the designation "his servant Moses" (משה עבדו, Ps 105:26), who was chosen (בחר, 105:26), and "Abraham, his servant" (אברהם עבדו, 105:42), in the context of God remembering his holy promise (דבר קדשו, 105:42). "Offspring of his servant Abraham" (זרע אברהם עבדו) is parallel to "his chosen ones" (בחיריו, 105:6), highlighting the connection between descending from Abraham and being chosen. Joseph's suffering is foregrounded when he is "sold as a slave"

16. "His servant" in Psalm 35:27 may refer to the "I" of the psalm.

17. "Your servant" in Psalm 89:40 may be a circumlocution of the "I," or a description by the psalmist.

(לעבד נמכר, 105:17), but he is then honored by Pharaoh. "Your servant" (עבדך) is not used in Book IV, and this is the only book in the Psalter where "servant" is not used to refer to David.

In Psalm 90, the plural noun "your servants" (עבדיך, 90:13, 16) evokes the relationship of the nation or the faithful to Yahweh in times of suffering, inviting God's compassion and favor. In Psalm 102 "your servants" (102:15) indicates loyalty to Yahweh and expresses confidence in the trustworthiness of Yahweh to establish security and maintain the relationship (102:29), possibly including other nations (see 102:16, 22).[18] In Psalm 105 "his servants" (עבדיו, 105:25) are suffering under oppression in Egypt.

THE "SERVANT" AND THE "SERVANTS" IN BOOK V (PSS 107–150)

The "Servant" in Book V

Deference and loyalty are affirmed in the first "servant" reference in Book V, where the "I" of the *ledavid* Psalm 109 refers to himself as "your servant" (עבדך, 109:28). The "I" is surrounded by words of hate: the wicked and deceitful return evil for good (109:1–5), pursue the weak to death, and love to curse (109:15–17). In his suffering, the "I" calls on Yahweh for help, using typical deferential strategies, invoking God's character (109:21, 26, 31), asserting his own weakness (109:22–25), and reminding God of the honor that will accrue to him when he acts (109:27, 30).[19] "Your servant" will rejoice at the downfall of his accusers (109:28–29) and promises praise because God stands at the right hand of the needy.

The (untitled) thanksgiving psalm, Psalm 116, contains the first use outside of the *ledavid* psalms of "your servant" (עבדך) as a circumlocution for "I." However, a connection to the *ledavid* psalms may be intended, as Psalm 116 reuses the distinctive phrase "the snares of death encompassed me" (אפפוני חבלי־מות, 18:5; 116:3) from *ledavid* Psalm 18, calling (אקרא) on Yahweh while in danger of Sheol (שאול, 18:6; 116:3).[20] The "I" of Psalm 116 also models his relationship to Yahweh on David's self-description in *ledavid* Psalm 86:16. "I am your servant, the child of your serving girl" (בן־אמתך, 116:16) recalls the only other use in the Psalter of the phrase "the child of your

18. Bridge, "Loyalty," 374.
19. Bridge, "Loyalty," 377.
20. Federico Villanueva, *Psalms 1–72: A Pastoral and Contextual Commentary*, Asia Bible Commentary Series (Carlisle: Langham Global Library, 2016), 110.

serving girl" (בן־אמתך, 86:16), which in Psalm 86 is also in grammatical apposition to "your servant" (עבדך, 86:16).[21]

The "I" of (untitled) Psalm 119 indicates deference and loyalty to Yahweh by using "your servant" (עבדך, 119:17, 23, 38, 49, 65, 76, 84, 122, 124, 125, 135, 140, 176). This self-designation occurs in the context of the plotting of the insolent (119:17–24), disgrace (119:38–40), taunting (119:49–51), the arrogant (119:65–70, 76–78), persecution (119:84), the godless (119:122), the wicked (119:124, 125), oppression (119:135, see 134), contempt, trouble, and anguish (119:140–143), and a longing for rescue and help (119:169–175). The "I" of Psalm 119 may be royal, as he is opposed by princes (שרים, 119:23, 161), and speaks before kings (מלכים, 119:46).[22] The "I" of Psalm 119 uses some expressions only used in Books I–III by the "I" of the *ledavid* psalms, such as "save me" (הושיעני, 119:94, 146) and "my persecutors" (רדפי, 119:84, 150, 157), and refers to his "zeal" (קנאה, 119:139), as in *ledavid* Psalm 69:10.[23]

Psalm 132 in the Psalms of Ascent focuses on David's status as "your servant David" (דוד עבדך, 132:10), which is linked with "your anointed" (משיחך, 132:10), referring to the Davidic descendant, and "your throne" (כסא־לך, 132:12) and "his crown" (נזרו, 132:18), invoking kingship. The appeal in Psalm 132 "for your servant David's sake" (בעבור דוד עבדך, 132:10) reminds God of his oath and covenant obligations to the Davidic descendant.[24] The "crown" (נזר), which occurs in the Psalter only here and in Psalm 89:40, will now gleam. Zion, people, and priests will be blessed along with the Davidic descendant (132:11–18). As in Psalms 18 and 89, Psalm 132 connects David, "servant," "anointed," the royal promises, and the Davidic descendant. Suffering is briefly addressed in Psalm 132, mentioning David's hardships (ענותו, 132:1), but the focus is on status and relationship.[25]

The "I" of *ledavid* Psalm 143 expresses deference and loyalty as "your servant" (עבדך, 143:2), and recites his sufferings, having been crushed to the ground (143:3) and numbed with horror (143:4). Recalling past rescue, he reaches out to God (143:5–6) with affirmations of trust, submission, and

---

21. The similarity could be through imitation, or even that Psalm 116 is from the same hand as the *ledavid* psalms in Books I–III.

22. See also Will Soll, *Psalm 119: Matrix, Form, and Setting*, CBQMS 23 (Washington, DC: Catholic Biblical Association of America, 1991), 135–42; Adam D. Hensley, *Covenant Relationships and the Editing of the Hebrew Psalter*, LHBOTS 666 (London: T&T Clark, 2018), 176.

23. Psalm 79:5 refers to the zeal of God, not of the "I" as in Psalm 69:10 and Psalm 119:139.

24. See Carleen Mandolfo, "Language of Lament in the Psalms," in Brown, *The Oxford Handbook of the Psalms*, 126.

25. For ענותו (Ps 132:1), see Leslie C. Allen, *Psalms 101–150*, rev. ed, WBC 21 (Nashville: Nelson, 2002), 264n1a.

loyalty in the face of his enemies (143:8–12), including "you are my God" (אתה אלוהי, 143:10), and "I am your servant" (אני עבדך, 143:12). Psalm 143:12 has the last use of the deferential phrase "your servant" (עבדך) in the Psalter. Psalm 143 is connected to the *ledavid* Psalms of Books I–III by its heading and other shared language and trustful stance, including מהר ענני ("answer me quickly," Pss 69:18; 143:7), and בך בטחתי("in you I trust," Pss 25:2; 143:8).[26]

Psalm 144 features the final reference to a servant in Book V. The psalm names David's status as "his servant David" (דוד עבדו, 144:10), and celebrates God's faithfulness in giving victory to Israel's kings (תשועה למלכים, 144:10), with wording similar to Psalm 18, where Yahweh gives victory to David, his king (ישועות מלכו, 18:51). The psalm requests God's continued help for David's lineage, using phrases recalling *ledavid* psalms of Book I, especially Psalm 18:10, 15, 17 (see 144:5–7).[27] The "I" sets his current plea for help against a background of past victory, requesting God to again reach down from on high (144:7; 18:17), and save him from "mighty waters" (מים רבים) and foreigners (בנינכר, 144:7, 11; 18:17, 45). Blessing is also envisaged for the whole community, as in Psalm 132:9–18, with plentiful food and flourishing of the people (144:12–15).

The "Servants" in Book V

Psalm 113 is the first psalm in Book V to call on "the servants of Yahweh" (עבדי יהוה, 113:1) to praise Yahweh. The plural imperative invites praise of God's name, as he is exalted (113:4), yet he looks down on the earth, caring for the poor and needy (113:5–9).

In Psalm 119, one use of a plural noun proclaims, "all things are your servants" (הכל עבדיך, 119:91), alongside thirteen uses of the singular עבדך (your servant), 119:17.[28] In the Pslams of Ascent, the masculine plural "servants" (עבדים, 123:2) is used alongside the feminine singular "maid" (שפחה) in a request for favor in a surfeit of contempt (בוז, 123:3, 4) and scorn (לעג, 123:4). This simile of servants carefully watching the hand of their master suggests deference, loyalty, and trust in Yahweh.[29]

---

26. For more detail on distinctive ledavid language in Psalms 140–143, see Gillian C. Firth, "The Re-Presentation of David in Psalms 140–143" (PhD diss., Australian College of Theology, 2016).

27. W. Dennis Tucker Jr., and Jamie A. Grant, *Psalms, Volume 2*, NIVAC (Grand Rapids: Zondervan, 2018), 973, list Psalms 144:1, 2//18:1–4, 46–47; 144:3//8:4; 144:4//39:5–6; 144:5//18:9; 144:6//18:14; 144:7, 11//18:16, 45, 46; 144:9//33:2–3; 144:10//18:0 (superscription); 144:15//33:12 (ET).

28. Psalm 119:17, 23, 38, 49, 65, 76, 84, 122, 124, 125, 135, 140, 176.

29. Bridge, "Loyalty," 362.

Perhaps invoking loyalty, Psalm 134 calls on "all the servants" of Yahweh (כל־עבדי יהוה, 134:1) to bless Yahweh. In Psalm 135, the "servants" of Yahweh (עבדי יהוה, 135:1) are invited to celebrate God's goodness, his choice (בחר) of Jacob, his acts of creation and deliverance (135:3–12), and his superiority to idols (135:15–18). The fate of "all [Pharaoh's] servants" (כל־עבדיו, 135:9) is contrasted with Yahweh's compassion on "his servants" (עבדיו, 135:14), to whom he gave the land as a heritage (135:12). The house of Israel, along with the priestly houses, is called to bless Yahweh (135:19–20).

Psalm 136 invites praise for Yahweh's eternal steadfast love (חסד) in creation, exodus, conquest, and continued providence (136:4–25), exemplified in giving land to "his servant Israel" (ישׂראל עבדו, 136:22). This is the only use in the Psalter of the singular term "servant" to refer to the nation, unlike in the Prophets, where Israel and Jacob are addressed as "my servant" (Isa 41:8, 9; 44:1; 45:4), and "his servant" (Isa 48:20).[30] The deferential singular term "your servant," always used referring to individuals elsewhere in the Psalter, is not found in Psalm 136.[31]

Building on this survey of עבד (servant) with reference to status, loyalty, and dependence, and in relation to David, kingship, and suffering, I now consider the servant and his suffering at the end of the Psalter in the context of perceived changes in David and kingship in Book V.

SINGULARITY, STATUS, AND STANCE OF THE SERVANT IN BOOK V

The use of the noun "servant" at the end of Book V has been seen by some as a collectivized or generic term, or as diminishing the royal connotations

30. For a discussion, see Joseph Blenkinsopp, "The Servant and the Servants in Isaiah and the Formation of the Book," 155–75, in *Writing and Reading the Scroll of Isaiah: Studies of an Interpretive Tradition*, ed. Craig C. Broyles and Craig A. Evans, VTSup 70/1 (Leiden: Brill, 1997); Joseph Blenkinsopp, *Isaiah 40–55: A New Translation with Introduction and Commentary*, AB 19A (New York: Doubleday, 2002), 80–87; Ulrich Berges, "Who Were the Servants? A Comparative Inquiry in the Book of Isaiah and the Psalms," in *Past, Present, Future: The Deuteronomic History and the Prophets*, ed. Johannes C. de Moor and Harry F. van Rooy (Leiden: Brill, 2000), 1–18; Hensley, *Covenant Relationships*, 174–77.

31. Bridge, "Loyalty," 369.

of the David figure.[32] Based on this study, I offer some brief contributions to these larger debates.[33]

Collective or Kingly Care?

Some have claimed that David is collectivized after Psalm 89, or in Psalm 144, so that the figure of David represents corporate Israel or the faithful.[34] However, the Psalter distinguishes between an individual "servant" and plural "servants" even where they appear together in the same psalm, as in Psalm 69 where "your servant" refers to the "I" of the psalm, but "his servants" refers to "those who love his name" (69:18, 37). Psalm 105 names Moses and Abraham as "his servant" but Israel as "his servants" (105:6, 25, 26, 42). In Psalm 119, "your servant" is the "I" (119:17), but "your servants" are "all things" (119:91).[35]

The term "his servant Israel" (Ps 136:22) is an anomaly in the Psalter, as it is the only use of the singular noun "servant" with a corporate referent in the Psalter, though this usage is well-known in Isaiah and other texts (e.g., Isa 41:8).[36] In all other occurrences in Book V, worshipers and the nation of Israel are described with the plural noun, such as "the servants" of Yahweh (113:1; 134:1; 135:1) and "his servants" (135:14). The "I" and the community are not fused after Psalm 136, as the term "your servant" (עבדך, 143:2, 12) has only been used by an individual voice elsewhere in the Psalter, the final occurrence of the lexeme עבד in the Psalter names "his servant David" (דוד עבדו, 144:10), and Psalms 145 and 146 distinguish between the voice of the "I"

32. Wilson, "King, Messiah," 401–5; Egbert Ballhorn, *Zum Telos des Psalters: Der Textzusammenhang des Vierten und Fünften Psalmenbuches (Ps 90–150)*, BBB 138 (Berlin: Philo, 2004), 379–80; Hossfeld and Zenger, *Psalms 3*, 589–90; Tucker, *Constructing*, 182–83; J. Clinton McCann Jr., "The Shape and Shaping of the Psalter: Psalms in their Literary Context," in Brown, *The Oxford Handbook of the Psalms*, 361.

33. For an introduction to canonical readings of the Psalter, see Michael K. Snearly, *The Return of the King: Messianic Expectation in Book V of the Psalter*, LHBOTS 624 (London: T&T Clark, 2016), 1–104. For recent critiques of canonical readings, see David Willgren, *The Formation of the "Book" of Psalms: Reconsidering the Transmission and Canonization of Psalmody in Light of Material Culture and the Poetics of Anthologies*, FAT 88 (Tübingen: Mohr Siebeck, 2016), 1–20, 392; Alma Brodersen, *The End of the Psalter: Psalms 146–150 in the Masoretic Text, the Dead Sea Scrolls, and the Septuagint* (Waco, TX: Baylor University Press, 2017), 278.

34. See Peter C. W. Ho, *The Design of the Psalter: A Macrostructural Analysis* (Eugene, OR: Pickwick, 2019), 253–55; Ballhorn, *Zum Telos*, 369; Tucker and Grant, *Psalms*, 974; McCann, "Shape and Shaping," 361.

35. Psalm 89:40 and 89:51 might be another example if the form in Psalm 89:51 was plural.

36. Charles A. Briggs and Emilie G. Briggs, *A Critical and Exegetical Commentary on the Book of Psalms*, vol. 2, ICC (Edinburgh: T&T Clark, 1907), 483, propose "a different hand."

(145:1, 2, 5, 6; 146:1, 2) and corporate Israel (145:4, 6, 7; 146:8, 9). Ancient kings were responsible for their community, so while an overly individualistic approach to the "I" would be anachronistic, a collectivized interpretation is not required for the "I" at the end of the Psalter.[37]

Everyman or Royal Example?

Scholars including Christoph Buysch have argued that David has become a generic praying figure in Book V.[38] However, while the "I" is an exemplar for prayer, the servant is strongly identified with David in Book V, as in Books I–III, where the only named individual servant is David, and "your servant" is always the "I" of the *ledavid* psalms or the Davidic descendant. In Book IV, the deferential phrase "your servant" is not used, and though Abraham and Moses make cameo appearances as "his servant" in Book IV, they do not reappear in Book V. Two untitled psalms use "your servant" (Pss 116 and 119) in Book V, but the "I" of Psalm 116 adopts David's experiences and self-description from *ledavid* Psalms 18 and 86, and the "I" of Psalm 119 reuses Davidic language, and may himself be royal, as his enemies are kings and princes. These psalms are followed by Psalm 132, which names David four times and reasserts promises to "your servant David" (132:10); and the final *ledavid* psalms with "your servant" (143:2, 12) and "his servant David" (144:10) reflect distinctive language from the *ledavid* psalms of Books I–III, as well as mentioning both David and kingship in Psalm 144:10.

Diminution or Deference?

Gerald Wilson has argued that, after Psalm 89, David is no longer a king, but only a servant. Frank-Lothar Hossfeld and Erich Zenger have suggested that in Psalm 144 the king is demilitarized, "disempowered" and "dependent," and Dennis Tucker argues that in Psalm 144, the royal theme is "diminished" and David is "without power."[39] However, David's status as "your servant David" (Ps 132:10) and "his servant David" (144:10) is affirmed in Book V in connection with Yahweh's promises and past faithfulness, just as the status of "his servant Abraham" and "his servant Moses" were connected in Book IV with God's promises and being chosen (105:2, 26, 42). "His

37. See John G. F. Wilks, "The Suffering Servant and Personhood," *The Evangelical Quarterly* 77 (2005): 209.

38. Christoph Buysch, *Der letzte Davidspsalter: Interpretation, Komposition und Funktion der Psalmengruppe Ps 138–145*, SBB 63 (Stuttgart: Katholisches Bibelwerk, 2009), 16.

39. Wilson, "King, Messiah," 402–5; Hossfeld and Zenger, *Psalms 3*, 588–90; Tucker, *Constructing*, 182–83.

king" (מלכו) refers to David in Psalm 18:51, and "kings" (מלכים) denotes the Davidic kings in Psalm 144:10,[40] where the relational phrase "his servant David" (דוד עבדו, 144:10) also emphasizes God's covenant with David and the faithful dependence of the "I" on God as rescuer.

In Book V, David's self-description as "your servant" (עבדך, 109:28; 143:2, 12) is not a diminution of his status but consistent with deferential language in Books I–III, and of the initiation of the royal covenant in 2 Samuel 7, where God twice addressed David with the relational and honorific term "my servant David" (לעבדי לדוד, 2 Sam 7:5, 8), appointing him as "ruler" (נגיד, 2 Sam 7:8). In reply, David ten times used the deferential and loyal term "your servant" (עבדך, 2 Sam 7:19, 20, 21, 25, 26, 27 [x2], 28, 29 [x2]). The word מלך (king) was not used in speeches by God or David in 2 Samuel 7, but "the king" and "King David" occur four times in the framing narrative (2 Sam 7:1, 2, 3, 18).[41]

Claims that David is no longer a royal or warlike figure at the end of Book V have focused on a comparison of Psalm 18 and Psalm 144.[42] In the well-known *relecture* of Psalm 18 in Psalm 144, God's dramatic rescue in Psalm 18 is reprised in a request for a repeat performance in Psalm 144 (18:10, 15, 17; 144:5–7).[43] By changing indicatives into imperatives, the genre of thanksgiving for past help in Psalm 18 is transformed to a plea for future deliverance in Psalm 144, leading to a different rhetorical strategy. Dennis Tucker comments on the lack of description of David's own martial activity in Psalm 144, compared with Psalm 18,[44] but Amy Cottrill notes "the consistent denial of instrumental agency in the language of violence" in the laments.[45] Hossfeld

---

40. Wilson's claim in "King, Messiah," 402–4 that Psalm 144:10 refers to foreign kings is disputed by Tucker, *Constructing*, 132; see also Hans-Joachim Kraus, *Psalms 60–150: A Commentary*, trans. Hilton C. Oswald (Minneapolis: Augsburg Fortress, 1989), 543. For recent defenses of David's royalty in Book V, see Snearly, *Return*, 187–95, and Hensley, *Covenant Relationships*, 255–63.

41. John H. Eaton, *Kingship and the Psalms*, 2nd ed. (Sheffield: JSOT Press, 1986), 25, says kings were reticent to use the term מלך to refer to themselves. Brevard S. Childs, "Psalm Titles and Midrashic Exegesis," *JSS* 16 (1971): 147, notes the term מלך was avoided in psalms describing David's conflict with Saul.

42. Tucker, *Constructing*, 134; Hossfeld and Zenger, *Psalms 3*, 589–90; Tucker and Grant, *Psalms*, 973–74, 983.

43. For *relecture* in Psalm 144, see Joseph A. Alexander, *The Psalms Translated and Explained* (Grand Rapids: Baker Academic, 1975), 550–52; Ballhorn, *Zum Telos*, 279; Hossfeld and Zenger, *Psalms 3*, 588–90; Tucker, *Constructing*, 130; Nancy L. deClaissé-Walford, Rolf A. Jacobson, and Beth LaNeel Tanner, *The Book of Psalms*, NICOT (Grand Rapids: Eerdmans, 2014), 984; Tucker and Grant, *Psalms*, 973.

44. Tucker, *Constructing*, 131.

45. Cottrill, *Identity*, 88n94.

and Zenger lament that "there is no synergy between God and the king,"[46] but David's celebration of his strength and success as in Psalm 18 (18:33–46) would be out of place in a lament, since the rhetorical strategy of the lament enlists God's help by claiming to be needy and weak (86:1; 109:22).[47]

The genre conventions of lament emphasizing trouble and affliction do not mean that a king has become powerless or has been dethroned.[48] Examples from the ancient Near East support this understanding of a plea for deliverance. Adad-šumu-usur uses a hyperbolic description of powerlessness to emphasize his utter dependence on the king: "My eyes are fixed on the king, my lord ... there is not a single friend of mine ... who would ... speak for me. May the king, my lord, have mercy on his servant."[49] Ashurbanipal, a powerful king, foregrounds his troubles in a prayer for help:

> In the country discord and at home wild quarrelling never leaves my side;
> Sedition and evil talk are constantly plotted against me ...
> In agony of heart and wretchedness I lament day and night ...
> How long will you inflict this on me, O God?[50]

In the lament psalms, as John Eaton explains, "The situation of battle is sometimes clearly indicated (Psalms 3; 27; 35; 54; 55; 56; 57; 59, etc.) but hardly ever does the king envisage himself in action. The action is to come from Yahweh, the omnipotent warrior."[51] Reference to the warlike efforts of the "I" would be out of place in Psalm 144, as it would diminish the effectiveness of this plea to gain God's help.[52] A description of royal might is not to be expected in a plea for deliverance, as found throughout the Psalter (such as Pss 22; 31; 36; 69; 86; 143), including in Psalm 144.

---

46. Hossfeld and Zenger, *Psalms 3*, 589.
47. Cottrill, *Identity*, 117. See also Roger Tomes, *"I Have Written to the King, My Lord": Secular Analogies for the Psalms*, HBM 1 (Sheffield: Sheffield Phoenix, 2005), 64–95.
48. See also Bridge, "Loyalty," 360–78.
49. Quoted in Tomes, *"I Have Written,"* 92.
50. Ashurbanipal inscription in Hans-Joachim Kraus, *Psalms 1–59: A Commentary*, trans. Hilton C. Oswald (Minneapolis: Augsburg, 1988), 56.
51. Eaton, *Kingship and the Psalms*, 140. See also David M. Howard Jr., "The Proto-MT Psalter, the King, and Psalms 1–2: A Response to Klaus Seybold," in *Jewish and Christian Approaches to the Psalms: Conflict and Convergence*, ed. Susan E. Gillingham (Oxford: Oxford University Press, 2013), 186.
52. Edward J. Bridge, "Self-Abasement as an Expression of Thanks in the Hebrew Bible," *Bib* 92 (2011): 272.

CONCLUSION

David's status as "servant" of Yahweh (Ps 18:1) and "his servant David" (Ps 144:10) bookends the use of עבד in the Psalter. In Books I–III, only David or his descendant are referred to using the terms "servant" of Yahweh (עבד יהוה) or "my servant" (עבדי). In Book IV, Abraham and Moses are named as "his servant" (עבדו), but in Book V, the only named individual servant is David, where his status is affirmed as "your servant David" (132:10) and "his servant David" (144:10). The royal promises are reaffirmed to David's descendant in Psalm 132, evoking the servant, anointed, king, and royal descendant of Psalms 18 and 89, and Psalm 144 draws on David's royalty and the Davidic covenant from Psalm 18.

Dependence and loyalty, not diminution, are expressed in the circumlocution "your servant" (עבדך), found in Books I–III only in *ledavid* psalms, and perhaps in the mouth of the Davidic descendant in Psalm 89:40. "Your servant" (עבדך) is not used as a circumlocution for the "I" in Book IV. In Book V, the "I" calls himself "your servant" (עבדך) in the untitled Psalm 116, which draws on Davidic language, and in Psalm 119, where the "I" may be royal, and in *ledavid* Psalms 109 and 143, so "your servant" (עבדך) is not a generic term.

The plural term "servants" (עבדים) is found in every book, including Book V, and can refer to Israel or the faithful, Pharaoh's servants, or "all things," and may include other nations. One singular noun uses the honorific "his servant Israel" (Gillingham, ישראל עבדו, Ps 136:22). The "I" is not collectivized, though the king is concerned for the well-being of his community.

Most occurrences of "servant" in the Psalter occur in the context of suffering from enemies. David's dependence on Yahweh amid suffering is consistently exhibited through the "servant" theme in the Psalter (Pss 18; 27; 31; 69; 86; 89; 109; 132; 143; 144), and in Book V, the final "servant" image is of the individual suffering royal servant in Psalms 143 and 144, still surrounded by his enemies, but awaiting deliverance. These final references foreground the servant's loyalty in suffering and persecution from enemies (Ps 143:12) but maintain the status of "his servant David" and his descendants (Ps 144:10), who continue to trust in Yahweh for help.

A number of scholars have suggested that Psalms 1, 2, and 3 together form a hermeneutical gateway to the Psalter.[53] According to Rolf Rendtorff, Psalm

53. James L. Mays, *The Lord Reigns: A Theological Handbook to the Psalms* (Louisville: Westminster John Knox, 1994), 123; Patrick D. Miller, "The Beginning of the Psalter," in *The Shape and Shaping of the Psalter*, ed. J. Clinton McCann Jr., JSOTSup 159 (Sheffield: Sheffield

1 shows an exemplary righteous king, and Psalm 2 shows a "messianic king" enthroned on Zion, but the most common picture in the *ledavid* psalms is the powerless fugitive of Psalm 3, "who asks for God's succor in his need, and who trusts in God's help."[54] The term "servant" occurs in Torah psalms (Pss 19; 119) like Psalm 1, in royal psalms (Pss 18; 21; 89; 132; 144) like Psalm 2, and in laments (including Pss 22; 31; 69; 109; 143) in the face of enemies, like Psalm 3. Thus, a righteous, royal, suffering servant is seen throughout the Psalter, including in Book V.

In the New Testament, the portrayal of the suffering servant relies not only on quotes or allusions to specific psalms (such as Pss 22 and 69), but on the Psalter's background imagery of the royal but persecuted servant. David's struggles with his enemies create a "symbolic world ... within which the death of Jesus is retold and received," says Richard Hays, in which Jesus is "inhabiting and reshaping ... the role of the Davidic king."[55]

The suffering David has been an exemplar for many, including Jesus and the New Testament writers, in line with the observation of psychologist Carl Rogers that "what is most personal is most general."[56] The story of a woman literature teacher, who was grossly humiliated and assaulted by a student and a former academic colleague, is used by Miroslav Volf to convey the depth of personal suffering and social breakdown in the former Yugoslavia.[57] Listening to Martin Luther King Jr. was transformative for writer Alice Walker: "The life of Dr. King ... because of all he had done and suffered, offered a pattern of strength and sincerity I felt I could trust. ... What Dr. King promised was not a ranch-style house and an acre of manicured lawn for every black man, but jail and finally freedom."[58] Stephen Ahearne-Kroll comments on the Psalter that "the way David grapples with

---

Academic, 1993), 87; Rolf Rendtorff, "The Psalms of David: David in the Psalms," in *The Book of Psalms: Composition and Reception*, ed. Peter W. Flint and Patrick D. Miller Jr. (Leiden: Brill, 2005), 56; Frank-Lothar Hossfeld and Till Magnus Steiner, "Problems and Prospects in Psalter Studies," in *Jewish and Christian Approaches to the Psalms: Conflict and Convergence*, ed. Susan E. Gillingham (Oxford: Oxford University Press, 2013), 240–58; Dan Wu, "The Role of Lament in the Shape of the Psalter," in *Finding Lost Words: The Church's Right to Lament*, ed. G. Geoffrey Harper and Kit Barker, ACT Monograph Series (Eugene, OR: Wipf and Stock, 2017), 140.

54. Rendtorff, "Psalms of David," 63.

55. Hays, *Echoes*, 162, 327.

56. Carl R. Rogers, *On Becoming a Person: A Therapist's View of Psychotherapy* (Boston: Houghton Mifflin, 1961), 26.

57. Miroslav Volf, *Exclusion and Embrace: A Theological Exploration of Identity, Otherness, and Reconciliation* (Nashville: Abingdon, 1996), 111.

58. Alice Walker, *In Search of Our Mothers' Gardens: Womanist Prose* (London: Phoenix, 2005), 124.

God in the midst of his suffering … allows the Gospel writers to tell the story of Jesus in such richly human ways. … The Psalms hold in tension kingship … and shameful suffering, neither one cancelling the other out."[59]

59. Ahearne-Kroll, "Psalms," 272–73.

7

Excavating the "Fossil Record" of a Metaphor: The Use of the Verb *Nasa'* as "To Forgive" in the Psalter

C. Hassell Bullock

Since some object or action generally lies behind a metaphor, this article attempts to uncover that information in relation to the Hebrew verb "to forgive" (nasa'), whose literal meaning is "to bear/carry away/lift up," especially as it is used in the Psalms. My proposal is that the use of this verb in Leviticus 16:22, describing the live goat "bearing" Israel's sins into the wilderness, is the key to understanding this metaphor. Thus the implied suffering of that action attaches itself subliminally to the figurative use of the verb "to forgive" and gives it a trace of vicarious suffering.

Metaphor is a literary device that seeks to illustrate and clarify. Our purpose in this study is to look at the Hebrew verb *nasa'* (נשׂא), whose literal meaning is to "bear/carry away/lift up," and try to discover whether its figurative meaning in the Psalter (and other texts), "to forgive," bears any residual nuance of the literal meaning. We may compare our method to an archaeological excavation that examines ancient artifacts in situ—that is, where time and earth have concealed them (literal meaning)—and further speculates on how they functioned in the real world (figurative meaning).

THE LITERARY PHENOMENA OF METAPHOR AND METALEPSIS

A metaphor is an implied comparison, based on both similarity and dissimilarity, sometimes involving equivalence.[1] Perhaps the most familiar of the myriad of metaphors in the Psalms is "The LORD is my shepherd" (Ps 23:1).[2] David could work from both terms of the comparison—in this case, an equivalence. "Shepherd" as the metaphorical trigger would, both for the writer and the reader, elicit a mental transfer of the shepherd's various functions to the deity, evoking a cadre of subimages: sheep, pastures, streams of water, danger, and so on. All of these features fall into the category of similarity because they are terms of real life that we are familiar with. The dissimilarity comes into play when the psalmist makes the master statement equating "shepherd" and "LORD": "The LORD is my shepherd." Obviously, this is an announcement of enormous proportions, since David's master claim has to be based on more than empirical observation. With this announcement we enter a transcendent understanding that David has acquired about his God. We know, of course, especially from the Psalms and the books of Samuel and Kings, that David's personal encounter with Yahweh was an ongoing relationship throughout his life that, despite his failures, brought him into an intimate encounter with his God (see 1 Sam 13:14). Out of that encounter David's spiritual person grew to proportions that taught him the lessons of his youthful avocation.

As we consider David's master declaration, "The LORD is my shepherd," even though he quotes no sacred texts, we know that the Hebrew Scriptures are the referent of the major terms, "LORD" and "shepherd." In the three other instances in the Psalms where Yahweh (LORD) is referred to as a shepherd, Yahweh is the "shepherd" of Israel, not of an individual (Pss 77:20; 78:52; and 95:7). What then is going on in David's mind? We can detect two dynamics that are operative here: (1) the writer's understanding of the textual terms alluded to, "LORD" and "shepherd," and (2) the reader's understanding of the conversation going on between the writer and text or textual terms. The latter is what Richard B. Hays in his studies on intertextuality calls "the conversion of the imagination."[3] Hays uses 1 Corinthians to demonstrate this phenomenon, noting that Paul reapplies Israel's status as

1. See Leland Ryken, "Metaphor in the Psalms," *ChrLit* 31 (1983): 9–30.

2. Scripture quotations are from the English Standard Version (ESV), unless otherwise noted. English numbering is used with MT references in brackets for the Psalms.

3. Richard B. Hays, *Echoes of Scripture in the Letters of Paul* (New Haven: Yale University Press, 1989); Hays, *The Conversion of the Imagination: Paul as Interpreter of Israel's Scripture* (Grand

the people of God to the gentile believers.[4] Basic to his method is the literary device known as "metalepsis," which Hays defines as

> a rhetorical and poetic device in which one text alludes to an earlier text in a way that evokes resonances of the earlier text *beyond those explicitly cited*. The result is that the interpretation of a metalepsis requires the reader to recover unstated or suppressed correspondences between the two texts."[5]

As we have already observed, even though David in Psalm 23 does not quote an Old Testament text per se, he deals with familiar terms of the sacred text as well as the culture that he and his readers were familiar with. In terms of the scant details of this text, Hays's comment may be applicable that "allusions are often most powerful when least explicit."[6] As we have observed above, David, a shepherd himself, was quite capable of describing the shepherd's life, and he introduced one of the boldest theological metaphors in all of Scripture: "The Lord is my shepherd." By that one clause he made an astounding assertion, proclaiming the Lord's presence, not *like* a shepherd (a simile), but equating "Lord" and "shepherd." That David, the shepherd of Israel, should himself have a shepherd, and that his shepherd was equivalent to his God, was a dazzling truth. What was more astounding still was that the Lord would stoop so low as to assume one of Israel's most menial roles. And while David was certainly aware of the dissimilarity he had set up, Christian interpreters, quite appropriately, think in dimensions of the incarnation of God in Jesus of Nazareth, augmenting the wonder and incredulity of the truth that the Lord would take upon himself human flesh: "And the Word became flesh and dwelt among us" (John 1:14), and Jesus's claim, "I am the good shepherd" (John 10:11). That further means for David, and for us, that our Shepherd, figuratively speaking, can and does lead us beside "still waters," takes away our fear in the dangerous valleys of our world, sets a banquet table for us to celebrate victory over our enemies, and, with the divine Shepherd's powerful attributes, "goodness and mercy," guides us safely into the Lord's house that he has prepared for us (see John 14:1–3).

Rapids: Eerdmans, 2005) [a collection of his essays over several years]; Hays, *Echoes of Scripture in the Gospels* (Waco, TX: Baylor University Press, 2016), 11–12.

4. Hays, "The Conversion of the Imagination: Scripture and Eschatology in 1 Corinthians," in Hays, *The Conversion of the Imagination: Paul as Interpreter of Israel's Scripture*, 1–24.

5. Hays, *Echoes of Scripture in the Letters of Paul*, 2 (italics original).

6. Hays, *Echoes of Scripture in the Letters of Paul*, 17.

In addition to evoking the words and images of the larger text, in this case, the context, *metalepsis* also activates the reader's imagination that often leads to a reapplication of the cited text, not unlike Paul's reapplication mentioned above.[7] A cautionary note, however, must be sounded that the sacred text cannot be made to say anything the readers wish to hear, but its meaning is conditioned by the historical/lexical relationship to the texts quoted and alluded to. So, exercising our imagination, we begin to think about those circumstances of our personal world that required solicitous care, including both physical and emotional wounds we have suffered, and the "shepherds," too numerous to name, who came to our aid. Psalms is a seedbed of this literary phenomenon, which we will seek to illustrate in this essay,[8] and this powerful collection of religious songs already in a formal way illustrates this method. That is, the psalmists themselves lay out a pattern of reapplication of other texts to new circumstances. For example, Psalm 14 is reissued as Psalm 53 and expands the truth of 14:5, that "God is present in the company of the righteous" (NIV), by introducing an instance when God demonstrated his presence by scattering the bones of those who attacked Israel (53:5).[9] Psalm 53 turns the theory of 14:5 into reality. A similar illustration is the duplication of Psalm 40:13–17 as Psalm 70, with minor variations, where Psalm 70, occurring at the end of Book II, makes a transition between Books II and III by reapplying David's lament, "I am poor and needy" (40:17) to the new and uncertain era of his successor Solomon, and sadly, beyond that to the destruction of the temple[10] (see 74:4–8; 79:1–4). This hermeneutical exercise that the synagogue and church have followed through the centuries has been laid out by the psalmists themselves.

THE LITERAL USE OF THE VERB *IN SITU*: LEVITICUS 16:22, *NASA'*, "TO BEAR/CARRY AWAY"

Words have different levels of meaning, and the literal and figurative connotations can stand alongside each other. Even if the orthographic form changes, the astute reader will perceive the different nuances, some of

7. See my discussion of how Psalm 23 evokes the larger context of Scripture: the language of the exodus draws upon Moses's Song of the Sea (Exod 15:13); the "quiet " (lit., "waters of rest") may allude to the "place of rest" to which the ark of the covenant guided Israel (Num 10:33); "I lack nothing" recounts Israel's lack of nothing during the wilderness experience (Deut 2:7), etc.; C. Hassell Bullock, *Psalms 1–72* (Grand Rapids: Baker Academic, 2015), 169–71.

8. See also my essay, C. Hassell Bullock, "The Psalter and Intertextuality: Voices Once Heard and Still Speaking," in *Presb* 46 (Spring 2020): 24–35.

9. Bullock, *Psalms 1–72*, 404.

10. Bullock, *Psalms 1–72*, 530–31.

which are subliminal. The verb *nasa'* is our case in point, and, as we have already recognized, it has a literal meaning, "to bear/carry away," as well as a figurative meaning, "to forgive." So let us look at the various levels of meaning that the verb attaches to itself.

The proverbial saying is still true: "A word is known by the company it keeps." Early in our discussion we should observe that the verb *nasa'* is surrounded by a cloud of witnesses that uses this verb to speak about some aspect of sin, forgiveness, and atonement. The verb is overwhelmingly transitive and generally requires a direct object. I suggest, given the literal meaning of the verb and its association with the cult-related denotations (figurative), that its primal occurrence, its in situ form, to use our own metaphor, is Leviticus 16:22. There the verb means quite literally "to bear/carry away/lift up," and the idiom in its cultic setting[11] is related to forgiveness, thus uniting the two aspects of the verb. The real-life situation is the Day of Atonement when the high priest sent one of the two goats into the wilderness, bearing Israel's sins: "The goat shall bear [וְנָשָׂא] all their iniquities on itself to a remote area, and he shall let the goat go free in the wilderness." The object of the verb—all the iniquities of the people of Israel, and all their transgressions, all their sins—associates the verb with the concept of sin and forgiveness, as the preceding verse attests: "And Aaron shall lay both his hands on the head of the live goat, and confess over it all the iniquities of the people of Israel, and all their transgressions, all their sins. And he shall put them on the head of the goat and send it away into the wilderness by the hand of a man who is in readiness" (Lev 16:21).

Aaron laying his hands on the head of the goat is a symbolic gesture of transferring the people's sins to the scapegoat ("live goat"), making it a substitute for the worshipers.[12] The goat then "bears" (נשא) their transgressions into the wilderness (Lev 16:22).

---

11. I am using the word "cult" to refer to the sacrificial system and temple worship.

12. Benjamin J. Noonan, "*Solo Sacrificio or Sola Fide*? On the Efficacy of the Levitical Sacrifices," a paper read at the Evangelical Theological Society annual meeting, November 17, 2017, deals with three views of the high priest's laying his hands on the goat on the Day of Atonement: transference, possession, and identification. He opts for the third view, identification, as most plausible. While this is not the concern of this study, it is of some import as we try to understand the pertinent witnesses that surround the verb *nasa'* as it is used in Leviticus 16:22. All three views, in fact, reveal the personal dynamic of this act on the Day of Atonement as worshipers interact with Yahweh in hope of forgiveness.

NASA' IN ISAIAH 53 AS AN ECHO OF LEVITICUS 16:22

Isaiah, whose language in chapters 40–66 is often reflective of psalmic language, and vice versa, shares both the language and imagery of Leviticus 16:22 to describe the suffering servant's atoning work. When we look at the larger picture of the servant's atoning work in Isaiah 53, there are striking similarities to the language and imagery of the scapegoat sent into the wilderness. First, the servant "bore the sin of many" (וְהוּא חֵטְא־רַבִּים נָשָׂא וְלַפֹּשְׁעִים יַפְגִּיעַ, Isa 53:12). The language "to bear" (נָשָׂא) and "to lay on (hands)" (Lev 16:21, סָמַךְ, a synonym of יַפְגִּיעַ, Isa 53:12), coupled with the transfer of the image of Aaron the priest in Leviticus 16:21 to Yahweh as the priest, and the live goat of Leviticus 16 to the servant in Isaiah 53, comes close to the bold metaphor of "the LORD is my shepherd" in Psalm 23.

Second, the suffering of the servant, only implied in Leviticus 16 in the live goats bearing the enormous sins of Israel, is distinctive of Isaiah 53. If the servant is primarily Israel, as some scholars believe, then Israel has become a kingdom of priests, as Yahweh intended (Exod 19:6), and the suffering servant has become a suffering priest:

> "He was despised and rejected by men, a man of sorrows, and acquainted with grief" (53:3)
>
> "Surely he has *borne* our griefs and carried our sorrows" (53:4)
>
> "But he was pierced for our transgressions; he was crushed for our iniquities" (53:5)
>
> "He was oppressed, and he was afflicted, yet he opened not his mouth; like a lamb that is led to the slaughter, and like a sheep that before its shearers is silent" (53:7)
>
> "He *bore* the sin of many, and makes intercession for the transgressors" (53:12).

The final verse of Isaiah 53 is a summary of the servant's ministry, with the second occurrence of *nasa'*, "to bear/carry away/lift up" (53:4, 12), intoned metaleptically against the backdrop of Leviticus 16. Our assumption is that the implied suffering of bearing the weight of Israel's sins becomes an inherent nuance of this verb.

THE IDIOMATIC USE OF THE VERB NASA', "TO BEAR ONE'S OWN GUILT/PUNISHMENT"

To continue surveying the company of witnesses that illustrates the cultic setting of this verb, we will follow the entries in Ludwig Koehler and

Walter Baumgartner's *The Hebrew and Aramaic Lexicon of the Old Testament*. The first entry that calls for our consideration is the list of several instances of the verb with the meaning "to bear" one's own guilt/punishment.[13] In this case the sense of the verb is punitive, implying the absence of forgiveness, while intimating the need of it.

The Idiomatic Use of the Verb *Nasa'*, "To Bear" Another's Guilt

This is also true of another cadre of lexical occurrences listed by Koehler and Baumgartner where the verb *nasa'* has the sense of "to bear" another's guilt.[14] The weight of this idiom, like bearing one's own guilt, involves emotional and spiritual trauma. As we have observed above, Isaiah's suffering servant, much like the scapegoat of Leviticus 16, engages in a vicarious bearing of Israel's sins (Isa 53:4, 12). This is also true of Ezekiel's peculiar performance of lying on his side (Ezek 4:4–5). Ezekiel, himself a priest, like Isaiah's suffering servant, bore Israel's sins vicariously. And in this case, as that of Isaiah's servant, we can assume that the ancient readers would have thought of the live goat bearing the transgressions of a whole nation, with the implied suffering of the enormity of their transgressions. Clearly the idea is that of "bearing a burden," a sense of the verb that is verified by its use in Job 34:31; Psalm 55:12 [13]; and Proverbs 18:14; 30:21. *The Theological Dictionary of the Old Testament* (*TDOT*) calls attention to this nuance particularly when the verb is associated with the objects of "scorn, abuse,"[15] "disgrace,"[16] and other such words of disparagement.

The Figurative Use of the Verb *Nasa'*, "To Atone"

A nuance that moves closer to the figurative meaning of the verb *nasa'* is found in the group of biblical texts that use the verb in the sense of "to atone."[17] The lexical occurrences of the verb shed the story of the scapegoat,

---

13. Bearing one's own guilt: Exodus 28:43; Leviticus 5:1; 7:18; 17:16; 19:8; 22:9; Numbers 9:13; or bearing one's own sin: Leviticus 20:20 (Ludwig Koehler and Walter Baumgartner, *The Hebrew and Aramaic Lexicon of the Old Testament* [Leiden: Brill, 2001], 2:772). The article by D. N. Freedman et al. in *TDOT*, ed. G. J. Botterweck, H. Ringgren, and H.-J. Fabry, trans. D. W. Stott (Grand Rapids: Eerdmans, 1999), X:24–40, provides an excellent and fuller discussion of the nuances of this verb with their theological implications.

14. Bearing another's guilt: Isaiah 53:12; Ezekiel 4:4–6; 18:19–20 (Koehler and Baumgartner, *The Hebrew and Aramaic Lexicon of the Old Testament*, 2:772).

15. Psalm 69:8 [7]; Jeremiah 15:15; 31:19; Ezekiel 36:15; Micah 6:16 (*TDOT*, X:30).

16. Ezekiel 16:52, 54; 32:24–25, 30; 34:29; 36:6–37; 44:13 (*TDOT*, X:30).

17. "To atone": Exodus 28:38; Numbers 14:34; 18:1; Ezekiel 44:13; 23:35 (Koehler and Baumgartner, *The Hebrew and Aramaic Lexicon of the Old Testament*, 1:726).

which stands behind the metaphor, and move to the core of the Leviticus 16 narrative, which is, of course, atonement for sin. That is what the story is about, and the metaphor has faded into the core message of the story, becoming one and the same. We will now examine the use of the verb in the formula of grace (Exod 34:6–7) as a driving force in its figurative use.

The Figurative Use of the Verb *Nasa'*, "To Forgive," in the Formula of Grace

The book of Psalms is a unique collection of Israel's prayers and meditations prayed and sung through the centuries of national and personal tragedies and triumphs. Israel's history is inscribed in their prayers, and their heart and soul are deposited in the Psalms like no other book. J. Gordon McConville writes: "Of all the Old Testament's testimony to and resources for spiritual transformation and growth, primacy belongs to the book of Psalms. The Psalms are unique in the Old Testament because they gather up the full range of Israel's past, present, and future with God in the context of worship."[18]

It is difficult to retrace the plot line of Israel's great theological ideas as they have wrapped themselves in metaphoric language, but we have the product, even though we may not be able to recreate the process. When, however, the product is found in Israel's creedal forms,[19] with their central and enduring place in religious life, we can expect them to have had widespread influence in the biblical literature. Moreover, we can expect them to have been stored in the minds of the psalmists and their readers/hearers as a whole text rather than a fragmentary one. One of the most important of these creedal formulas is the formula of grace (Exod 34:6–7) given to Moses as a postlude to the devastating tragedy of the golden calf (Exod 32). The golden calf event, historically speaking, lays the foundation for Israel's tragic involvement in idolatry; yet in that context the Lord revealed himself to Moses as a compassionate and forgiving God. And interestingly, Yahweh's identity as given in the formula of grace is probably the most

18. J. Gordon McConville, *Being Human in God's World* (Grand Rapids: Baker Academic, 2016), 192.

19. The Hebrew faith was not *creedal* in the sense that Christianity is *creedal*. The latter, in contradistinction, means that the faith is articulated and confessed in certain creedal forms, but Israel confessed their faith nevertheless in such forms as the Ten Commandments (Exod 20/Deut 5), the Shema (Deut 6:4–9), the formula of grace (Exod 34:6–7), and Deuteronomy 26:5–10. While none of these forms are intended to be a comprehensive outline of the Hebrew faith, they catch certain moments and circumstances of Israel's faith and ritual (for example, Deut 26:5–10 is a "historical" review recited at the presentation of firstfruits).

widely dispersed character description of God in the Hebrew Bible generally and in the Psalms particularly.[20] The formula has two parts:

> Part 1 (Exod 34:6): "The Lord, the Lord, a God merciful and gracious, slow to anger, and abounding in steadfast love and faithfulness,"
>
> Part 2 (Exod 34:7): "keeping steadfast love for thousands, *forgiving* iniquity and transgression and sin [נֹשֵׂא עָוֺן וָפֶשַׁע וְחַטָּאָה], but who will by no means clear the guilty, visiting the iniquity of the fathers on the children and the children's children, to the third and the fourth generation."

Judging from the prominence of this covenant text, it is not surprising that the Psalter contains many allusions to the formula and quotes the first half (Exod 34:6) three times, each occurrence positioned in a psalm attributed to David and located at a strategic place in each of the final three books of the Psalter: Book III: 86:15; Book IV: 103:8; Book V: 145:8.[21] While the first half of the formula (Exod 34:6) predominates, any allusion to the formula or quotation of one part but not the whole presupposes the other part. That is, an allusion to the verb *nasa'*, "to forgive," in Part 2 (Exod 34:7) is a textual summons to Yahweh's compassionate, gracious, and loving character of Part 1 (Exod 34:6). This literary phenomenon, metalepsis, discussed above, is a shorthand method of calling memory into service. To illustrate, there are two phrases from Part 1 of the formula that occur in distinctive form and constitute a shorthand reference or mental "citation" of the larger formula: "gracious and compassionate," and "abounding in steadfast love." In the case of the three quotations of Part 1 of the formula (mentioned above), these quotations also function in a metaleptical way to call forth Part 2 of the formula that speaks of forgiveness and uses our verb *nasa'*. In fact, we have an illustration of this phenomenon in Psalm 103, where an extensive meditation on forgiveness (Ps 103:9–14) follows directly upon the quotation

20. In addition to the three quotations of the formula of grace mentioned above, I have looked for allusions in the Psalter which include the distinctive pair of terms "gracious" (רחום) and "compassionate" (חַנּוּן) in the space of one or two contiguous verses, and/or the unique phrase "abounding in steadfast love and faithfulness" (וְרַב־חֶסֶד וֶאֱמֶת). They are: Book I: 25:10; 26:3; 40:12; Book II: 57:3[4]; 61:7[8]; 69:13[14], 16[17]; Book III: 85:10[11]; 86:5; 88:11[12]; 89:1[2], 2[3], 14[15], 24[25], 33[34], 49[50]; Book IV: 92:2[3]; 98:3; 100:5; 106:45; Book V: 108:4[5]; 111:4; 112:4; 115:1; 116:5; 117:2.

21. See my essay, "Covenant Renewal and the Formula of Grace in the Psalter," *BibSac* 170 (2019): 18–34.

of Exodus 34:6 (Ps 103:8). Thus the use of the verb as "to forgive" in a key creedal formula (Part 2) means that the gracious and compassionate Lord, who is slow to anger and abounds in steadfast love and faithfulness, is the forgiving God. That is, Part 1 of the formula of grace (Exod 34:6) gives us a description of Yahweh's character out of which flows Yahweh's forgiveness affirmed in Part 2 (Exod 34:7). In Numbers 14:18b–19 metalepsis works in the reverse direction: "forgiving [נֹשֵׂא] iniquity and transgression, but he will by no means clear the guilty, visiting the iniquity of the fathers on the children, to the third and the fourth generation" (Part 2), immediately summons Part 1 to mind. The setting is that of the Hebrew spies' terrifying report of the formidable challenges the anticipated conquest of Canaan posed for the Israelites. When the Lord thought to disown them, Moses appealed to the Lord on the basis of the formula of grace, appealing to the Lord's "steadfast love," which was foundational to Yahweh's forgiveness: "Please pardon the iniquity of this people, according to the *greatness of your steadfast love* [alluding to Part 1], just as you have forgiven this people [alluding to Part 2], from Egypt until now" (Num 14:19). Moses's prayer reveals the formula operating as a whole piece of cloth, even though Part 1 is abbreviated.

The Figurative Use of the Verb *Nasa'*, "To Forgive," in the Psalter

There is a cadre of texts in the Hebrew Bible generally, and in the Psalter particularly, that use our verb in the full metaphorical or figurative sense "to forgive."[22] Psalm 99:8 is a leading text because it harks back to the time of Moses and Aaron and the time of Samuel, citing these men as examples of "priests ... who called upon his [Yahweh's] name" (Ps 99:6). And the signature that the Lord left on the palette of their lives was that of "a forgiving God": "O Lord our God, you answered them; you were a *forgiving God to them* [אֵל נֹשֵׂא הָיִיתָ לָהֶם], but an avenger of their wrongdoings" (Ps 99:8). Here the divine name, "forgiving God," like other examples in the Old Testament,[23] takes the form of a participle (sometimes a finite verb) to express God's nature, suggesting Yahweh's active role in Israel's life and his magnanimous activity of forgiveness. This text connects to the formula of grace in two

22. Leviticus 10:17; Numbers 14:18; Joshua 24:19; 1 Samuel 15:25; 25:28; Isaiah 2:9; 33:24; Hosea 1:6; 14:2; Micah 7:18; Psalms 25:18; 32:1, 5; 85:3; 99:8; Job 7:21 (Koehler and Baumgartner, *The Hebrew and Aramaic Lexicon of the Old Testament*, 2:772).

23. For example: Genesis 16:13, "a seeing God" (אֵל רֳאִי); Isaiah 43:3, "your Savior" (מוֹשִׁיעֶךָ); Exodus 15:26, "the Lord your healer" (יְהוָה רֹפְאֶךָ), and many others.

ways: the use of our verb "to forgive" (נָשָׂא) and the verb "to avenge" (נָקַם), both occurring in Part 2 of the formula. The metaleptical method of interpretation means that these allusions summon to mind the character of Yahweh as the merciful, gracious, and loving God of Part 1.

Further, Psalm 99 is contained in Book IV of the Psalter (Pss 90–106), which proclaims that "Yahweh reigns" (Pss 93:1; 96:10; 97:1; 99:1; cf. 95:3; 98:6), and as the reigning God, he is also the forgiving God; both attributes are juxtaposed in this psalm (99:1, 8). This portrait of Yahweh is one of the most potent and consoling descriptions of Yahweh in the entire Psalter. Of what benefit is a deity who reigns but does not forgive, especially when his people are guilty of idolatry, the sin of all sins—a defiant challenge to Yahweh's existence and integrity! And what benefit is a deity who forgives but does not reign, and who is thus incapable of imputing the grace of forgiveness to his people?

Having established Yahweh as the reigning and forgiving God, Book IV closes with a poetic treatise on Israel's past, first recalling the historic event of the golden calf that began Israel's idolatrous career (106:19–23), then the shameful reputation they incurred with their espousal of the cult of Baal of Peor upon their entrance into Canaan (106:28–31), and finally the appalling Baal cult of Canaan where the Israelites "mixed with the nations and learned to do as they did," which involved sacrificing their children to the Canaanite idols (106:34–39). Book IV closes on the theme of idolatry with its abhorrent practices and blatant defiance of the first commandment, "You shall have no other gods before me" (Exod 20:3), but not before the portrait of the reigning and forgiving Yahweh has been hung in the anteroom of Israel's primal transgression. Then, as part of a powerful transition to Book V, leading toward the nation's rejection of idolatry as their national sin, the psalmist prays for an end to the exile (106:44–47), which, in both a historical and spiritual sense, as we have already mentioned, paralleled the golden calf debacle. That is, the sin of idolatry that proved to be Israel's detriment in Moses's day, also brought about the Babylonian exile. Israel had, according to Ezekiel, gone into exile because of their idolatry (Ezek 36:16–18; implied in 14:11 and 39:23). In view of the theological stage the editor(s) of Book IV laid out, Book V (Pss 107–150) follows with what we might call a virtual confession and repudiation of Israel's idolatry, calling forth two textual witnesses that Israel had forsaken their idolatrous ways (Pss 115:4–8; 135:15–18). So sincere and profound was the decision, evidently made in the exile, that they never returned to their idols.

Four other occurrences of *nasa'* as "to forgive" are found in the Psalter: 25:18; 32:1, 5; and 85:3. In Psalm 25 the psalmist fortifies his prayer for forgiveness by first alluding to Yahweh's "steadfast love and faithfulness" (חֶסֶד וֶאֱמֶת), connecting it to the Sinai covenant and the formula of grace: "All the paths of the LORD are steadfast love and faithfulness, for those who keep his covenant and his testimonies" (Ps 25:10; see Exod 34:6). And then the psalmist prays, using our verb: "Consider my affliction and my trouble, and *forgive* all my sins" (שָׂא לְכָל־חַטֹּאותָי, imperative; Ps 25:18). David's sin is a burden to him: "I am lonely and afflicted. The troubles of my heart are enlarged; bring me out of my distresses" (Ps 25:16–17). While Yahweh's role in bearing that burden is not explicit, we should nevertheless hear the overtones of the verb *nasa'*, sensing the relief of the burden that Yahweh's forgiveness brings to David.

The verb *nasa'* appears twice in Psalm 32 (vv. 1, 5). The first is a passive particle singling out that person "whose transgression is forgiven" (נְשׂוּי). Subsequently the psalmist reports the heavy burden his sin had become: "For day and night your [Yahweh's] hand was heavy upon me; my strength was dried up as by the heat of summer" (32:4). Then the psalmist confessed: "I acknowledged my sin to you, and I did not cover my iniquity; I said, 'I will confess [אוֹדֶה, the *hiphil* of the verb ידה, "to confess"] my *transgressions* to the LORD,' and *you forgave* (נָשָׂאתָ) the *iniquity* of my *sin*" (32:5). The Day of Atonement ritual is likely in view here as the psalmist, like the high priest on Israel's behalf, confessed the nation's sins[24] with the result that the Lord forgave (the italicized words are also contained in Leviticus 16). Moreover, the verb "counts" (אַשְׁרֵי אָדָם לֹא יַחְשֹׁב יְהוָה לוֹ עָוֹן, 32:2), which the writer of Genesis uses to describe Abraham's faith (Gen 15:6), and the use of the noun "righteous ones" at the end of the psalm (שִׂמְחוּ בַיהוָה וְגִילוּ צַדִּיקִים, 32:11), evidently suggested to Paul an Abrahamic imputed faith, and Paul quotes Psalm 32:1–2 in Romans 4:7–8 ("Abraham believed God, and it was counted to him as righteousness," Rom 4:3). Although there is no vicarious transfer of sins here as in the Levitical story, contextually our verb under consideration certainly carries that nuance of a weight lifted by forgiveness. Identification, to cite Noonan again,[25] or even substitution, is the view here.

---

24. The verb "to confess" is called a denominative verb, meaning that it derives from a noun, and in this instance the noun is "hand" (יָד), which seems to allude to the high priest laying his hands on the scapegoat.

25. Noonan, "*Solo Sacrificio or Sola Fide?*"

Psalm 85:2 shares the vocabulary of Psalm 32, using the verbs "to forgive" (*nasa'*) and "to cover" (*kassah*, in the *piel* stem), with Yahweh as the subject: "LORD, you were favorable to your land; you restored the fortunes of Jacob. You *forgave* the iniquity of your people; you *covered* all their sin" (85:1–2). In Psalm 32:1 the psalmist pronounces blessing on "the one whose transgression is forgiven, whose sin is covered," expressed in the passive voice, leaving us to assume the subject of the participles is Yahweh. That is, Yahweh is the one who forgave their transgression and covered their sin—both powerful metaphors—and indeed, Psalm 85:2, using the same two verbs, identifies Yahweh as the one who "forgave the iniquity of your [Yahweh's] people; you covered all their [Israel's] sin." In these examples the metaphor "to forgive" is figurative but implies the nuance of "to bear/carry away."[26]

CONCLUSION

The subtleties of metaphor are both intriguing and challenging, and this essay has attempted to deal with both perspectives: the literal and idiomatic/figurative uses of *nasa'*. First, we have identified Leviticus 16:22 as the in situ story of our metaphor, and insisted that suffering inheres in the verb *nasa'* when it reflects the story of the scapegoat sent into the wilderness on the Day of Atonement. That is, if the literal sense of the verb is "to bear/carry away/lift up," suffering is implied. On the other hand, if the figurative sense is to "forgive," the nuance of "to bear" a heavy load still inheres in the use of the verb, and sometimes, as in Isaiah 53:12, vicarious suffering is explicit, pointing again to the scapegoat bearing/carrying away Israel's sins. Second, this essay has attempted to show that the metaphorical (figurative) sense of the verb may very likely owe its fixation in biblical language to the power of the creedal formula of grace (Exod 34:6–7). Further, by metalepsis, Part 1 of the formula, Yahweh's character description summons to mind Part 2, Yahweh's nature of forgiveness, and vice versa. The creedal statement functions as a whole piece, and either half summons the other half to mind. We illustrated this from Psalm 103 and the occurrence of the formula in Numbers 14:18–19. We have also insisted that the verb *nasa'* in Leviticus 16:22 carries the implication of suffering; and drawing upon the similar language of the suffering servant in Isaiah 53, the point is made that the Day of Atonement ritual of the scapegoat that "bears/takes away/lifts up" Israel's

26. My thanks to my former student and friend, Bryan Eklund, whose keen eye and kind hand of direction have helped to shape this article, even though he is not responsible for any inaccuracies that might inhere to its content.

sins interweaves the suffering servant and the Day of Atonement ritual together in an adaptive way.

Our conclusion is that the implied suffering of the live goat of Leviticus 16 is inherent in the figurative use of the verb in the psalmic contexts. The spiritual lesson to be drawn from this data is that in the act of forgiveness someone has to "bear" the burden of guilt, which implies suffering. In Leviticus it is the live goat in a symbolic sense; in other texts it is a human person who bears his/her own guilt or another's; in Isaiah 53 and the psalmic texts that we cited, it is Yahweh in a theological sense who, in forgiving, "bears" the guilt of the sinner. That ultimate act of forgiveness may very well be why David prayed: "Against you, you only, have I sinned and done what is evil in your sight" (Ps 51:4); Yahweh is the ultimate transactor. Forgiveness is like love, it is such an authentic attribute and act of God's essential being that when we forgive our brother or sister as a reflex of the forgiving God, we "bear" the burden of guilt vicariously for the person forgiven; and when we forgive someone by common grace, it, like love, is not so much a reflex of God's love as it is a mere reflection of the forgiving God who "bears" the burden of the guilt of the forgiven. In this regard, Psalm 130:4 and 7 has a grammatical phenomenon that comes close to an equivalence of 1 John 4:8 ("God is love"). The psalmist uses the nouns "forgiveness" and "steadfast love" with the definite article ("the"), an irregular practice, which carries the meaning that Yahweh is the essence of forgiveness and the essence of steadfast love (his true nature): "with you [Yahweh] there is *the* forgiveness," and "with the Lord there is *the* steadfast love." God is the essential essence of forgiveness as he is of love. George MacDonald spoke a memorable word to this effect: "Never a cry of love went forth from human heart but it found some heavenly chord to fold it in."[27]

27. George MacDonald, *Paul Faber, Surgeon*, ch. 7 (1900; repr., Project Gutenberg, 2004), https://www.gutenberg.org/ebooks/12387.

8

The Art of Lament in Lamentations

May Young

This chapter on the book of Lamentations is included to provide additional insight on how the broader genre of lament outside the Psalter also reflects a movement from despair to greater hope. It explores the extent to which five key poetic features in the book of Lamentations work together to bring cohesion or dissonance to the message in this book. The overall findings of this study show that these poetic devices work both in consonance and dissonance to highlight particular structures and themes found in the book. The book begins with clear correspondences among these literary devices, which then progressively unravel, requiring a completely different structure in chapter 5, the book's conclusion. Astonishingly, this transition also highlights how the message in Lamentations mirrors a process of lament that moves progressively from an attitude of despair to one of greater hope.[1]

INTRODUCTION

Art historians agree that artistic vision entails both the intricacies of detailed techniques on smaller fragments, as well as how these sections come together to form a large-scale composition or masterpiece. While this can be said of most great works of art, this is particularly highlighted in the work of Rogier van der Weyden, a Flemish artist in the fifteenth century. His work, *The Descent from the Cross*, or *The Escorial Deposition*, (c. 1435) can

1. This essay summarizes and provides the theological conclusions of my dissertation: May Young, "Making Sense Out of Suffering: Prominent Poetic Features as Interpretive Matrix in the Book of Lamentations" (PhD diss., Trinity Evangelical Divinity School, 2015).

be found in the Museo del Prado, Madrid. In this piece, the composition, spacing, colors, lighting, facial expressions, and even bodily contortions all contribute to the greater message that the artist is trying to convey. "He compresses the figures and actions onto a shallow slate, to concentrate the observer's attention. … A series of lateral, undulating movements gives the group a unity, a formal cohesion."[2] Though not immediately obvious, "the false perspectives engender feelings of unease. The viewer cannot fail to be disturbed by them. Christ's head is on a horizontal axis, which seems unnatural, and his nose is twisted out of perspective to make a more assertive horizontal. Since the whole picture is strongly lit from the right, Rogier can illumine Christ's face from below so that the parts normally in shadow are brightly illuminated."[3] Van der Weyden uses several artistic devices to highlight the grace, beauty, and agony of Christ's sacrifice, as well as the attempt to understand the different emotional responses of those depicted in this work. While great artistic mastery can be recognized by focusing on the individual artistic elements, a greater understanding of the masterpiece is grasped when one recognizes how these artistic devices work together to bring out the greater message depicted by the work as a whole.

Similarly, the literary art of Hebrew poetry uses various techniques to highlight the individual components of a composition that simultaneously contribute to the rest of the work in order to exhibit greater depth and beauty to the whole. The book of Lamentations is an example of such Hebrew poetry. The theological message in this book is enhanced by poetic devices that mirror the process of lament in this carefully constructed literary masterpiece. The book begins with clear correspondences among these literary devices, which then progressively unravel, requiring a completely different structure in chapter 5, the book's conclusion. We will walk through these specific transitions to highlight how the message in Lamentations mirrors a process of lament that moves progressively from an attitude of despair to one of greater hopefulness.

Lamentations is known for its usage of diverse literary devices. In the last fifty years, scholarship on Lamentations has given greater attention to the presence of prominent poetic literary features such as acrostic structure,

2. Horst De La Croix, Richard G. Tansey, and Diane Kirkpatrick, *Gardner's Art through the Ages: Renaissance and Modern Art*, 9th ed. (Orlando, FL: Harcourt Brace Jovanovich, 1991), 707.

3. Comments from the website of the Museo del Prado on this work: https://www.museodelprado.es/en/the-collection/art-work/the-descent-from-the-cross/856d822a-dd22-4425-bebd-920a1d416aa7. One may also Google "Museo del Prado Weyden, Rogier Van Der The Descent From the Cross" to access the painting and comments.

parallelism, enjambed lines,[4] shift in voice, and repetition of key images and words. The exploration of literary aspects in this book has enhanced our understanding of this poetic text. My work builds on these previous studies and provides additional examination on how these poetic devices work together to contribute to the theology of lament in Lamentations. More specifically, it highlights how the correspondence of these devices in the first four chapters deliberately contrast with the final chapter to enhance the theological message of the book.

A SUMMARY OF THE MATRIX APPROACH

A survey on the research of Lamentations indicates that the following five poetic devices have been consistently seen as significant literary techniques employed in the book: the acrostic structure, parallelism, enjambment, change in voice, and repetition of lexemes and images. My study uses a matrix approach to analyze the correspondence of the literary devices employed in this book. It begins with the basic identification of the acrostic structure because this offers a starting point in which to make observations on how the other poetic techniques function in correspondence to this structural device. Next, the occurrence of enjambed lines and parallel lines are noted with respect to their placement in the acrostic structure. These three poetic devices—acrostic structure, enjambment, and parallelism—can be observed from a stanzaic and clausal level, but change in voice and the repetition of key words, images, and motifs require a more detailed analysis. Change in voice is observed through change in verb subject (overt or implied), change in addressee, independent pronouns, prefixed pronouns, or suffixed pronouns. This draws attention to places in the text where there are grammatical changes that signal a shift in speaker, as well as a change in addressee. Lastly, the repetition of key words, images, and motifs are identified. The clustering of key words, as well as an examination of repetitive imagery, are also highlighted to identify important themes.

Acrostic Structure

The acrostic structure, though integral to the structure of the book, is not uniform across all five poems. Only chapters 1–4 have an alphabetic acrostic

4. Watson defines enjambment/enjambed lines as "when a sentence or clause does not end when the colon ends but runs over into the next colon. Hence the alternative name 'run-over line.' " Wilfred G. E. Watson, *Classical Hebrew Poetry: A Guide to Its Techniques*, LHBOTS 26 (Sheffield: Sheffield Academic Press, 2009), 333. In English, it is referred to as a "run-on line."

structure. Secondly, even though chapters 1, 2, and 3 have sixty-six lines and twenty-two stanzas (three lines per stanza), only the first two chapters begin each stanza with a consecutive alphabetic letter. Chapter 3 has an intensified acrostic with a triple repetition of the same letter for each line in the stanza. Chapter 4 has been reduced to forty-four lines, but like chapters 1–2 it begins each stanza with a consecutive alphabetic letter. In contrast, chapter 5 does not have the alphabetic sequence at the beginning of each line. Additionally, the number of lines per stanza or verse have decreased successively to only one line in the last chapter.

The following table gives a visual representation of this structure:

Figure 8.1

CHAPTER 1	CHAPTER 2	CHAPTER 3	CHAPTER 4	CHAPTER 5
22 stanzas (verses) Three-line stanzas. One letter per stanza 66 lines total a______ ______ ______	22 stanzas (verses) Three-line stanzas. One letter per stanza 66 lines total a______ ______ ______	22 stanzas (3 verses per stanza) Three-line stanzas. Three letters per stanza 66 lines total a______ ______ ______	22 stanzas (verses) Two-line stanzas. One letter per stanza 44 lines total a______ ______	22 stanza (verses) One-line stanzas. No alphabetic sequence 22 lines total ______

Enjambed and Parallel Clauses

Analyses of Lamentations consistently highlight the lack of parallel lines in the first four chapters of the book. Only chapter 5 regularly exhibits the standard bi-colon structure of parallelism as defined by Bishop Robert Lowth.[5] Delbert Hillers made a similar observation that highlighted the presence of single sentences that cannot be divided into the standard two-cola lines found in parallel structures. According to his research, chapter 5 has 86 percent parallel lines versus 59 percent in chapters 1–4 combined.[6] Even though the presence of this distinction was recognized early on, it was F. W.

5. Robert Lowth, *Lectures on the Sacred Poetry of the Hebrews*, De Sacra Poesi Hebraeorum Praelectiones Academicae, 1753, ed. Johann David Michaelis, trans. G. Gregory (London: Thomas Tegg, 1835); Robert Lowth, *Isaiah: A New Translation* (1778; repr., London: Routledge/Thoemmes Press, 1995). Although Lowth was not the first to recognize parallelism, his work promoted its study in the biblical text. See James L. Kugel, *The Idea of Biblical Poetry: Parallelism and Its History* (Baltimore: Johns Hopkins University Press, 1981), 96–286.

6. Delbert R. Hillers, *Lamentations*, AB 7A (Garden City, NY: Doubleday, 1972), 19–20.

Dobbs-Allsopp who identified and provided an exhaustive classification of the types of lines found in this book. More specifically, he identified the prominence of enjambment over parallelism in the first four chapters.[7]

My study notes that the dispersal of enjambed and parallel clauses in the acrostic shows a specific pattern that highlights the initial and midpoint, stanzas and a couple of secondary stanzas.[8] Additionally, the dispersal of lineation across the acrostic structure confirms an ordered structure in the initial chapters that seems to coincide with obvious section breaks that indicate significant shifts in content or other literary markers—for example, change in speaker or addressee.

Change in Voice/ Imagery

The array of voices employed in the book of Lamentations is a significant feature of this poetic work. Each voice or persona adds to the complex dynamic embodied in the book.[9] While this literary aspect of Lamentations received some initial consideration in scholarship, William F. Lanahan pioneered the systematic analysis of voice (1974).[10] His research shifted the conversation regarding speaking voice away from historical authorship to

---

7. F. W. Dobbs-Allsopp, "The Enjambing Line in Lamentations: A Taxonomy (Part 1)," *ZAW* 113 (2001): 219–39. F. W. Dobbs-Allsopp, "The Effects of Enjambment in Lamentations (Part 2)," *ZAW* 113 (2001): 370–85. The categories defined by Dobbs-Allsopp have been adopted for my analysis of lineation.

8. More specifically, my study marks these stanza divisions at the aleph (א) and lamed (ל) (primary) stanzas, and the khet (ח) and qoph (ק) (secondary) stanzas. Young, "Making Sense Out of Suffering." These observations are in alignment with Michael Barré's and A. R. Ceresko's research on the significance of the beginning and center lines/stanzas of an acrostic poem. Michael L. Barré, "'Terminative' Terms in Hebrew Acrostics," in *Wisdom, You Are My Sister: Studies in Honor of Roland E. Murphy, O.Carm., on the Occasion of His Eightieth Birthday*, ed. Michael L. Barré, CBQMS 29 (Washington, DC: Catholic Biblical Association of America, 1997), 207–15. Anthony R. Ceresko, "The ABCs of Wisdom in Psalm Xxxiv," *VT* 35 (1985): 99–104. Anthony R. Ceresko, "Endings and Beginnings : Alphabetic Thinking and the Shaping of Psalms 106 and 150," *CBQ* 68 (2006): 32–46.

9. According to the *Princeton Encyclopedia of Poetry and Poetics*, defining voice in written poetry "poses a problem, for there is no literal voice in the poem: voice is an oral metaphor employed in the description and analysis of the written word." E. Richards, "Voice," in *The Princeton Encyclopedia of Poetry and Poetics*, ed. Roland Greene, 4th ed. (Princeton: Princeton University Press, 2012), 1525–27. Although voice is more abstract and conceptual than "persona," my study uses these terms synonymously. "The *persona* is not to be thought of as a fiction. It is a creative procedure in the displacement of the poet's imagination beyond the limitations of his single viewpoint so that he may gain a manifold insight into the human experience." William F. Lanahan, "The Speaking Voice in the Book of Lamentations," *JBL* 93 (1974): 41.

10. Lanahan, "The Speaking Voice," 93. My study also provides more detailed analysis on the number of voices and speech boundaries. Young, "Making Sense Out of Suffering," 98–153.

that of "stylistic concerns." He introduced the term "persona" into the discussion and proposed five discernible personae in the book. In doing this, he mitigated the need to identify speakers with historical characters and centered the attention on this phenomenon as a literary device.

Observations from Lamentations Chapter 1

The significance of the initial, midpoint, and secondary stanzas are highlighted through a change in voice, as well as imagery, especially in the first two chapters of Lamentations. Additionally, as the chapters progress, a breakdown in correlation appears. In chapter 1, the middle stanza is highlighted through the change in speech boundaries. The following is the sequence of speeches/speakers in the first half of the poem: narrator, Jerusalem, narrator, Jerusalem, and Jerusalem. This same sequence is repeated in the second half. Moreover, the double speeches of Jerusalem are differentiated by different addressee(s), namely Yahweh and "all who pass by the way," in the first half of the poem. In the second half of the poem, the double speeches of Jerusalem end the poem, with the speech directed to Yahweh showing an inverse relationship to the pair in the first half of the poem. Yahweh is now the second addressee rather than the first.

The lineation also highlights the secondary division stanzas with a clear break that precedes the speeches directed to Yahweh (1:9, 20). These divisions are further reinforced through the repeated usage of the second-person imperative of *ra'ah* ("to see"). This form of the verb initiates every speech directed to Yahweh by Jerusalem in this chapter. It is evident that these devices work together to highlight certain speech boundaries in Jerusalem's discourse.

Observations from Lamentations Chapter 2

Just as I have noted in Lamentations 1, there is also definite correspondence between the acrostic structure, lineation, and speech boundaries in chapter 2. However, a slight "regression" or unraveling of structure and continuity can be observed in this chapter. As in chapter 1, scholars also recognize a clear division at the center of this poem. More specifically, the break between 2:12 and 2:13 is noted through a definite shift to second-person discourse. However, chapter 2 only exhibits one secondary break that precedes a speech directed to Yahweh in verse 20. Like Lamentations 1, Zion's speech to Yahweh in verse 20 begins with the usage of the second-person imperative of *ra'ah* ("to see"). As indicated earlier, this form of the verb initiates every speech directed to Yahweh by Jerusalem.

The consistent alternation between the two main speakers continues in chapter 2, but quoted speeches of others are interspersed in the chapter—for example, infants and babes (2:12b), passersby (2:15c), enemies (2:16c).[11] This incorporation of quoted speech by others, as well as the addition of clustering pronominal suffixes, foreshadows the discontinuity exhibited in the later chapters.

Observations from Lamentations Chapter 3

Chapter 3 exhibits an even greater unraveling of structure with the incorporation of even more new voices. Instead of only hearing Jerusalem and the narrator, there is the addition of *hageber* ("the man") and the people in this chapter. There is also a quoted speech by Yahweh (3:37).

Additionally, this chapter exhibits a definite "regression" or unraveling of structure and correspondence. For example, there is not a speech division in the middle of the poem in this chapter. Instead, the division comes at verse 40, where the discourse shifts from third-person singular to first-person plural.[12] After reading the first two chapters, a reader would expect to find a break at the center of the acrostic but will be surprised to discover that it occurs later, resulting in a subtle shift that exhibits increased discordance.

The increased number of voices, as well as the lack of patterned alternation of speakers contributes to the increased dissonance between the poetic devices. Although Jerusalem and the narrator continue to speak in this chapter, the speech of *hageber* ("the man") and the people (collectively), as well as the quoted speech of Yahweh, compose half of the poem (thirty-three verses). The narrator's voice is heard only in verses 25–39 and Jerusalem's voice in verses 48–66 (excluding 3:57, where Yahweh's quoted speech is found). Perhaps the attribution of half the poem to the previous speakers and half to new speakers gives them equal weight. These additional voices bring added perspective to that of the two main voices heard in the previous two chapters. However, as in real life, the addition of new voices and perspectives can seem to engender greater chaos. Because of this, past scholars have attributed inconsistencies in perspectives to the presence of

11. Knut Heim categorizes these as separate utterances: utterance 7, 9, and 10. Knut M. Heim, "Personification of Jerusalem and the Drama of Her Bereavement in Lamentations," in *Zion, City of Our God*, ed. Richard S. Hess and Gordon J. Wenham (Grand Rapids: Eerdmans, 1999): 151–53.

12. The break comes after the *mem* (מ) stanza, which is one stanza after the center *lamed* (ל) stanza.

composite pieces.[13] However, Charles Miller rightly argues that "when one takes seriously the speaker shifts that exist within the poem, one can easily understand the inconsistencies. That is to say, the apparently problematic contradictions are, in fact, examples of the dialogue that exists between and among the various speakers, each of whom offer their own perspective."[14]

To be sure, chapter 3 still exhibits some correspondence among the literary devices, albeit less than that of chapters 1–2. Even though the center of the acrostic is not highlighted through change in voice or speech, the two secondary subdivisions still show correspondence with speech boundaries. More specifically, the speech of the people, which begins in verse 22, is the first sign of hope given in this book. The subdivision marked by verses 55–57 clearly identifies a shift in addressee to Yahweh through the predominant usage of second masculine singular (2ms) pronominal suffixes, 2ms verb forms, as well as the usage of the proper noun "Yahweh." Again, as in chapters 1–2, Jerusalem's speech to Yahweh ends the chapter. However, the usage of the second-person imperative of *ra'ah* ("to see") is not present in this chapter. Instead, there is a fronted repetition of this same verb, *ra'ah* ("to see") in the 2ms perfect (3:59, 60). As indicated earlier, the 2ms imperative form of the verb initiates every speech directed to Yahweh by Jerusalem so far, but in this chapter the verb form is no longer an imperative but a perfect.

Although some recent scholars have identified these forms as precative perfects expressing a desire or request,[15] Robin Parry rightly argues that the traditional simple past-time interpretation is the more plausible option.[16] First, given the context of the passage, an imperative would be more rhetorically effective than a precative perfect. Second, interpreting these perfect forms as precatives results in the same translation for all the perfects, imperatives, and imperfects in this passage (3:52–66).[17]

13. E.g., Claus Westermann, *Lamentations: Issues and Interpretation* (Minneapolis: Fortress Press, 1994), 191.

14. Charles William Miller, "Poetry and Personae: The Use and Function of Changing Speaking Voices in the Book of Lamentations" (PhD diss., University of Denver Iliff School of Theology, 1996), 179–80.

15. Hillers, *Lamentations*, 59; Adele Berlin, *Lamentations: A Commentary*, OTL (Louisville: Westminster John Knox, 2002), 97; Iain W. Provan, "Past, Present and Future in Lamentations III 52–66: The Case for a Precative Perfect Re-Examined," *VT* 41, 2 (1991): 164–75.

16. Robin Parry, *Lamentations*, Two Horizons Old Testament Commentary (Grand Rapids: Eerdmans, 2010), 123–24.

17. Parry, *Lamentations*, 124.

Although adopting the traditional interpretation for the perfect forms of the verb *ra'ah* ("to see") contributes to discontinuity from the two previous chapters, it ironically signals a progression in Jerusalem's disposition. More specifically, it moves from desperate imploring in the two earlier chapters to one of confidence, which is reinforced by the twofold repetition that affirms acknowledgment of Yahweh's action. As Paul W. Ferris Jr. observes, "The poet goes on to affirm that God hears the pleas of the faithful, that he is present even when the circumstances seem to the contrary."[18] The imagery still retains the idea of sight in correlation with Yahweh, but in this poem, if these statements are seen as past time interpretation, it expresses a hopeful confidence of faith. Kathleen O'Connor notes that "because the strongman, hageber (the man), has been seen and heard, because he has a witness for his suffering, he is able to hope and look toward the future."[19]

This shift comes at the center chapter of the book of Lamentations, which has been considered by some to be pivotal, as well as central to the book. Johan Renkema states, "From a structural perspective, the present literary twist constitutes the centre of the book of Lamentations."[20] Conversely, even though Parry does not believe that chapter 3 is the climax of the book, he asserts that it is central.[21] To be sure, this chapter fluctuates between hope and grief, which can also be observed through the dissonance between the acrostic structure, lineation, and breaks in speech. More specifically, this is highlighted in the delay of the break in speech after the midpoint of the poem. This delay reminds the reader, who may come to expect a break at the center of the acrostic, that expectations are not always predictable, which, in turn, mirrors the circumstances of this poem. However, as the reader continues to the end of the poem, a sense of hope rather than the desperate imploring found in the two previous chapters can be found.

Observations from Lamentations Chapter 4

Chapter 4 incorporates the same number of speakers as chapter 3. However, the voice of Jerusalem is not in this poem. Like chapter 3, the addition of new voices has complicated the observation of clear speech boundaries, structures, and correspondence that are visible in the previous chapters.

---

18. Paul W. Ferris Jr., "Lamentations," in *Jeremiah-Ezekiel*, The Expositor's Bible Commentary 7, 2nd ed. (Grand Rapids: Zondervan, 2010), 624.

19. Kathleen M. O'Connor, *Lamentations and the Tears of the World* (Maryknoll, NY: Orbis, 2002), 106.

20. Johan Renkema, *Lamentations*, Historical Commentary on the Old Testament (Leuven: Peeters, 1998), 344.

21. Parry, *Lamentations*, 18.

An even greater "regression" or unraveling of structure and correspondence can be observed moving from chapters 1–3 to chapter 4. The acrostic structure in chapter 4 has decreased to only two lines per stanza from three lines per stanza in the first three chapters. Moreover, the correspondence between the primary and secondary boundaries of speech are completely absent in this chapter. While chapter 3 only lacks correspondence between midpoint and new speech boundaries, this chapter does not display any correspondence with the boundaries that have been highlighted through lineation. Thus, there are no shifts in speakers or speech boundaries. Moreover, unlike chapters 1–3, which end their respective chapters with a prayer to Yahweh, the last speech in this chapter is not a prayer.

This chapter also includes additional voices, as well as the lack of patterned alternation of speakers. Jerusalem's voice is no longer heard, but the narrator continues to speak. However, the narrator's speech is only limited to six verses (twelve lines) or 27 percent of the total lines in this poem. Unlike chapter 3, which allots 50 percent of the discourse to Jerusalem and the narrator, this chapter has decreased that. A member of Jerusalem, the people, an authoritative voice, as well as quoted speech of unclean priests and xenophobic foreigners compose the remaining three-fourths of the poem (73 percent) or sixteen verses (thirty-two lines). The locution by others besides Jerusalem and/or the narrator increases as the chapters unfold in the book.

From the standpoint of literary structure and correspondence between the devices, this chapter shows the least correspondence. Not only are the lines "shrinking" from three- to two-line stanzas, but the expected correspondence to specific structural references (e.g., breaks in speech boundaries at the primary and secondary stanzas) are also missing and familiar voices are fading, but surprisingly the chapter ends with more hope than the previous chapters. Kenneth Hanson notes this growing sense of hope in this chapter:

> A muted but real sense of hope lies behind the progression. From a detached description of destruction, to a communal sense of loss, to an announcement proclaiming a reversal of fortunes, the poem climaxes at its conclusion. … The announcement falls naturally at the

> conclusion since it speaks a word of hope to the distress articulated in the dirge and communal lament.[22]

Likewise, Iain Provan notes, "It is clear that we have here the first and last real note of unfettered hope in the book. In contrast to the marked lack of hope throughout chaps. 1 and 2, and the tortured vacillation between faith and doubt in chap. 3, here at last is a note of assurance."[23]

Observations from Lamentations Chapter 5

Chapter 5 stands in stark contrast to the previous four chapters. The text lacks the acrostic structure, shows a decrease in lines per stanza, displays a different type of lineation, and has only one corporate speaking voice. These differences give chapter 5 a unique function in relation to the previous chapters.

The only corporate speaking voice is the community/people of Jerusalem. According to Lanahan, the choral voice is "not simply the reporter, the city, the veteran and the bourgeois speaking together; the chorus has its own character, subsuming each individual persona in an act of prayer which transcends the viewpoints and the inadequacies which the poet perceived and expressed through the first four chapters."[24]

This poem has been described by most scholars as following more closely to a communal lament. More specifically, it contains the following three basic sections that can be identified in communal laments: an appeal to Yahweh (5:1), a complaint (5:2–18), and a prayer for restoration (5:19–22).[25] These sections frame the prayer by the community. Miller posits that even though there is no change of speaker, this chapter continues the dialogue that began in chapter 1 because it reflects many of the themes and motifs found in the previous poems. In fact, he argues that "every word is drawn from the previous four poems and functions to direct the reader's attention back to the terrible predicament in which Jerusalem had found herself and the dialogue that had been going on about the reasons for her pitiful situation."[26]

The chapter opens with a threefold appeal to Yahweh to remember, look at, and see. This set of imperatives ends with the familiar imperative "see"

22. Kenneth C. Hanson, "Alphabetic Acrostics: A Form Critical Study" (PhD diss., Claremont Graduate School, 1984), 278–79.

23. Provan, *Lamentations*, 123.

24. Lanahan, "The Speaking Voice," 48.

25. Miller, "Poetry and Personae," 212.

26. Miller, "Poetry and Personae," 215.

found in chapters 1 (1:9, 11, 20) and 2 (2:20) in Jerusalem's prayers to Yahweh. It is no coincidence that chapter 4 does not contain a prayer, while chapter 5 is itself a prayer. The community is collectively imploring the Lord to "see" their reproach and dire state.

As noted earlier, the correspondence between the poetic devices displays disintegration with the progression of each chapter. Although the correspondence between the literary structure and other literary devices exhibits disintegration, the sense of hope gradually builds as one reads through the book. Correspondence would seem to project stability, and yet, hope takes hold as correspondence slips away. This inverse correlation catches the reader by surprise because one would expect the structural breakdown to mimic a loss of hope. It is precisely this unexpected change that sets the reader up for the final chapter of the book. At chapter 5, the increased dissonance that has been progressively exhibited now calls for the need of a drastically new structure and form. I propose that this unexpected inverse correlation mirrors the process of lament, which calls for a necessary breakdown of neatly ordered expectations in order to make room for voices that can inspire greater hope.

CONCLUSION: MIRRORING LAMENT

Scholarship on Lamentations has consistently recognized the striking difference between chapter 5, the last chapter of the book, and its previous four chapters. These obvious differences have caused speculation concerning the function of this last chapter as it relates to the rest of the book. For example, Kathleen O'Connor understands the shortening of the poems and the shrinking alphabetic form as a mirror of the exhaustion and increasing numbness of the poet(s), but she also argues that the loosening of structures indicates sustained confidence in God and in the future.[27] Likewise, Parry suggests this last chapter functions as a climax for the rest of the book. He argues that chapter 5 is the community's response to the ongoing suffering described in the previous four chapters. Parry believes that chapter 5 is the response to the promise of salvation at the end of chapter 4.

While these suggestions do have merit, I believe that the contrast between the final chapter and the previous four chapters strategically functions to mirror the process of lament in this poetic masterpiece. More specifically, the stark differences observed in chapter 5 provide a new structure that has

27. O'Connor, *Lamentations*, 14.

resulted from the progressive unraveling of correspondences between the prominent poetic devices observed in the previous four chapters.

When we or our community experience grief and lament, the pain can become so blinding that we cannot see beyond the "structures" of pain that have been built. In times of suffering our voices can be confined to our own experiences. We only grasp one aspect of truth because our perspective is limited. We feel alone and isolated from others, and oftentimes we construct these psychological defenses or "structures" to protect ourselves from further harm. If we remain behind these isolated barriers, we will sink deeper into our grief, hopelessness, and despair. The echo chambers of our minds with their limited perspectives will inevitably become the primary voices that reinforce the downward spiral of our disillusionment and discouragement. Psychologists have recognized that "moving beyond victimization requires expanding a narrative of danger to a narrative of hope and promise."[28] But how do we expand our narrative? This involves the willingness to break down our "structures" of isolation to make room for other voices. In humility, we must be willing to allow others to speak into our situations and pain. O'Connor notes, "After worlds collapse, survivors need a new story." [29] This new story often requires a completely new "structure," which inevitably issues a call to be open to a new narrative. This progression is what we witness in the book of Lamentations. The isolated and alone Lady Jerusalem (Lam 1:1) who opens up chapter 1 is no longer alone in chapter 5. This final chapter reflects a completely different structure, which mirrors the increased hope in the book that could only arise from the rubble of the previously constructed order exhibited in the initial chapters of the book.

It is important, however, that these observations are not meant to discourage the expression or minimize the experience of pain. In fact, giving voice to our pain can bring us to a place of greater faith. The book of Lamentations honors the voice of suffering and pain and does not try to minimize it by resolving it with trite answers. This is mirrored in the book itself. The art of lament is one that gives expression to real pain, while making room for new voices. Jerusalem's experience is not minimized. Lady Jerusalem's voice is given prominence in the first couple of chapters, indicating that the author gives room for her to express the depth of her sorrow and shame. This truthful expression is often raw and difficult to witness, but it is acknowledged, nonetheless. However, the expression of pain must

28. Sheri Heller, *A Clinician's Journey from Complex Trauma to Thriving: Reflections on Abuse, C-PTSD and Reclamation* (New York: independently published, 2017), 54.

29. O'Connor, *Lamentations*, 93.

not devolve into a mire of self-pity or self-loathing. This is why other voices are critical, and we see this in the usage of poetic devices in this book.

As mentioned earlier, the increased number of voices contributes to the disintegration between the structural correspondences, but also gives way to greater hope. It is only when we cry out and hear other voices in response that we can move beyond the perspective that we have become accustomed to. The progressive unraveling of correspondence among the literary devices offers the reader an illustration of this journey through lament. With each new chapter, the unraveling of structural correspondences is accentuated through the addition of more voices and different perspectives. This addition reinforces the necessity for openness to new voices and structures. In fact, the usage of a corporate voice in chapter 5 suggests a sense of hope. O'Connor writes:

> Lamentations becomes a mirror of our sorrow, loss and doubt. It creates a framework, a larger world to which individual and community suffering can be related. We are no longer alone in our suffering because it is called forth, acknowledged and named, no matter how indirectly, no matter how veiled by the text's metaphors and images. Art that leaps across the centuries can mirror our lives, echo our circumstance, and validate our experience of divine absence.[30]

A recent study on the usage of pronouns during times of trauma or traumatic events found that the "more depressed a person is, the more likely he or she will use I-words in writing or speaking." Conversely, the usage of first-person plural we-words were associated with more positive experiences.[31] Therefore, it is not surprising that the progression through chapters 1–4 culminates in a communal prayer (chapter 5) that breaks all the literary and structural conventions found in the previous four chapters. But this prayer could not have been spoken by Jerusalem's people had she stayed in her constructed experience of pain. The increased locution of other voices besides those of Jerusalem and the narrator help to broaden the perspective of this text. The polyphonic and multivalent character of this book allows for greater growth and development in the voices. Instead of hearing a univocal or even bi-vocal point of view throughout the poem, the multiple voices engage in a dialogic relationship. Each voice is not immune

30. O'Connor, *Lamentations*, 102.

31. James W. Pennebaker, *The Secret Life of Pronouns: What Our Words Say About Us* (New York: Bloomsbury Press, 2011), 106, 108.

to the other voices in the text, for they form a relationship by being placed side by side, and they must orient themselves to one another. Moreover, this last chapter recounts much of the significant imagery presented in earlier chapters. In reiterating these themes and motifs the community is giving voice to the pain expressed.

Chapter 5 does not end on a positive note, but rather in an unsettled and precarious manner. What begins as a request for restoration in verse 21, ends with a question and uncertainty: "Or have you utterly rejected us?"[32] Mikail Bakhtin notes that at times this dialogical intersection may not result in a resolution.[33] The open-ended quality of the nonfinalized dialogic truth implies that a text does not give the final word within a dialogue but is open to future words. It is precisely this desperate yet tempered openness to Yahweh's response that allows the community to continue to wait for him. Yahweh has not given his final word in the text. Therefore, all hope is not lost. Just as Jerusalem's community waited in expectation for a future word, communities experiencing great pain and suffering can move together toward earnest receptivity for Yahweh's response.

As I noted in the introduction, just as visual masterpieces use a myriad of artistic devices to reinforce their message, literary masterpieces do so as well. Poetic literary devices do not exist in a vacuum to be viewed as individual gems, but they function together to enhance the message of the entire work. Lamentations is an example of such artistry, which enhances its theology through these devices and mirrors the process of lament.

32. My translation; see Gordis for a detailed assessment on how 5:22 has been translated by previous scholars. Robert Gordis, "Conclusion of the Book of Lamentations (5:22)," *JBL* 93 (1974): 289–93.

33. Mikhail M. Makhtin, *The Dialogic Imagination: Four Essays*, ed. Michael Holquist, trans. Caryl Emerson and Michael Holquist (University of Texas Press: Austin, 1981), 365.

9

The Psalms of Lament and the Theology of the Cross

Rolf A. Jacobson

This essay explores the relationship between the theology of the cross and the psalms of lament. The theology of the cross is briefly defined as a theology (1) for discerning God's presence and action in the world, (2) that refuses to reason backward in causal faction from tangible experience to theological conclusions, (3) that "calls a thing what it is" rather than calling it its opposite, and (4) that always must be preached. This theology is then related to the psalms of lament, arguing that although the cross itself is not present in the psalms, this way of doing theology is present in many of the lament psalms.

I say to God, my rock,
  "Why have you forgotten me?
Why must I walk about mournfully
  because the enemy oppresses me?"
As with a deadly wound in my body,
  my adversaries taunt me,
while they say to me continually,
  "Where is your God?"
Why are you cast down, O my soul,
  and why are you disquieted within me?
Hope in God; for I shall again praise him,
  my help and my God. (Psalm 42:9–11)[1]

1. Scripture quotations are taken from the NRSV unless otherwise noted.

The "theology of the cross" has been treated at great length and depth in recent years by theologians of many theological traditions, disciplines, and hermeneutical approaches.[2] The relationship of the theology of the cross to the Old Testament, however, is a field that has yet to be satisfactorily plowed. For many years, I have hoped to pursue such an investigation. Here, as a beginning point, a brief investigation of the theology of the cross in relationship to the Psalms is offered.

THE THEOLOGY OF THE CROSS IN BRIEF

The theology of the cross is more about how one does theology than it is about the content of one's theology, as Gerhard Forde makes explicit in *On Being a Theologian of the Cross* and as Martin Luther implies in the way he words theses 19–21 of the Heidelberg Disputation (1518):

> 19. That person does not deserve to be called a theologian who looks upon the invisible things of God as though they were clearly perceptible in those things which have actually happened.
>
> 20. [One] deserves to be called a theologian, however, who comprehends the visible and hindmost things of God as visible in the suffering and the cross.
>
> 21. A theologian of glory calls evil good and good evil. A theologian of the cross calls a thing what it actually is.[3]

Although some translations miss the point, in the Heidelberg Disputation Luther does not write about the "theology of the cross" but rather about "the theologian of the cross." He writes about the person who "does not deserve to be called a theologian," about the person who does "deserve to be called a theologian," about the "theologian of glory," and about the "theologian of the cross." The point is that the theology of the cross is first and

2. I have found these volumes to be helpful: Walther von Loewenich, *Luther's Theology of the Cross* (Minneapolis: Augsburg, 1976); Gerhard Forde, *On Being a Theologian of the Cross: Reflections on Luther's Heidelberg Disputation, 1518* (Grand Rapids: Eerdmans, 1997); Douglas John Hall, *Lighten Our Darkness: Toward an Indigenous Theology of the Cross* (Louisville: Westminster John Knox, 1971); Jürgen Moltmann, *The Crucified God*, 4th ed. (Minneapolis: Fortress, 2015); Deanna Thompson, *Crossing the Divide: Luther, Feminism, and the Cross* (Minneapolis: Fortress, 2004); Andrew Root, *Christopraxis: A Practical Theology of the Cross* (Minneapolis: Fortress, 2014); Eberhard Jüngel, *God as the Mystery of the World: On the Foundation of the Theology of the Crucified One in the Dispute between Theism and Atheism* (London: T&T Clark, 2014).

3. "Heidelberg Disputation," *LW* 31:52–53.

foremost about how one does theology. As my colleague Andrew Root puts it, "The theology of the cross is a hermeneutic for [understanding] how God acts in the world. It affirms a dialectical shape to God's action—God is found in places God should not be, but this is what makes God God."[4]

And how does a theologian of the cross "do" theology? According to Luther, how the theologian of the cross does theology can be expressed both negatively and positively. Stated in the negative, the theologian of the cross does not do theology by looking "upon the invisible things of God as though they were clearly perceptible in those things which have actually happened."[5] That is, by trying to reason backward from the perceivable realities of life (in a fallen creation) in order to draw conclusions about the imperceivable nature of God. Stated in the positive, the theologian of the cross does theology by observing "the visible and hindmost things of God as visible in the suffering and the cross"[6]—that is, both by taking seriously what Christ accomplished for us on the cross and by assuming that the cross is the model for how God normally works.

Luther contrasts the theologian of the cross with the theologian of glory. The theologian of glory does theology hypothetically, by observing life in the visible creation and reasoning backward toward what sort of God might be behind such a creation. Reformation historian Ken Sundet Jones puts it this way: "Theologians of glory are inveterate believers in Newtonian physics: all of creation is a realm of causation."[7] With regard to salvation, this means that since "the present has been caused by the past, then the future is also subject to our present actions. Using the tools at hand, we can exert our efforts to achieve a desired future. When it comes to salvation, the seemingly logical tool to pull out of the box on our workbench is the Law."[8] Thus for the theologian of glory, salvation comes through works of the law.

4. Andrew Root, personal correspondence, May 27, 2020. Root engages the theology of the cross throughout his vast corpus of publications, but especially in *Christopraxis: A Practical Theology of the Cross*.

5. "Heidelberg Disputation," *LW* 31:52.

6. This is the translation of the Reformation Historian Hans Wiersma, of Augsburg University, personal correspondence, May 27, 2020. Wiersma notes that the translation in *Luther's Works* by Harold Grimm misses the allusion in Luther's Latin to a favorite passage of Luther, Exodus 33:23, where God places Moses in a cleft in the rock and passes in front of him, but Moses is only allowed to see God's "backside" (*posteriora mea*).

7. Ken Sundet Jones, personal correspondence, May 26, 2020. Jones later published a version of this correspondence at https://www.1517.org/articles/what-makes-a-theologian-of-the-cross.

8. Jones, personal correspondence, May 26, 2020.

Further, with regard to "suffering" on the one hand, and "success" on the other hand, working in the framework of causation means that the theologian of glory assumes someone has "caused" suffering or success. That someone is usually God—who has rewarded those who keep the law with success or punished those who have not kept the law with suffering. Job's friends—Eliphaz, Bildad, and Zophar—are well-meaning theologians of glory. As Eliphaz says to the suffering Job, "Think now, who that was innocent ever perished?" (Job 4:7a).

The theologian of the cross, by contrast, starts with the suffering of the Son of God on the cross. When it comes to the matter of salvation, the theologian of the cross accepts the evangelical promise of the New Testament that "while we were still weak, at the right time Christ died for the ungodly. ... That while we still were sinners Christ died for us. ... While we were enemies we were reconciled to God through the death of his Son" (Rom 5:6, 8, 10). The threefold repetition in this passage of the phrase "while we were" with threefold references to Christ's death emphasizes that Christ's death on the cross effected salvation for us from outside of our will or our agency. Salvation (justification) comes not through works of the law, but it is a free and gracious gift. Gone is the way of doing theology that operates out of "Newtonian physics" based on belief in the free will and operating from causation. When it comes to suffering and success, the theologian of the cross must eschew causation. If God's power to save is made evident in the cross, then neither suffering nor success can be assumed to have been "caused" by someone—neither by God, nor the one experiencing suffering or success. Many—but not all—of the psalmists, I will argue below, were theologians of the cross. They recognized that their suffering was not caused by any act of the free will—either their own or God's.

The theologian of the cross understands that the cross is not just a one-time event, through which Christ overcame the power of death (although that is certainly true). As already mentioned, the cross sets the pattern for God's presence and action in the world—the cross is a hermeneutic for discerning how God shows up in the world. God will be found in suffering; suffering is not the absence of God, but the place God has most promised to show up.

Further, the cross is not simply the content of Christian theology, but an active, speaking, and preaching agent. The cross itself speaks and preaches about God's action and presence with "the power of God." In 1 Corinthians 1:18, Paul speaks about "the word of the cross" (Ὁ λόγος γὰρ ὁ τοῦ σταυροῦ).

> For the word of the cross is foolishness to those who are perishing, but to those of us who are being saved, it is the power of God. ... Has not God made foolish the wisdom of the world? For since, in the wisdom of God, the world did not know God through its wisdom, God was pleased, through the foolishness of preaching, to save those who believe. For Jews demand signs and Greeks desire wisdom, but we preach Christ crucified, a scandal to Jews and foolishness to Greeks, but to those of us who are called—both Jews and Greeks—Christ the power of God and the wisdom of God. (1 Cor 1:18, 20b–25, my translation)

The NRSV and NIV unhelpfully render this phrase "the message about the cross" and "the message of the cross," respectively. Older translations such as the KJV ("the preaching of the cross") or the *Luther Bible (Das Wort vom Kreuz)* more effectively maintain the ambiguity of Paul's Greek phrase. The "word of the cross" can be construed as both a subjective genetic and an objective genitive. It can be understood as both "the word about the cross" but also "the word that the cross speaks to us"—*what the cross does to us*. The cross offends us, repulses us, causes us incredulity, humbles us, and mocks our wisdom and strength. The cross also saves us, kills us and gives us new life, and empowers us—"to those of us who are being saved, it is the power of God" (1 Cor 1:18).

The cross also teaches us how to do theology, according to Paul. Paul writes, "For since, in the wisdom of God, the world did not know God through its wisdom, God was pleased, through the foolishness of preaching, to save those who believe" (1 Cor 1:20). The cross teaches us that we did not and indeed we cannot know God through human wisdom. No theologian or philosopher could have foreseen the cross. Thus the cross makes a fool of human wisdom—including speculative theology about the nature and actions of God: "Has not God made foolish the wisdom of the world? ... The world did not know God through its wisdom" (1 Cor 1:20b). Thus, when we do theology, we must do so in the mode not of speculation but of proclamation and preaching, announcing to the world what has been done for it by Christ. Because "God was pleased, through the foolishness of preaching, to save those who believe," according to Paul (1 Cor 1:21b). As Jones puts it, another "thing that makes a theologian of the cross is Christ preached, and him crucified. Christ is not preached in his glory but in his ignominy, his utter shame, degradation, and desolation. ... If a theologian of the cross sees a thing and calls it what it is, then the thing is this: The cross, Christ's and yours, is where, like some mafioso, you are 'made.' "[9]

Calling a thing what it is does not stop with naming what Christ has done on the cross, however. As Deanna Thompson says,

> Theologians of the cross call sinful structures and forces of evil that threaten to destroy God's good creation by their names. Because it takes its cue from the crucifixion, a theology of the cross limits its theologizing to this world, to God's coming to us and meeting us where we live; it highlights God's giving and our receiving. ... A cross-centered theology understands God as hidden in the suffering of this world, and that God's righteousness works within the pain and awfulness of our lives to bring about justification and new life.[10]

By way of summarizing this brief theology of the cross (or a brief guide to being a theologian of the cross), the following precepts are offered:

1. *The theology of the cross is a hermeneutic for discerning God's presence and action in the world.* God shows up most profoundly in the cross and in suffering. Therefore the theologian of the cross looks for God in suffering, precisely where the "wisdom of the world" would never look for God.
2. *The theologian of the cross eschews the temptation to reason backward in a causal fashion from what is visible in creation to drawing conclusions about the invisible God.* Regarding salvation, Christ's death on the cross has done it all. Regarding God's nature, the cross reveals what needs to be known. Speculation is dangerous.
3. *Unlike the theologian of glory, who calls a thing its opposite, the theologian of the cross calls a thing what it is.* This includes calling suffering what it is—suffering. It also includes naming the sinful structures of this world and all of the forces that defy the life-giving will of the Triune God.
4. *The theologian of the cross must therefore always be a preacher—working through the category of promise.* The theologian of the cross promises that in Christ's death and resurrection all that is sufficient for salvation and sanctification has already been

9. Jones, personal correspondence, May 26, 2020.

10. Deanna Thompson, personal correspondence, May 26, 2020. Thompson's feminist exposition of the theology of the cross is found in *Crossing the Divide: Luther, Feminism, and the Cross.*

achieved for you. There is nothing to be added, no further works are necessary.

THE PSALMISTS OF LAMENT AS THEOLOGIANS OF THE CROSS

In Luther's second series of Psalm lectures (1519–1521), commenting on Psalm 5:11—"Let all who take refuge in you rejoice"—the Reformer wrote: "The CROSS alone is our theology." It is apt that Luther uttered these words about a lament psalm. In context, Luther was offering theological reflection about how the great Christian virtues of "faith, hope, and love are not able to be achieved except through suffering: By suffering, I say, within the working of God."[11]

How odd, one might reflect, that the "working of God" is to use suffering to bring about faith, hope, and love. But according to Luther, the soul is led into "its own resting place" by a strange kind of "leading." "This leading ... this shaping torments it miserably. For it is difficult and the way is narrow," Luther comments. But "by faith, hope, and love alone I live, and I am weak (that is, I suffer), indeed when I am weak, then I am strong." Luther casts doubt upon theologians who see this as accomplished by our own actions or agency. Rather, Luther sees the creation of faith, hope, and love as the result of Christ's work on the cross—that is, through Christ's agency on the cross. And thus, for Luther, "the cross alone is our theology."[12] By implication, therefore, the Christian theologian can expect to experience and discern the agency of the crucified and resurrected Christ in the sufferings of God's people as a whole and in the sufferings of individual Christians. The cross marks both the moment of God's atoning and reconciling action for all of creation and the ongoing nature and place of God's transformative agency. To be clear, the cross indicates that God showed up most profoundly in the death and resurrection of Christ to reconcile all creation to himself. And the cross also indicates where and when God will continue to show up—that is, in our suffering.

Although the literal theology and proclamation of the cross of Christ are obviously not present in either the Old Testament or the Psalter, the major themes of the theology of the cross as laid out above are present in the

11. Translation from *Weimarer Ausgabe* (complete Latin and German edition of Luther's Works) 5:175–76 by Christopher C. Smith, personal correspondence, July 14–15, 2020. Emphasis in original.

12. *Weimarer Ausgabe*, trans. Smith, personal correspondence, July 14–15, 2020.

Psalter. And therefore it is appropriate—and indeed helpful—to regard at least some of the psalmists as theologians of the cross. In particular, it is helpful to regard the psalmists of lament as theologians of the cross.

The lament psalms (or, better, the "prayers for help") compose one of the primary Old Testament genres of the theology of the cross, because the lament psalms refuse to reason backward from the experience of suffering to any conclusion about either God or the psalmist. For the most part, the psalmists of lament refuse to regard their own suffering as evidence of God's absence, lack of power, or judgment against the psalmist. The psalmists of lament refuse to regard their own suffering as evidence that they've committed some unknown sin or that they've been rejected by God. (The psalms of penitence are exceptions, to the extent that in these prayers the psalmists know the sins they have committed and actively repent of them.) Rather, the psalmists of lament contend with God actively. They demand that the Lord be faithful to the divine promises and show up in ways that manifest the divine character.

The psalmists of lament—those suffering individuals who pray prayers for help—can be said to be theologians because they make statements about God. In context, of course, these theologians are in the midst of intense suffering, trauma, or crisis, and they are speaking to God in the midst of these circumstances. The statements they make about God are in the context of speaking to God—that is, in prayer. But the fact that the psalmists are praying does not make their statements about God any less theological. After all, *lex orandi, lex credendi*—"the law of what is to be prayed [becomes] the law of what is to be believed." In other words, what we pray spiritually becomes what we believe theologically.

And as these theologians suffer, they are surrounded by other theologians—let's call at least some of them theologians of glory—who also make theological statements about God. I will start with some of the theological statements of these other theologians. Consider how the psalmists characterize those around them, and especially how these other voices regard the suffering of the psalmists:

- Many are saying to me, "There is no help for you in God." (3:2)
- How can you say to me, "Flee like a bird to the mountains; for look, the wicked bend the bow ... what can the righteous do?" (11:1–3)
- They close their hearts to pity; with their mouths they speak arrogantly. (17:10)

- I am ... scorned by others and despised by the people. All who see me mock at me. ... "Commit your cause to the LORD; let him deliver—let him rescue the one in whom he delights!" (22:6–8)
- At my stumbling they gathered in glee, ... they impiously mocked more and more. (35:15–16)
- They think that a deadly thing has fastened on me, that I will not rise again from where I lie. Even my bosom friend in whom I trusted, who ate of my bread, has lifted the heel against me. (41:8–9)
- They say to me continually, "Where is your God?" (42:10, see also 42:3)
- It is not enemies who taunt me ... it is you, my equal, my companion, my familiar friend, with whom I kept pleasant company; we walked in the house of God with the throng. (55:12–14)

Summed up, these "theologians of glory" believe that the psalmists are beyond God's help. They believe God has either turned against them or that God lacks the effective power to act on the psalmists' behalf. Some of them delight—at least secretly—in the psalmists' suffering, with a peculiar sort of *Schadenfreude*. They even mock, deride, and taunt those suffering. They mock the sufferer, the sufferer's faith in God, and even directly mock the sufferer's God. Others simply seem to have abandoned the psalmists—to have given them up for dead.

To be clear, I am contending that the psalmists who are suffering are not "theologians of glory." Rather, I am contending that the other "theologians"—those who say things such as "there is no help for you in God," or "they think a deadly thing has fastened on me," or "Where is your God?"—these others are the theologians of glory, because they do not look for or discern God's presence in suffering.

In contrast to them, the psalmists of lament contend with both God and neighbor. They demand that God prove visibly present and show up with the power to save. And in words of confession that are one part defiance—defiance of both their adversaries and of God—and one part faith, they confess the faithful character and effective power of God. There are too many examples, so just a few will have to suffice, selected from the same psalms from which the sample statements of the theologians of glory were taken:

- Deliver me, O my God! ... Deliverance belongs to the LORD. (3:7–8)
- The LORD is righteous; ... the upright shall behold his face. (11:7)
- I shall behold your face in righteousness; when I awake I shall be satisfied, beholding your likeness. (17:15)

- You are holy, enthroned on the praises of Israel. ... I will tell of your name to my brothers and sisters; in the midst of the congregation I will praise you. (22:3, 22)
- Say evermore, "Great is the LORD, who delights in the welfare of his servant." (35:27)
- By this I know that you are pleased with me: ... You have upheld me because of my integrity. (41:11–12)
- Hope in God; for I shall again praise him, my help and my God (42:5–6, 11; 43:5)
- I call upon God, and the LORD will save me. (55:16)

These few examples could be multiplied many times over. Again and again in the Psalter, the psalmists of lament refuse to regard their present suffering and trauma either as proof of their own sin (this is true especially in the psalms of innocence, such as Pss 17 and 26), of God's absence, or of God's lack of effective power to save. In the face of the suffering that others take as evidence of these things, the psalmists of lament confess God's faithful character and trust in God's effective power. They expect—even demand—that God show up in suffering with the power to save and transform imminent death into what Paul later called new creation. And as noted earlier, all of these things make the psalm of lament one of the most important Old Testament genres of the theology of the cross. In these psalms, we see what Deanna Thompson describes as a basic aspect of life as a theologian of the cross: the way of living life and doing theology "before the crucified God." She writes, "It begins with affirmations of a righteous, loving God who desires goodness for God's creation. But it quickly moves to ... working to peel away the illusions perpetuated by theologians of glory who focus on human attempts at salvation of themselves and the whole creation." Such a "cross-centered theology understands God as hidden in the suffering of this world, and that God's righteousness works within the pain and awfulness of our lives to bring about justification and new life."[13]

The lament psalmists, as theologians of the cross, have come to expect that suffering is neither the evidence of God's absence nor is trauma the necessary precursor of death. They expect and demand that God will show up precisely where it seems that God cannot be—in disease, trauma, and death. This is not to say that God can only show up there or that God is absent in joy and triumph. For of course God will be known and recognized in

13. Thompson, personal correspondence, May 26, 2020.

joy and triumph. But God will also show up—perhaps even preferentially so—in those places where God's absence will be assumed by the world and the theologians of glory.

Because the world and the theologians of glory will always assume that God is not present in suffering, the psalmists of lament are continuously preaching and proclaiming God's imminent presence and power—even in the midst of suffering and God's seeming absence. They demand it of God: "Deliver me, O my God! … Deliverance belongs to the LORD" (3:7–8) and "I shall behold your face in righteousness; when I awake I shall be satisfied, beholding your likeness" (17:15). They proclaim it to their neighbors and the theologians of glory: "The LORD is righteous; … the upright shall behold his face" (11:7) and "Say evermore, 'Great is the LORD, who delights in the welfare of his servant'" (35:27). And, at times, when there is no preacher around to preach this hopeful word of the cross to them, they will even preach it to themselves. Note in Psalms 42 and 43 how the homiletical injunction to "hope in God" is actually addressed by the psalmist to himself:

> Why are you cast down, O my soul,
> and why are you disquieted within me?
> Hope in God, for I shall again praise him,
> my help and my God. (Ps 42:11)

The "word of the theology of the cross" in the psalms of lament must be preached in order to be believed, because it is not a theology that one can arrive at on one's own either by reason or by experience. As Paul wrote, "God was pleased, through the foolishness of preaching, to save those who believe" (1 Cor 1:21b). The cross alone is our theology. The cross is also the theology of the psalmists of lament.

CONCLUSION: WHEN REAL LIFE IS SIMPLY AWFUL

Five years ago, at the age of thirty-five, my friend Kate Bowler was diagnosed with stage four incurable cancer. Bowler has chronicled her journey with cancer and offered theological reflection on living life fully in the face of death in an article, a book, and a podcast.[14] In the initial article, which first appeared in *The New York Times* in 2016, Bowler described what I would

14. Kate Bowler, "Death, the Prosperity Gospel, and Me," *The New York Times* (February 13, 2016); *Everything Happens for a Reason: And Other Lies I Have Loved* (New York: Random House, 2018); and the podcast "Everything Happens with Kate Bowler."

call a particularly American version of theology of glory—the theology of the so-called prosperity gospel.

According to Bowler, the word "blessed" plays a key role in this version of Christian theology: "One of the prosperity gospel's greatest triumphs is its popularization of the term 'blessed.' ... 'Blessed' is the shorthand for the prosperity message."[15] She continues, "Blessed is a loaded term because it blurs the distinction between two very different categories: gift and reward. It can be a term of pure gratitude." And again, "If Oprah could eliminate a single word, it would be 'luck.' 'Nothing about my life is lucky,' she argued on her cable show. 'Nothing. A lot of grace. A lot of blessings. A lot of divine order. But I don't believe in luck. For me luck is preparation meeting the moment of opportunity.' This is America, where there are no setbacks, just setups. Tragedies are simply tests of character."[16]

Notice in this theology how the agency of God ("gift") becomes blurred with the agency of the human ("reward"). And notice how, according to Bowler, this theology does not call a thing what it is, but rather calls a thing its opposite. Tragedies are not tragedies; they are tests of character. Setbacks are not setbacks; they are setups. The theology of glory here is motivated by the impulse to keep things positive, to find a positive label to slap on a tragedy in order to cover it up theologically.

This impulse to cover up a negative experience with a positive label is a uniquely American expression of the theology of glory. The impulse can be discerned in many of the euphemisms Americans use in response to various forms of loss. These include: "When God closes a door, God opens up a window." "Whatever doesn't kill me makes me stronger." "Every cloud has a silver lining." "God has a purpose for everything." And the greatest of all, "Everything happens for a reason."

In her 2016 article, Bowler described when

> a neighbor knocked on our door to tell my husband that everything happens for a reason.
>
> "I'd love to hear it," my husband said.
>
> "Pardon?" she said, startled.
>
> "I'd love to hear the reason my wife is dying," he said, in that sweet and sour way he has. My neighbor wasn't trying to sell him a spiritual guarantee. But there was a reason she wanted to fill that silence

15. Bowler, "Death, the Prosperity Gospel, and Me."
16. Bowler, "Death, the Prosperity Gospel, and Me."

around why some people die young and others grow old and fussy about their lawns. She wanted some kind of order behind this chaos. Because the opposite of #blessed is leaving a husband and a toddler behind, and people can't quite let themselves say it: "Wow. That's awful." There has to be a reason, because without one we are left as helpless and possibly as unlucky as everyone else.[17]

I would call attention to the need for "some kind of order" and the rationalization that "there has to be a reason," or we are left "helpless" and "unlucky," or #unblessed. The theology of glory cannot stand the lack of order, the feeling of helplessness, the lack of explanation. It demands that life be rational. It clings to the idea that the human will—our own sense of agency—has the last word. As mentioned above, when it comes to salvation, the theology of glory sees in the law—God's commands about what we are to do and not to do—a tool via which the self can have agency in its own salvation and blessing. The theologian of glory reasons, "If I follow God's law, God will bless and save me—that must be why God gave me the law." Because the self demands agency in life. And then when the bottom drops out and suffering comes out of nowhere, the self demands that things make sense. Forty years ago today (a biblical number), as a fifteen-year-old boy I was diagnosed with cancer on a Monday and had my right leg amputated two days later on a Wednesday. This human need for order and causality is why one woman in our church said to my mom, "If you had fed your family the right diet of high-antioxidant, cancer-fighting fresh fruits and vegetables, your son would not have gotten cancer." Ah, the theology of glory and the mirage of control. Sometimes suffering just happens and all we can say—all we should say—is: "that is awful."

Kate Bowler, in her own story of cancer's sudden onslaught, names suffering as a spiritual and physical reality that we will all face eventually. Suffering is spiritual space, one in which the powers of sin, death, disease, the devil, and the sinful world take over and leave the Christian feeling helpless. This is a space where the Christian is faced with unbearable suffering, with chaotic lack of spiritual order, and a debilitating sense of helplessness.

And the spiritual space of suffering is the place for the psalms of lament to go to work. This is a good place for the psalms of lament, which do theology along the lines of the theology of the cross, because the psalms of lament refuse to relabel suffering with some sort of positive euphemism.

17. Bowler, "Death, the Prosperity Gospel, and Me."

After all, mired in our own suffering, we look to Christ in his suffering, who is remembered in the Gospels as having twice quoted the psalms while dying on the cross.

Moments of suffering and death create great disorder spiritually and rationally. The psalms of lament refuse to retreat into a euphemism that tries to impose order where there can be no order (the sort of euphemism that says something about how God acts). Instead, the psalms of lament turn directly to God—where they pray, they scream, they question, they challenge, and they shout at God: "My God, my God, why have you forsaken me?" (22:1) Or "How long, O Lord? Will you forget me forever?" (13:1). The psalms of lament give us the language to say to God (and to each other), "Wow! This is awful!" In fact, the psalms of lament say, "Hey God, this is awful! Do something about it!"

Perhaps the greatest gift of the psalms of lament in a time of suffering is that they turn us to speak to God rather than about God. If we only talk about God, our human need for order, for understanding, for meaning, and for cause-and-effect reasoning kicks in. And when that happens, pretty soon we find ourselves mouthing sentences that try to impose human reason and the human need for order and meaning unto the sovereign Lord. And not long after that we are saying things like, "Everything happens for a reason."

But rather than talk about God, the psalms of lament give us visceral language to cry out to God. To say, "I am languishing" (6:2); "Why do you hide yourself in times of trouble?" (10:1); "Help, O Lord, for there is no longer anyone who is godly" (12:1).

Then the psalms of lament demand that God change the awful reality, that God bring salvation and redemption. They plead, "Save my life!" (6:4); "Rise up!" (10:12); "Answer me, O Lord my God!" (13:3). And in the end, when faced with suffering, raging against God and demanding that God show up and be tangibly present and powerful is not a bad way to do theology. Mired in our own suffering, we look to Christ in his suffering, and we try to discern God's presence and activity. And we do so precisely by praying, "Save me!"

10

"In Sheol, Who Can Give You Praise?" Death in the Psalms

Philip S. Johnston

Western Christians often struggle with the portrayal of death in the Psalter. As in the Old Testament generally—in marked contrast to the New—the dead seem to subsist lifelessly in the underworld of Sheol, far removed from God's presence. This is presented typically in Psalm 6 and dramatically in Psalm 88. We examine a few verses which may glimpse beyond this: possibly in Psalms 16, 49, and 73; less likely in Psalms 1, 17, 23, 79, and 139. And we note how the dominant view coheres with ancient Israel's theology, while the few glimpses point beyond its shadows.

TYPICAL CHRISTIAN READING OF HALF THE PSALTER

In practice, most of us use only half the Psalter, mainly the second half (Pss 90–150).[1] We gladly celebrate God's rule, which dominates Book IV (Pss 90–106). We enjoy the psalms of victory and praise that open Book V (Pss 107–118). We identify with the more personal Psalms of Ascent (Pss 120–134) and many of the sentiments of the next ten assorted psalms (Pss 135–145). And we rejoice in the exuberant worship of the final hallelujahs (Pss 146–150). The second half is full of life, marked by confident faith and dominated by praise of God. The praise is sometimes quiet and reflective (as in Ps 139), but more often full-throated and boisterous, declaring and

1. This approximate division serves a heuristic purpose here and has a scholarly reflection in the canonical approach of Gerald H. Wilson, *The Editing of the Hebrew Psalter*, SBLDS 76 (Chico, CA: Scholars Press, 1985), and others.

celebrating who God is and what he does, both for the world in general and for his people in particular. And this leads in turn to affirmation of trust and renewal of confidence on both individual and communal levels. It is a faith easily transferred across the Testaments.

But most of us find the first half of the Psalter much heavier. Here it is only the occasional psalm we treasure, whether for reasons similar to those just noted, or because of occasional further insights (like Pss 8, 15, 19), or New Testament appropriation (like Pss 2, 16, 22), or sublime encapsulations of faith (Ps 23). Otherwise this first half seems dominated by enemies and violence, suffering and pain, horror and despair, isolation from humans and alienation from God himself; and over all this hovers the ever-present specter of death. Insecurity is omnipresent; indeed, two-thirds of the psalms in Book I (Pss 1–41) mention enemies in one form or another, usually threatening life itself.[2] So those of us who read systematically through the Psalter in personal devotions or sing through it in liturgical settings often breathe a sigh of relief as we move from the first half to the second.

There are two key reasons for this disparity. One is experiential: most Christians in the developed world, most of the time, experience neither the overbearing prevalence of human enemies nor the haunting threat of death. By and large we live in tolerant societies, and we trust modern medicine for our ailments. And when life is threated, especially for the nonelderly, we instinctively pray for healing rather than prepare for death. This is certainly not to disparage those with different experiences, whether of extreme intolerance, harsh persecution, or tragic death. But, however viscerally painful and ideologically challenging, these situations are mercifully rare in our circles. Most of us know little of the edge-of-life experiences of our fellow believers in other parts of the contemporary world, or of our Christian forebears of previous centuries.

The other reason is theological: as Christians we have a different perspective on enemies, pain, suffering, and ultimately death. This is due, of course, to Christ, the center of our faith through his ministry, death, and resurrection. As 2 Timothy 1:10 reminds us: "Our Savior Christ Jesus …

2. Pslams 2, 3, 5, 6, 7, 8, 10, 11, 12, 13, 14, 17, 18, 21, 22, 23, 25, 27, 28, 31, 35, 36, 37, 38, 40, 41 (i.e., twenty-six out of the forty-one psalms). This list doesn't even include more general references to the wicked, as in Psalm 1. For "enemies" as a synonym of the wicked in binary opposition to the righteous, see Jerome F. D. Creach, "The Righteous and the Wicked," in *The Oxford Handbook of the Psalms*, ed. William P. Brown (Oxford: Oxford University Press, 2014), 531–32.

abolished death and brought life and immortality to light through the gospel."[3] He lifted the shroud of death (see Isa 25:7), preached and practiced forgiveness in this life, proclaimed divine judgment in the next, and above all promised continued blissful communion between God and his people. This has enabled countless Christians of all eras to live, suffer, and die, faithful to the same God as their Israelite predecessors, but with more light and a more positive expectation than theirs.

DEATH IN THE PSALTER: TWO ILLUSTRATIVE PSALMS

Two psalms vividly illustrate Old Testament perspectives on death and its consequence of descent to Sheol.[4] Occurring respectively near the beginning and end of the first half, they frame it and encapsulate its somber mood.[5]

Psalm 6 is a typical short lament, painting in a few vivid brushstrokes an anguished soul who languishes under a sense of divine rebuke (6:1) yet pours out their troubles to the same deity—shaking with terror, weeping all night, and wasting away through grief and anxiety (6:2–3, 6–7). This harrowing description surrounds a prayer for deliverance (6:4), including its motivation clause (6:5):

> For in death there is no remembrance of you;
> in Sheol who can give you praise?

Unless Yahweh intervenes, the psalmist envisages death and consignment to Sheol with no further memory of, or recourse to, God. But then the final verses are strikingly different. The psalmist now has a new confidence:[6] Yahweh has not just heard but accepted the prayer, and he will dispel all their enemies.

---

3. Scripture quotations are taken from the NRSV unless otherwise noted, mainly because of its rendering of Old Testament death terminology (see below). Verses are cited in their English numeration, which differs from the Hebrew in some psalms.

4. Much of this essay builds on research published in Philip S. Johnston, *Shades of Sheol: Death and Afterlife in the Old Testament* (Leicester: Apollos; Downers Grove, IL: InterVarsity, 2002).

5. A count of twenty-four psalms mentioning death and/or the underworld is given by Carleen Mandolfo, "Language of Lament in the Psalms," in Brown, *The Oxford Handbook of the Psalms*, 124.

6. The reason for such assurances in the laments has been much discussed. It has often been attributed to cultic prophecy, but a more plausible explanation is that laments were written after their prayers had been heard. See Hugh G. M. Williamson, "Reading the Lament Psalms Backwards," in *A God So Near*, ed. Brent A. Strawn and Nancy R. Bowen (Winona Lake, IN: Eisenbrauns, 2003), 3–16.

By contrast, Psalm 88 is both longer and darker. Indeed, it is often called the bleakest of all the psalms.[7] A sense of gloom and despair pervades all eighteen verses, and the psalm's last word in Hebrew as in most English translations is "darkness." Here the psalmist writhes under divine wrath, in tears night and day, abandoned by friends and assaulted by divine terrors that close in like a flood. This includes a lengthy reflection on the psalmist's impending fate (88:3–6, 10–12), the most extended of all such biblical descriptions:

> For my soul is full of troubles,
> and my life draws near to Sheol.
> I am counted among those who go down to the Pit;
> I am like those who have no help,
> like those forsaken among the dead,
> like the slain that lie in the grave,
> like those whom you remember no more,
> for they are cut off from your hand.
> You have put me in the depths of the Pit,
> in the regions dark and deep. …
>
> Do you work wonders for the dead?
> Do the shades rise up to praise you?
> Is your steadfast love declared in the grave,
> or your faithfulness in Abaddon?
> Are your wonders known in the darkness
> or your saving help in the land of forgetfulness?

The same themes as in Psalm 6 are writ large here: the psalmist approaches Sheol, also referenced by its synonyms "Pit" and "Abaddon" ("destruction"); the dead (here called shades) are entirely removed from all memory of life and from further interaction with both humans and God. But unlike Psalm 6 and most other laments, there is no flicker of hope, no vow of recommitment, no sense of a divine response, no premonition of

---

7. See W. S. Prinsloo, "Psalm 88: The Gloomiest Psalm?," *OTE* 5 (1992): 322–45; David M. Howard Jr., "Psalm 88 and the Rhetoric of Lament," in *"My Words Are Lovely": Studies in the Rhetoric of the Psalms*, ed. Robert Foster and David Howard, LHBOTS 467 (New York: T&T Clark, 2008), 132–46; David M. Howard Jr., "Preaching the Darkest Psalm: Psalm 88," in *Text Message: The Centrality of Scripture in Preaching*, ed. Ian Stackhouse and Oliver Crisp (Eugene, OR: Wipf and Stock, 2014), 54–66.

divine deliverance.[8] The best that can be said is that the psalmist is still alive and still able to pray.

While Psalms 6 and 88 present these views paradigmatically, they are far from unique. Similar views are frequent elsewhere: for example, "The dead do not praise the LORD" (115:17); "Turn your gaze away from me, that I may smile again, before I depart and am no more" (39:13); "My enemies wonder in malice when I will die and my name perish" (41:5). The rupture in relationship caused by death even affects Yahweh himself, as one psalmist boldly asserts: "The death of the devout costs Yahweh dear" (116:15, JB).[9]

DEATH AND SHEOL IN THE OLD TESTAMENT

These psalms illustrate certain key features of the Old Testament's portrayal of death and Sheol, the underworld, which we need to summarize briefly.[10] In common with other ancient Semitic cultures,[11] Israel envisaged a dark, gloomy underworld where the shades of the dead (*repāʾîm*) had some form of pathetic, flaccid existence. This was a place of no return, possibly gated and barred.[12] Ezekiel 32:20–30 envisages a vast cavern where uncircumcised warriors lie in their ethnic groups. Isaiah 14:9–11 imagines the somnolent shades being roused to greet the mighty king of Babylon with the devastating comment, "You have become weak like us." These sparse passages are the only biblical descriptions of Sheol. Instead, the prominent aspect of Sheol is that it is cut off from Yahweh, and its denizens are incapable of interaction with him, as noted above. (There is a minority conservative view that Sheol is simply the grave, as frequently translated in the NIV.[13] However, the arguments for this implicitly result from reading New

8. Contra the assertion of Claus Westermann, *Praise and Lament in the Psalms* (Atlanta: John Knox, 1981), 74: "There are no psalms which do not progress beyond petition and lament" (similarly at 266). Westermann does not discuss Psalm 88 or the almost equally bleak Psalm 39.

9. For this meaning, see also Derek Kidner, *Psalms 72–150*, TOTC (London: IVP, 1975), 410–11; and Nancy deClaissé-Walford, Rolf A. Jacobson, and Beth LaNeel Tanner, eds., *The Book of Psalms*, NICOT (Grand Rapids: Eerdmans, 2014), 861–62.

10. The following summary largely follows Philip S. Johnston, "Sheol," in *New Interpreter's Dictionary of the Bible*, Katharine D. Sakenfeld, vol. 5 (Nashville: Abingdon, 2009), 227.

11. But not Egypt; for this, see amongst many others Philip S. Johnston, "Death in Egypt and Israel: A Theological Reflection," in *The Old Testament in Its World*, ed. Robert P. Gordon and Johannes C. de Moor, OTS 52 (Leiden: Brill, 2004), 94–116.

12. Job 7:9 (despite Job's own wish, 14:13); 17:16.

13. Notably R. Laird Harris, "The Meaning of the Word Sheol as Shown by Parallels in Poetic Texts," *BETS* 4 (1961): 129–135; R . Laird Harris, "*šeʾôl*" in *Theological Wordbook of the Old Testament*, ed. R. L. Harris et al. (Chicago: Moody, 1980), 829–90. Harris argues inter alia that Psalm 88 refers only to the tomb, and Isaiah 14:9 is at most a figure of speech. As a senior translator

Testament afterlife perspectives back into the Old Testament, and they do not allow the older texts to speak for themselves in their own religio-cultural context.)

This Israelite view differs markedly from the more common ancient Near Eastern fascination with the underworld, as illustrated in several texts from the polytheistic Mesopotamia world—e.g., *Gilgamesh, The Descent of Ishtar*, and *Nergal and Ereshkigal*. One posited explanation for the contrast is that Israel may once have had a similar perspective but later orthodox redactors largely excised this.[14] However, the available evidence belies this view. The biblical text itself stresses the uniqueness of Yahweh as sole deity and his distinctive concern with life and the living, not death and the dead.

The Hebrew term *šeʾôl* is a proper name, occurring sixty-six times.[15] However, its occurrence has a very distinct profile. First, given the frequent mention of death in the many literary genres and historical contexts of the Hebrew Bible, this is a remarkably low number of occurrences. In comparison, the stem *m-w-t*, meaning "die/death," occurs one thousand times. This strongly suggests that the underworld was not a major Israelite preoccupation.[16]

Secondly, the term occurs unequally across the types of Hebrew literature: psalmodic, twenty-one times; wisdom, twenty times; prophetic, seventeen times; and narrative, eight times.[17] In sum, it occurs predominantly in reflective literature with personal engagement; conversely it occurs very seldom in narrative accounts with their more detached reporting, and then

---

Harris decisively influenced the NIV on this point; see Harris, "Why Hebrew She'ol was translated 'Grave', in *NIV: The Making of a Contemporary Translation*, ed. Kenneth L. Barker (London: Hodder & Stoughton, 1987), 72–92. However, it is noteworthy that the NIV could not maintain this interpretation consistently, needing alternatives like "depths of the grave" (Amos 9:2) or "realm of death" (Deut 32:22); for further critique see Johnston, *Shades of Sheol*, 73–75. The ESV avoids interpretation and renders *šeʾôl* without translation as "Sheol," like the NRSV.

14. This view, countered at length in *Shades of Sheol*, is frequent in scholarship; see, e.g., several articles in Alan Avery-Peck and Jacob Neusner, eds., *Judaism in Late Antiquity* 4, Handbook of Oriental Studies 1:49 (Leiden: Brill, 2000), including John Goldingay, "Death and Afterlife in the Psalms," 61–85.

15. Like other names, it never has the definite article ("the"). The total includes one generally accepted emendation, Isaiah 7:11. There are a few synonyms, notably *bôr/beʾēr, šaḥat* ("pit," "grave") and *ʾabaddôn* ("destruction"); these are less frequent, and their use complements that of *šeʾôl*.

16. Contra many scholars, including the oft-cited N. J. Tromp, *Primitive Conceptions of Death and the Nether World in the Old Testament* (Rome: Pontifical Biblical Institute, 1969). Tromp was heavily influenced by his doctoral supervisor Mitchell Dahood.

17. Psalms 6:5; 9:17; 16:10; 18:5; 30:3; 31:17; 49:14 (x2), 15; 55:15; 86:13; 88:3; 89:48; 116:3; 139:8; 141:7. Note that "psalmodic" here includes the psalms of Hannah, Hezekiah, and Jonah; and "wisdom" includes Deuteronomy 32.

only in direct speech.[18] Further, it is noticeably absent from nearly all narrative accounts of death. This implies that the term is only used in contexts of personal involvement.

Thirdly, the term occurs with different connotations: occasionally the cosmological extremity opposite the heavens above; or a general reference to the abode of the dead; or death's personification as a devourer of humans.[19] However, in well over half of its occurrences (some thirty-nine times), *še'ôl* indicates the fate of human beings. Here it connotes personal and emotional involvement, whether in regard to one's own destiny or that of one's perceived enemies. This supports the observation above that the Hebrew Bible is largely disinterested in speculating about the underworld per se and much more concerned with it as a human destiny.[20]

Regarding human fate, Sheol is predominantly one to which the ungodly are consigned.[21] These are often described in general terms as wicked, sinners, foolish rich, scoffers, and the immoral.[22] They can be named individuals, for example, Korah (and company), Joab, and Shimei. They can also be national enemies, for example, the king of Babylon, the Egyptians, and many uncircumcised warriors.[23] This identification of the underworld with the wicked is paramount.[24]

Sheol also occurs occasionally as the prospect for the apparently righteous (Jacob, Hezekiah, Job, and a psalmist), but arguably these are all in adverse situations interpreted as divine judgment.[25] In particular, in the case

18. There is a single, partial exception, where the narrator simply repeats Moses's words: Numbers 16:30, 33.

19. For example, see respectively: Job 11:8; 17:13; Hab 2:5.

20. By contrast, some have portrayed Sheol as a power invading life; see particularly Johannes Pedersen, *Israel: Its Life and Culture I-II* (London: Oxford University Press, 1926); Christoph F. Barth, *Die Errettung vom Tode in den individuellen Klage- und Dankliedern des Alten Testamentes* (Zollikon: Evangelischer, 1947; reissued by B. Janowski, ed., Stuttgart: Kohlhammer, 1997). This view is accepted by some later scholars, e.g., Hans-Joachim Kraus, *Psalms 1–59* and *Psalms 60–150* (Minneapolis: Augsburg, 1988 and 1989). While the prospect of Sheol undoubtedly influenced the living, this strand of scholarship is ill-founded; see Johnston, *Shades of Sheol*, ch. 4.

21. Also noted by James Barr, *The Garden of Eden and the Hope of Immortality* (London: SCM, 1992), 29; and Jon D. Levenson, *Resurrection and the Restoration of Israel* (New Haven: Yale University Press, 2006), 72–73.

22. Wicked: Job 21:13; Pss 9:17; 31:17; 141:7; Isa 5:14; sinners: Job 24:19; foolish rich: Ps 49:14; scoffers: Isa 28:15, 18; immoral: Prov 5:5; 7:27; 9:18.

23. Respectively Num 16:30, 33; 1 Kgs 2:6, 9; Isa 14:11, 15; Ezek 31:15–17; 32:18–32.

24. Similarly for the synonyms of *še'ôl*, e.g., *bôr*: Pss 28:1; 143:7; Isa 14:15, 19; Ezek 26:20 (x2); 31:14, 16; 32:18–30 (x5); *šaḥat*: Job 33:18–30 (x5); Ps 55:23; Isa 51:14; Ezek 28:8.

25. Gen 37:35; 42:38; 44:29, 31; Isa 38:10; Job 14:13; Ps 88:3. Later references to Jacob's death in Genesis 46–50 mostly use "die/death," but also "lie down with my ancestors" and "gathered to

of Jacob there is a marked contrast between him fearing that his gray hairs will descend to Sheol following the misfortune of his favorite sons, and later references to his eventual death with no mention of Sheol. Finally, two exceptional texts imply that everyone goes to Sheol; but one is in a historical context of disastrous judgment and the other in a skeptical context.[26] These few texts may attenuate the distinct bias noted, but they hardly negate it.

The Psalms clearly reflect this distinct bias. Many a psalmist in difficulty fears their own descent to Sheol, or rejoices in God's deliverance from it. Many implore God to bring their enemies down to Sheol, as fitting punishment for their antagonism to God's people and/or to God himself. However, both these observations need nuancing. For the latter, it is noteworthy that Sheol is never described as a place of punishment. Descent to it is the desired fate on the ungodly, to be permanently separated from family, humanity, and Yahweh. This itself is the punishment, and entails a continued, dreary, somnolent nonexistence. Punishment after death is a later development, arguably on the margins of the Old Testament but certainly not present in the Psalms.[27]

For the psalmists, the obvious question is whether they envisaged any alternative for themselves. The simple answer is that, by and large, they did not. The overwhelming majority of psalms (and other Old Testament texts) have a this-worldly perspective. After all, Yahweh is preeminently the God of life, not death![28] Their goal was continued communion with Yahweh here and now, then eventually after a full and fulfilling life to "go the way of all the earth."[29] Most Israelites seemed content with this. But a very few seemed to glimpse further, as discussed in the next section.

DEATH AND A POSITIVE AFTERLIFE?

The general perspective just outlined is so widely attested as to be incontrovertible and uncontroversial. But many readers and some scholars see at least occasional glimpses of an alternative fate. We will first examine the most likely three texts, then comment briefly on a few others.

---

my/his people" (Gen 47:30; 49:29, 33).

26. Ps 89:48; Eccl 9:10.

27. The AV/KJV's frequent translation of *šeʾôl* as "Hell" is clearly unhelpful since it retrojects later doctrine into the ancient Israelite world.

28. Notably in the grand finale of the longest Mosaic discourse (Deut 30:19–20).

29. See Josh 23:14; 1 Kgs 2:2.

Psalm 16 opens with a plea for protection, an affirmation of allegiance, and a repudiation of alternatives (16:1–4).[30] It continues with declarations of assurance, blessing, gratefulness, and confidence (16:5–9). It then concludes with this confidence extended into the future (16:10–11):

For you do not give me up to Sheol,
  or let your faithful one see the Pit.

You show me the path of life.
  In your presence there is fullness of joy;
  in your right hand are pleasures forevermore.

For most scholars, the psalmist envisages deliverance from imminent death in verse 1 and further communion with Yahweh in this current life, but accepts that this avoidance of Sheol is only temporary.

However, regardless of whether verse 1 envisages untimely death, this psalmist may have felt that Sheol was inappropriate for Yahweh's "faithful one" and instead affirmed an instinctive confidence in deliverance from it and some form of continued postmortem communion with Yahweh. But that form remains tantalizingly vague: no location is specified or named (unlike "Sheol"), no other beneficiaries are acknowledged, in fact no details are given at all. Only Yahweh's presence and blessing are clear (16:11). Faced with an underworld primarily for the ungodly, the psalmist at least affirms that some alternative is appropriate for the faithful, but goes no further.

Psalm 49 opens by addressing all humanity with proverbial wisdom (49:1–4),[31] and immediately poses the age-old riddle of why the wicked prosper (49:5–6) while the righteous suffer at their hands. It then responds in several stages: no amount of wealth can provide ransom from the grave (49:7–9);[32] regardless of wisdom or fame, all humans die like animals and leave their wealth to others (49:10–12); this applies specifically to the foolishly self-confident, who are assigned to Sheol (49:13–14).

---

30. Regardless of textual difficulties. On Psalm 16 see further Philip S. Johnston, "'Left in Hell'? Psalm 16, Sheol and the Holy One," in *The Lord's Anointed*, ed. Philip Satterthwaite, Richard Hess, and Gordon Wenham (Carlisle: Paternoster, 1995), 213–22; also Johnston, *Shades of Sheol*, 201–2.

31. See Johnston, *Shades of Sheol*, 202–4, for discussion of the many textual issues and a slightly different analysis (as two responses, in 49:7–14 and 49:15 respectively). Also, for more on Psalm 49 including its date, see Philip S. Johnston, "Psalm 49: A Personal Eschatology," in *"The Reader Must Understand": Eschatology in Bible and Theology*, ed. Kent Brower and Mark Elliott(Leicester: Apollos, 1997), 73–84.

32. Here *šaḥat* more likely means "pit of grave" than "underworld."

But then comes a remarkable affirmation: God himself will ransom the psalmist from Sheol (49:15).[33] Here, more explicitly than anywhere else in the Hebrew Bible, consignment of the ungodly to Sheol is contrasted with ransom of the godly from it. Many scholars interpret verse 15 as rescue from imminent death rather than from eventual fate. But this fails to do justice to the psalm generally, since the presenting issue is not only immediate persecution needing temporary relief but also a constant injustice needing full resolution.[34]

The psalm then concludes by repeating that the contented wealthy leave everything behind (49:16–20). They join their ancestors in the grave,[35] never again to see the light. The final verse reprises the refrain of verse 12, which concludes the similar earlier section on the renowned rich. This underlines that the foolish and famous wealthy, presumably ungodly, perish forever, in marked contrast to the wise psalmist.

Psalm 73 is another wisdom psalm that ponders the prosperity of the wicked. The psalmist openly envies them (73:1–14), but then enters the sanctuary and perceives their ruinous end (73:15–20). Realizing his own stupidity, he affirms that continued communion with God forms the very essence of personal existence (73:21–28). The psalm's turning point is the act of entering the sanctuary (73:17), and its highpoint is the terse affirmation (73:24): "afterward you will receive me with honor." Here the final term means "honor" or "dignity";[36] it never elsewhere indicates the afterlife, and its traditional translation here as "glory" unhelpfully connotes later Christian theology. The verb "take/receive" (*l-q-ḥ*) is sometimes seen as a conscious echo of Enoch in Genesis 5:24. But *l-q-ḥ* is as common a term in Hebrew as is "take" in English, with just as wide a semantic field,[37] so any such echo is at best tenuous. In sum, these two terms are at best ambiguous.

---

33. Peter C. Craigie, *Psalms 1–50*, WBC 19 (Waco, TX: Word, 1983), 360, reads verse 15 as the foolish hope of the self-confident, but this is unlikely both textually and interpretatively; cf. T. D. Alexander, "The Psalms and the Afterlife," *IBS* 9 (1987): 9; Johnston, *Shades of Sheol*, 204.

34. Also the final verb, "will receive," may imply more than mere preservation in life. The same verb l-q-ḥ occurs in Psalm 18:16 of immediate rescue, as made explicit in the parallel lines. But the context of Psalm 49 is quite different.

35. For the similar phrases "gathered to his people" and "slept with his fathers," see Johnston, *Shades of Sheol*, 33–35.

36. There is no preposition to indicate "'in/with" (though Hebrew poetry is not always syntactically precise).

37. P. J. J. S. Els lists seventeen different "linguistic and theological nuances" of the dominant qal form: : *"lqḥ"*, *NIDOTTE* 2:812–17.

The crucial term is therefore "after(ward)," which can be taken in different ways. Some see this as "after the present oppression," noting that there is no mention of death. The psalm ends by celebrating God's nearness and activity, presumably to a human audience; and a this-world interpretation fits the general view of the Psalms and the Hebrew Scriptures. Others counter that there is no obvious reference point for the adverb other than "after death"; verse 25 denies that the psalmist has any other concern "in heaven [or] on earth," and verse 26 contrasts his failing "flesh and heart" with God as his "portion forever."[38]

Like Psalm 49, Psalm 73 is often described as postexilic or late. Thematically, wisdom literature's wrestling with human suffering and divine wisdom is often placed at a late phase of Israel's theological development. Further, linguistically Psalm 73 has several Aramaisms, abstract plurals, and other features more common in late biblical literature. These arguments are certainly suggestive of a late date, though not conclusive. Form-critical and cult-functional study add little since wisdom psalms have no clear form and avoid cultic reference. However, redactional study may add insights. Some argue that Psalm 73 is strategically placed at the Psalter's midpoint between obedience (Ps 1) and praise (Ps 150), so its positioning was a final element of the book's composition.[39] Perhaps the Psalter's redactors picked it as one of the best examples of hope and saw it as pointing beyond death.[40]

Other psalms have sometimes been seen to point to a postmortem fate for the righteous other than Sheol. Psalm 1 concludes: "The wicked will not stand in the judgment" (1:5). Early Jewish and Christian commentators often read the passage eschatologically because of its reference to judgment and the use of "stand" (*q-w-m*) elsewhere for rising from the dead.[41]

However, while Psalm 1 may be among the latest written, neither this psalm in particular nor the Psalter in general suggests a significant belief

38. See, e.g., Kraus, *Psalms 60–150*, 91; more recently Janet Smith, *Dust or Dew* (Cambridge: James Clarke & Co., 2012).

39. Notably Walter Brueggemann, "Bounded by Obedience and Praise: The Psalms as Canon," *JSOT* 50 (1991): 63–92; reprinted in *The Psalms and the Life of Faith* (Minneapolis: Fortress, 1995), 189–213.

40. For a similar argument that various psalms have been reinterpreted in an eschatological redaction, see David C. Mitchell, *The Message of the Psalter*, JSOTSup 252 (Sheffield: Sheffield Academic, 1997).

41. Hypothetical in Job 14:12; foreseen in Isaiah 26:14, 19. Further points, arguably more tenuous, are noted by John F. A. Sawyer, "Hebrew Words for the Resurrection of the Dead," *VT* 23 (1973): 232.

in resurrection. Most scholars think Psalm 1 originally referred to the present life, with "judgment" indicating some civil or religious procedure in the gathered community. The psalms refer regularly to the worshiping community and occasionally to the personal integrity required to join it (Pss 15, 24). Psalm 1 itself has a present-life perspective, both in the opening description (1:1–3) and crucially in the final verse following this reference to judgment (1:6). Also, *q-w-m* is one of the most common Hebrew verbs and refers predominantly to ordinary physical movement. Psalm 1 was certainly later read in eschatological terms, but this was more a rereading than the original intent.

Psalm 23 ends, "And I will dwell in the house of the LORD for ever," in the ubiquitous traditional version (23:6, KJV/AV). However, the Hebrew here is not the common *lᵉʿôlām* ("for ever") but rather the unusual *lᵉʾôrek yāmîm,* literally "for length of days," as reflected in modern translations like the NRSV: "my whole life long."[42] This parallels "all the days of my life" in the previous line; it does not extend the verse's affirmation beyond this life.

Psalms 17 and 139 refer to waking: "When I awake, I shall be satisfied, beholding your likeness" (Ps 17:15b); "When I awake, I am still with you" (Ps 139:18b RSV, NIV). The verb *q-y-ṣ* normally means waking from sleep in life, but occasionally from the sleep of death, notably in the only two clear Old Testament references to personal resurrection.[43] Hence interpretation in the common era has taken one or both of these as an expectation of seeing God after death.[44]

However, in neither case is this obvious or necessary. In Psalm 17, though surrounded by threatening enemies, the psalmist refers not to death but to nocturnal testing (17:3), so the psalmist likely desires to wake more from sleep than from death. Psalm 139 doesn't even refer to sleep, let alone death, though it does mention night's darkness earlier. The immediate context is of divine vastness, hence some versions and scholars translate verse 18b instead as "I come to the end."[45]

---

42. Also in footnotes from pre-twentieth century versions onward, e.g., RV (1885), RSV (1952), NASB (1960). The immediate perspective is further underlined by the MT's verb "return" (rather than the LXX's "dwell"), as followed by deClaissé-Walford, Jacobson, and Tanner, *The Book of Psalms*, 240.

43. Isa 26:19; Dan 12:2; see Johnston, *Shades of Sheol*, 224–27. Also wakening from death: 2 Kgs 4:31; Job 14:12; Jer 51:39, 57.

44. Johnston, *Shades of Sheol*, 206–7, notes Christian sources for the former and Jewish for the latter.

45. So NRSV (from *qēṣ*, not *q-y-ṣ*). Also Leslie C. Allen, *Psalms 101–150*, WBC 21 (Waco, TX: Word, 1983), 253. Allen describes the afterlife interpretation as "both contextually inappropriate ...

Several elements recur in the psalms just discussed: textual ambiguity, late composition of psalms, even later compilation of the Psalter, and reinterpretation in light of developing theology. This is easily explained. The Qumran scrolls (especially 11QPs[a]) suggest there was still canonical fluidity of the Psalter in the immediate pre-Christian period, leading many to conclude with Nancy deClaissé-Walford: "The book of Psalms appears to be one of the latest books of the Old Testament to achieve ... final form."[46] The French term *relecture* ("rereading") was first used by scholars to describe the process of biblical editors reinterpreting older material when resetting it in a new context. But the term can extend to reinterpretation of older texts without necessarily resetting the original or emending its wording. In this way, these psalms can be seen to illustrate *relecture*. While the Old Testament texts generally exhibit no concept of a positive afterlife, hints of this emerged in response mainly to the catastrophe of exile and the political uncertainties of the ensuing centuries. And as this concept developed, older texts were reread and new texts written to reflect it.[47]

A PROPER CHRISTIAN READING OF ALL THE PSALTER

So, as Christians with a different understanding of death and the afterlife, how should we read these psalms? How can we use them devotionally—or can we even do this at all? Arguably there are three important steps.

First, we remember that the Psalms, as part of the Old Testament, contain much else that doesn't translate easily into Christian theology or devotion. Ancient Israel was an ethnic people, in a specific geographical location, with a divinely chosen capital city, and a human king who fought physical battles. They had a legal system incorporating religious responsibilities as well as civil punishments. They had a single temple for the whole nation, where animal sacrifices were performed daily by a hereditary priestly clan. They fulfilled vows and presented obligatory tithes. They prayed enthusiastically for vengeance and the demise of their enemies. By contrast, nothing in this long list applies to Christians. We tend to lose sight of this when reading the Psalter, mainly because the psalms express the essence of faith more than its structure, and they engage our emotions before our intellect.

---

and probably theologically anachronistic."

46. deClaissé-Walford, Jacobson, and Tanner, *The Book of Psalms*, 24.

47. For a fuller exploration of this with respect to messianism, see Philip S. Johnston, "Suffering Saints, Glorious Kings and Divine Deliverance: Context and *Relecture* in the Psalms," in *The Seed of Promise*, ed. Paul R. Williamson and Rita F. Cefalu, GlossaHouse Festschrift Series 3 (Wilmore, KY: GlossaHouse, 2020), 142–61.

As a result, when we meet such elements in our reading, we either omit them (as we often do in public reading, especially the vengeful verses) or we mentally translate them into a Christian equivalent. This reflex has become so instinctive that we think of the Psalter as almost Christian.[48] So the first step is to note these pre-Christian elements, and simply acknowledge them without feeling the need to baptize them in some way or other.

Secondly, we note that the standard Israelite perspective on death and Sheol interconnects with other aspects of Old Testament theology. When there is no general prospect of an afterlife, this life is all the more precious. When there is no righting of wrongs after death, in order for God to be truly supreme, his justice must be seen in this life; so those who oppose him must be punished in the here and now. The Israelite view on death is integrated into many other aspects of their faith—a faith which forms the bedrock of ours, but is not the same as ours.

Thirdly, we see glimpses of an alternative. As noted, this is clearest in Psalm 49, and is perhaps also present in Psalms 16 and 73, and possibly elsewhere, at least as the psalms were later interpreted. Just as some psalmists or later editors may have glimpsed beyond the Israelite king to a super-king, so some glimpsed beyond the apparently final separation of death to continued life with God. We can note these as foretastes of what was to come, of the light which would eventually break through in the gospel of our Savior Christ Jesus. And we can rejoice in this inspired prescience without having to impute the same insight into the majority of texts which retain the standard view of death as separation from the God of life.

48. Scholarly introductions to the Psalms abound with quotes to this effect, from Athanasius and Augustine to Luther, Calvin, and beyond; see most recently W. H. Bellinger, *Psalms as a Grammar for Faith* (Waco, TX: Baylor University Press, 2020), 2–3.

11

Psalm 32: More Accurately a Declarative Praise than Penitential Psalm

Daniel J. Estes

For centuries, Psalm 32 has traditionally been considered one of the seven penitential psalms. Although it does touch on the psalmist's repentance for his sin, the psalm is actually a song of thanksgiving as the psalmist reflects on the joy he has received after experiencing God's forgiveness. In this spirit, he calls on other worshipers to follow his pattern by confessing their sins and by rejoicing in the blessing of the Lord's forgiveness and the happiness that forgiveness gives.

Psalm 32 has traditionally been included among the seven penitential psalms, along with Psalms 6, 38, 51, 102, 130, and 143,[1] but a careful reading of this psalm calls that familiar designation into question. Although Robert Alter insists that this psalm is "a confession in the perfect sense: the speaker admits he has transgressed, affirms that he has confessed his transgression, and that as a result God has granted him forgiveness,"[2] Psalm 32 is rather different from a truly penitential psalm like Psalm 51, in which the psalmist presents a confession of sin as a performative act of contrition. There is, to be sure, penitential content in Psalm 32 in the psalmist's retrospection in verse 5, but its overall form corresponds closely to the standard pattern of

1. See, for example, the discussions in Beth Tanner, "Preaching the Penitential Psalms," *Word & World* 27 (2007): 88–98, and in Harry P. Nasuti, *Defining the Sacred Songs: Genre, Tradition and the Post-Critical Interpretation of the Psalms* (Sheffield: Sheffield Academic, 1999), 30–56.
2. Robert Alter, *The Book of Psalms* (New York: Norton, 2007), 110.

declarative praise (call to praise, report of deliverance, conclusion), with the initial benediction functioning as a proclamation to praise in verses 1–2, the psalmist's report of deliverance in verses 3–10, and a concluding call to praise in verse 11.

The psalmic superscriptions cannot be dated with certainty, but they do at least constitute the earliest extant interpretive comments on the psalms. In this case, the superscription links Psalm 32 to David, and this could plausibly reflect the historical record in 2 Samuel 11–12 that narrates David's adultery with Bathsheba, his arranged murder of her husband Uriah, and his subsequent long refusal to confess his sin. H. C. Leupold suggests that Psalm 32 may have been the fulfillment of the vow made in Psalm 51:13 (MT 15),[3] a psalm also attributed to David, when the psalmist says, "Then I will teach transgressors your ways, so that sinners will turn back to you."[4] There is no way to prove definitively this setting for Psalm 32, but it is the kind of situation that fits the content of the psalm, and it would match the description of the psalm as a *maśkîl*, an instruction psalm,[5] and its sapiential language in verses 8–10. What is undeniable is that the psalmist, identified as David by Paul in Romans 4:6–8, relates a cautionary tale from his own experience. In effect, he says to his audience, "I am telling you this so that you will learn from my mistakes." As he discloses how the Lord has delivered him from his guilt, the psalmist instructs others so that they will learn from his example how to turn to the Lord with their sins, so that they can receive his forgiveness and live joyfully in it.

EXPOSITION OF PSALM 32

Benediction (32:1–2)

Similar to the structure of Psalm 73, in which the psalmist's experience traced in verses 2–28 is summarized in the opening thematic statement in verse 1, the text of Psalm 32 begins where the experience of the psalmist ended. The two opening benedictions speak of people who are happy (*'ašrê*), not because they are perfect in their sinlessness, but because they have been forgiven of their sins by the Lord. As Peter Craigie notes, "The

3. H. C. Leupold, *Exposition of the Psalms* (Columbus, OH: Wartburg, 1959), 269.

4. All Scripture citations are from the NIV 2011, unless otherwise noted.

5. James Limburg, *Psalms*, Westminster Bible Companion (Louisville: Westminster John Knox, 2000), 103, notes that *maśkîl* also appears in verse 8, where it refers to the Lord's instruction concerning the way the psalmist should go.

psalmist views humans as sinning beings, whose possibility of happiness lies in the removal and forgiveness of that sin."[6] Three of the most common Old Testament words for sin are used in verses 1–2, *peša'*, which connotes rebellion against God's rule;[7] *ḥaṭṭā't*, which indicates missing the mark of God's will;[8] and *'āwōn*, which features distortion of God's desires.[9] These are overlapping synonyms that together span the full range of evil human actions and attitudes against God. The blessed person, however, has been forgiven, with the effect that *peša'* has been lifted and removed, *ḥaṭṭā't* covered from sight, and *'āwōn* not placed on the legal record. In explaining the sense of the verb *ḥšb* in verse 2, John Hartley observes, "Yahweh's granting forgiveness is here stated in a metaphor from accounting in order to communicate that such a person has full assurance that nothing will ever be exacted from that one for past sin."[10]

What is suggested by the passive verbs in verse 1 (cf. Ps 85:2 [MT 3]) is specified by the divine subject of the verbs in verse 2a, as the Lord is the one who graciously provides forgiveness for sinners (cf. Ps 130:4). This forgiveness, however, is not cheap grace, because the Lord requires honest, genuine repentance by one "in whose spirit is no deceit" (32:2b; cf. 52:2 [MT 4]; 101:7; 120:2–3). The Lord is not fooled by phony words and empty promises, so to receive his forgiveness a sinner must be totally candid with him. As Artur Weiser states, "We must be absolutely truthful in our relationship with God and with ourselves; for man's absolute truthfulness in his relationship with God and with his own self form, together with God's grace, the two foundation-pillars not only of penitence but of man's whole relationship with God."[11]

---

6. Peter C. Craigie, *Psalms 1–50*, WBC 19 (Waco, TX: Word, 1983), 266.

7. See discussions by Eugene Carpenter and Michael A. Grisanti, *NIDOTTE* 3:706–10, and by H. Ringgren and H. Seebass, *TDOT* 12:133–51.

8. See discussions by Alex Luc, *NIDOTTE* 2:87–93 and by K. Koch, *TDOT* 4:309–19.

9. See discussions by Alex Luc, *NIDOTTE* 3:351 and by K. Koch, *TDOT* 10:546–62.

10. John E. Hartley, *NIDOTTE* 2:305.

11. Artur Weiser, *The Psalms: A Commentary*, OTL, trans. Herbert Hartwell, 5th ed. (Philadelphia: Westminster, 1962), 283–84. Similarly, Allen P. Ross, *A Commentary on the Psalms Volume 1 (1–41)*, Kregel Exegetical Library (Grand Rapids: Kregel Academic & Professional, 2011), 711, explains: "Those who are truly penitent will have no such deceit in their confession—they will fully acknowledge their sin. The absence of 'guile' is a qualification for the forgiveness. God knows whether the confession is genuine or the individual is simply going through a confessional

This initial section of Psalm 32 takes the form of a benediction or exclamation of happiness. At the same time, in opening this declarative praise psalm, this benediction takes the place of what is customarily the call to praise. In effect, then, verses 1–2 function as an invitation to those who hear and sing this psalm to appropriate it as their own, as will become explicit in the final verse of the psalm. With these words, the psalmist urges other people to join with him in a response to the Lord that will result in their own celebratory thanksgiving to him.

Report of Deliverance (32:3–10)

The psalmist has not always felt the happiness he expresses in the benedictions in verses 1–2. Beginning in verse 3, he takes his readers on the journey that led him to the happiness of forgiveness, sharing his story as an example from which others can learn. After his sin, the psalmist's first impulse was to keep silent, and thus to deny his sin. As Adam and Eve hid from the Lord after their disobedience (Gen 3:8), so the psalmist's silence refers to his refusal to confess his sin (contra Ps 32:5). His silent denial, however, only tore him apart with guilt, for he discloses, "My bones wasted away through my groaning all day long." This intense internal turmoil that penetrated even to his bones (cf. Pss 6:2 [MT 3]; 31:10 [MT 11]; 38:3 [MT 4]; 42:10 [MT 11])[12] reflects the high price tag for the guilt of unconfessed sin.

The longer the psalmist refused to yield to the Lord and kept silent about his sin, the more he experienced the heavy hand of God's conviction upon him (32:4). In passages such as Isaiah 41:10, the hand of the Lord refers to his strength to help his people in their needs, but it can also refer to his judgment and conviction of sin, as here and in 1 Samuel 5:6 and 11. This divine conviction weighed upon him perpetually, throughout the day and night, with debilitating effect.[13] The psalmist discloses that as a result of God's

---

but without remorse for the sin or desire to change. There is full forgiveness for the one who confesses, but the confession must be honest."

12. Robert B. Chisholm, *NIDOTTE* 3:500, observes, "The bones were often viewed as the seat of one's physical strength and health. ... Those overcome by fear spoke of their bones shaking, while those enduring intense physical pain or emotional distress frequently complained that their bones were weakened." The high price of guilt is the prominent theme in William Shakespeare's play, *Macbeth*.

13. Craigie, *Psalms 1–50*, 267, explains, "The 'heavy hand' of God, experienced within the mind and conscience, indicates an awareness of the need for repentance, but a stubborn refusal to yield to God. And the sinner's silence, aggravated by the heavy hand of God, contributed to the dry curling of the tongue, as in one desperate for water in a desert; so long as the tongue refused to speak the words of repentance, it curled in speechless pain."

hand pressing upon him his vitality "was sapped as in the heat of summer." He felt as though his bodily fluids were dried up by the summer drought,[14] as unrelenting conviction immobilized him. He experienced what many others have learned through their own struggles: that unconfessed sin paralyzes, crushes, and enslaves those who refuse to acknowledge their sinful faults.

If Psalm 32 emerges from the experience of David, as Romans 4:6–8 indicates, and if it specifically refers to David's adultery with Bathsheba recorded in 2 Samuel 11–12, which is a credible possibility although it cannot be determined with certainty, then David in that experience kept silent about his sin for at least nine months, until after their son was born. Only after being confronted by the prophet Nathan did David confess his sin to the Lord (2 Sam 12:13). Until that time, he lived under the heavy hand of God's conviction. Whether or not this is the specific occasion for Psalm 32, it is the kind of confession reflected in verse 5. In continuing his narrative, the psalmist indicates, "Then I acknowledged my sin [*ḥaṭṭā't*] to you and did not cover up my iniquity [*'āwōn*]. I said, 'I will confess my transgressions [*peša'*] to the Lord.'" Using the same three terms as in verses 1–2, he did not soft-pedal his offenses against the Lord, but all that he had long denied he at last admitted honestly and completely. When he did that, the Lord in keeping with his gracious character (see Exod 34:6–7; Num 14:18; Ps 85:2 [MT 3]) responded by removing the iniquity of his sin, for as 1 John 1:9 states, God is always ready to forgive the sins of those who truly confess them to him.[15] As a result, the psalmist's heavy burden of guilt was lifted from him, and he began to experience the freedom of forgiveness.

The introductory "therefore" in verse 6 signals that what the psalmist has experienced personally he now applies more broadly to others: "Therefore let all the faithful pray to you while you may be found." He has learned through his pain while resisting the Lord's conviction that it is better to yield to the Lord than to have to endure his heavy hand. The Lord can turn up his pressure to break a stubborn heart. Changing his image, the psalmist now pictures God's conviction as the rising of mighty waters,

14. Allen P. Ross, *NIDOTTE*, 4:452 observes: "Cakes or breads were often prepared with oil. The word *lāšād* describes a cake baked with olive oil, or one that has the taste of fresh oil. The basic idea of the word is moist or moisture; in fact, it is used in Ps 32:4 for the fluids and moisture of the body."

15. Douglas McC. L. Judisch, "Propitiation in the Language and Typology of the Old Testament," *CBQ* 48 (1984): 233, concludes, "Only those people of the Old Testament era enjoy eternal life with God who trusted in the propitiation of God which the Messiah was to accomplish."

which in Psalm 69:1–2 (MT 2–3) speak of the torrential rain of divine discipline. The term here is *šēṭep*, which is used six times in the Old Testament, usually with the nuance of judgment (see Neh 1:8; Dan 9:26). The flood of divine conviction is indeed powerful in its destructive potential, but those mighty waters do not reach the faithful who pray to the Lord,[16] confessing their sins. They, like the psalmist, will come to experience that God's grace is able to deliver them from the flood of divine judgment that would otherwise consume them.

As long as the psalmist refused to confess his sin, he experienced the pain of divine conviction upon him (32:3–4). What was it that prompted him to turn to the Lord in repentance in verse 5? In verse 7 he articulates his confession of trust in the Lord that caused him to view the Lord as the solution rather than the problem. The psalmist came to recognize that the Lord was not his enemy, but rather his champion who protects and preserves him, a familiar truth in the Psalms, for example in Psalms 27:5; 31:20 (MT 21); 61:4 (MT 5); 91:1; and 119:114. The Lord is not someone from whom to hide, but he is in fact the hiding place for the psalmist. Instead of bringing trouble upon the psalmist, the Lord is the one who protects him from trouble. The Lord is the deliverer who encircles those who trust in him (see Ps 32:10; Deut 32:10), protecting them on all sides, so that they can rejoice with songs celebrating his deliverance of them.

The words of instruction in verses 8–9 have been construed in two different ways by commentators. Weiser links these verses with verse 10, arguing that "the poet now turns to the community of the godly ones whom he wants to spare the bitter experience of his own struggle."[17] However, several times in the Psalms the Lord is described as teaching humans his way (16:11; 25:9), or individuals call on the Lord to teach them his way (27:11; 86:11), so Hans-Joachim Kraus is likely right when he concludes that verses 8–9 "are to be understood as the words of a divine statement quoted in a song of thanksgiving."[18] This is the divine truth that the Lord has taught

16. P. A. Verhoef, *NIDOTTE* 4:1062, notes, "To pray is an act of faith in the almighty and gracious God, who responds to the prayers of his people. It is a privilege, but also a responsibility to pray. It is a privilege to communicate one's deepest needs and wishes to a God who hears, but at the same time it is a great responsibility to pray in such a manner that the prayer is acceptable to God."

17. Weiser, *The Psalms*, 286.

18. Hans-Joachim Kraus, *Psalms 1–59*, 5th ed., trans. Hilton C. Oswald, Continental Commentary (Minneapolis: Fortress, 1993), 371. Similarly, Willem A. VanGemeren, "Psalms," in *Expositor's Bible Commentary*, ed. Frank E. Gaebelein (Grand Rapids: Zondervan, 1991), 5:274 observes, "He quotes Yahweh, who has promised to instruct his children, give them wisdom, and watch over them."

the psalmist as he has meditated on his painful experience. Verse 8 has a concentration of wisdom terms, including "instruct" (*śkl*), "teach" (*yrh*), "way" (*derek*), and "counsel" (*y'ṣ*). The psalmist previously took his own way into sin and guilt (see Prov 14:12), but he has come to realize that the Lord has a much better way for him to go. The Lord calls the psalmist to lay down his stubborn resistance and denial, and to surrender to divine leadership that gives true direction for life. All the while, the Lord will keep his eye upon him, as he attentively looks out for the welfare of his pupil.

The pronouns in verse 8 are singular, but in verse 9 they are plural, signaling that the instruction by the Lord is not directed to the psalmist alone, but it is intended for all humans, and this parallels the psalmist's own address to all the faithful to learn from his personal example in verse 6. When the Lord instructs people in the way they should go, he desires their willing compliance as they accept their role as students in his school. However, stubborn refusal to accept the Lord's counsel by not confessing sin (see 32:3–4) is an invitation to sterner measures by the Lord, as the psalmist has learned only too well from his experience. It is unreasonable to resist the Lord by holding on to sin, and indeed it is the path of folly, as Proverbs 26:3 admonishes: "A whip for the horse, a bridle for the donkey, and a rod for the backs of fools!" Here in Psalm 32:9, the Lord cautions, "Do not be like the horse or the mule, which have no understanding but must be controlled by bit and bridle or they will not come to you."[19] Animals without understanding have to be compelled by force, but humans should respond to the Lord's wise counsel by confessing their sins to him. If they do not, then they, like the psalmist, will feel the force of the heavy hand of divine conviction upon them.

The psalmist draws his report of deliverance to a conclusion in verse 10, as he contrasts the two paths he has taken in his experience. He has walked down both paths, so he knows which is better by far. At first, he took the wicked path as he held on to his sin rather than confessing it to the Lord (32:3). During that protracted time, he felt the full force of the woes of the Lord's discipline (Ps 32:3–4; see also Jer 30:15; Lam 1:12, 18). By contrast, once he confessed his sin honestly and completely (32:5), he came to realize that "the LORD's unfailing love surrounds the one who trusts in him" (32:10). In this verse, the psalmist generalizes from his personal experience to the

19. Leupold, *Exposition of the Psalms*, 267, comments, "Refusal to let oneself be guided by the Lord's kindly direction puts one in the class of the brute beasts that must at times be controlled by forcible and harsh means when they refuse gentle guidance." Similar imagery is used in Psalms 49:20 (MT 21) and 73:21–22.

broader reality that holding on to sin only increases sorrow for those who are wicked, but those who trust in the Lord experience his protective love. This is what he has learned and what he now teaches as his cautionary tale to others.

Call to Praise 32:11

In the final verse of the psalm, the psalmist calls on other righteous people to join him in rejoicing in the Lord. He uses three verbs that are all in the semantic field of joy, as he exhorts those who like him have experienced God's forgiveness to rejoice (*śimḥû*), be glad (*gîlû*), and sing (*harnînû*). These three imperatives may possibly crescendo from private gladness to public declaration as those who are upright in heart proclaim their joy in the Lord. Previously, when the psalmist refused to confess his sin, he was silent (32:3), because his sin stole his song. He has learned, however, that the Lord's forgiveness fills the heart with joy. This concluding note of rejoicing is the tone in which Psalm 32 begins in verses 1–2, as the psalmist rejoices in the forgiveness the Lord has graciously given to him, and he urges others to join with him as they follow his example.

THEME OF PSALM 32

VanGemeren observes well that in Psalm 32 "contrition is viewed ... in its truly biblical context as a deep sorrow for sin coupled with and followed by confession, forgiveness, and an openness to the wisdom of God."[20] As the psalmist addresses the issues of sin and guilt, he brings to light what humans too often endeavor to hide, and he makes clear that confession of sin is a crucial part of maintaining one's relationship with the Lord. The initial benediction formula and the concluding calls to rejoice that frame the psalm indicate that its theme is that true happiness comes from accepting the Lord's forgiveness, and "this is presented in stark contrast to the spiritual depression and sorrow under divine discipline that comes from stubbornly refusing to confess sin."[21] By relating his own cautionary tale, the psalmist exhorts his readers to learn from his painful example the wisdom of confessing their sins early and honestly to the Lord, with the assurance that he will graciously forgive their sins and restore their joy. In many respects, Psalm 32 unpacks and expands the truth stated in Proverbs 28:13: "Whoever conceals their sins does not prosper, but the one who confesses

---

20. VanGemeren, "Psalms," 5:270.

21. Ross, *A Commentary on the Psalms Volume 1 (1–41)*, 705.

and renounces them finds mercy." Paul in Romans 4:6–8 cites Psalm 32:1–2 as an example of God graciously crediting righteousness to David apart from works.[22] Because of this New Testament citation, Christians have long read Psalm 32 "in the light of the pardon offered to faith in Jesus Christ."[23]

RESPONSE TO PSALM 32

Psalm 32 was composed originally as the thanksgiving song of an individual who, after denying his sin and experiencing the force of divine conviction, had at last confessed his sin and was now rejoicing in the blessing of the Lord's forgiveness. Its inclusion in the Psalter signals its broader appropriation by the people of God. Both the ancient Israelites and the early Christians sang the psalms in their worship (see 1 Cor 14:26; Eph 5:19; Col 3:16; Jas 5:13), as have the people of the Lord up to the present time as they turn to him across the range of their experiences. In articulating Psalm 32 as their response to the Lord, worshipers are prompted by the psalm to deal honestly with their sin by confessing it fully, and then to rejoice in the assurance of forgiveness that is available from their gracious Lord.

Like the psalmist, whose first impulse was to deny his sin (32:3), humans are prone to try to ignore the issue of their sin and guilt, but they cannot. Finding it difficult to admit when they are wrong, they attempt to deny, to hide, and to rename their faults. When confronted about their sins, their typical impulse is to attack the messenger rather than accept the message. Their stubborn pride is a barrier to their holiness and indeed to their true happiness.

In his cautionary tale in Psalm 32, the psalmist provides a pattern that needs to be followed by God's people, a pattern he has learned through his own painful experience. First, stop ignoring or denying the problem of sin. Rather than redefining it away, for example by calling it "inappropriate" instead of acknowledging that it is wrong and evil, call sin by its proper name. In reality, sin is rebelling against God's rule, missing God's mark, and distorting his desires. Second, honestly confess the sin to God, as well as to those who have been wronged. The Lord is faithful in forgiving sins when they are confessed to him (see 1 John 1:9), because his grace is greater than

22. Andrew Hassler, "Ethnocentric Legalism and the Justification of the Individual: Rethinking Some New Perspective Assumptions," *JETS* 54 (2011): 327 reasons that the citation of Psalm 32:1–2 in Romans 4:6–8, as well as the citations of Psalm 143:2 in Galatians 2:16 and in Romans 3:20, support an individual element in justification: "how the individual is counted as righteous before God apart from works and in spite of sin."

23. James L. Mays, *Psalms*, Interpretation (Louisville: John Knox, 1994), 146.

human sin. Third, and this is the prominent tone of Psalm 32 (verses 1–2, 11), those who have been forgiven by God must accept the blessing of the happiness that his forgiveness gives. People are sometimes heard to say, "I know that God has forgiven me, but I cannot forgive myself for what I did." That kind of false guilt in effect says that the person has a higher standard for herself than the Lord does, and therefore cannot feel fully forgiven. By contrast, what Psalm 32 and the entire biblical testimony teaches is that God's forgiveness in response to honest confession is total and unconditional, and it must be accepted as such by the recipients of his grace. That is what David experienced when he at last confessed his sin with Bathsheba, and it is the experience that all of God's people are invited to enjoy, as they appropriate for themselves the pattern set forth in the declarative praise song in Psalm 32.

12

Theology of the Nations in the Book of Psalms

Ryan J. Cook

The Psalter references other nations or people groups frequently and in richly diverse ways. This essay seeks to understand the role and function of these references in the book of Psalms. It conducts this study by outlining the diverse roles the nations play in the Psalter. Israel's relationship with the nations was a key part of its identity and helped Israel to understand its own mission and purpose, providing it with a compelling eschatological vision.

INTRODUCTION

The Psalter is a uniquely appropriate place to embark on a theology of the Old Testament.[1] There are many reasons for this. The Psalter includes texts from the earliest periods of Israel's history through the postexilic period. This allows theological emphases from different eras to be collected. Additionally, individual psalms come from a variety of contexts in ancient Israel and reflect their origins (e.g., royal psalms, northern psalms, psalms from a familial worship context, and psalms from the temple). This diverse collection of poems was then edited and structured in the Second Temple

1. W. H. Bellinger Jr., "The Psalms as a Place to Begin for Old Testament Theology," in *Psalms and Practice: Worship, Virtue, and Authority*, ed. Stephen Breck Reed (Collegeville, MN: Liturgical Press, 2001), 28–39; Robert Wallace, "The Psalms as a Place to Begin for Old Testament Theology," *PRSt* 44 (2017): 239–48; Patrick D. Miller, "The Psalter as a Book of Theology," in *Psalms in Community: Jewish and Christian Textual, Liturgical, and Artistic Traditions*, ed. Harold Attridge and Margot Fassler (Atlanta: SBL Press, 2003), 87–98.

period, which brought an additional sense of unity to the collection.[2] Thus, on almost any theological topic, the Psalter embodies both the rich diversity and the underlying unity of the Old Testament canon as a whole. This is especially true of Israel's relationship with the nations.

The Old Testament canon displays a conceptual tension between nationalism and universalism in its relationship with the nations.[3] As John Goldingay describes it, "On the one side, the whole world is called to revere Yhwh, its maker, the one who asserted control of the forces of disorder by a word of power. ... On the other side, Yhwh frustrates the intentions of the nations and insists on being the only one whose plan gets fulfilled, and this explicitly works for the benefit of Israel."[4] That this tension exists is not surprising when one considers how Israel's situation vis-à-vis the nations changed throughout the course of its long history. This essay will explore five themes relating Israel and the nations from the Psalms, which are grounded in Israel's understanding of God's character and of God's plan for them and the world.

THE NATIONS AS CREATED BY GOD

One of Israel's foundational beliefs was that God created the world. Naturally, many Psalms celebrate this fact.[5] In a few contexts, celebrating Yahweh as Creator includes a consideration of the nations. After praising Yahweh as Creator, Psalm 33 compels the nations to recognize his sovereignty, "Let all the peoples fear Yahweh, all who dwell in the cultivated land stand in awe of him" (Ps 33:8). The implication behind this call to praise is that as Creator, Yahweh has jurisdiction over all peoples.[6]

This theme does not surface frequently in the Psalter and is not structurally highlighted. It functions more as a presupposition that the psalmists work from. This underlying belief comes to the surface in Psalm 24:1–2:

2. For a discussion of the current state of editorial criticism on the Psalms, see Nancy L. deClaissé-Walford, ed. *The Shape and Shaping of the Book of Psalms: The Current State of Scholarship* (Atlanta: SBL Press, 2014).

3. Duane Christensen, "Nations," ed. David Noel Freedman, *ABD* (New York: Doubleday, 1992), 4:1037.

4. John Goldingay, *Old Testament Theology: Israel's Gospel*, vol. 1 (Downers Grove, IL: IVP Academic, 2003), 59.

5. See Geoffrey Grogan, *Prayer, Praise, and Prophecy: A Theology of the Psalms* (Ross-shire, UK: Christian Focus, 2001), 77–81.

6. Gordon Wenham, *The Psalter Reclaimed: Praying and Praising with the Psalms* (Wheaton, IL: Crossway, 2012), 165.

Belonging to YHWH is the earth and its fullness,
the cultivated land and those who live in it.
For he has founded it upon the seas,
and established it on the rivers.[7]

The psalm asserts that Yahweh is God, not only of the Israelites and their land, but of the entire earth and its population.[8] The basis for this assertion is found in verse 2. The terms "seas" (יַמִּים) and "rivers" (נְהָרוֹת) reflect ancient Near Eastern cosmology. In most Canaanite thinking the waters are personified as gods who have to be conquered and tamed for the world to exist. However, the psalmist uses the terms "in a demythologized and depersonified sense," and so, "depicts forcefully the Lord's creation of an ordered world."[9] The psalm declares that Yahweh owns the entire world and all who live in it because he is the one who created and established them. Because of this, Yahweh has a relationship with and responsibility for all people. God owns both Israel and the nations. In this sense, Israel and the nations stand on equal footing before Yahweh. They are both called to praise and demonstrate allegiance to Yahweh.

Despite God's ownership of all the nations, the Psalter is clear that he has a unique relationship with Israel. Yahweh is known as the "God of Israel" (Pss 41:13; 59:5; 68:8; 106:48), the God of Abraham and Jacob (e.g., Pss 20:1; 24:6; 46:7, 11; 47:9). He declares, "I am YHWH, your God" (Pss 50:7; 81:10).[10] In God's covenant with Israel, not only did Israel take on an identity as the people of Yahweh, God also took on an identity as their God.[11]

In the Psalter, Israel is frequently described as God's inheritance (נַחֲלָה) (Pss 28:9; 68:9; 74:2; 78:71; 79:1; 94:5, 14; 106:40). The word's basic meaning refers to the transfer of land and property within a kinship structure.[12]

7. All translations are the author's unless otherwise indicated.

8. If one views Psalm 24 as a unified composition, then this verse has a dramatic impact on how one understands the rest of the poem. This has led Lohfink to argue that Psalm 24 is actually about a pilgrimage of the nations to Zion. See Norbert Lohfink and Erich Zenger, *The God of Israel and the Nations: Studies in Isaiah and the Psalms*, trans. Everett Kalin (Collegeville, MN: Liturgical Press, 2000), 61–64.

9. Peter Craigie and Marvin Tate, *Psalms 1–50*, rev. ed., WBC 19 (Nashville: Nelson, 2004), 212.

10. See the thorough discussion of divine titles in the Psalter in Hans-Joachim Kraus, *Theology of Psalms*, CC (Minneapolis: Fortress, 1992), 17–31.

11. John Walton, *Old Testament Theology for Christians: From Ancient Context to Enduring Belief* (Downers Grove, IL: IVP Academic, 2017), 107.

12. Christopher J. H. Wright, "נַחֲלָה," *NIDOTTE*, 3:77.

In the ancient Near East, most deities were understood to own a particular territory, and the deity required loyalty from whoever the occupants happened to be. The Psalter demonstrates that the God of Israel's inheritance was not a territory, but a people.[13] Yahweh did not receive his people as an inheritance through an arbitrary means. Rather, he *chose* them (Ps 33:12). Additionally, he delivered them from Egypt and gave them their territorial inheritance, thus creating a landed state (Pss 47:4; 78:55; 105:11; 135:12; 136:21–22). So, while it is true that in one sense the nations and Israel stand on equal footing before God as their Creator, there is another sense in which they do not. God has uniquely elected and chosen Israel as his special people. This creates a complexity in the network of relationships between Israel and God, the nations and God, and Israel and the nations.

THE NATIONS AS SOURCES OF VIOLENCE, CHAOS, AND EVIL

The Psalter most frequently portrays the nations as forces of violence and evil.[14] Although all people were created by God, there is something about the nations that is naturally hostile to him. The nations first appear in Psalm 2, where they are conspiring against Yahweh and his anointed.[15] Their default stance is in opposition to God and what he is doing in the world.[16] This aligns well with the canonical description of the nations, which were founded as the result of a unified rebellion against God (Gen 11:1–9).

The nations plot and scheme against God's people seeking to annihilate Israel, seemingly for no reason.[17] One of the few things that can unite violent and brutal nations is their opposition to Israel, and hence to Yahweh himself. The nations exult themselves rather than God (66:7), they defile God's temple (79:1), they do not call on the name of God (79:6), and they

13. Daniel Block, *The Gods of the Nations: Studies in Ancient Near Eastern National Theology*, 2nd ed. (Eugene, OR: Wipf & Stock, 1988), 90.

14. For a moving iconographic portrait of foreign nations as a hostile power, see Othmar Keel, *The Symbolism of the Biblical World: Ancient Near Eastern Iconography and the Book of Psalms*, trans. Timothy Hallett (Winona Lake, IN: Eisenbrauns, 1997), 100–109.

15. For a more thorough treatment of Psalm 2 see, Ryan Cook, "'They Were Born There': The Nations in Psalmic Rhetoric," *HBT* 39 (2017): 16–30.

16. Derek E. Wittman, "Let Us Cast Off Their Ropes from Us: The Editorial Significance of the Portrayal of Foreign Nations in Psalms 2 and 149," in *The Shape and Shaping of the Book of Psalms*, ed. deClaissé-Walford, 56; Harris Birkeland, *The Evildoers in the Book of Psalms* (Oslo: Dybwad, 1955), 31.

17. Kraus puts it this way, "Denounce and destroy—that is the determined will of the peoples and their rulers," *Theology of the Psalms*, 125.

taunt God's people (79:12; 137:3, 7). Even worse, one psalm portrays the nations as leading Israel into idolatry (106:34–39).

The Psalms movingly depict the violence and recalcitrance of the nations by portraying them as primeval sources of chaos and destruction. Psalm 46 envisions a world coming apart at the seams:

Therefore, we will not fear when the earth shakes,[18]
and when the mountains sway[מוט] in the heart of the seas.
Its waters roar [הָמָה], they foam;
the mountains quake at its arrogance. (Ps 46:2–3)

In these verses, the poet presents a dizzying and apocalyptic scene of mountains tumbling into the sea and the waters arrogantly rising up to envelop all things.[19] The sea is a common symbol of a chaotic power in the ancient Near East, which needs to be tamed for life to flourish. Here it is a menacing threat. However, as the psalm continues it becomes clear that the psalmist is not talking about literal seas, but about the destructive force of the nations. The same verbs of "shaking" and "roaring" are applied to the nations (46:6). As William Brown describes the scene, "The kingdoms are shown to be both perpetrators and victims of their own chaos: they 'roar' and they 'totter'; they whip up chaos while collapsing in the very tumult they provoke."[20]

The violence of the nations is premeditated, carefully planned, and almost always directed at Israel. Psalm 83 describes their process.[21] Our focus here will be on the first two strophes (83:1–10). Strophe 1 says:

O God, do not be at rest! Do not be silent!
    And do not be peaceful, O El!
For look, your enemies are tumultuous
    And those who hate you lift up their head.
Against your people, they concoct crafty plans,
    And they take a stand against your sheltered ones.

18. בְּהָמִיר is an unusual form, not attested elsewhere. It is possible to either read this with the LXX and point it as a *niphal* infinitive, or to read it as a *niphal* infinitive from מוג. This assumes that the final ג was misread as ר by a scribe (the two letters are orthographically close in Paleo-Hebrew script).

19. For a more complete description of the imagery of this psalm, see Ryan Cook, "Prayers that Form Us: Rhetoric and Psalms Interpretation," *JSOT* 39 (2015): 451–67.

20. William Brown, *Seeing the Psalms: A Theology of Metaphor* (Louisville: Westminster John Knox, 2002), 116.

21. This section is adapted from Cook, "They Were Born There," 18–19.

They said, "Come and let us wipe them out as a nation,
And the name of Israel will be remembered no more."

The psalmist here begs God not to relax or to be indifferent. The reasons why are spelled out in the two כִּי clauses (83:2, 5). The nations are portrayed as people who hate God and arrogantly defy him (83:2). They scheme against Israel, his people (83:3). The enemies of God want to annihilate Israel so that her name will no longer be remembered, thus undoing God's promise to Abram in Genesis 12:2.

The second strophe continues this theme and gives a further reason for God not to be silent.

For they conspire together,
Against you, they make a covenant.
The tents of Edom and the Ishmaelites,
Moab and the Hagrites
Gebal and Ammon and Amalek,
Philistia with the inhabitants of Tyre,
Even Assyria has joined with them,
They have become an arm to the sons of Lot.

Verse 5 contains a striking use of "covenant" (בְּרִית). In contrast to Yahweh's covenant with Israel, which was intended to bring blessing to the nations, the nations have made their own covenant opposing what Yahweh is doing through Israel. Or, put more simply, the covenant of the nations is attempting to undo Yahweh's covenant with Israel. Verses 6–8 give a catalog of ten nations that have united in their opposition to God's people. This list comprises nine smaller powers who are Israel's neighbors climaxed by a tenth superpower, Assyria. This list makes clear that the psalmist is not reflecting on a historical situation. Rather, they "are emblematic for the world of nations experienced and feared by Israel throughout its history."[22]

The Psalms picture the nations as arrogant, rebellious, and violent. Everything God is trying to do through his covenant with Israel, the nations are opposed to and try to undermine. The nations are not a neutral party. In order for life to flourish, they need to be tamed and their plans need to be thwarted (Ps 65:7). Yet, it is for their redemption that God called and elected Israel.

22. Frank-Lothar Hossfeld and Erich Zenger, *Psalms 2: A Commentary of Psalms 51–100*, ed. Klaus Baltzer, trans. L. M. Maloney, Hermeneia (Minneapolis: Fortress, 2005),

THE NATIONS AS COVENANT CURSE IMPLEMENTERS

The destructive power of the nations is at times harnessed by God and used by him to punish Israel for their violation of the covenant.[23] This theme is particularly highlighted in the Asaphite collection (Pss 50; 73–83). The Psalms of Asaph form a cohesive group that recount a dialogue between the religious leaders, the people, and God.[24] This dialogue is centered around questions relating to the destruction of the temple as the people seek to maintain their identity and their understanding of God despite the loss of the temple and triumph of their enemies.

Regarding the nations, three themes stand out as the psalmists reflect on the experience of exile. First, the nations destroyed and humiliated Israel with a special focus on the temple. The destruction of the temple is graphically described:

> Your foes have roared in the midst of your meeting place;
> they set up their own signs for signs.
> They were like those who swing axes
> in a forest of trees.
> And all its carved wood
> they broke down with hatchets and hammers.
> They set your sanctuary on fire;
> they profaned the dwelling place of your name,
> bringing it down to the ground. (Ps 74:4–7, ESV)

> O God, the nations have come into your inheritance;
> they have defiled your holy temple;
> they have laid Jerusalem in ruins.
> They have given the bodies of your servants
> to the birds of the heavens for food,
> the flesh of your faithful to the beasts of the earth.
> They have poured out their blood like water
> all around Jerusalem,
> and there was no one to bury them. (Ps 79:1–3, ESV)

23. John Goldingay, *Old Testament Theology: Israel's Faith*, vol. 2 (Downers Grove, IL: IVP Academic, 2006), 761–62.

24. For an attempt to read the Asaphite psalms as a unit, see, David C. Mitchell, *The Message of the Psalter: An Eschatological Programme in the Book of Psalms*, JSOTSup 252 (Sheffield: Sheffield, 1997), 90–107, and the critiques by Christine Jones, "The Psalms of Asaph: A Study of the Function of a Psalm Collection" (PhD diss., Baylor University, 2009), 7–61.

The nations are good at this kind of work. In addition to bringing destruction, they scoff, taunt, and mock Israel (74:10; 79:4; 80:6). Second, the destruction of the temple and humiliation of Israel is understood to be God's hand of judgment (74:1; 79:8; 80:4). This is seen as a regular pattern for how God has dealt with Israel's rebellion. When Psalm 78 reflects on the period of the Judges, the psalmist declares, "When God heard, he was full of wrath ... and delivered his power ... to the hand of the foe" (78:59–61). Third, the nations seem to relish their role as God's hand of judgment a bit too much. Of course, they do not understand themselves as agents of Israel's God. They have their own agenda. Because of their pride, cruelty, and disregard of God, the psalmists beg God to judge them (74:10–11, 18, 22–23; 79:6–7, 12).

THE NATIONS AS OBJECTS OF JUDGMENT

The inhumanity and cruelty of the nations and their treatment of Israel often provoke God's judgment.[25] This theme is especially highlighted in Psalm 9/10.[26] While the precise circumstances of its composition are difficult to construct, it has a summative, or comprehensive quality.[27] Patrick Miller has argued that this psalm(s) was intended to bring together many of the basic themes of the Psalter into one work with the king as the speaker.[28] The sections that discuss the judgment of the nations are what concern us here (9:5–6, 15–20; 10:15–16).

The psalm opens with a resolve to give thanks to Yahweh because of all of his "wonderful deeds" (9:1). These deeds begin to be enumerated in verses 3–4 and continue into verses 5–6.

> You have rebuked the nations, you have destroyed the wicked;
> you have blotted out their name forever and ever.
> The enemies have vanished in everlasting ruins;
> their cities you have rooted out;
> the very memory of them has perished. (NRSV)

---

25. The texts here are numerous: Pss 2:9; 9:5–8, 15–20; 10:16; 33:10; 44:2; 46:6; 56:6–7; 59:5–13; 78:55; 79:6–7; 83:16; 96:13; 98:9; 108:9; 110:5–6; 135:8–12; 137:7–9; 149:6–9.

26. These psalms combine to form one (albeit broken) acrostic; also the LXX combines the two, and Psalm 9 ends with a *selah*, which indicates that the work is not finished. See the discussion in Peter C. Craigie, *Psalms 1–50*, WBC 19 (Waco, TX: Word, 1983).

27. Patrick D. Miller, "The Ruler of Zion and the Hope of the Poor: Psalms 9–10 in the Context of the Psalter" in *The Way of the Lord: Essays in Old Testament Theology* (Tübingen: Mohr Siebeck, 2004), 170–71.

28. Miller, "The Ruler of Zion and the Hope of the Poor," 168–69.

The first line in verse 5 describes in general terms what Yahweh has done to the nations. The verb "rebuke" (גָּעַר) is frequently used to describe Yahweh's taming of the seas.[29] The nations are here cast in the role of chaotic power opposed to Yahweh.[30] Rather than being a problem for Yahweh, the psalmist declares that he simply destroys them. This destruction takes the form of Yahweh blotting out their name and causing any memory of them to be lost.[31] This is a complete destruction—not only are the nations defeated, no one even remembers they existed!

This destruction of the nations is further described in 9:15–20. Here it is not Yahweh punishing the nations directly, but rather, "the nations have sunk in the pit that they made; in the net that they hid has their own foot been caught" (9:15, NRSV).[32] Their own evil has rebounded upon them. Craigie calls this the "boomerang" effect of evil, which is also seen as the work of Yahweh (9:16).[33] The end of the nations is *Sheol*, the "realm of separation from God."[34] The reason for this is given in the second half of verse 17: the nations forgot God. There is a functional atheism at work among the nations, as particularly brought out in 10:4, 11, and 13, which enables the nations to act as if they were their own god.[35] Yahweh's punishment on the nations is to serve the purpose of reminding the nations "that they are only human [אֱנוֹשׁ]" (9:20). However, this causes a bit of a tension here: God's judgment was said to be total, yet it also serves as a corrective to the nations.

As we briefly turn to the rest of the Psalter, we see the judgment of the nations described in these terms: their "plans" and "counsel" are brought to nothing (33:10); among the nations, the psalmist wants "none to be spared" (59:5); they are to be "consumed until they are no more" (59:13); their faces are filled with shame (83:16); and climactically they are judged by God through Israel: "Let the high praises of God be in their throats and two-edged swords in their hands, to execute vengeance on the nations and

---

29. Psalm 106:9.

30. Isaiah 17:13 brings this connection between "nations" and "waters" out directly: "The nations roar like the roaring of the many waters, but he will rebuke [גָּעַר] them, and they will flee far away" (NRSV).

31. It is interesting that this "blotting" out of a name is something that Yahweh threatened to do to Israel (Deut 9:14).

32. The imagery here is based on ancient Near Eastern hunting practices of digging pits and using nets. Kings often used this imagery to talk about how they "trapped" other nations. Here the nations get caught in their own trap. See Keel, *The Symbolism of the Biblical World*, 89–95.

33. Craigie, *Psalms 1–50*, 120.

34. Hans-Joachim Kraus, *Psalms 1–59*, CC (Minneapolis: Fortress, 1993), 196.

35. For an excellent discussion of functional atheism in Psalms, see Craigie, *Psalms 1–50*, 126–27.

punishment on the peoples" (149:6–7). In summary, the nations are the just recipients of God's wrath because of their tendencies toward autonomy and injustice. This judgment is described as total and complete, although there are hints that some will be spared. Sometimes the nations are judged directly by God, other times their own evil comes back to haunt them, and still other times the nation of Israel is the instrument of God's judgment on them.

THE NATIONS AS OBJECTS OF SALVATION

Numerous psalms go beyond simply describing the nations as being judged and envision the nations as joining Israel in worship of Yahweh, thus being included within the congregation.[36] Hans-Joachim Kraus summarizes this theme well:

> In innumerable significant passages in the Psalter we can note the openness of songs of praise, the prayers, and the didactic psalms to the world of nations. In the *todah*, the individual praying wants kings of the nations to join him in offering thanks. ... The Psalms raise the banner of proclamation and communication. In the old Zion traditions Jerusalem is the "joy of all the earth," the center of creation, the place where kings and nations gather to worship and adore.[37]

A few examples will suffice to demonstrate this theme. Psalm 47:10 visualizes the nations gathering "with the people of the God of Abraham" in ritual worship.[38] Psalm 87, which "programmatically summarizes the theme of 'Israel and the nations' in the Psalter," has a dramatic view of the inclusion of the nations.[39] The psalmist here states that other nations were actually

36. A partial list of psalms that address this issue include: 2:11–12; 22:27–31; 47:1–9; 66:2–8; 68:32; 69:34; 83:16–18; 86:9; 87:1–7; 94:8–12; 98:4–9; 99:1–3; 102:18–22; 105:45; 107; 117; 138:4–5; 148:7–11.

37. Kraus, *Theology of the Psalms*, 16. This vision of the nations as joining Israel in worship is a theme that has been elaborated on in several studies on the Psalter. See Charles Scobie, "Israel and the Nations: An Essay in Biblical Theology," *TynBul* 43 (1992): 283–305; Eckhard Schnabel, "Israel, the People of God, and the Nations," *JETS* 45 (2002): 35–57; Christopher J. H. Wright, *The Mission of God: Unlocking the Bible's Grand Narrative* (Downers Grove, IL: IVP Academic, 2005), 454–500; Walter Kaiser, *Mission in the Old Testament: Israel as a Light to the Nations* (Grand Rapids: Baker Academic, 2000), 29–38; Lohfink and Zenger, *The God of Israel and the Nations*; Mitchell, *The Message of the Psalter*.

38. The addition of "with" (עִם) is based on the LXX and assuming haplography. So also, Craigie, *Psalms 1–50*, 347.

39. Lohfink and Zenger, *The God of Israel and the Nations*, 126–27.

born in Zion (87:4–6), the nations are registered among God's people (87:6), and they "know" God (יָדַע).[40]

In the Psalter, the nations are encouraged to "serve the Lord with fear" (2:11); they are called on to praise God (67:3); and to seek his name (83:16); they are told to fear Yahweh (102:15); and are encouraged to obey God's law (105:45). The ingathering of the nations to Zion is not only a prominent theme in the Prophets but is also reflected in the Psalter.

THE NATIONS IN ISRAEL'S WORSHIP

Thus far this essay has been mostly descriptive. It has attempted to analyze all the various ways the book of Psalms describes the nations. However, in order to frame it theologically, we must try to put the pieces together into some kind of coherent whole. As stated at the outset, there is a tension between the concepts of nationalism and universalism in the Psalter.[41] That is, there are several psalms that indicate that the nations will be judged so completely that the very memory of them will have vanished (9:6); while on the other hand, other psalms hold out hope that the nations will join Israel in worshiping Yahweh, even hinting that they will somehow be included in the people of God.

From an editorial perspective, Psalms 1–2 work together to serve as an introduction to the entire book.[42] The themes raised in these two psalms are to guide the reader and shape the reading of the rest of the Psalter. Most scholars would argue that Psalm 2 originally was used as a part of an enthronement ceremony.[43] However, James Watts has argued, "The incorporation of the royal psalms [like Ps 2] into the Psalter has deprived them of their original royal and cultic context, so that they no longer seem to refer to the present or past, but speak of hope for the future. Royal ideology has been replaced by eschatology."[44] One could argue about whether or not eschatology was a part of the religious context of these psalms; however, he

40. This language of "knowing" God is often used in the Old Testament to describe Israel's unique relationship to Yahweh (e.g., Amos 3:2; Exod 33:12–16).

41. Christensen, "Nations," 4:1037.

42. Some of the connections that indicate these psalms should be read together in an introductory way are: (1) the absence of a title in both psalms, whereas every other psalm in the first three books either has a title or is closely connected to the psalm before it (e.g., Pss 9–10); (2) the *inclusio* between 1:1 and 2:12 of אַשְׁרֵי ("blessed"); (3) the final repetition of אָבַד ("destroy") in 1:6 and 2:12; (4) the repetition of the verb הָגָה ("meditate"/"plot") in 1:2 and 2:1. See also, Robert Cole, "An Integrated Reading of Psalms 1 and 2," *JSOT* 98 (2002): 75–88.

43. John Eaton, *Kingship and the Psalms*, 2nd ed. (Sheffield: Sheffield, 1986), 112.

44. James W. Watts, "Psalm 2 in the Context of Biblical Theology," *HBT* 12 (1990): 73.

is clearly on the mark when he states that Psalm 2 functions eschatologically in its canonical placement.[45] One piece of evidence that Psalm 2 has an eschatological orientation is the content of verse 8: "Ask of me, and I will make the nations your heritage; and your possession, the ends of the earth." The speaker here, as throughout the psalm, is the king.[46] Beginning in verse 7, the king recounts a decree he received from Yahweh. This decree states that he is God's son.[47] The king then declares that Yahweh has offered him the nations as his heritage (נַחֲלָה).[48] The land of the nations is promised to become the land of Israel's king. We know that it is not simply the land of Canaan in view because of the parallel between "nations" and "ends of the earth." This is a striking and universal claim. The "anointed one" of a small Near Eastern country is claiming that the "ends of the earth" are his possession. The difficulty with this psalm is that it did not ever take place in Israel's history. Even if one looked to the time of Solomon during the united monarchy as the historical context for this psalm, it would still be quite hyperbolic. When one combines that fact with this psalm's place in the introduction to the Psalter, it is clear the psalm points beyond itself to some kind of future fulfillment.

This eschatological orientation can also be seen in the editorial conclusion to the book. Psalms 146–150 are all united by the superscription הַלְלוּ־יָהּ ("hallelujah").[49] These psalms were either written intentionally as the conclusion to the Psalter or brought together for this purpose. In these psalms, one can see the various roles of the nations being brought together. Psalm 147 celebrates the unique relationship between Israel and Yahweh. The psalmist declares that God cares particularly for Israel (147:1–2) and encourages Israel to praise Yahweh for his blessings (147:12–15). The psalm closes with the assertion, "He has not dealt thus with any other nation; they do not know his ordinances" (147:20). This psalm by itself does not say anything

45. "Eschatology" is a notoriously difficult word to define. Following Gerhard von Rad, I mean it in the sense of the "expectation of something soon to happen," or that "there is a break which goes so deep that a new state beyond it cannot be understood as the continuation of what went before" (*Old Testament Theology*, vol. 2, trans. D. M. G. Stalker [New York: Oliver & Boyd, 1965], 114–15).

46. John Goldingay, *Psalms 1–41* (Grand Rapids: Baker Academic, 2006), 96.

47. Much ink has been spilled trying to discern what the psalmist meant by the phrase, "You are my son." For a good overview see Watts, "Psalm 2 in the Context of Biblical Theology."

48. This word denotes "hereditary division of property between an individual or the family as their share of the booty," *HALOT* 2:687.

49. On the editorial function of Psalms 146–150, see Michael Snearly, *The Return of the King: Messianic Expectation in Book V of the Psalter*, LHBOTS 624 (New York: T&T Clark, 2016), 171–84.

directly about the fate of the nations, but it is a striking statement, especially when compared to the statement in 148:11. In this verse, the psalmist encourages all people to join with Israel in worship, "Praise the Lord. … Kings of the earth and all peoples, princes and all rulers of the earth!" (148:7a, 11). There is at least some idea of inclusion in this psalm, even if there is still a focus on Israel (148:14).

Psalm 149 has a different take on the nations. This psalm rouses Israel to be God's instrument of judgment on them (149:6–9). Finally, the Psalter closes with the words, "Let everything that breathes praise the Lord! Praise the Lord!" (150:6). The nations would presumably be included in "everything that breathes." Thus, judgment and inclusion are brought together and not considered to be contradictory. The perspective of the nations as judged and included within Israel is best understood eschatologically. That is, there will be a future day when the nations will be judged, but some from all the nations will seek Yahweh and worship him as well.

CONCLUSION

The Psalter embodies the whole range of perspectives Israel had on the nations. The nations are viewed as an existential threat and a force of chaos and evil. The nations are seen as a tool in the hand of God to implement his wrath on Israel. But the nations are also seen as the beneficiaries of God's promise to Abraham to be a "blessing to the nations" (Gen 12:3). Israel understood that its relationship with Yahweh had a global significance. Religious gatherings at the temple in Jerusalem became anticipations of an eschatological ingathering of the nations to worship Yahweh.[50] In sum, one helpful way to understand the complex and various roles of the nations in Israel's worship is to interpret these roles within the context of a future-oriented theology. Ultimately, this study supports Walter Brueggemann's conclusion that "scholarly categories which separate cult from eschatology artificially divide what belongs together in the act of worship in Israel."[51] Israel's understanding of how Yahweh has acted in the past and will act in the future is central to their religious life, so one should not be surprised to find evidence of these perspectives in their worship.

50. Christensen, "Nations," 4:1045.

51. Walter Brueggemann, *Israel's Praise: Doxology against Idolatry and Ideology* (Philadelphia: Fortress, 1988), 5.

13

Psalm 87 and the Promise of Inclusion

Jamie A. Grant

Psalm 87 is something of an outlier within the Psalter. It is a Zion psalm but an unusual one even within that subgenre. The song celebrates the belonging of Israel's enemies—both historic and painfully recent—as part of the worshiping community gathered in Jerusalem. It presents an image of ingathering that echoes the voice of the Old Testament prophets but that is almost unheard of within the spiritual vocabulary of the Psalter. This essay discusses the role that Zion played in the mindset of the worshiping community, especially in the postexilic period. It also examines Psalm 87's voice of radical, cross-cultural inclusion and belonging—a voice that serves as a challenge for the people of God in every generation.

INTRODUCTION

To describe Psalm 87 as an outlier in the Psalter would be an understatement. A theme that is common enough in the Prophets—the ingathering of the nations to worship with Israel in Zion—finds voice in a unique way in this composition. There are, of course, flashes of this proleptic ideology in the Psalter: Psalm 47:9 comes close to the ideas of Psalm 87, the Yahweh *mālāk* psalms (Pss 93–100) are replete with public invitations to the nations to join the covenant community in worship, and the missionary vision of this poem seems to spring from a short declaration of faith in the preceding lament (Ps 86:8–10). However, there is nothing *quite* like the tone, language, and ideas of Psalm 87 elsewhere in the book.[1]

It must have been a startling composition for the original singers of this psalm. The dual titles in the superscription ("A psalm. A song.") most likely indicate that this composition was part of the public worship of Israel. Psalm 87 was a song to be sung in worship of Yahweh. It is hard to imagine singing out loud the names of your most vociferous enemies in praise of your God.[2] The staggering nature of the psalm is compounded by the geopolitical realities of the day. There was no peaceful cohabitation of nation-states in the days of the psalmist—you either ruled or you were ruled. What is more, some of the nations listed were enemies, ancient and modern, who had perpetrated atrocities against the people of Israel, the type of atrocities that live long in the memory. Yet God's people were expected to *sing* of their belonging as part of the community of faith. Psalm 87 is also startling from a religious perspective as well as a political perspective. These nations worshiped *other* gods. These were gods that commanded the sacrifice of children and the practice of cultic prostitution and other things that were, at least supposedly, heinous in the eyes of God's people. Of course, the belonging that the psalm envisages comes from the nations' ultimate allegiance to Yahweh, but that must have seemed like a desperately unlikely possibility in the day of the original singers.[3]

The covenant community were asked to sing a song of praise that celebrated the belonging of their worst enemies, who also presently worshiped false gods. It is difficult to imagine such a worship song gaining popularity in the contemporary church in these years of the war on terror, is it not? A song celebrating the belonging of rogue nation-states who follow

1. Goldingay comments on the unusual tone: "It is simultaneously one of the most particularist and one of the most universalist of psalms" (John Goldingay, *Psalms Volume 2: Psalms 42–89*, BCOTWP 2 [Grand Rapids: Baker Academic, 2007], 632). And Allen discusses the obscurity of the psalm within the life of the church when compared to the continuing "popularity" of Newton's paraphrase, "Glorious things of thee are spoken" (Ronald B. Allen, "Psalm 87, A Song Rarely Sung," *Bibliotheca Sacra* 153 [1996]: 131–40).

2. David Clyde Jones, "The Multiracial City," *Presb* 21.2 (1995): 68.

3. There is, indeed, something profoundly universalizing about Psalm 87, but it is not universalist in the sense that allegiance to God is neither here nor there. Yahweh's role in the psalm is limited but significant. He "loves" the gates of Zion (87:2) and he "records" the belonging of the nations (87:6). These two actions are equally vital. Yahweh causes his presence to dwell in Zion. It is through *his* presence in *that* place that the remarkable inclusion of Psalm 87 occurs. The third action of Yahweh is implicit in verse 4: he speaks. It is Yahweh who declares the belonging of the nations within the worshiping community before recording that inclusion in his register. As Goldingay comments, the psalm is both particularist and universalist.

the ideologies of Islam or Communism or a personality cult based around one "glorious leader" or another. Yet Psalm 87 was part of Israel's liturgical practice.[4] Liturgy is designed to shape the way in which we think and act, so what was the intended impact of this poem? How did it shape God's people? And how should it be read as Christian Scripture in the light of the New Testament?

THE SPIRITUALITY OF ZION

Psalm 87 is clearly a Zion psalm, but it is a Zion psalm unlike the others that we come across in the Psalter.[5] Zion is central to the rhetoric of the composition but in a way that is not typically associated with the other Zion psalms. Psalms 46 and 48, for example, focus on the military impregnability of Jerusalem. The neighboring psalm, Psalm 84, centers on the temple as the dwelling place of the Lord of armies and as a place of rest and blessing for his people. All of the Zion-centered psalms share a theological construct: Zion is the tangible dwelling place of Yahweh on earth, and in some sense, he presides over all of the events of humanity from that place. It is not that the Hebrews believed that their God was restricted to the confines of the building or the geography of the city (see, for example, Solomon's prayer of dedication and Yahweh's response in 2 Chr 6–7), but Zion functioned as a physical sign of the presence and power of God to intervene in the human sphere. As Erich Zenger puts it, "Zion/Jerusalem is the seat of the king and place of the throne of the Most High God. From here he holds cosmic chaos at bay. The chaotic assault of the nations shatters against the mountain of God."[6]

This view of Zion is a theological construct as it reflects a perspective on reality that belies observable circumstances. While the historical locus of the writing of this psalm—like most psalms—is difficult to ascertain with any degree of certainty, it is located in Book III of the Psalter, which is a collection focused around lament at the losses suffered in the fall of Jerusalem.

4. See Gordon J. Wenham, *Psalms as Torah: Reading Biblical Song Ethically*, Studies in Theological Interpretation (Grand Rapids: Baker Academic, 2012), for a helpful discussion of the formative nature of the psalms as liturgy.

5. Among the psalms of Zion, Psalm 87 makes the most positive, explicit statement about the nations. In the preceding songs "kingdoms fall" (46:6), "kings" and their "forces" are "destroyed" (48:4–7), and the "neighbouring lands" and "kings of the earth" bring tribute after a stunning defeat (76:11–12), but here they are "born in Zion"! (Craig C. Broyles, *Psalms*, NIBCOT [Carlisle: Paternoster, 1999], 350).

6. Frank-Lothar Hossfeld and Erich Zenger, *Psalms 2: A Commentary on Psalms 51–100*, trans. Linda M. Maloney, Hermeneia (Minneapolis: Fortress, 2005), 379.

The confidence of Psalms 46 and 48 is a thing of the past. Jerusalem has fallen, the Davidic line is broken, the temple is destroyed, the return from exile is something of a disappointment, and throughout all of this Judah/Israel is nothing more than a puppet state in the hands of a succession of dominant world powers. Humanly speaking, nothing is ruled from Zion. Yet Psalm 87 remains a surprising voice of hope and a statement of faith among the laments that surround it.[7] According to Psalm 87, hope is still centered around Zion and that hope is not just for the returning Hebrews but also for their bitterest enemies and, by implication, for all nations. So, how does this work?

Some scholars suggest that Psalm 87 is a postexilic rereading of classical Zion theology.[8] The military security celebrated in Book I is reread in a new and forward-looking manner. Zion is no longer *just* the physical symbol of the presence of Yahweh on earth as a marker of hope for the covenant community. In the more internationalized setting of the postexilic era, Zion has become a marker of hope *for all nations*. The vision is of an expansive and expanding covenant community that transcends ethnic and national lines.[9] Yahweh is present on *the earth*, he is active in all of the events of *humanity*, he is working out his purposes and developing his plans and economy *for the whole world*.[10] Zion becomes a symbol of hope for the nations, not just the nation.

This much is clear from Psalm 87, yet it is important to note that it is Yahweh's beloved city (87:2) and Yahweh's permanent record (97:6) that are in play here. Hope is premised on the activity and call of Israel's God. The psalmist is not advocating any sort of vague Near Eastern pluralism, rather he envisions a reality where the sovereignty of Yahweh is recognized internationally and interculturally. It is a vision of a future reality that would have seemed all but impossible to the exilic and postexilic communities

7. Note that this voice of future hope is the center-point of four laments. Psalms 85 and 89 speak with the voice of communal complaint, and Psalms 86 and 88 are individual laments, but the editors saw fit to include or retain Psalm 87 as a voice of future hope in the midst of cataclysmic loss.

8. Hossfeld and Zenger, *Psalms* 2, 382. C. Briggs and E. Briggs suggest a historical location in the exile, which fits with the "voice" of Book III, although the rationale for their exilic conclusion is not, of course, premised on editorial considerations (*The Book of Psalms*, ICC [Edinburgh: T&T Clark, 1906], 390–91). However, it is important to remember John Eaton's reminder that the "theme of Zion's universal significance is very ancient" (*The Psalms: A Historical and Spiritual Commentary with an Introduction and New Translation* [London: T&T Clark International, 2003], 311). It is, as always, difficult to be definitive about the historical origins of Psalm 87.

9. Konrad Schaefer, *Psalms*, Berit Olam (Collegeville, MN: Liturgical Press, 2001), 213–14.

10. Briggs and Briggs, *Psalms*, 392.

of faith. Yahweh's name had been "blasphemed among the nations" (Ezek 20, 36). Firstly, his name was profaned by Israel's failures in terms of singularity of worship and maintenance of social justice in the land (Ezek 20). However, Yahweh's name was also blasphemed among the nations by the loss of the land, city, and temple and the presence of God's people in Babylonian exile (Ezek 36). Yahweh appeared to be a "failed god" in the eyes of the nations, unable to protect his people and mocked by the worshipers of other gods (Ps 137).[11] Yet the psalmist envisions a time when all nations recognize the true identity of Yahweh. "However much they may differ from each other in language and appearance, they are all united in *one* faith, believing in the *one* God whom they jointly profess."[12] This singular faith is premised on a singular place: Zion.

Herein lies one of the key biblical-theological questions of Psalm 87. It is often argued that we see a significant movement away from the physicality of Zion in the Old Testament, as exemplified in this psalm, to spiritualized and nontangible versions of divine place in the New Testament. The classic example of this process and argument is seen in Jesus's conversation with the Samaritan woman in John 4:19–24.

> "Sir," the woman said, "I can see that you are a prophet. Our ancestors worshipped on this mountain, but you Jews claim that the place where we must worship is in Jerusalem."
>
> "Woman," Jesus replied, "believe me, a time is coming when you will worship the Father neither on this mountain nor in Jerusalem. You Samaritans worship what you do not know; we worship what we do know, for salvation is from the Jews. Yet a time is coming and has now come when the true worshippers will worship the Father in the Spirit and in truth, for they are the kind of worshippers the Father seeks. God is spirit, and his worshippers must worship in the Spirit and in truth."[13]

The idea seems clear: Jesus is moving new-covenant believers away from the physicality of land, city, and temple to a *spiritualized* notion of belief in

11. See Christopher J. H. Wright, *The Mission of God: Unlocking the Bible's Grand Narrative* (Nottingham: Apollos, 2006), especially chapter 3, for a fuller discussion of the missional impact of the exile.

12. Artur Weiser, *The Psalms: A Commentary*, OTL, trans. H. Hartwell (Philadelphia: Westminster, 1962), 580.

13. Scripture citations taken from NIVUK, unless otherwise noted.

the divine presence on earth. Believers no longer need to make a pilgrimage to Jerusalem or to make sacrifices in the temple. These concepts of worship have been spiritualized once and for all in the work of Christ. Therefore, people of faith encounter God *wherever* they are; they can approach in prayer without first offering sacrifice in the temple and so on. Along with John 4, the dispersal of the Jerusalem church in Acts 8 is often cited as necessary divine action because the nascent church had failed to fully grasp the work of Christ in the expansion of the covenant community. The first Christians had not quite grasped that the city and (second) temple no longer played the same role as before. The temple, as Paul indicates, is now a body of people rather than a physical place (1 Cor 3:16–17).[14] However, as it was made up—at least initially—of largely Jewish-background believers, it was hard for the early church to move beyond the physicality of land, city, and temple buildings, so action was required to move them out of Zion.

Frequently, in biblical-theological terms, there is an assumption of movement from the "tangible" to the "essential" in our understanding of the physical signs of the Old Testament covenant promises. There is much discussion of sign and significance.[15] The signs of the Old Testament covenant promises—promised land, chosen city, dwelling place of the divine name, and a "house" for David—are, indeed, all physical. So, the assumption goes, there has to be a marked change in the new covenant community's understanding of these symbols. Zion, as it is most pertinent to our discussion of Psalm 87, is transformed from the physical temple building to the universal church (incorporating both Jews and Gentiles) as the sign of God's presence on earth. The underlying implication is that the physical signs were nothing more than poor precursors of a more meaningful spiritualized concept that ultimately comes to display the *essential* divine intent from the beginning. So, the physical temple was meaningful only as a precursor of the incarnation, for example. The building itself, regardless of its grand nature, was in fact a poor representation of the Immanuel principle that is revealed in the Christ-event.

This is an understanding of the external signs of the Old Testament covenant promises that is worth challenging. Not because there is no expansion of these concepts in Christ—there clearly is a fuller understanding of the covenant revealed in the person and work of Jesus. Nevertheless, the assumption that there was *no* understanding of the broader spiritualized

---

14. Peter seems to agree (1 Pet 2:4–10).

15. A classic example would be Geerhardus Vos, *Biblical Theology: Old and New Testaments* (London: Banner of Truth, 1975), but there is an abundance of such examples.

significance of these physical signs among the Old Testament people of God is patently ridiculous. Without doubt, the Old Testament community's engagement with the external signs of the covenant has a checkered history. The Major Prophets make it clear that, in periods of Judah's history, there was an unhealthy focus on the external. Arguably, this is most clearly evidenced in Jeremiah 7:1–8,

> This is the word that came to Jeremiah from the LORD: "Stand at the gate of the LORD's house and there proclaim this message:
>
> 'Hear the word of the LORD, all you people of Judah who come through these gates to worship the LORD. This is what the LORD Almighty, the God of Israel, says: reform your ways and your actions, and I will let you live in this place. Do not trust in deceptive words and say, "This is the temple of the LORD, the temple of the LORD, the temple of the LORD!" If you really change your ways and your actions and deal with each other justly, if you do not oppress the foreigner, the fatherless or the widow and do not shed innocent blood in this place, and if you do not follow other gods to your own harm, then I will let you live in this place, in the land I gave your ancestors for ever and ever. But look, you are trusting in deceptive words that are worthless.' "

Yahweh's word to Jeremiah indicates that a majority within Judah, especially its leadership, had come to focus on the external signs of the covenant, specifically here the temple, in an almost talismanic fashion. Their trust was in the mere presence of the physical symbol in their midst rather than in the remembrance of the semiotics of divine presence. The temple signified Yahweh's communion presence in their midst and yet the people had forgotten their obligations regarding singularity of worship and a concern for social justice that stemmed from Yahweh's predilection for the marginalized. Clearly, there were times when the people were overly focused on the externality of the signs of the covenant and had lost sight of their essential meaning.

However, it is unlikely that this was true for everyone in Judah, nor was this true throughout all of Israel/Judah's history. Even in the time of Jeremiah, there would have been those whose desire was to remain faithful to Yahweh, who remembered the essential truth of divine presence and their obligations to their God.[16] Throughout the existence of the temple its symbolic nature was frequently recognized in Scripture. From its origin[17] to its demise,[18] the emblematic nature of the temple as the "site" of divine dwelling is well-attested in the Old Testament. Yahweh is really and powerfully present everywhere (Ps 24), so tabernacle and temple have always functioned as tangible *signs* of that presence in a manner that reflected a fuller spiritual and intangible reality behind the external.

How does this speak to the biblical theology of Psalm 87? This unusual composition, rather than positing a strong disconnect between Old and New Testament realities of worship, points toward a meaningful continuity of expectation in terms of the *missio Dei*. The psalmist attests that Zion was central to the global purposes of Yahweh in drawing to himself an international, cross-cultural, multiethnic community of worship. It seems highly unlikely, however, that the psalmist expected the imagery of Psalm 87 to be fulfilled in historical reality. The logistics of ingathering would be physically impossible in ancient Jerusalem.[19] Rather, Psalm 87 is an Old Testament precursor to a theology of worship that belies the requirement of special places or practices. All nations—even enemy nations—belong. They belong to Yahweh and, therefore, they enjoy belonging within the city and space that marks his presence. The LXX translation of 87:7 (86:7), though apparently remote from the Masoretic Text, is interesting:

> *ὡς εὐφραινομένων πάντων ἡ κατοικία ἐν σοί*
> How delighted are all those at home in you![20]

Samuel Terrien captures well the sense of the verse in the Greek and the sense of the psalm as a whole:

---

16. As evidenced by Jeremiah's notable disciples—Baruch (Jer 32), the Rekabites (Jer 35), and Ebed-Melek (Jer 38). A further indication of the less than total turning away from Yahweh in the preexilic period is seen in the role of Isaiah's disciples (e.g., Isa 8).

17. "But will God really dwell on earth? The heavens, even the highest heaven, cannot contain you. How much less this temple I have built!" (1 Kgs 8:27).

18. See, for example, the symbolic departure of the "glory of the Lord" from the temple out to the east of the city in Ezekiel 10 and its equally symbolic return from the east in Ezekiel 43. This imagery of divine presence in, withdrawal from, and return to the temple goes against the formative theological background that "the glory of the Lord fills the whole earth" (וְיִמָּלֵא כְבוֹד־יְהוָה אֶת־כָּל־הָאָרֶץ, Num 14:21).

19. Goldingay, *Psalms* 2, 640; see also Briggs and Briggs, *Psalms*, 392.

20. See Samuel Terrien, *The Psalms: Strophic Structure and Theological Commentary*, ECC (Grand Rapids: Eerdmans, 2003), 623.

> The word [κατοικία] designates not a house but a state of mind, such as "feeling at home with." This precise wording is significant. "Dwelling in God" or rather "feeling at home with," tactfully contradicts "dwelling in the temple." The Greek word, which translates an unknown Hebrew original, hints not at a geographic location but at the psychological sentiment of happiness in communion. ... "To feel at home with God" no longer requires a sacred edifice, even sacred in a unique way, but acclimation to the new temple at the end of days.[21]

With all that we know of the significance of the temple in Old Testament thought and practice, this seems counterintuitive, yet there also seems to be an externalizing trajectory throughout Psalms 84–87. In 84:5–6 the people on pilgrimage to Zion transform the Valley of Baka into a place of springs (i.e., places beyond the temple, foreign places). Psalm 85:10–11 points to a God who fulfills the obligations of the covenant that we are unable to keep ourselves (i.e., faithfulness and justice are supplied graciously and creationally, apart from sacerdotal practice). Psalm 86:8–10 opens the reader's eyes to the presence of the nations as part of the worshiping community of Yahweh (i.e., those who worship other gods, by implication; therefore they are not present in the temple but will somehow recognize Yahweh's greatness and glorify him). Zion is, of course, significant to all these realities, but they point to a vision of worship and belonging that extends far beyond the symbol.

Eaton is helpful here and worth quoting at length:

> The weighty and visionary content of this psalm is expressed abruptly in vv. 1 and 7. Perhaps this abruptness is connected with its prophetic character, shafts of meaning merging from the mysterious depths. ... It is a transfigured city that is described, Zion according to her meaning in God's purpose. That he himself founded her, and on the mountains that reach into heaven and bear the very traffic of heaven—all this to say that she is one with the heavenly sanctuary. ... The psalm shows how the worshippers in the temple in Jerusalem might see through to

21. Terrien, *The Psalms*, 623. Albert Pietersma's translation of 86:7 [Heb 87:7] in the LXX is as follows: "The habitation of all, when they are glad, is in you" (*A New English Translation of the Septuagint* [Oxford: Oxford University Press, 2000]). Interestingly, the online version is slightly different: "Seeing that they are glad, the habitation of all is in you," http://ccat.sas.upenn.edu/nets/edition/24-ps-nets.pdf. In either case, however, the translation echoes that sense of belonging in Yahweh, rather than belonging in or through the temple.

> an immense meaning; because they encountered there the Lord, the Most High, maker of all people, they saw in Zion a summit carrying them into heaven. Around this throne of the Creator all people must gather; his pleasure must be in the songs and dances of all. With a visionary leap beyond all historical divisions and enmities, the psalmist sees the Lord enrolling all peoples as natives of Zion. How this could come about is not explained; only that it has been "spoken," created beforehand by the divine word.[22]

There is a real sense in which this psalm of Zion points the worshiper beyond the physicality of city and temple to a spiritual reality that encompasses and transcends both. Zion is key to Yahweh's purposes because his purposes were never intended to be limited to geographic Jerusalem. The holy city was always, in some sense, a means to an end, and that end was always meant to include the nations worshiping around the throne of the Creator and King. Jesus's discussion of true worship with the woman of Samaria surely encompassed the psalmist's vision of worshipful reality. And it is not hard to imagine John the apostle calling the words of Psalm 87 to mind as he penned his powerful images of apocalyptic worship in Revelation 5 and 7. To suggest that the Old Testament people of God had no insight into that eschatological reality seems to run counter to the imagery of Psalm 87. The relationship between the Testaments is complex—pretending that it is otherwise is not helpful. Psalm 87 illustrates that the Old Testament people of God were well able to see beyond signs to their essential meaning.

WORSHIP AND RADICAL INCLUSION

One other aspect of Psalm 87 seems to speak powerfully from the perspective of biblical theology, namely its voice of radical inclusion.

There is, of course, debate about the identity of the recipients of the divinely decreed citizenship of Zion.[23] Some, like Bernard Duhm, limit the identity of these "foreign" citizens of Zion to Jews in the diaspora, spread throughout the Near East following the Babylonian exile.[24] Hermann Gunkel expands this definition slightly by including gentile proselytes along with

22. Eaton, *Psalms*, 213–14.
23. For a thorough and well-reasoned discussion of the options, see Hossfeld and Zenger, *Psalms 2*, 379–82.
24. Bernard Duhm, *Die Psalmen eklärt*, KHC 14 (Freiburg: Mohr Siebeck, 1899), 218–19.

diaspora Jews.[25] Andreas Stadelmann, far from seeing this as an expansive picture of inclusion, argues that Psalm 87 is a clarion call to Jews of the dispersal, reminding them that—though small and sidelined—Jerusalem has been rebuilt and Zion still exists. Thus, for Stadelmann, the poem remains nationalistic in its scope.[26] This seems unlikely, however, because although Psalm 87 is unusual as an example of Zion theology in the Psalter, its ingathering emphasis echoes themes found in the Prophets (primarily in Isaiah and Micah)[27] and its expansive voice of transnational inclusion within the worshiping community of Israel is far from unique within the broader book of Psalms. The Yahweh *mālāk* psalms (Pss 93–100) are marked by this internationalizing focus, with "all the earth" (e.g., 96:1; 98:4) called to join the community of worship in praising Yahweh.[28] So, although this image of the nations' belonging is unusual for the Zion psalms, it is not particularly unusual for the Psalter (especially Books IV and V), and it is not unusual for the Old Testament.[29]

However, even taking the view that the psalmist is presenting some sort of amorphous eschatological picture of the ingathering of the gentile nations into the body of Yahweh's people,[30] one can still imagine that the song must have grated somewhat whenever it was sung.[31] It is easy to imagine that there must have been something (at least, slightly) jarring about Psalm 87 for the original reader/singer. In many ways, it is hard to imagine Psalm 87

25. Hermann Gunkel, *Introduction to the Psalms: The Genres of the Religious Lyric of Israel*, trans. James D. Nogalski (Macon, GA: Mercer University Press, 1998), 379–80.

26. Andreas Stadelmann, "Psalm 87(86): Theologischer Gehalt und gesellschaftliche Wirkung," in *Ein Gott, eine Offenbarung: Beiträge zur biblischen Exegese, Theologie und Spiritualität*, ed. Friedrich V. Reiterer (Würzburg: Echter Verlag, 1991), 333–56.

27. Goldingay, *Psalms 2*, 632.

28. Jamie A. Grant, "Creation and Kingship: Environment and Witness in the Yahweh Mālāk Psalms," in *As Long as Earth Endures: The Bible Creation and the Environment*, ed. Jonathan Moo and Robin Routledge (Nottingham: Apollos, 2014), 92–106.

29. Zenger is correct in his observation that the different interpretative perspectives tend to be driven by one's view of *Sitz im Leben* and the structure of the psalm. The central rhetoric of the psalm revolves around the "glorious things" (87:3) that are laid out plainly in 87:4–6, the unlikely (perhaps even unthinkable) declarations of birth in Zion which bring an unmistakably expansive eschatological vision to mind. See Hossfeld and Zenger, *Psalms 2*, 382, and also Thijs Booij, "Some Observations on Psalm 87," *VT* 37.1 (1987): 16–25. Several of the commentators associate Psalm 87 with the prophetic tradition (see, e.g., A. F. Kirkpatrick, *The Book of Psalms* [Cambridge: Cambridge University Press, 1910], 518, who suggests that it may well be the oracular nature of the poem that resulted in its awkward Hebrew text).

30. "Amorphous" in the sense that there is no clear discussion of mechanism. It is far from clear as to how this image will occur, simply that it will happen.

31. See the helpful discussion in Jones, "The Multiracial City."

ever being a popular composition in the sense of "yes, let's sing the one about Egypt and Babylon." Annually, the people remembered the brutal oppression of their forebears by "Rahab" (Egypt) in the Passover festival (Exod 12:1–30; Deut 16:1–8). The very founding identity of the nation is rooted in that story of miraculous release from a brutally oppressive superpower. Yet, here, that very oppressor's belonging is celebrated. Babylon's rise to power and violent association with Judah would have been much more recent but, for all that, fresher in the memory. It would have been hard to see beyond the brutalities of the fall of Jerusalem to sing this proleptic expression of brotherhood with a whole heart and loud voice.

Yet, that is precisely the responsibility that the psalmist lays upon the singer: she or he is to look beyond past injustices—brutal and real as they were—to a future reality of boundary-defying inclusion. The Egyptians did not stop being identifiably Egyptian, but they were to be deemed "born in Zion." The Babylonians were still recognizably such, but they were "born in her." There is an unmistakable voice of radical inclusion in the psalmist's presentation of Yahweh's eschatological kingdom.[32]

The biblical-theological ramifications of Psalm 87's unusual imagery are not difficult to discern. Christl Maier, for example, points out the intertestamental echoes that likely shape Paul's thought in Galatians 4:26: "But the Jerusalem that is above is free, and she is our mother."[33] However, it strikes me that the ramifications of Psalm 87 resonate loudly throughout much of the New Testament epistles in particular. Maier's argument specifically regarding Galatians 4:26 is particularly poignant and well-grounded in exegetical reflection on the LXX text of Psalm 87 (MT 86), but this pericope is, of course, part of a much broader discussion of the place of Jewish and gentile background believers together in the infant church. In the previous chapter, by way of example, Paul states:

32. Note Smith's helpful comments on the structure of Psalm 87 which focuses attention on the central statement that "this one and that one were born in her" (87:5). See Mark S. Smith, "The Structure of Psalm LXXXVII," *VT* 38.3 (1988): 357–58.

33. Christl M. Maier, "Psalm 87 as a Reappraisal of the Zion Tradition and Its Reception in Galatians 4:26," *CBQ* 69.3 (2007): 473–86. She concludes: "In sum, Gal 4:26 is one example of a highly sophisticated exegesis that is based on an idea unique in the Hebrew Bible. The vision of Psalm 87 that God grants the nations citizenship in Jerusalem may be a Utopian political concept. Its reception in the LXX and Galatians 4, however, shows that Paul's idea of God's people consisting of Jews and Gentiles alike has a root in Scripture. It is therefore no coincidence that this Zion song today is used in Christian communities as a baptismal psalm." The LXX, it should be pointed out, translates Zion as *μήτηρ Σειών*, "mother Zion," the eschatological mother of the nations (see Joachim Schaper, *Eschatology in the Greek Psalter*, WUNT 2 [Tübingen: Mohr Siebeck, 1994], 99–101).

> Πάντες γὰρ υἱοὶ θεοῦ ἐστε διὰ τῆς πίστεως ἐν Χριστῷ Ἰησοῦ· ὅσοι γὰρ εἰς Χριστὸν ἐβαπτίσθητε, Χριστὸν ἐνεδύσασθε. οὐκ ἔνι Ἰουδαῖος οὐδὲ Ἕλλην, οὐκ ἔνι δοῦλος οὐδὲ ἐλεύθερος, οὐκ ἔνι ἄρσεν καὶ θῆλυ· πάντες γὰρ ὑμεῖς εἷς ἐστε ἐν Χριστῷ Ἰησοῦ. εἰ δὲ ὑμεῖς Χριστοῦ, ἄρα τοῦ Ἀβραὰμ σπέρμα ἐστέ, κατ' ἐπαγγελίαν κληρονόμοι.
>
> For you are all children of God through faith in Christ Jesus. For as many of you who were baptized into Christ, have clothed yourselves in Christ. There is neither Jew nor Greek, there is neither slave nor free, there is neither male nor female; for all of you are one in Christ Jesus. And if you are of Christ, then you are Abraham's seed and heirs according to promise. (Gal 3:26–29, author's translation)

While not directly in terms of word choice, conceptually, in this message of union and shared inheritance, Paul also echoes the imagery of Psalm 87. The privileged "birthright" of Zion is extended to all, regardless of ethnic origin, social status, or gender. All are children. All are heirs. All belong.

It is interesting to note how much of the New Testament epistolary content is devoted to the relationship between Jewish- and gentile-background believers within the church. This was, of course, the original contention of Krister Stendahl with regard to Romans, an argument that has sparked a great deal of debate over the years.[34] Ignoring the broader issues surrounding the New Perspective on Paul, there is something in Stendahl's original contention: the relationship between Jewish- and gentile-background communities within the church draws a great deal of apostolic attention throughout the epistles. Whether it is in Romans, Galatians, or Ephesians, issues of inclusion and belonging seem to be central to Paul's thought. As well as being theologically important to the "apostle to the nations," the merging of diverse communities into a singular church gave rise to a great many practical and cultural ramifications. Whether it was the relative equity of treatment for Jewish- or Greek proselyte-background believers in the early Jerusalem church (Acts 6), or the stipulations that would be applied to the (increasingly) non-Jewish background church (Acts 15), or leadership conflicts based around the continuation or otherwise of former practices (Gal 2), the practical ramifications of cross-cultural inclusion have always been real and difficult to navigate. Yet the voice of Psalm 87 points to an

34. Krister Stendahl, "The Apostle Paul and the Introspective Conscience of the West," *HTR* 56 (1963): 199–215.

eschatological image of complete belonging that transcends all culture, all historic harms, and all hatreds, whether they be petty or deep-rooted and fully justified.

It is the ongoing task of the universal church to work toward the creation of that reality in the here and now, as a foretaste of the eschatological norm. Inclusion is an essential aspect of the gospel and will always be an essential indication of the transformation that an encounter with Christ brings. "Thy Kingdom come, thy will be done, on earth as it is in heaven"—whether we mumble it mindlessly or not—is a prayer for radical societal transformation. The Christian church should always be about the importation of eschatological norms into historical reality. The future-focused imagery of Psalm 87 is of enemies celebrating the worship of Yahweh together with a sense of common belonging and a shared core identity. That which one day will be our unceasing norm should increasingly become our present historical reality.[35]

All too often it feels like our theology speaks in and into a vacuum, without reference to the world around us. It is impossible in 2020 to write about Psalm 87 without some consideration of contemporary events. Worldwide we live in cultures that are increasingly polarized, a world where views that would have been deemed extreme just five years ago have become normalized. Communities no longer communicate; they shout at each other. People are separated along lines of race, class, wealth, gender, language, age, and a whole host of other markers. Surely, Psalm 87—this obscure and unusual ancient Hebrew song—speaks into our present realities powerfully. The church should always be marked by *radical* inclusion. The eschatological image of shared citizenship should be ever-increasingly visible in the life of the Christian church today.[36]

CONCLUSION

How then does Psalm 87 speak from a biblical-theological perspective? Firstly, it seems to challenge some of the careless methodological maxims that are common in discussion of the relationship between the Testaments. There may be some truth in the broadly held premise of movement from the literal in the Old to the spiritual (nonliteral) in the New, but the interpreter

35. Jones, "The Multiracial City."

36. "The church suffers from the same temptation as Jerusalem. It is constitutionally inclined to forget that God's purpose is to make all nations its citizens and so becomes gloomy and closed in on itself. The psalm thus sets God's vision before it. ... The psalm offers a promise of an ethnically diverse church" (Goldingay, *Psalms* 2, 641).

should be careful not to overstate that movement because there is strong evidence that Old Testament believers clearly saw the spiritual realities that were the real underpinning of the physical markers of the covenant. Psalm 87 is one such indicator. Secondly, Psalm 87 prepares the reader for the important voice of inclusion that rings out so clearly in and from the Gospels. It speaks of the vital importance of radical inclusion, and it probably implies that such inclusion is never going to be easy. It may never be easy, but the merging of diverse and separated communities in worship is a marker of belonging—a belonging that is both ordained and indelibly recorded by Yahweh. That *is* the real reality. The challenge is to make it so in our churches in the turbulent world in which we live.

14

Yahweh among the Gods: The Trial for Justice in Psalm 82

Andrew J. Schmutzer

This study considers Yahweh's interaction with other "gods" in the Psalms, especially Psalm 82, an Asaph psalm. Israel's historical exodus, led by the sovereign God who hears and responds, is replayed in the neighboring Asaph psalms. The only offense mentioned in Psalm 81 is Israel's worship of other gods. The message is clear: the pagan gods do not hear, nor do they rescue the needy. Drawing on genre and linguistic factors, it is argued that Psalm 82 depicts a courtroom scene, in which God indicts the incompetent international gods (82:1b, אלהים), for abandoning the needs of the oppressed under their care.

INTRODUCTION

It may come as a surprise to some, but the God who miraculously delivered Israel out of Egypt, cherishing her like a mother and gardener ("You brought a vine out" Ps 80:8a ESV),[1] still faced a host of competitors for Israel's affection. In possibly the oldest poetry of the Hebrew Bible (Exod 15), Moses leads the liberated Israelites in a triumphant song that includes the question, "Who is like you among the gods, O Lord?" (באלם יהוה, 15:11a NLT). This is a stunning juxtaposition, indeed, placing Yahweh among the pagan gods![2]

1. All Scripture citations are the author's translation, unless otherwise noted.

2. Robert Alter quips, "This line has inspired a good deal of rather nervous commentary," but quickly adds, "Hebrew writers had no difficulty in conceding the existence of other deities,

There is a reason Egypt occurs no less than fifteen times in the psalms (esp. Pss 105, 106).[3] There are related reasons why gods and idols also occur in the psalms (eleven and six times respectively in 105 and 106).[4] The situation gets worse when Israel arrives in Canaan. In just one psalm, for example, we are told that God's covenant people: "mingled with the nations [גוים]," "worshiped their idols [עצבים]," and "sacrificed their sons and daughters to demons [שדים]" (Ps 106:35–37). This is a dark picture. Why would the Psalter include such language in Israel's "Book of Praise"? Actually, this is not unique to the psalms, nor does historic treason diminish worship. The Psalter functions as a "theological pantry," stocked with testimonies of the righteous and historical reflections on the uniqueness of Israel's God. While much of our study will focus on Yahweh and the gods in Psalm 82, it is necessary to observe some key terms and themes that form the religious backdrop to the Psalter.

History Recounted

In Deuteronomy 1:6–4:40, Moses sketched the nation's recent journey from Sinai, through the wilderness and into Moab. The suffering Israel experienced was the result of the nation's rebelliousness against Yahweh—in no way was Yahweh weak, unjust, or absent in the face of national disasters.[5] Moses's exhortation was designed to remind Israel that their worship and service to Yahweh lies exclusively in God's uniqueness as the transcendent, covenant-making God. The terms employed here are significant: "so that you might know that the Lord is God (האלהים); besides him there is no other" (Deut 4:35), and "acknowledge ... that the Lord is God (האלהים) in heaven above and on the earth below. There is no other" (4:39 NIV). Any

---

though always stipulating, as here, their absolute inferiority to the God of Israel" (*The Five Books of Moses: A Translation with Commentary* [New York: Norton, 2004], 400). The key uses of אלם ("gods") in poetry are Exodus 15:11; Psalms 29:1; 89:6; Daniel 11:36; cf. 1QM 1:10; 14:16; see Frank M. Cross, "אל," *TDOT*, 1:254.

3. See Psalms 68:31; 78:12, 43, 51; 80:8; 81:5, 10; 105:23, 38; 106:7, 21; 114:1; 135:8, 9; 136:10.

4. See for "gods," Psalms 82:1, 6; 86:8; 95:3; 96:4, 5; 97:7, 9; 135:5; 136:2; 138:1; for "idols," 96:5; 97:7; 106:36, 38; 115:4; 135:15. Sometimes both nouns are directly equated, "For all the *gods* of the nations are *idols*" (96:5).

5. Marvin A. Sweeney, *Tanak: A Theological and Critical Introduction to the Jewish Bible* (Minneapolis: Fortress, 2012), 149.

alternatives are not real gods, just "other gods." These two verses form the climax of two sections in Moses's reminder (4:32–35, 36–39).[6]

Figure 14.1

PANEL 1 (Deut 4:32–35)	PANEL 2 (Deut 4:36–39)
"earth [ארץ] ... heavens [שמים] (32) heard ... voice ... out of a fire (33) any god [אלהים] ... out of another nation (34) know YHWH is God [האלהים] (35a) beside him there is no other" [אין עוד] (35b)	"heaven [שמים] ... earth [ארץ] (36a) heard ... words ... out of the fire" (36b) his presence ... before you nations (37b-38a) acknowledge ... YHWH is God [האלהים] (39a) heaven above ... earth below (39b) there is no other" [אין עוד] (39c)

This is a daring "confession of incomparability."[7] In these texts, the reiteration that "the Lord is [the true, only] God (האלהים)" (4:35, 39) highlights not only the consequence of Israel's election but the distinctiveness of God's revelation. This robust creed became a desperate affirmation: "Give thanks to the God of gods" (לאלהי האלהים, Ps 136:2). The effect is to elevate the supreme power of Yahweh on behalf of a nation that is obligated to recognize him as their unique God. At the Red Sea, they began celebrating Yahweh as a "warrior" who "reigns" (Exod 15:3a, 18a). In Joshua, Rahab's confession (Josh 2:7–11) is potent, "He is God in heaven above and on earth below" (2:11b; see also 1 Kgs 8:23). Notice too, that the core of her confession (2:9b–11a) recounts Israel's soteriological experience: the exodus, the drying up of the Red Sea, the fear of the nations, and the execution of Og and Sihon.[8]

The combined theological message of the First Commandment and the Shema shows that Deuteronomy does not deny the existence of other gods; it presupposes them.[9] Such creedal statements demand Israel's exclusive devotion to Yahweh alone. Thomas Mann observes, "In effect, the Shema

6. A definitive study on this: Nathan MacDonald, *Deuteronomy and the Meaning of "Monotheism,"* FAT 2/1 (Tübingen: Mohr Siebeck, 2003).

7. The language of W. H. Schmidt, "אלהים," *TLOT*, 1:124.

8. For quality discussions of Rahab's confession, see David M. Howard Jr., *Joshua*, NAC 5 (Nashville: Broadman & Holman, 1998), 102–5; Thomas B. Dozeman, *Joshua 1–12: A New Translation with Introduction and Commentary*, The Anchor Yale Bible 6B (New Haven: Yale University Press, 2015), 223–46.

9. Richard Bauckham, "Biblical Theology and the Problems of Monotheism," in *Out of Egypt: Biblical Theology and Biblical Interpretation*, ed. Craig Bartholomew et al., vol. 5, Scripture and Hermeneutics Series (Grand Rapids: Zondervan, 2004), 190.

is an extension of the first of the Ten Commandments (5:6–7). There are two primary foci: first, the confession that only Yahweh can be Israel's God (rather than that Yahweh is the only God); and second, that this confession carries with it the demand to love Yahweh ... technical treaty language for loyalty" (see Matt 22:34–40).[10] In these creeds, Israel pledged their allegiance to Yahweh and no other. These themes only rise in intensity: "For the LORD your God is God of gods and Lord of lords" (Deut 10:17a). When Israel betrayed their loyalty to Yahweh, who acted so majestically to deliver and sustain his people, it pushed God to a sarcastic anger that he unloaded on Jeremiah, confiding that Israel has "as many gods [אלהים] as you have towns" (Jer 11:13 NIV).

The insights we can glean from these texts include the following: (1) Yahweh's claim to be God (האלהים) is more soteriological than ontological, though they are related.[11] Israel's covenant relationship is rooted in a cherished recital of God's historical acts for his people. (2) Both Yahweh's presence and power fill the dynamic realms of "heaven and earth," where other national deities have staked out territories (see Deut 10:14). (3) God's unrivaled power is not only what Israel recognizes by experience, but what the theater of gods must concede by comparison—"worship him, all you gods!" (Ps 97:7). (4) His supreme power—"God of gods ... the great God" (Deut 10:17)—is unmatched precisely because he is powerful enough to make his election and defense *effective* in ways that are beyond the power of other gods (see 1 Kgs 8:23).[12] (5) Finally, the creedal epithet, "there is no other" (אין עוד, Deut 4:35b, 39c), reinforces the uniqueness of Israel's covenant God. With didactic force, Moses claimed that God was both universal ("heaven and earth") and peerless ("no other"). For this reason, Yahweh's jealousy for his people has a warrant of distinctiveness; he detests betrayal—"they aroused his jealousy with their idols" (Ps 78:58b).

10. Thomas W. Mann, *The Book of the Torah*, 2nd ed. (Eugene, OR: Cascade Books, 2013), 184.

11. MacDonald, *Deuteronomy*, 215. The definite article appears with God (האלהים) approximately 370 times out of over 2,600 occurrences. These could be called a "naming" or "solitary" use of the article (Gen 5:22; 1 Kgs 18:39; Bill T. Arnold and John H. Choi, *A Guide to Biblical Hebrew Syntax* [Cambridge: Cambridge University Press, 2003], 2.6.3, 2.6.4).

12. W. H. Schmidt, "אלהים," *TLOT*, 1:124; Bauckham, "Problems of Monotheism," 195.

THE ASAPH COLLECTION

Our particular study of Psalm 82 is one of twelve psalms associated with Asaph (50; 73–83) and located near the midpoint of the Psalter.[13] A Levite appointed by David to lead worship, Asaph's duties continued under Solomon (2 Chr 5:11–14),[14] even singing at the dedication of Solomon's Temple.[15] The descendants of Asaph extended this service, both in the cleansing of the temple under Hezekiah (2 Chr 29:13), and further service after the exile (Ezra 2:41; Neh 12:46).[16] Later, we will observe some linguistic and thematic connections that bring significant rhetorical movement to this collection, but for now, we note some central themes.

Several core theological themes reverberate through the Asaph collection. God is the judge (Pss 50:6; 75; 76:9; 82:1, 2, 3, 8), and he shows divine anger toward his people (50:22; 76; 78:58, 62; 79; 80:5). Amazingly, the nation's constant rebellion is matched by God's ongoing grief (78:40–41).[17] This relationship finds God vulnerable, not mechanical.[18] Clearly, God's anger is not the final image, for God is exalted as the ultimate judge of the earth

13. Notice that the psalm of Asaph is also found in 1 Chronicles 16:8–36. Close inspection reveals editorial changes drawn from Psalms 105:6, 8, 12; 96:6, 8, 10, and 106:48. The themes of nations, gods and idols, and the Lord as a reigning judge all reappear, as found in other Asaphite psalms. According to Nancy L. deClaissé-Walford, it is arguable that there was a much larger collection of Asaph psalms, from which only the twelve in the Psalter became "authoritative" for the postexilic Jewish community, struggling without their temple and cultic apparatus (*Reading from the Beginning: The Shaping of the Hebrew Psalter* [Macon, GA: Mercer University Press, 1997], 73–74).

14. In 2 Chronicles 29:30, a reference is made to Levites singing "praises to the Lord with the words of David and of the seer, Asaph." This kind of formula could suggest that Asaph was a composer of liturgical hymns alongside David. See the discussion of Alastair G. Hunter, *An Introduction to the Psalms*, T&T Clark Approaches to Biblical Studies (London: T&T Clark, 2008), 21–24.

15. See 1 Chronicles 6:39; 15:17; 16:7; 26:1; 2 Chronicles 5:12; Nehemiah 12:46.

16. The author of 1 Esdras writes that among those returning after the exile were "the Levites … the temple singers: the descendants of Asaph, one hundred twenty-eight (1 Esdras 5:26–27).

17. Terence E. Fretheim, *The Suffering of God: An Old Testament Perspective*, OBT (Philadelphia: Fortress, 1984), 111.

18. Rolf A. Jacobson, "'The Faithfulness of the Lord Endures Forever': The Theological Witness of the Psalter," in *Soundings of the Theology of the Psalms: Perspectives and Methods in Contemporary Scholarship*, ed. Rolf A. Jacobson (Minneapolis: Fortress, 2011), 121.

(82:8).[19] God has the moral resolve and emotional wherewithal necessary to bring justice continually and without compromise.[20]

God is also identified as the one who saves (Pss 50:23; 76:9; 78:22; 79:9; 80:3), delivers (Pss 50:22; 79; 82), and redeems (Pss 74; 77). In fact, only three of the twelve Asaphite psalms have no terms for God's salvific activity.[21] The final theme we note is that of creation. God not only creates (Ps 74:12–17), he also sustains a tottering earth (Ps 75:3; see also 82:5c). Of course, there is also the linguistic "theme" of the divine name אלהים ("God") that dominates these psalms. The broader Elohistic Psalter (Pss 42–83) has a distinct, though inconsistent preference for אלהים ("God") over יהוה ("Yahweh"), in reference to deity.[22] Maybe the *universality* of God is highlighted in this way, especially given the fact that nations and enemies are common themes in the Asaph collection (see Pss 74, 78, 82, 83). The God of Israel's history is also the God of the world.[23] However, one should not overstate the use of "Elohim" in these psalms, as Frank-Lothar Hossfeld and Erich Zenger astutely observe,

> Each Asaph psalm mentions the name YHWH at least once, even be it "only" in the short form; this must be intentional, not merely coincidental. The only exception, Psalm 82, actually proves the rule, since the setting of this psalm takes place in *the trial of the gods in heaven.* Psalm 82 is not about the historical revelation of YHWH to his people, but about *his superior divinity in comparison with the other doomed gods.*[24]

---

19. Christine Brown Jones, "The Message of the Asaphite Collection and Its Role in the Psalter," in *The Shape and Shaping of the Book of Psalms: The Current State of Scholarship*, ed. Nancy L. de-Claissé-Walford (Atlanta: SBL Press, 2014), 74. The insights of Jones's study are evident in this presentation of the Asaphite collection.

20. William P. Brown, *Seeing the Psalms: A Theology of Metaphor* (Louisville: Westminster John Knox, 2002), 182.

21. Jones, "Message of the Asaphite Collection," 75.

22. In the "Elohistic Psalter" (42–83), Yahweh occurs only 45 times and Elohim 210 times. But Psalms 1–41 and 84–150 find Yahweh occurring 584 times and Elohim 94 times. Outside 42–83, Yahweh is predominantly in colon "a" and Elohim in "b"; but within 42–83 the situation is reversed. Strangely, we find the names are also reversed in synoptic psalms (compare 14:2, 4, 7 with 53:2, 4, 6; 40:13 [MT 14], 17 with 70:1 [MT 2], 5. The observation of Bruce K. Waltke is that there is no consensus to explain these dynamics of Psalms 42–83 (*An Old Testament Theology: An Exegetical, Canonical, and Thematic Approach* [Grand Rapids: Zondervan, 2007], 884).

23. W. H. Schmidt, "אלהים," *TLOT*, 1:118.

24. Frank-Lothar Hossfeld and Erich Zenger, "The So-Called Elohistic Psalter: A New Solution for an Old Problem," in *A God So Near: Essays on Old Testament Theology in Honor of Patrick D.*

If the Asaphite psalms (Pss 50, 73–83) lift up God as judge over the nations, the surrounding Korahite psalms (Pss 42/43–49, 84–85, 87–88) stress God's *royal* nature. It should be no surprise, then, that the Asaphite collection contains the highest concentration of divine discourse in the entire Psalter, and this richly informs our study of Psalm 82 (vv. 2–7).[25] In the Asaphite psalms, God routinely speaks in judgment or warning. He also calls Israel, people groups, and even the gods to account (e.g., Pss 50, 76, 81, 82).

Divine judgment has the first and last word (cf. Pss 50, 82–83), with God's anger registered in the middle (Pss 74, 77–80). Psalm 50, the opening Asaph psalm, sets the tone for the entire corpus: as judge, God rebukes Israel, specifically for not offering their sacrifices with a heart of thanksgiving (50:4, 6). Those who hate God's "instruction" will never be ready to "honor" him (50:15b, 17a). The God who once delivered still hears cries for national rescue. As William P. Brown notes, "Calling upon God for deliverance and acknowledging God's salvific work are the two performative poles of this collection."[26] The distressed community still cries out for aid—because their temple has been destroyed (see Pss 74, 79, 80, 83).

For good reason, needy people still recite God's mighty acts (Pss 73:28; 77:11; 78:4). History can repeat itself in "updates" to older phrases. For example: "He remembers his covenant for ever" is reissued in an Asaph psalm as: "Remember [plural imperative] his covenant forever" (cf. Ps 105:8 with 1 Chr 16:15). In a time of national difficulty, a new identity is enacted for a new audience.[27] By highlighting God's role in creation (Ps 50:1, 5)—for Israel's political straits and the governance of the whole cosmos—the Asaphite psalms declare that God is sovereign over all (50:12), and he remains powerful, despite the nation's recent defeat.[28] We now turn our attention toward Psalm 82.

Miller, ed. Brent A. Strawn and Nancy R. Bowen (Winona Lake, IN: Eisenbrauns, 2003), 48; emphasis added.

25. See Psalms 50:5, 7–15, 16–23; 75:2–5, 10; 81:6–16; 82:2–4, 6–7.

26. William P. Brown, *Psalms*, Interpreting Biblical Texts (Nashville: Abingdon, 2010), 95.

27. Terry Giles and William J. Doan, *Twice Used Songs: Performance Criticism of the Songs of Ancient Israel* (Peabody, MA: Hendrickson, 2009), 93.

28. Jones, "Message of the Asaphite Collection," 76–77.

THE COSMIC KING DEMOTES THE GODS (PS 82)

Genres, Gods, and Myths

It is the particular terms, divine discourse, and heavenly theater of Psalm 82 that make it a rather unique psalm. In the estimation of Marvin E. Tate, "It is *sui generis* in the psalter"—without parallel.[29] Because of this, equally unique classifications or descriptions have been proposed, such as, "Petition for Divine Justice,"[30] "gods-complaint,"[31] "Prophetic Tribunal,"[32] and "oracle of sarcasm against other gods."[33] Given the oracular character of the psalm, some describe it as "prophetic liturgy,"[34] and still others, a form of protest/lament.[35] More recently, some commentators simply do not classify the psalm,[36] or declare it "unclassifiable."[37] Yet, as Brown reminds us, noting genre types is not pointless, as they still provide flexible templates to appreciate what is both common and distinctive.[38]

While some interpreters may see ancient Near Eastern mythological elements in Psalm 82,[39] it is far harder to deny the reality of the Divine Assembly (בעדת אל, "in the assembly of *El*," 82:1) or "council" in other psalms

29. Marvin E. Tate, *Psalms 51–100*, WBC 20 (Dallas: Word, 1990), 332.
30. Richard J. Clifford, *Psalms 73–150*, AOTC (Nashville: Abingdon, 2003), 330.
31. Daniel McClellan, "The Gods-Complaint: Psalm 82 as a Psalm of Complaint," *JBL* 137 (2018): 833–51.
32. Tate, *Psalms 51–100*, 332; referencing D. M. Fleming, "The Divine Council as Type-Scene in the Hebrew Bible" (PhD diss., The Southern Baptist Theological Seminary, 1989), 334–35.
33. C. Hassell Bullock, *Psalms*, vol. 2, Teach the Text Commentary Series (Grand Rapids: Baker Academic, 2017), 75.
34. Hans-Joachim Kraus, *Psalms 60–150*, CC, trans. Hilton C. Oswald (Minneapolis: Fortress, 1983), 154; Craig C. Broyles, *Psalms*, New International Biblical Commentary (Peabody, MA: Hendrickson, 1999), 335; similarly, Geoffrey W. Grogan, *Psalms*, The Two Horizons Old Testament Commentary (Grand Rapids: Eerdmans, 2008), 146.
35. John Goldingay, *Psalms, Volume 2: Psalms 42–89*, BCOTWP (Grand Rapids: Baker Academic, 2007), 559; Tremper Longman III, *Psalms*, TOTC (Downers Grove, IL: IVP Academic, 2014), 305.
36. Nancy deClaissé-Walford, Rolf A. Jacobson, and Beth LaNeel Tanner, *The Book of Psalms*, NICOT (Grand Rapids: Eerdmans, 2014), 641–44; W. Dennis Tucker Jr. and Jamie A. Grant, *Psalms*, vol. 2, NIV Application Commentary (Grand Rapids: Zondervan, 2018), 214–27.
37. Brown declares Psalm 82 as "unclassifiable" (*Psalms*, 147), including Psalms 50; 73; 115; 133.
38. Brown, *Psalms*, 58.
39. Clifford, *Psalms 73–150*, 63–66; Frank-Lothar Hossfeld and Erich Zenger, *Psalms 2: A Commentary on Psalms 51–100*, Hermeneia; trans. Linda M. Maloney (Minneapolis: Augsburg Fortress, 2005), 329–30; John W. Hilber, "Psalms," in *Zondervan Illustrated Bible Backgrounds Commentary*, vol. 5, ed. John H. Walton (Grand Rapids: Zondervan, 2009), esp. Pss 29 (344–48), 74 (380–83), 82 (388–89), 89 (395–98).

(cf. בסוד ... אל, "El ... in the council," 89:7).[40] Myth and eschatology operate as metaphor systems for theological interpretation of historical events—"you crushed the heads of Leviathan" (רצצת ראשי לויתן, Ps 74:14).[41] At times, ancient Near Eastern Canaanite (Ugaritic) mythology was repurposed in a psalm (Ps 104:3b–4; see also Ps 29).[42] For this reason, the Lord's triumph over the nations is also his victory over their national gods, who are then summoned to take their place in his entourage: "Bow down, all gods [כל־אלהים], before him" (Ps 97:7). Clearly, the psalmists do not deny the existence of idols or other beings, just their deity.[43] In his helpful treatment, *Theology of the Psalms*, Hans-Joachim Kraus gives an appropriate description of the interplay between mythology and pagan deities:

> *[In] the Psalter there are tendencies toward transcendence that draw on the field of mythology.* But they have no function of their own that would revive and employ the total myth. ... References to mythology are found also in the praise that speaks of the overcoming of the gods. The gods of the peoples are as nothing before Yahweh (Ps. 96:5). Scorn is heaped on the idols (Ps. 135:15–18). In all these allusions it is astonishing that Yahweh, in contrast to the gods of the surrounding nations who had to overcome the chaos, did not have to wage a toilsome war with the primeval powers, and that there is not a single word about a victory in battle against the foreign gods. The God of Israel reigns over the hostile powers in unchallenged sovereignty. They have been stripped of all power. *It is only as relics that they make their appearance.*[44]

Three points of perspective are in order. First, regarding the function of myth, as I am using it, Israel never requests a divine intervention that is not well-grounded in the unity and continuity of their salvific past. In particular, the historical events of creation and the exodus provide the theological "prism" that sharpens a covenantal focus and fuels confidence for their

40. So BDB 417.1; *HALOT* 2:790; Heinz-Josef Fabry, "עדה," *TDOT*, 10:477 [468–81].

41. G. B. Caird, *The Language and Imagery of the Bible* (Grand Rapids: Eerdmans, 1980), 219.

42. The Lord is the one "who rides on the clouds" (Ps 68:4) in divine-warrior theology. This is ancient Near Eastern storm-god imagery, particularly of Baal mythology, and used elsewhere in the Old Testament (Deut 33:26; Pss 18:9; 104:3b–4; Isa 19:1; Nah 1:3); see Tremper Longman III and Daniel Reid, *God Is a Warrior* (Grand Rapids: Zondervan, 1995).

43. Caird, *Language and Imagery*, 236.

44. Hans-Joachim Kraus, *Theology of the Psalms*; trans. Keith Crim (Minneapolis: Fortress, 1992), 129; emphasis added.

immanent recurrence.[45] The message of Psalm 82 thrives in a theological tension between the birth of deliverance and the culmination of enduring hope. Second, if the ontology of the gods is a sticking point for some interpreters, the biblical writers focus more on the ethical obligations and moral *competence* of these deities. Third, and building on these prior points, I take Psalm 82 as rooted in historical rather than imaginary impulse. If metaphorical language is used, it is not based on what is excluded from a writer's view of reality.[46] For good reason then, the theology of Yahweh's cosmic kingship forms the backdrop for the *legal trial* of Psalm 82—what W. H. Schmidt calls, "the mythical judgment scene."[47] This connects the "Most High" (עליון, Pss 47:2; 97:9) with the nations' gods (95:3; see also 29:1; 96:4–5; 97:7, 9), in a concern for international justice and world stability (93:1b; 96:10–13; 98:7–9).

The Israelite community is now called to live in this divine reality of Yahweh's supreme kingship— כי אל גדול יהוה ומלך גדול על כל־אלהים ("For a great God [*El*] is the Lord, and a greater King over all gods," 95:3; cf. Pss 47:2; 135:5). However, God's cosmic rule will not be recognized internationally until a later eschatological time. Because the Israelite people are experiencing God's deliverance from wicked powers (Pss 97:8, 10–12), God's final judgment of the nations is yet to be realized (96:10–13; 98:9). Yet because the covenant community has been given insight into the heavenly council and God's ensuing decree, they must now regard God as the cosmic caring king and ultimate judge whose unrivaled kingship will bring all promises to fulfillment.[48] This is the context in which the nations' gods are mentioned because, they in turn, highlight Yahweh's world dominion. Psalm 82 has a unique contribution to make.

Rhetorical Elements in Psalm 82

Exploring the message of Psalm 82 reveals that God's judgeship searches out all "corners" of the world. Beyond the nations, even the gods in the heavenly

45. Michael Fishbane, *Biblical Interpretation in Ancient Israel* (Oxford: Clarendon Press, 1988), 356.

46. Michael S. Heiser, "Divine Council," in *Dictionary of the Old Testament Wisdom, Poetry and Writings*, ed. Tremper Longman III and Peter Enns (Downers Grove, IL: IVP Academic, 2008), 115.

47. W. H. Schmidt, "אלהים," *TLOT*, 1:120.

48. Broyles, *Psalms*, 338.

realm can be arraigned. The following chiastic arrangement helps elucidate the linguistic contour and thematic movement of the psalm.[49]

A God judges in the divine assembly (v. 1)
B Charge laid against the gods (v. 2)
C Charge violated by the gods (vv. 3–4)
D CENTER: Result of the failure of the gods (v. 5)
C′ Proclamation of the gods' former status (v. 6)
B′ Sentence of judgment on the gods (v. 7)
A′ Plea for God to rise and judge the earth (v. 8)

The observer of the heavenly tribunal is not identified, unlike Isaiah's or Micaiah's "I saw" statement (Isa 6; 1 Kgs 22; Hab 3:7). However, in the drama of the dethronement of the gods (אלהים, Ps 82:1b), it is the God (אלהים) of Israel who frames the opening and closing of the psalm (82:1a, 8a). It is speech, probably divine, that fills the center. Overlapping terms with the God of Israel (and so somewhat baffling), the gods are addressed as both "sons of the Most High" (בני עליון, 82:6b) and "gods" (אלהים, 82:1b, 6a). Verses 3–4 outline the legal charge against the gods: they have abdicated their role in protecting the helpless under their care—the quintessential task for a god was to advocate for the people in their domain. Shockingly, the gods have been *inactive* toward the helpless, and instead, have been despicably *active* in other ways: defending the unjust and showing favoritism to the malicious (82:2).

Indictment can be instructional.[50] The gods' violations are itemized by listing the *positive* measures that should have defined their commission by four imperatives: "vindicate" (שפט), "maintain the right" (צדיק), "rescue" (פלט), and "deliver" (נצל, 82:3–4). In turn, this series of imperatives highlight a stunning catalog of helpless groups: "weak" (דל), "orphan" (יתום), "poor" (עני), "oppressed" (רוש), "weak" (דל), and "needy" (אביון). Six terms are used to describe the helpless requiring protection (see Lev 19:15; Deut 24:14). By stacking terms that are virtually synonymous, the passage "conveys a sense of gross malfeasance."[51]

49. Adapted from Tate, *Psalms 51–100*, 334.
50. Allen P. Ross, *A Commentary on the Psalms*, vol. 2, Kregel Exegetical Library (42–89) (Grand Rapids: Kregel Academic, 2013), 722.
51. Clifford, *Psalms 73–150*, 65.

With the poet's great rhetorical skill, notice that the "wicked" (רשעים) utterly surround the "weak" (82:2b, 4b and 3a, 4a).[52] Elsewhere, when the godless abuse the godly "the foundations are destroyed" (Ps 11:3; 82:5c). Repeated terms create both a portrait and emphasis: רשעים—דל—דל—רשעים. Along with the gods who have colluded in the ethical crimes, the wicked are also in the plural—an *archetype* of guilt and profusion. The most miserable and desperate people are entirely hemmed in.

The center of the psalm is the declaration of result, "the plight of the misgoverned and misled,"[53] and employs a longer tricola (82:5).[54] The change is also grammatical. Preceding imperatives and second-person plurals now give way to four third-person plurals. Verse 5 functions as a thematic and linguistic fulcrum, pointing backward and forward. The ב preposition[55] ties verse 5a to verse 1 and verse 8, while כל and ארץ of verse 5b look forward to ארץ and כל of verse 8. The gods' culpability is acute—knowing God means caring for the needy (Ps 72:1–4, 12–14).[56] Rhetorically, the lack (לא) of "knowledge" (ידע) and "understanding" (בין, 82:5) among the gods (אלהים, 82:1b), who have failed to "vindicate" (שפט, 82:3), requires the cosmic God (אלהים) to rise and "judge" (שפט, 82:8). Establishing the primary theme of the psalm (the *Leitwort*), the verb שפט ("judge") occurs four times (82:1b "judgment," 2a "defend," 3a "defend," 8a "judge"). Whereas God is the subject of the first and last uses (82:1b, 8a), the accused are called out in between (82:2a, 3a).

A strong "inclusion" is created by three elements: "God-realm-judge" (82:1), or "God-judge-realm" (82:8). Emphasis is achieved by repeating

52. Significant for our study of Psalm 82 and its judicial character, the root רשע ("guilty, wicked person") "refers primarily to those who on the basis of their deeds should expect to be declared guilty in court" (Helmer Ringgren, "רשע," *TDOT*, 14:3). The plural noun רשעים ("wicked") occurs eighty-two times in the Psalter and generally as adversaries of the "righteous." One wonders if the helpless groups in Psalm 82 function in *counterpoint* to the "wicked" and so are implicitly viewed as "righteous."

53. Derek Kidner, *Psalms 73–150*, TOTC (Downers Grove, IL: InterVarsity, 1975), 298.

54. On the poetics of Psalm 82, see W. S. Prinsloo, "Psalm 82: Once Again, Gods or Men?" *Biblica*, 76 (1995): 219–28.

55. The gods "wander in darkness" because they lack insight into justice and righteousness. As a result, they perpetually "live" בחשכה ("in darkness"). The preposition could be classified as a ב of *condition* or *state* (Ronald J. Williams, *Williams' Hebrew Syntax*, 3rd ed., revised and expanded by John C. Beckman [Toronto: University of Toronto Press, 2007], 100).

56. Mignon R. Jacobs, "Toward an Old Testament Theology of Concern for the Underprivileged," in *Reading the Hebrew Bible for a New Millennium: Form, Concept, and Theological Perspective*, vol. 1, Studies in Antiquity and Christianity, ed. Wonil Kim et al. (Harrisburg, PA: Trinity Press International, 2000), 210.

multiple terms, especially "judge"; Alonso Schökel calls this "strong inclusion."[57] Note this rhetorical framing: the God of Israel is introduced as "standing in/among" (-נצב ב, v. 1a), and the psalm concludes with another active role, namely "take possession ... among" (-נחל ב, v. 8b). The concerns of heaven are the conditions of earth. This movement is revealing. Descending from the heavenly sphere to the earthly (vv. 1, 8 הארץ), a ב of *realm*[58] marks the domain of "the gods" (אלהים) who stand in counterpoint to "the nations" (הגוים)—the offenders over against the helpless, now under the new judicial care of God. Simon B. Parker writes, "Thus Ps 82 rhetorically acknowledges the gods' claims to be rulers of the nations, but does so only to demonstrate their failure and the justice of Yahweh's replacing them as ruler of the world."[59] The logic of the psalm suggests that those who appeal to God for justice are the helpless ones who have suffered from the gods' treachery.

Drama in the Heavenly Court

The heavenly court is a standard scene in the Old Testament and the ancient Near East, especially evident, for example, in 1 Kings 22:19–23; Job 1:6–12, and 2:1–6 (cf. בני אלהים, "sons of God").[60] Just as the prophet Isaiah is commissioned within the heavenly court (Isa 6:1–13), Psalm 82 ushers the reader into a divine assembly, but these voices are not always identified (cf. Isa 40:1–8). Not surprisingly, the phrases in 82:6, אלהים אתם ובני עליון ("gods are you, and sons of *Elyon*") share similar terms for the "assembly of the gods"

57. Luis Alonso Schökel, *A Manual of Hebrew Poetics*, SubBi 11 (Rome: Editrice Pontificio Istituto Biblico, 1988), 78; similarly, Psalm 73.

58. See *HALOT*, 1:104.4; Kraus, *Theology of the Psalms*, 25; with similar terms and function, עליון על־כל־האץ ("*Elyon* over all the earth" [Ps 83:18]; "*among* the nations" [Deut 4:27]).

59. Simon B. Parker, "Sons of (the) God(s)," in *DDD*, ed. Karel van der Toorn, Bob Becking, and Pieter W. van der Horst, 2nd ed. (Grand Rapids: Eerdmans, 1999), 797.

60. Other standard biblical texts of the heavenly court include: Zechariah 1:7–17; 3:1–5; Isaiah 40:1–8. The better treatments are Matitiahu Tsevat, "God and the Gods in Assembly," *HUCA* 40 (1969): 123–37; E. T. Mullen Jr., *The Assembly of the Gods: The Divine Council in Canaanite and Early Hebrew Literature*, HSM 24 (Chico, CA: Scholars Press, 1980). For insight into the ancient Near Eastern texts and background of the divine council, see Hilber, "Psalms," in *Zondervan Illustrated Bible Backgrounds Commentary*, vol. 5, ed. John H. Walton (Grand Rapids: Zondervan, 2009), esp. Psalms 29 (344–48), 74 (380–83), 82 (388–89), 89 (395–98). Contemporary Old Testament theologies have standard address of the heavenly court, see John Kessler, *Old Testament Theology: Divine Call and Human Response* (Waco, TX: Baylor University Press, 2013), 326–27; R. W. L. Moberly, *Old Testament Theology: Reading the Hebrew Bible as Christian Scripture* (Grand Rapids: Baker Academic, 2013), 248; John Goldingay, *Old Testament Theology: Israel's Faith*, vol. 2 (Downers Grove, IL: Inter-Varsity Press, 2006), 44–46, 57–67; Bernhard W. Anderson, *Contours of Old Testament Theology* (Minneapolis: Fortress, 1999), 67–68; Waltke, *Old Testament Theology*, 213–15, 273.

found in Psalm 29:1, בני אלים ("sons of gods," see also Pss 58, 75, 89). As we find these terms in Psalm 82, I agree with Kraus that "all the אלהים ('gods') are בני עליון ('sons of the Most High') and thus stand in the service of God 'Most High' (Ps. 82:6)."[61]

On the one hand, Elohim is Yahweh (Ps 95:3); therefore, Israel is summoned to "kneel before יהוה [Yahweh]. For he is our אלהים [God]" (95:6b–7a). On the other hand, "Elohim" can carry an element of polemic, even in doxology; after all, Yahweh is Elohim (יהוה אלהים)—a remarkable combination in Psalm 84:12—and this supplies both a role and an identifying name.[62] "Elohim" can also function as a name within the Asaph psalms, since abstract concepts would lack all reality.[63] As a proper name, Elohim often appears without an article, even serving as a vocative of direct address (Pss 5:11; 51:3). "He is Israel's God, and as such he is the Lord of the nations (Psalms 96; 98). ... He is אלהים (*Elohim*) who fights in the midst of and for his people against the gods and powers that want to control Israel."[64] Psalm 96:5 even uses a derogatory term for the foreign gods, calling them "worthless idols" (אלילים), possibly an intentional disfigurement of אלהים.[65] This term is used as part of a *contrast motif* in hymns exalting Yahweh as king (cf. Pss 96:5; 97:7). This usage also has an eschatological thrust since the coming of Yahweh will signal the end of idols (Ps 19:1, 3; Isa 2:6–22).[66] In the case of Psalm 82, the assembly of the gods is summoned by the Most High (עליון) to stand trial (see Ps 58). Yet there are more terms in Psalm 82 that help define the divine assembly.

According to Heinz-Josef Fabry, the "assembly of El" (עדת אל, 82:1) "is the only passage that transfers the notion of a human legal assembly to

61. Kraus, *Theology of the Psalms*, 25.

62. Kraus, *Theology of the Psalms*, 22. As Psalm 84 is the first psalm following the Asaph collection, it is glaring and delightful to see *both* divine names occurring seven times throughout the psalm.

63. Kraus, *Theology of the Psalms*, 23. In the Psalter, Yahweh is called Elohim or *Eloah* 365 times, and *El* 75 times.

64. Kraus, *Theology of the Psalms*, 23.

65. S. Schwertner, "אליל," *TLOT*, 1:126; *HALOT*, 1:55–56. The stress is on the insignificance of the pagan gods (Ps 97:7). Hossfeld and Zenger describe the unique word as "a technical term of polemic against idols" (*Psalms* 2, 465). Much like 1 Chronicles 16:26, the contrast is intentionally struck between Yahweh as the unmatched Creator of the heavens and the cast-metal gods (see also Lev 19:4). Especially used for heathen gods, the LXX 95:5 reads "demons" (δαιμόνια; see also Deut 32:17; Pss 90:6; 105:37). The irony is that pagan gods are viewed as powerful, but rarely available.

66. Horst Dietrich Preuss, "אליל," *TDOT*, 1:286–87.

heaven by means of the expression עדת אל."[67] This means that the "gods" of Psalm 82:1 are the members of the heavenly עדה ("assembly").[68] In this way, the earthly order of kings and court officials is a reflection of the heavenly realm.[69] The heavenly beings comprise a juridical assembly that hears the legal cases of the whole world—God leads the heavenly עדה ("assembly"), just as Moses led the earthly one.[70] Significantly, the power of the governing El is marked by relatedness and this establishes profound congruency between heaven and earth.[71]

Are the אלהים Human Judges?

It is Yahweh, the God of Israel, who stands at the head of an assembly of heavenly beings, which Old Testament psalm texts often call "gods" (see Pss 29:1; 82:1, 6; 89:5; 96:4–5; 103:20).[72] While my analysis has built a broad argument for reading אלהים as supernatural beings, nevertheless, there is a view that persists, claiming that the אלהים in Psalm 82:1, 6 refers to earthly judges under the honorific term "gods." Following a Jewish tradition,[73] Franz Delitzsch argues passionately that "those in authority are God's delegates and bearers of His image, and therefore as His representatives are also themselves called *elohim*, 'gods.'" For God's question "seeks to bring

67. Heinz-Josef Fabry, "עדה," *TDOT* 10:477. Within Jewish apocalyptic and liturgical literature, angels serving in the celestial temple are common, yet significantly, the terms mirror those of Psalm 82:1 in the Hebrew Bible, e.g., "O divinities of all the most holy ones … attendants of the Presence in the inner chamber of His glory, in the assembly belonging to all the gods of divinities" (4Q400 1:2–5a). In his commentary, James R. Davila states, "Compare the phrase 'in the assembly belonging to all the gods' to 'in the assembly of god' in Ps 82:1; 11Q13 ii:10; 4Q427 7i:14 and 'the assembly of the gods' in 1QM i:10; 1Q22 iv:1; 4Q491^{c} 1:5" (*Liturgical Works: Eerdmans Commentaries on the Dead Sea Scrolls* [Grand Rapids: Eerdmans, 2000], 97, 101).

68. Heinz-Josef Fabry, "עדה," *TDOT* 10:477.

69. Robin Routledge, *Old Testament Theology: A Thematic Approach* (Downers Grove, IL: IVP Academic, 2008), 121.

70. Some Hebrew terms are ancient loanwords from the cognitive environment of Mesopotamia, but the theology present is from Yahweh for his covenant people, so I see little convincing reason to argue that Yahweh actually shows deference to *El*, reflecting organic connection to Ugaritic myth, standing in a multitiered assembly (i.e., "the council of *El*"), or that *El* was programmatically revised to Elohim (so the History of Religions approach; see Frank M. Cross, "אל," *TDOT* 1:242–61, esp. 254).

71. Walter Brueggemann, "Divine Council," in *Reverberations of Faith: A Theological Handbook of Old Testament Themes* (Louisville: Westminster John Knox, 2002), 56.

72. Hilber, "Psalms," 388; also, Heiser, "Divine Council," 112–16, offers some contextual reasons why human judges are not in view. Some of these I've developed.

73. This precritical view was common until the mid-twentieth century: see BDB, 43; Targum Onkelos (דיניא, "judge," cf. Ezra 7:29); *HALOT* 5:1853; Exod LXX ("before the court of God" [21:6], also "place of God's decision" [22:8]).

the 'gods' of the earth to their right mind."[74] Similarly, Allen P. Ross sees "a strong polemic against the pagan world," evident in human judges who are controlled by spirits.[75] Whether the "elohim" are earthly judges, kings, or elders, I find this line of argument overwrought. When interpretations press so hard for a polemic, it not only minimizes the cognitive environment from which the psalms emerged, ironically, it also ignores the more text-dominant points of evidence.[76] My reasons for seeing supernatural beings are as follows.

First, the lexical data overwhelmingly supports divine beings. Standard lexica identify the אלהים of Psalm 82:1, 6 as "gods."[77] In fact, the biblical texts typically used to support the view of human judges are not convincing and may better serve as references to God (see Exod 18:19; 21:6; 22:8, 9, 28; 1 Sam 2:25). For example, under Moses's oversight, cases are brought before God for judgment (Exod 18:19), much as Moses is לאלהים ("has the place of God") for Aaron (Exod 4:16).[78] Brevard S. Childs claims that the instruction to have the person "brought to God [האלהים, Exod 21:6]" is "a stereotyped term signifying to the nearest sanctuary" (so Exod 22:8, 9),[79] and he translates these phrases: "before God = at the sanctuary."[80] These complex texts lead W. H. Schmidt to conclude, "*Elohim* does not have the meaning 'judge.'"[81] The role of human

74. Carl F. Keil and Franz Delitzsch, *Old Testament Commentaries: Psalm 78 to Isaiah 14*, vol. 4 (Grand Rapids: Associated Publishers and Authors, 1960), 36, "God Himself speaks in ver. 5 of the judges" (p. 37).

75. Ross, *A Commentary on the Psalms*, 2:719.

76. See, for example, the strong polemical interpretation of Psalm 82:6 in John 10:34 by Andreas J. Köstenberger, "John," in *Commentary on the New Testament Use of the Old Testament*, ed. G. K. Beale and D. A. Carson (Grand Rapids: Baker Academic, 2007), 464–67.

77. *HALOT*, 1:53.1; David Cline, ed., *Dictionary of Classical Hebrew* (Sheffield: Sheffield Phoenix, 2011), 1:285.

78. William L. Holladay, *A Concise Hebrew and Aramaic Lexicon of the Old Testament* (Grand Rapids: Eerdmans, 1988), 17, 3.b. Nahum M. Sarna translates, "playing the role of God to him," noting the parallel text of 7:1 that stipulates "your prophet" as the spokesman for God (*The JPS Torah Commentary: Exodus* [Philadelphia: JPS, 1991], 22).

79. Brevard S. Childs, *The Book of Exodus: A Critical, Theological Commentary* (Louisville: Westminster John Knox, 1974), 469. Rashi glosses אלהים as "judges," and Ibn Ezra as "angels" (see Jon D. Levenson, *Creation and the Persistence of Evil: The Jewish Drama of Divine Omnipotence* [San Francisco: Harper & Row, 1988], 5–9). For an intriguing discussion of how Christian interpreters uncritically accepted traditional Jewish (Tannaitic) interpretation about Jethro being a pagan, therefore shaping his language about God and practical recommendations for Moses, see Childs, *Exodus*, 332–34. Childs's observation about early streams of Christian interpretation is glaringly evident in Quentin F. Wesselschmidt, ed., *Psalms 51–150*, ACCS 8 (Downers Grove, IL: InterVarsity, 2007), esp. "82:1–8 A Word of Judgment on Unjust Rulers and Judges," 145–48.

80. Childs, *Exodus*, 475.

81. W. H. Schmidt, "אלהים," *TLOT*, 1:118.

agents representing divine authority is clear enough, but this responsibility does not suspend God as the referent—the giver of that authority. This is the focus of the lexical usage.[82]

Second, the dramatic scene of Psalm 82 unfolds on a cosmic stage with distinct parties and unique terms. Even the shaking of the earth's foundations (82:5c) is language of universal turmoil (see also Pss 11:3; 46:3, 7; 60:4; 93:1).[83] Goldingay observes, "When the ineffectiveness of the divine aides imperils earth's foundations by threatening world judgment, Yhwh intervenes in their working and thus keeps earth's pillars steady (Ps 75:3; 82:5)."[84] Clearly, the cosmic scope of Psalm 82 does not support God presiding over a council of humans, nor would some rogue rulers shake the earth's foundations. While the presenting concern regards life on earth, the occasion in Psalm 82:1 is a divine trial that distinguishes God from foreign gods (Ps 82:1a; see also Isa 41:21–29). Furthermore, the grammar separates the cosmic judge from the international gods (אלהים, Ps 82:1b). Whereas singular verbs identify God (82:1a, 8), the "gods" are governed by a prepositional phrase (בקרב, "among/midst of," 82:1b)[85] and plural words in apposition (82:6). In this way, both the setting and the grammar bring clarity. The cosmic stage of the heavenly tribunal is significant because the judges of Israel never had legal jurisdiction over "all the nations" (82:8).

Thirdly, the rhetorical movement of the psalm climaxes in the legal sentence of mortality for the gods (82:6–7), using standard trial language (second-person plural). The unjust divine beings—"sons of the Most High [בני עליון]"—are unmasked! But this stunning demotion loses all force if the convicted "elohim" (אלהים, v. 1b) are merely humans. Keep in mind that the thrust of this psalm is not about the gods' metaphysical status but their moral behavior.[86] So Hossfeld and Zenger describe this exposing as one of the most spectacular of biblical texts, because "it announces the death of *all* gods … and the disempowerment of the systems of dominance that rely

82. For example, the Exodus texts show that: קרב אל האלהים ("come near to God") always communicates approaching a place of God's presence, typically for a ritual purpose (see Exod 18:19; 21:6; 22: 8, 28). For further discussion of these texts, see John I. Durham, *Exodus*, WBC, vol. 3 (Waco, TX: Word, 1987).

83. Erhard S. Gerstenberger, *Psalms, Part 2, and Lamentations*, FOTL 15 (Grand Rapids: Eerdmans, 2001), 114.

84. Goldingay, *Old Testament Theology*, 2:697.

85. Cline, *Dictionary of Classical Hebrew*, 1:285.

86. Goldingay, *Old Testament Theology*, 2:56.

on these gods."[87] By "de-deifying" all other gods,[88] not least because of their failure to bring justice for the oppressed (82:3–4), the heavenly king formally takes up the rule of earth. Having demoted all patron deities of the nations, now "all nations are your inheritance" (82:8).[89] Clearly, following incapable gods can imperil a people. Now we must take a brief look at the contribution of the neighboring psalms to Psalm 82.

NEIGHBORING PSALMS AND "FOREIGN GODS"

Harry P. Nasuti is surely correct when he claims, "It is only through association with other texts that one knows how to approach any particular text."[90] By considering the psalms that reverberate around Psalm 82, we can bring a far richer interpretive lens to this text.

The Theo-Logic Surrounding Psalm 82

Psalm 82 is the climax of the Asaph psalms. This is achieved by a rotation of communal laments, divine oracles, and, finally, divine interventions. As Hossfeld and Zenger have ably shown, this theological stream advances through two broad cycles: 74–76 and 79–82.[91] National lament begins each cycle (Pss 74, 79–80). Evidently, the pain of exile mixes with the taunting of nations against God and his people, and this creates a theological crisis. "The sheep of your pasture" (Ps 74:1b; 79:13a) have been ruthlessly attacked by God's "foes" among "the nations" (74:4a; 79:1, 10). Israel needs God to plead their cause (74:22a; 79:10–12). Not surprisingly, numerous questions are aimed at God: "Why?" (74:1, 11; 79:10; 80:12) and "How long?" (74:10; 79:5; 80:4). It is sobering to hear God himself use the language of lament: "O that

87. Hossfeld and Zenger, *Psalms* 2, 334; emphasis original. Adam and Eve also lost their immortality (Gen 3:16–19, 22). However, I'm not convinced that כאדם ("like a man," 7a) is referring to the story of Adam in Genesis.

88. Patrick D. Miller, "The Psalms as a Meditation on the First Commandment," in *The Way of the Lord: Essays in Old Testament Theology* (Grand Rapids: Eerdmans, 2004), 101.

89. On the patron deities of the nations, see Daniel I. Block, "Other Religions in Old Testament Theology," in *The Gospel According to Moses: Theological and Ethical Reflections on the Book of Deuteronomy* (Eugene, OR: Cascade Books, 2012), 200–236.

90. Harry P. Nasuti, *Defining the Sacred Songs: Genre, Tradition and the Post-Critical Interpretation of the Psalms*, JSOTSup 218 (Sheffield: Sheffield Academic, 1999), 52–53.

91. Hossfeld and Zenger, *Psalms* 2, 2:250, 257–58, 271, 305, 307, 317, 325–26, 336; also David Emanuel, "An Unrecognized Voice: Intra-Textual and Intertextual Perspectives on Psalm 81," *HS*, 50 (2009): 85–120; Jones, "Message of the Asaphite Collection," 71–85. Several terms associated with God connect Psalm 78 and 79: "wrath," "memory," "compassion," and "shepherd" (cf. 78:38–39, 52, 59 with 79:5, 8–9, 13).

my people would listen to me!" (81:13 NRSV; cf. Isa. 65:1–2).[92] For God, intimacy desired became intimacy spurned. But it is 82:2 that concludes with God's own desperate question—"How long?"—thrust at the international gods. The national plea of the opening lament, "Rise up, O God, plead your cause" (74:22a) culminates in the prayer of the oppressed—"Rise up, O God, judge the earth!" (82:8a). The desire that "the poor and needy praise your name" (74:21b) is resolved when he, "whose name is the LORD ... the Most High," is known "over all the earth" (83:18).

God's response to these laments follows in Psalms 75 and 81. These divine oracles do not provide answers; they provide instruction.[93] Returning to his role in the exodus, God challenges Israel to trust him again. (Only three Asaph psalms omit any exodus reference, see Pss 73, 75, 83). God not only reassures Israel, "I will judge with equity ... when the earth totters" (75:2b–3a; see also 82:5c), he also reproves (81:8–14). The one who relieved Israel's "burden" in Egypt (81:5b, 6a) still calls them to uncompromising loyalty. Here is the rich interplay between Psalm 80 and 81: the people call for God to "turn again" (80:14a) and God responds to their cry by pleading for Israel to "listen" (81:8a, 11a, 13a). The theological significance of this oracle cannot be missed—God returns to the historic template: "You called, and I rescued you" (81:7a).

The only offense that God mentions is Israel's worship of foreign gods (81:9)! Israel begged for restoration (80:3, 7) and, significantly, God responds by reciting the language of the Shema—"Hear, O my people" (Ps 81:8a; see Deut 6:4) and the first commandment—"There shall be no strange god (אל) among you" (Ps 81:9a; Exod 20:3). By starting with the Shema, God elevates the positive form of the first commandment (Ps 81:8a, 10a), followed by the phrase of self-presentation: "I am the LORD your God who brought you up out of the land of Egypt" (Ps 81:10a; see Exod 20:2a). The latter is a typical lead-in when God commands Israel to reject foreign gods (see Deut 5:9; Hos 13:4).[94] For the first time, the name Yahweh is used in Psalm 81. Moreover, Psalm 81 uses the most explicit reference to the first commandment in the entire Psalter.[95]

While the people pled for God to "look down from heaven" (80:14), claiming, "We will never turn back from you" (80:18); God, however, raises a condition: they must reject the "strange god" (אל זר, see also Ps 44:20) and the "foreign god" (אל נכר, 81:9). Only eight verses later, the "gods" (אלהים, cf. אל)

92. Fretheim, *Suffering of God*, 117–18. Emanuel also claims that God laments here ("An Unrecognized Voice," 115).

93. Jones, "Message of the Asaphite Collection," 78.

94. Emanuel, "An Unrecognized Voice," 102.

95. Miller, "Meditation on the First Commandment," 99.

are again encountered in Psalm 82:1. The placement of these psalms adds additional layers of meaning. Israel's cry for deliverance is wed to God's call for obedience ... again.[96] It is as if to say, "I, the LORD, am the only one who answered you (see 81:7a)—no other gods responded, did they?" His tactic is both powerful and brilliant.

The third element of the cycle is divine intervention (Pss 76, 82). Psalm 76 strikes a note of hope for a nation beaten down: "From the heavens you uttered judgment" (76:8a). "When God rose up to establish judgment, to save all the oppressed of earth" (76:9), this is the aid Israel needed. In Psalm 82, the intervention plays out in heaven, where cosmic order is reestablished. God judges the gods for their corruption (82:1). Small wonder that the oppressed plea for God to "rise up" and "judge the earth" (82:8a). "The 'strange god among' Israel in Ps. 81.9 is, in Psalm 82, stripped of divine status by God who reigns over all."[97]

Put another way, Psalm 82 takes the offense of worshiping other gods in Psalm 81 and illustrates why it is utterly misguided.[98] Just as the forefathers were condemned to follow the dictates of their hearts (81:12), so the international gods are condemned to die like mortals (82:7). Placed together, these psalms form a theological *merism*, showing that God is judge of both heaven and earth.[99] Eschatological and doxological messages emerge. Against the backdrop of a destroyed temple, decimated land, spurned ethics, and a scattered people—all concerns of the Asaphite leaders—this kind of hope assures a future with justice.

As Patrick D. Miller observes, the nations of the world are officially brought under the oversight and protection of God, since "the First Commandment is *universalized* and made applicable to all the nations."[100] Based on Deuteronomy 32:8, Tucker and Grant correctly argue that "the gods have failed Yahweh's expectation of them."[101] God's verdict in the tribunal represents a seismic shift from Deuteronomy 32:8, when "*El Elyon* apportioned the nations ... according to the number of the sons of God" (cf. Dan 10:13–21).[102] Fittingly, *El Elyon*—the name of the Lord's universal

96. Jones, "Message of the Asaphite Collection," 75.

97. Howard N. Wallace, *Psalms*. Readings: A New Biblical Commentary (Sheffield: Sheffield Phoenix Press, 2009), 140.

98. Jones, "Message of the Asaphite Collection," 81.

99. Emanuel, "An Unrecognized Voice," 111.

100. Miller, "Meditation on the First Commandment," 101; emphasis added.

101. Tucker and Grant, *Psalms*, 2:217, 221–22.

102. Many scholars believe that a Qumran fragment (4QDeut^{j}) holds the preferred reading, בני אלהים ("sons of God," ESV), instead of the MT, בני ישראל ("sons of Israel," CSB, NASB);

sovereignty—highlights a rising doxological theme (see Num 24:16; Pss 47:2; 78:35; 82:6; 83:18). This mounting doxology is evident at the close of the Asaph psalms, the communal lament against hostile nations: "Let them know that you alone, whose name is the LORD [שמך יהוה], are the Most High [עליון] over all the earth" (Ps 83:18; see also 1 Kgs 8:42b–43a; Isa 37:16, 20). This forms a doxological conclusion to the Asaphite psalms (see also Ps 73:28).

CONCLUSION

Our analysis has focused on the Lord's relationship to the "gods" in the Psalter, particularly from a biblical-theological perspective. Exactly why the most passionate texts of worship should also speak of other gods strikes one somewhere between odd and irreverent. To explore this, we focused on Psalm 82, with its dramatic portrayal of the cosmic king indicting other אלהים ("gods"). We found that the collection of Asaph psalms contributes a rich theology of God as divine judge and is very aware of the international threats to Israel. We also discovered a high degree of divine speech in the Asaph collection. Myth, as I defined it, provided a theological "prism" in which the psalmists could reflect God's past acts onto a desperate present, thereby stirring confidence for their future.

Psalm 82 clearly functions within the heavenly stage of the divine assembly, entirely fitting for a legal tribunal. In fact, it is this legal court scene in heaven that helps solve the identity of the "gods" (82:1). We determined that the combination of lexical terms, coupled with the psalm's cosmic setting and God's sentence of mortality, argued for the Elohim being international gods, albeit utterly incompetent. These gods are guilty of not bringing justice to the poor and oppressed in their charge—the quintessential responsibility of deity.

Finally, our study considered the argument of the neighboring psalms that gives shape and function to Psalm 82. Observing a cycle of communal

similarly LXX[848 106c] "angels of God" (Aquila). Other translations read: "number of the gods" (NRSV), "number of the heavenly assembly" (NET) or "number in his heavenly court" (NLT). Contemporary translations overwhelmingly side with the Dead Sea Scrolls fragment. The MT may assume that "sons of God" includes Israel (Hos 1:10), while the LXX reflects the angelic assembly (Pss 29:1; 82:1, 6; 89:6). For theological reasons a scribe appears to have changed בני אל to בני ישראל as an antipolytheistic alteration. For further discussion, see Emanuel Tov, *Textual Criticism of the Hebrew Bible*, second rev. ed. (Minneapolis: Fortress, 1992), 267–69. Interestingly, another Qumran fragment (4QDeut[q]) for Deuteronomy 32:43 reads: "Rejoice, O heavens, together with him; and bow down to him all you gods [אלהים]" (similarly, LXX, "angels"). This is essentially the same line as Psalm 97:7 (see John W. Wevers, *Notes on the Greek Text of Deuteronomy*, SCS 39 [Atlanta: Scholars Press, 1995], 533–35).

laments, divine oracles, and divine interventions, we discovered that the lead up to Psalm 82 finds Israel reliving the cries for help that defined her suffering in Egypt. Again, God hears their cry for help, but insists that they must show their obedience by rejecting all other gods and worship the Lord exclusively. If Israel found Egypt's gods irrelevant, they found Canaan's gods irresistible.[103] So it is significant that "gods" are mentioned in the Psalter in Psalm 81:9—only eight verses prior to their indictment in Psalm 82:1. The way the Lord admonishes his people through the familiar language of the Shema and the first commandment is very powerful. Psalm 82 then argues that God is entirely right to judge the international gods, since they are incompetent authorities, cannot defend or rescue, and unlike them, God actually hears and delivers the oppressed.

Extolling the Lord in the psalms necessarily raises the issue of "competing gods," as the practical question is unavoidable, "Can any Elohim hear and deliver the needy when they cry out?" Since none can, the Lord is owed exclusive loyalty, obedience, and praise. One day, every nation will understand this and praise the Lord as the only God capable of rescuing the needy. Not surprisingly, Psalm 82 lays the foundation for international recognition of God. We must touch on several implications that stem from this study.

Lingering Implications for Contemporary Readers

First is the struggle most Western cultures have with the concept that "other gods" exist. Psalm 82 makes no apologies. Our historic commitment to the sovereignty of self—evident in our education, rigid metaphysics, and utopian social experiments—has left little room for the spiritual realm. Biblically speaking, this is the fool's life, regardless of its cause (Pss 14:1; 53:1). The real enemy of the true knowledge of God is not aggressive atheism but always rival gods. Yes, that is a paradox, and teaching this theology in the church is no easy task. So it is necessary to affirm the eschatological victory that the King of kings will bring. Psalm 82 teaches us that God will judge the gods *within history*. In truth, the spiritual realm is inhabited by the demonic (Ps 106:37). Goldingay gives a fitting reminder:

> The heavenly powers were created in or by Christ and through and for Christ (Col. 1:15–16), and by dying Christ has defeated and dethroned them or divested himself of them, and triumphed over them (Col. 2:15).

103. Victor P. Hamilton, *Exodus: An Exegetical Commentary* (Grand Rapids: Baker Academic, 2011), 329.

They are subject to him (1 Pet. 3:22), and they cannot separate us from God's love (Rom. 8:38–39). Yet we still battle against them (Eph. 6:12). Evidently they are still capable of asserting themselves, and we still look forward to God's final judgment on them (1 Cor. 15:24–25). And we still pray for God's authority to be exercised over them in the now (Eph. 6:12, 18), as the psalm does.[104]

A sober reading of Scripture must face Israel's debilitating addiction to other gods, spanning the period of the entrance into the land to their exile from it (Exod 32:8; 1 Sam 8:8; Ps 106:28; Hos 3:1). Idolatry was no brief spiritual stumble. In our day, the contemporary lust for the novel masks a dangerous boredom with "old truths." Modern-day idols are also plentiful in the contemporary addiction to identities. As always, such idols obscure the true names of people. May God grant them a redemptive pain "so that people will seek your name, O Lord" (Ps 83:16b).

A second implication for our day is the dire need for social justice. In hardly any other biblical passage is the lack of social justice made the central thrust of God's accusation, like Psalm 82:2–6.[105] This generation has witnessed a profound sensitizing to the social plane of human frailty. The ultimate hope of the weak and oppressed remains the conviction that God will judge. The catalog of poor and vulnerable listed in Psalm 82 finds ample mention throughout the Psalter. God both *hears* and *helps* the poor (Pss 10:14, 17; 69:33; 107:41; 113:7; 132:15; 146:9). The ethical foundation is the laws of the Pentateuch, which contain exhortations and rules to help the vulnerable in every legal unit.[106] To describe oneself as "poor and needy" is to appeal to the character of the heavenly king (Pss 74:21; 140:12–13). Aid is the responsibility of the righteous king (Ps 72:12–14). Yet "poverty" is both a social position and an attitude toward those suffering. This means that poverty is never idealized in the Old Testament, like the "pious poor" of later Judaism.[107] But Jesus does make the plight of the poor a key aspect of his kingdom mission (Luke 4:18, quoting Isa 61:1).

But there are also some cautions that speak into the contemporary focus on "justice and liberation." For example, Scripture does not show a

---

104. Goldingay, *Psalms*, 2:570.

105. Gerstenberger, *Psalms*, 114.

106. Gordon J. Wenham, *Psalms as Torah: Reading Biblical Song Ethically* (Grand Rapids: Baker Academic, 2012), 116.

107. Hans Kvalbein, "Poor/Poverty," in *New Dictionary of Biblical Theology*, ed. Desmond Alexander and Brian Rosner (Downers Grove, IL: InterVarsity, 2000), 688.

"preferential option for the poor," nor do they have an "in" with God. In fact, the righteous were intended to prosper, which is why Asaph struggles so acutely in Psalm 73 when the wicked are the ones prospering. Moreover, the poor are never seen as immoral or a threat to social order. Similarly, helping the "sinners" and "babes" is no excuse for any sin or idealizing any ignorance (Matt 11:25; Mark 2:17). Such statements in Scripture highlight that "the kingdom is a gift given freely to those who are not able to repay it."[108] Aggressive aid for the poor is essential, but one's deeper identity stems from the new values provided by Christ in the gospel: "as poor, yet making many rich, as having nothing, and yet possessing all things" (2 Cor 6:10; see also 8:9).

When society is so obsessed with power and social standing, what does healing and resolution look like? The gods of the well-to-do usually outnumber the gods of the poor.[109] Truly, the hardships of the poor seem most intractable. Let us not forget the persecuted Christians scattered throughout the nations (Heb 13:3). The dire situation of Psalm 82 seems painfully relevant. Yet, just *how* a society seeks to heal such inequities can make the larger populace terminal. Sadly, a culture of shaming has lost the art of repentance. At present, there is a real danger of societies pursuing *social* atonements—demanding the king's aid but dismissing the king. This concern of Brevard S. Childs just may be timeless:

> The contemporary use of liberation is seriously marred by its dominantly political and economic connotations with heavy ideological overtones, which have robbed the word of its rich religious connotations. The term liberation, as currently used in theological circles fails to treat seriously those features basic to the Old Testament's understanding of God's intention, namely forgiveness of sin, response of faith, and the basic inability of all human schemes to accomplish genuine freedom. The hope of the biblical writers is not anchored to a human social programme, regardless of how well-meaning or pious, but to God's salvation which he is already bringing to fruition according to his eternal purpose.[110]

---

108. Kvalbein, "Poor/Poverty," 690.
109. Hamilton, *Exodus*, 329.
110. Brevard S. Childs, *Old Testament Theology in a Canonical Context* (Philadelphia: Fortress Press, 1985), 49.

15

Reclaiming Divine Sovereignty in the Anthropocene: Psalms 93–100 and the Convergence of Theology and Ecology

J. Clinton McCann Jr.

After a brief review of the recent history of interpretation of Psalms 93–100, this question is raised: Why further attention to these psalms? The answer is that the concerns of our contemporary context affect the way we hear the biblical text. As for Psalms 93–100, their affirmation of God's sovereignty over all creation invites the recognition that we human beings do not rule the world the way we seem to think we do. Plus, their portrayal of a harmonious, praise-oriented creational community (see especially Pss 96:11–13; 98:7–9) invites an appreciation of the convergence of theology and ecology.

WHY THE ENTHRONEMENT PSALMS AGAIN?

The collection of enthronement psalms—traditionally identified as Psalms 93 and 95–99, but more recently as Psalms 93–100—have been the focus of a great deal of scholarly attention from a variety of methodological perspectives.[1] The enthronement psalms figured prominently in Sigmund Mowinckel's form-critical/cult-functional approach, forming the centerpiece of his

1. For the logic of treating Psalms 93–100 as a group, see David M. Howard Jr., *The Structure of Psalms 93–100*, Biblical and Judaic Studies 5 (Winona Lake, IN: Eisenbrauns, 1997), 21–22. See also Frank-Lothar Hossfeld and Erich Zenger, *Psalms 2*, Hermeneia (Minneapolis: Fortress, 2005), 6–7.

magisterial proposal for an Enthronement Festival of Yahweh that he identified as part of the "feast of tabernacles in its character of new year festival."[2] Mowinckel's proposal enjoyed wide support in the third quarter of the twentieth century. Its popularity faded only as biblical studies moved beyond form-critical and cult-functional approaches toward the more literary perspectives represented by rhetorical criticism, and as pertains to Psalms studies, attention to the shape and shaping of the Psalter.

The movement in biblical studies did not result in any less attention devoted to the enthronement collection. Working from a very different methodological starting point than Mowinckel, Gerald H. Wilson also gave primary attention to the enthronement collection. In his analysis of the editorial shaping of the Psalter, Wilson concluded that Books I–III (Pss 1–89) had taken shape first, noting that they conclude with Psalm 89 that reflects the rupture of exile and thus the apparent failure of the Davidic covenant. In Wilson's words, "The Davidic covenant introduced in Ps 2 has come to nothing and the combination of three books concludes with the anguished cry of the Davidic descendants [Ps 89:46–51]."[3] In response to this crisis, Book IV "stands as the 'answer' to the problem posed in Ps 89 as to the apparent failure of the Davidic covenant with which Books One–Three are primarily concerned."[4] A major element of this "answer" is that, in the absence of an earthly king, Yahweh is king, which is the fundamental message of the enthronement psalms. Thus, Wilson concludes that "Pss 90–106 function as the editorial 'center' of the final form of the Hebrew Psalter."[5] And as the most obvious structural feature of Book IV, the enthronement collection is "the theological 'heart' " of the Psalter.[6]

While Wilson's work highlights the importance of the enthronement collection, even more detailed attention to Psalms 93–100 was given by David M. Howard Jr. His study reinforces Wilson's conclusion; as he puts it, his "study confirms the judgment of many scholars that the Kingship of YHWH psalms are the climax to which the Psalter builds throughout Books I-III."[7] But in making this case, Howard pays far more attention than

2. Sigmund Mowinckel, *The Psalms in Israel's Worship*, vol. 1, trans. D. R. Ap-Thomas (Nashville: Abingdon, 1962), 121.

3. Gerald H. Wilson, *The Editing of the Hebrew Psalter*, SBLDS 76 (Chico, CA: Scholars Press, 1985), 213.

4. Wilson, *The Editing of the Hebrew Psalter*, 215.

5. Wilson, *The Editing of the Hebrew Psalter*, 215.

6. Gerald H. Wilson, "The Use of Royal Psalms at the 'Seams' of the Hebrew Psalter," *JSOT* 35 (1986): 92.

7. Howard, *The Structure of Psalms 93–100*, 183.

Wilson did to structure, rhetorical features, and linguistic and thematic connections among Psalms 93–100. In effect, the work of Howard, Wilson, and Mowinckel represent the movement of Psalms studies over the past several generations—that is, from the form-critical/cult-functional approach (Mowinckel) to the more literary approaches represented by rhetorical criticism (Howard) and attention to the shape and shaping of the Psalter (Wilson and Howard). Given the application of these methods to the analysis of Psalms 93–100, one might well ask the question, "Why do we need another essay devoted to the enthronement collection in Book IV?"

The clue to answering this question lies in the recognition that the meaning(s) and significance of biblical texts cannot be confined simply to the application of scholarly methods nor to the historical, sociological, and literary data that these methods might uncover. In describing the process of biblical interpretation, Ellen F. Davis outlines "five movements," the middle three of which have to do with discovering "*literary data*," discerning "*social and historical* features that may lie in the background of the text's composition," and articulating "a *reasoned account* of how the interpreter chooses to draw inferences and conclusion on the basis of the literary and historical data."[8] But the first and last steps in the interpretive process are, in part, as follows:

1. Giving clear expression to the *presuppositions and prior concerns* with which the interpreter comes to the text. For biblical interpreters, these include the challenges—cultural, political, social—faced by the interpreter's own faith community, as well as those of her neighbor. ...
2. Remaining open to *continual revision* as the interpreter's own further work, challenges from others, and the changing landscape of contemporary concerns (see #1 above) disclose new problems and insights.[9]

The work of Mowinckel, Wilson, and Howard on the enthronement psalms remains useful, helpful, and compelling (even though Mowinckel was probably incorrect in his historical conclusion about an Enthronement Festival of Yahweh). What I want to do differently is to acknowledge and take seriously both the challenges facing my own faith community, and

8. Ellen F. Davis, *Opening Israel's Scriptures* (Oxford: Oxford University Press, 2019), 4.
9. Davis, *Opening Israel's Scriptures*, 4.

indeed the whole world, and to take into account what Davis calls "the changing landscape of contemporary concerns." In particular, I will consider the enthronement psalms in the historical context of what many are now calling the "Anthropocene," which is an unofficial designation to indicate that our contemporary era is one dominated by the impact of human activity on essentially everything, including every corner of the planet.[10]

Of particular concern are the ecological effects of human activity—for instance, air and water pollution; climate change, especially global warming; the presence of plastic particles in the remotest places on earth, including the highest mountains and the deepest oceans; the growing shortage of water; the increasing presence of invasive species; the dramatic loss of biodiversity; and the disappearance of plant and animal species at a rate approaching perhaps one thousand times the rate at which species have gone extinct in the course of natural history. These realities are interrelated, of course, but perhaps the most troubling current reality is the extinction rate, since human beings are also a species. Many scientists conclude that we are now in the midst of earth's sixth great "extinction spasm." The causes of the previous five are unclear, although the fifth was almost certainly caused by a huge meteorite that hit the earth and wiped out the dinosaurs about sixty-five million years ago. In any case, the cause of this sixth spasm is crystal clear: human beings, especially by way of our polluting, overpopulation, overharvesting of forests and fisheries, and destruction of habitats, either by our direct possession or by human-caused climate change.[11] The environmental destruction that we human beings have caused and are causing "stands as the single great crisis of our time, surpassing and encompassing all others."[12] This is life in the Anthropocene, and this is the monumental challenge in view of which I shall interpret the enthronement psalms in this essay.

YAHWEH *MLK*: "THE LORD REIGNS" AND WE DON'T

The most obvious feature of Psalms 93–100 is the occurrence of the Hebrew root *mlk*, either as a noun or a verb, in Psalms 93 and 95–99. While this root does not occur in Psalms 94 and 100, there are other items of

10. A good, basic source for defining the Anthropocene is S. Lewis and M. Maslin, "Defining the Anthropocene," *Nature* 519 (March 11, 2015): 171–80 (see https://doi.org/10.1038/nature14258).
11. See E. O. Wilson, *The Creation, An Appeal to Save Life on Earth* (New York: Norton, 2006), 73–75.
12. Bill McKibben, *The Comforting Whirlwind: God, Job, and the Scale of Creation* (Cambridge, MA: Cowley Publications, 2005), 15.

vocabulary that cohere with the proclamation that Yahweh is "King" or that "the LORD reigns."[13] In short, the overriding message of the enthronement collection is that God is sovereign. As the "answer" to Psalm 89 at the conclusion of Book III, the assurance is that despite the demise of the Davidic monarchy and thus the absence of an earthly king, there is still a ruling monarch for the people—Yahweh. As a response to the Babylonian exile and its aftermath, the proclamation of God's sovereignty would have had a polemical intent—that is, Yahweh reigns, and Marduk, the god of Babylon, does not.

But what is the impact of the proclamation of God's sovereignty in view of our contemporary concerns and challenges? In a real sense, there is still a polemical edge, but now the polemic is best understood as aimed at us—that is, human beings, the dominant feature of the Anthropocene. In short, the Lord reigns, and *we do not*. In other words, in view of contemporary concerns and challenges, we would do well to hear the fundamental message of the enthronement psalms as a warning rather than an assurance or a promise. To be sure, the enthronement psalms in their original context, both historically and literarily, were meant to convey good news.[14] If there is any good news to be heard in the proclamation of divine sovereignty in the Anthropocene, it may be the possibility that a contemplation of divine sovereignty may begin to dislodge the thorough-going anthropocentrism that currently rules the day. Despite the growing and indisputable evidence of human-caused environmental degradation and devastation, the human response has been less than enthusiastic. It may well be, as some scientists are saying, that we have passed the tipping-point for returning the earth to a stable foundation, and that the very future of humankind hangs in the balance. Even if these scientists are wrong, the stakes are extremely high. The book of Psalms has been a major resource for devotion and spirituality for hundreds, indeed thousands, of years; and it is a resource that is needed today more than ever. Attentiveness to the Psalter, especially to its "theological 'heart,'" Psalms 93–100, could serve to remind us what the Bible recognizes from the very beginning—that we human beings, *'adam*, have no

13. For instance, the appearance of the Hebrew root sh-p-t to describe Yahweh as "the one who establishes justice on earth" (Ps 94:2, author translation) anticipates what God has come to do in Psalms 96:13 and 98:9; and in fact, the root occurs in each of Psalms 96–99 (see also Ps 94:15 where the root occurs again). As for Psalm 100, its opening invitation occurs also in Psalms 95:1–2 and 98:4, indicating the appropriate way to greet a monarch. Scripture quotations are taken from the NRSV, unless otherwise noted.

14. See Psalm 96:2 where the NRSV "tell" translates the Hebrew root bsr, which would better be rendered as something like "proclaim good news."

livable future apart from the earth itself, the *'adamâ*, which is our home. The affirmation of divine sovereignty serves to put us human beings in our place, to de-center us, and thus to reconnect us to the earth that we cannot live without. The Lord reigns, and we do not.

"THE WORLD IS FIRMLY ESTABLISHED" (PS 96:10)—OR NOT

A detailed examination of Psalms 93–100 is not feasible nor necessary in this essay. Rather, I shall focus more briefly on several features of Psalm 96, which, as David Howard points out, "functions well at the head of the four closely related Kingship of YHWH psalms placed between Psalms 95 and 100," and which "contain[s] all of the major themes of the Kingship of YHWH genre."[15] Of particular interest and importance in my view is the observation that follows immediately the proclamation that "the Lord is king!" (96:10). It is this: "The world is firmly established; it shall never be moved" (96:10). This observation suggests another way that the enthronement collection in Book IV is an answer, or at least a response, to the content of Book III.

The verb translated "moved" is *môt*, and the claim that the world "shall never (*bal*) be moved" can be understood as a direct response to the dire situation described in Psalm 82:5 where "all the foundations of the earth are shaken [the verb *môt* again]." The "foundations of the earth" are the mountains that both hold up the domed firmament, keeping back the waters above, and that anchor the dry land in place, thus preventing a deluge from the waters below. The shaking of the mountains is a worst-case scenario, for it means nothing short of the undoing of creation—that is, the ordered cosmos is in danger of reverting to a watery chaos (see Gen 1:2).

As it turns out, the crisis is being caused by the injustice of "the gods" (Ps 82:1; the Hebrew root *sh-p-t* occurs in each verse of 1–3 to indicate that the issue is justice, or more accurately, the lack thereof), who "have neither knowledge nor understanding" (Ps 82:5). Biblically speaking, justice is not giving people what they deserve, but rather giving people what they need to survive and thrive, beginning with attentiveness to and provision for the most vulnerable: the "weak and the orphan ... the lowly and the destitute ... the weak and the needy" (82:3–4). As a result of their failure to understand justice so defined and thus their endangerment of the whole creation, the gods are demoted to the status of mortals. The voice of the Israelite God

15. Howard, *The Structure of Psalms 93–100*, 177.

announces that they will "fall like any prince" (82:7).[16] As if the demotion of the gods has left a vacuum of power, Psalm 82 concludes with a prayer: "Arise, O God, establish justice [*sh-p-t*] on earth; for *you* possess all the nations" (v. 8, author translation).

The request for God to act and establish justice among the nations anticipates exactly what happens in Psalm 96. Immediately following the observation that the world "shall never be moved," we are told—or more accurately, "the nations" are told—why stability has been restored. It is because God "governs [*dîn*] the peoples with equity" (Ps 96:10), as opposed to the gods who governed unjustly in Psalm 82. This explanation is the prelude to a creation-wide celebration that happens, in effect, because the prayer of Psalm 82:8 has been answered—that is, Yahweh "has come [reading the form of *bôʾ* here as a *qal* perfect rather than a participle]; for he has come to establish justice [*sh-p-t*] on earth. He establishes justice [*sh-p-t*] in the world with righteousness and among the peoples with his faithfulness" (Ps 96:13, author translation; see also CEB and note the nearly identical conclusion to Psalm 98 in v. 9).

As it turns out, the very important words "justice" and "righteousness" occur in each psalm of Psalms 97–99 as well (see 97:2, 6, 8 [where "judgments" could also be rendered "acts of justice"]; 98:2 [where "vindication" would be better than "righteousness"], 9; 99:4). These two words amount to a summary of the divine will, upon which the stability of the whole creation depends. As Psalm 82 indicates, injustice in the human community threatens the whole creation; and as Psalm 96 affirms, justice and righteousness are precisely what put the whole world on a stable foundation.

This affirmation is stated directly in Psalm 96:10, "The world is firmly established; it shall never be moved." And it is reinforced in verses 11–12 by the creation-wide celebration that accompanies God's arrival to "establish justice ... in the world with righteousness" (v. 13). The whole cosmos is involved: the heavens, the earth, the sea, and the field, along with the animals and plants (trees) that inhabit these realms. When Psalm 82 and the enthronement collection, especially Psalms 96 and 98, are heard together, we learn that the well-being of the human community and the well-being of the creation are inextricably related. It is at this point that theology and ecology begin to converge.

---

16. Lest Psalm 82:7 sound dangerously triumphalist and imperialist, it should be noted that in Psalm 89:38–45, God has caused God's "anointed" to fall. In short, God will demote or remove God's *own* "son" if that son fails to do the justice that God wills. God is not partial, except to favor justice. See below on Psalm 96:13.

THE INTERSECTION OF THEOLOGY AND CONTEMPORARY CONCERNS

At this point "the changing landscape of contemporary concerns" becomes particularly important. Having learned that the well-being of the human community and the well-being of the creation are inextricably related, we cannot help but notice that the contemporary condition of both the human community and the creation is dangerously unstable. Poverty, hunger, and malnutrition persist in a world that currently produces enough food to feed the whole human family. Even in the United States of America, perhaps the richest country in the history of the world, one in seven children regularly experience hunger and food insecurity; and worldwide, the growth of one in five children is stunted by hunger and/or malnutrition. The United Nations Refugee Agency estimates that 70.8 million people are now forcibly displaced from their homes, including 25.9 million refugees, more than ever in the history of the world; 41.3 million internally displaced persons; and 3.5 million asylum-seekers.[17] This represents nearly 1 percent of the global population.

In short, the human community is suffering; and as for the creation, as suggested above, the earth itself is being increasingly degraded in an unprecedented way. The irony is that what human beings are doing in the name of development or progress is the process of destroying the planet on which our life depends. Indeed, our unfettered and unprincipled push for progress, which has touched every parcel of dry land and even the deepest seas, is precisely why our current era is called the Anthropocene. Because of human beings, the world is *not* "firmly established."

For anyone familiar with the Bible, it should not be surprising that human beings regularly act to thwart God's purposes for the human family and for the creation; it has been happening since the third chapter of Genesis. Human self-assertion—that is, our attempt to be sovereign—does not mean that God is not sovereign. Rather, it means that God has chosen to enact God's sovereignty as love, not enforcement. Indeed, this divine choice takes us all the way back to Genesis 1 where human beings are given dominion (Gen 1:26–28), the responsibility to share with God the task of preserving the goodness of creation. But, of course, it does not take long for human beings to use their freedom to act over against God and God's purposes, hurting themselves and each other, as well as utterly frustrating God (Gen 6:5–6). As Terence Fretheim aptly concludes concerning the opening

17. See www.unrefugees.org.

chapters of Genesis, "The very act of creation thus might be called the beginning of the passion of God."[18] And God has been suffering ever since as we human beings have consistently failed to enact justice and righteousness in the human community and have failed to preserve the goodness of the earth on which our life depends.

The current destabilization of the earth invites us to appropriate the enthronement psalms in a particular way. Form-critically speaking, the enthronement psalms are songs of praise, but the current threat would not seem to elicit any sort of joyful response. Praise, however, is not only a celebrative liturgical act; but it is also, as Claus Westermann puts it, a "mode of existence"—in particular, a "mode of existence" that involves submission to God and God's purposes for human life and the life of the world.[19] In short, praise is a "mode of existence" that recognizes that God is sovereign and we are not. The recovery of praise as both a liturgical act and a "mode of existence," and thus the reclaiming of divine sovereignty, would mean that we human beings would confront our idolatrous, destructive, deadly sin of anthropocentrism. Ecologists are saying that our life depends on it. And indeed, so are biblical theologians. As Westermann puts it, "If the praise of God, as the Psalms express it, belongs to existence, then the directing of this praise to a man, an idea, or an institution must disturb and finally destroy life itself."[20] For God's sake, for our own sake as human beings, and for the sake of the integrity of creation, the enthronement psalms invite us to praise God. Submission to God and to God's purposes is the way toward a world that is "firmly established."

As we join God at moving the world in this direction, "the changing landscape of contemporary concerns" makes it especially important that we remember what is learned by reading both Psalms 82 and 96, separately and together—namely, injustice in the human community has an impact on the whole creation, an insight that suggests the degradation of creation has an impoverishing impact on the human community. For this reason, it is crucial, as Pope Francis reminds us, to be attentive simultaneously to the impoverishment of both the human community and the earth. In his encyclical letter entitled *Laudato Si' [Praise Be to You]: On Care for Our Common Home*, Pope Francis puts it like this: "Today, however, we have to realize that

18. Terence Fretheim, *The Suffering of God: An Old Testament Perspective*, OBT (Philadelphia: Fortress Press, 1984), 58.

19. Claus Westermann, *Praise and Lament in the Psalms*, trans. Keith R. Crim and Richard N. Soulen (Atlanta: John Knox, 1981), 160.

20. Westermann, *Praise and Lament in the Psalms*, 160–61.

a true ecological approach always becomes a social approach; it must integrate questions of justice in debates on the environment, so as to hear *both the cry of the earth and the cry of the poor.*"[21] And having learned from Psalms 82 and 96, we might add that a true theological approach will always be also an ecological approach.

CONCLUSION: BEYOND THE ENTHRONEMENT PSALMS

Given the likelihood that the enthronement collection forms "the theological 'heart'" of the Psalter, it is probably not coincidental that the Psalter moves toward its conclusion by a return to the theme of divine sovereignty. Psalm 145 is the final Davidic psalm in the book; and by changing the tone of the final Davidic collection (Pss 138–145) from lament (Pss 139–144) to praise, Psalm 145 serves as a transition to the Psalter's final collection, Psalms 146–150, which is a collection of songs of praise. Psalm 145 begins: "I will extol you, my God and King" (v. 1). Psalm 146, the opening psalm of the final collection, also features the root *mlk* by way of its concluding affirmation, "The Lord will reign forever" (v. 10); and like the enthronement collection, Psalm 146:7 describes God's work as justice. And Psalm 149 reminds the people that God is "their King" (v. 2), and that their calling as "the faithful" (vv. 1, 5; see v. 9) is to "do among them [the nations, peoples, and their leaders] the justice decreed" (v. 9).

Then too, like Psalms 96 and 98 especially, the concluding collection portrays the community of praise that God wills to gather as a world-encompassing one, even a universe-encompassing one. Particularly reminiscent of the creation-wide response to God's arrival in the world to establish justice (96:13; 98:9) is the final verse of the Psalter, "Let everything that breathes praise the Lord! Praise the Lord!" (150:6). While some interpreters restrict this invitation to human community, which would still make it impressively expansive (see Ps 82:8), such a restriction is unnecessary. The creatures have breath too (see Ps 104:27–30), and perhaps so do the trees and other plants, which, in any case, belong to God (see 104:16). Even more expansive than Psalm 150:6 though is Psalm 148, the centerpiece of the final collection. Psalm 148 invites praise not only from "everything that breathes," but also from *everything that is*. This includes inanimate features of creation (148:3–4, 9), as well as explicitly animals and plants (148:7, 9–10). The unmistakable

21. Pope Francis, *Laudato Si': On Care for Our Common Home* (Vatican City: Libreria Editrice Vaticana, 2015), 23 (section 49); see also Leonardo Boff, *Cry of the Earth, Cry of the Poor*, trans. Phillip Berryman (Maryknoll, NY: Orbis Books, 1997).

conclusion is that God is to be recognized as the universal sovereign, who wills the existence of a world where people, creatures, and the features of creation coexist in harmony. The psalmists even imagine that people, creatures, and the features of creation are partners in a worshiping congregation. Such will constitute a world that is "firmly established" (Ps 96:10). For this to happen, of course, we human creatures will need to affirm that God is sovereign, and we are not.

Finally, Psalm 72 suggests that the earthly kings had the responsibility for establishing on earth the justice and righteousness that God wills (esp. 72:1–7). The kings were known as God's "anointed" (see Ps 2:2; the Hebrew is traditionally transliterated as *messiah*, which came into Greek as *christos*) and God's "son" (see Ps 2:7; 2 Sam 7:14). These two titles became the primary ones for understanding who Jesus is (Mark 1:1). From the Christian point of view, the trajectory that begins with the Psalms culminates in Jesus, in whom "all things hold together" (Col 1:17) and through whom "God was pleased to reconcile to himself all things" (Col 1:20). In him we witness the ultimate expression of the convergence of theology and ecology.

16

A Theology of Glory: Divine Sanctum and Service in the Psalter

Jerome Skinner

The theme of God's glory in the Psalter brings heaven and earth together in interesting ways. The emphasis and background to many psalms that deal with God's glory show strong affinities with passages reflecting sanctuary settings in Israel's formative period as a nation and as a theocratic monarchy. An exploration of how the theme of God's glory emerges in these sanctuary settings shows the importance of God's divine sanctum in the Psalter and its implications for the life of his people.

From the heavens you uttered judgment; the earth feared and was still, when God arose to establish judgment, to save all the humble of the earth. *Selah*
—Psalm 76:8–9 ESV

The plethora of ideas, associations, images, and intertextual connections throughout the Hebrew Bible (HB) concerning Yahweh's glory that informs a reading of the Psalter warrants attention.[1] In the HB, the authors usually associate the glory of Yahweh with the spatial arena of Israel's sanctuary.[2] In its varied contexts in the Psalter, glory is associated with Yahweh, humanity,

1. In its varied grammatical forms, "glory" appears fifty-one times in thirty-three verses throughout the Psalter.
2. Exod 29:43; 40:34; Lev 9:6, 23; Num 14:10; 16:19; 1 Kgs 8:11; Isa 4:5; 6:1–3; Ezek 1–10; 40–48; Hag 2:7–9.

and the world. When Yahweh is in view, his dwelling place is usually the locus from which expressions of his glory burst forth. The psalmists assert, "O Lord, I love the habitation of thy house, and the place where thy glory dwells" (Ps 26:8); "So I have looked upon thee in the sanctuary, beholding thy power and glory" (63:2); "Honor and majesty are before him; strength and beauty are in his sanctuary. Ascribe to the Lord, O families of the peoples, ascribe to the Lord glory and strength!" (96:6, 7).[3]

The images of Yahweh's dwelling place are significant because, in addition to the usual religious and liturgical associations,[4] other vital ideas are in view. The Psalter shows that the combination of Yahweh, sanctum, and his divine action frequently occurs throughout the Psalter regarding his sovereignty and beneficence toward his people. Spread evenly throughout the Psalter, this combination covers a broad swath of descriptions, time, activity, and key theological dynamics inherent in the designations that refer to Yahweh's dwelling places.[5]

The parallels of language and images pertaining to a variety of architectural expressions about Israel's sanctuaries in the wilderness and Jerusalem highlight the centrality of God's divine sanctum and service in the Psalter.[6] Other expressions refer to aspects of ritual service,[7] as well as a broader spatial domain than Israel's local sanctuaries.[8] The Psalter's language alludes to God's divine presence among his people, often extending the scope of his reign and actions from his cosmic locus. In the Psalter, the implications of God's presence, manifested in his reign and character, address

3. Scripture quotations taken from the RSV, unless otherwise noted. For the Psalms, the Masoretic Text (MT) numbering is used, unless otherwise noted.

4. The Pentateuch expresses God's glory in theophanies and settings that explore acts of salvation and judgment. It is connected with the religious services such as covenant inauguration (Exod 24:1–17), tabernacle inauguration (Exod 40:34–35), ritual service inauguration (Lev 9: 6–23), and scenes of judgment (Num 14; 16; 20).

5. Steven Dunn, *The Sanctuary in the Psalms: Exploring the Paradox of God's Transcendence and Immanence* (Lanham, MD: Lexington Books, 2016).

6. Gordon J. Wenham, "Sanctuary Symbolism in the Garden of Eden Story," *WCJS* 9, A (1985): 19–25.

7. Jacob Milgrom, "The Cultic שגגה and Its Influence in Psalms and Job," *JQR* 58 (1967): 115–25.

8. Dragoslava Santrac, "The Psalmists' Journey and the Sanctuary: A Study in the Sanctuary and the Shape of the Book of Psalms," *JATS* 25/1 (2014): 23–42; and Santrac, *Sanctuary Cult in Relation to Religious Piety in the Book of Psalms* (Lambert Academic Publishing, 2013).

theodicy,[9] atonement and judgment,[10] and kingship.[11] The close association and overlap is seen in Yahweh's heavenly sanctum and merits an exploration of the Psalter's use of antecedent language and motifs. This larger literary corpus gives a more robust picture of divine presence and activity on humanity's behalf. These connections are most evident in a theological reflection on the Psalter's expression of Yahweh's glory.

DIVINE SANCTUM

In the Psalter, Yahweh's domain, sovereign acts, and glory are integrally tied to rich theological expressions about creation, salvation, judgment, enthronement, and doxology. These foci are part and parcel of the motif of divine presence and activity throughout glory-sanctum passages in the HB.[12] The Psalter emphasizes the cosmic aspect of God's glory by highlighting the convergence of the domains of heaven and earth in references to God's dwelling places, showing their complementarity.[13] This emphasis corresponds to Solomon's recognition of a heaven-earth fusion within the sphere of Yahweh's sovereignty, as expressed in his prayer at the dedication of the First Temple. His plea for Yahweh to act from his dwelling place in heaven while Israel's attention is turned to the earthly temple is twice recounted (1 Kgs 8; 2 Chr 6; cf. Pss 8:1; 11:4; 20:6; 57:3). His prayer contains language paralleling many of the prayers to Yahweh in the Psalter. It includes an expectation for Yahweh's covenant fidelity (1 Kgs 8:23–26; Ps 89:29), protection (1 Kgs 8:27–29; Pss 6:10; 39:13; 55:2; 86:16), justice (1 Kgs 8:31–32; Ps 82:3),

---

9. Martin Klingbeil, *YHWH Fighting from Heaven: God as Warrior and as God of Heaven in the Hebrew Psalter and Ancient Near Eastern Iconography*, OBO 169 (Gottingen: Vandenhoeck & Ruprecht, 1999), 5–37.

10. Pss 51; 73. Bruce Waltke, "Atonement in Psalm 51," in *The Glory of the Atonement: Biblical, Theological and Practical Perspectives: Essays in Honor of Roger Cole*, ed. Charles E. Hill and Frank A. James III (Downers Grove, IL: IVP Academic, 2004), 51–60.

11. Pss 93; 95–99. For a helpful analysis of this theme, see David M. Howard Jr., *The Structure of Psalms 93–100*, Biblical and Judaic Studies 5 (Winona Lake, IN: Eisenbrauns, 1997).

12. Cf. Exod 19; 24; 40; Num 14; Ezek 1–10. See also Elizabeth Bloch-Smith, "'Who Is the King of Glory?': Solomon's Temple and Its Symbolism," in *Scripture and Other Artifacts, Festschrift for Philip J. King*, ed. Michael D. Coogan, J. Cheryl Exum, and Lawrence E. Stager (Louisville: Westminster John Knox, 1994), 18–31.

13. On Psalm 102:20, Allen comments, "Zion is the place where the name is proclaimed in praise (v 22) and also the earthly counterpart of the heavenly temple." Leslie C. Allen, *Psalms 101–150 (Revised)*, WBC 21 (Dallas: Word, 2002), 22. Others use the term "heavenly sanctuary" in multiple instances. Hans-Joachim Kraus, *Psalms 1–59*, CC (Minneapolis: Fortress Press, 1993), 469; Frank-Lothar Hossfeld and Erich Zenger, *Psalms 3: A Commentary on Psalms 101–150*, Hermeneia (Minneapolis: Fortress Press, 2011), 654–59.

forgiveness (1 Kgs 8:34; Pss 25:11; 103:3), and vindication (1 Kgs 8:45, 49; Pss 9:5, 17; 99:4). Elsewhere in the HB, the covenantal promise of divine presence and restoration outside the spatial context of the temple in Jerusalem is addressed in Yahweh's proclamation of dwelling with his people (Ezek 11:16).[14] This affirms that Yahweh's expression of his glory and redemptive work was not confined solely to one locale or expressed in one sole expression of the divine presence.

The extensive terminology of God's dwelling places in the Psalter carries a broad semantic and thematic range that is fertile with historical allusions and echoes to Israelite sacred spaces when Yahweh's glory is in view.[15] The terms include variations of the noun *qodesh* (holy place),[16] *hekal* (palace),[17] *ohel* (tent),[18] *bet YHWH* (house of the Lord),[19] *khatser* (courtyard),[20] and *mishkan* (dwelling place, sanctuary).[21] These terms are all used in the Psalter when reference is made to Yahweh's glory on a cosmic scope. The chart below indicates the thematic context (activity) of each psalm focusing on some aspect of Yahweh's glory. These acts of God address the same themes that are evident in the main sanctuary scenes that allude to some aspects of his glory on earth. Enthronement, creation, salvation, judgment, and doxology are the main theological contexts of these previous revelations and the substance of these psalms listed in Figure 16.1.

14. Dirk Human, "YHWH, the Israelite High God Bends Down to Uplift the Downtrodden: Perspectives on the Incomparability of YHWH in Psalm 113," *JNSL* 30.1 (2004): 41–64.

15. Richard E. Averbeck, "Tabernacle," in *Dictionary of the Old Testament: Pentateuch*, ed. T. Desmond Alexander and David W. Baker (Downers Grove, IL: InterVarsity Press, 2003), 807–27.

16. The verb *qadash* "to set apart" is connected with Yahweh's glory and dwelling place (Exod 29:43). See also, 1 Chr 16:29 (LXX).

17. 1 Sam 3:3; 4:21–22; 1 Kgs 7:50–8:11.

18. Exod 29:42–44; 40:34–35; 9:23; Num 14:10; 16:19, 42; 20:6; 1 Kgs 8:4–11.

19. 1 Kgs 8:10–11; 2 Chr 7:1–3.

20. Ezek 8–10; 43:5.

21. Exod 40:34–38; Num 9:15–23.

Figure 16.1

GLORY PASSAGE	FOCUS	TEMPLE REFERENCE	ACTIVITY
3:4	YHWH	har qodesh	salvation
24:7–9	YHWH	qodesh	procession, creation[22]
26:8	YHWH	bet, mishkan	judgment
29:1–3, 9	YHWH	heykal	enthronement, doxology
57:6, 9, 12	YHWH	shamayim	salvation
63:3	YHWH	qodesh	doxology
66:2	YHWH	bet	doxology
72:19	YHWH	shem[23]	doxology
79:9	YHWH	qodesh, hekal	defilement, salvation
84:12	YHWH	ohel, mishkan	doxology
85:10–11	YHWH	shamayim	salvation, judgment
96:3, 7–9	YHWH	qodesh, miqdash, hatsrot	doxology
102:16–17	YHWH	qodesh	doxology, judgment
108:6–8	YHWH	qodesh	judgment
138:5	YHWH	qodesh, hekal	doxology
GLORY PASSAGE	**FOCUS**	**NO TEMPLE REFERENCE**	**ACTIVITY**
85:10	YHWH		salvation, judgment
104:31	YHWH		creation
113:4	YHWH		doxology
115:1	YHWH		doxology
145:5, 11, 12	YHWH		doxology

22. God's name can be associated with his temple. Deuteronomy's emphasis on Yahweh "making his name dwell" (infinitive construct of *shakan* + *shem*) in the place of his choosing is an overriding theme that focuses on the locus of Yahweh's glory (Deut 12:11; 14:23; 16:2, 6, 11; 26:2; Ps 74:7). Yahweh's name is subsequently associated with his glory for a multitude of reasons (Pss 8:1; 72:19; 102:15; 115:1; 106:47; 1 Chr 16:10, 29, 35). See J. G. McConville, "God's Name, God's Glory," *TynBul* 30 (1979): 149–63.

23. Psalm 104:31

SANCTUM REFERENCES

Har Qodesh

The first expression of God's glory in the Psalter is connected to Yahweh's *har qodesh* "holy mountain/hill" (Ps 3:4; see also 2:6). The phrase "holy hill," or some variation[24] points to God in a number of ways: (1) in his glorious majesty (Ps 87:1–3); (2) as the benefactor of divine protection and moral holiness (Pss 15:1;[25] 24:3); (3) as defender of the oppressed (Ps 43:2–3); and (4) as the one who addresses injustice. These notions of God's glory are further enriched by references to his holy mountain as indestructible because of his abiding presence (Ps 48:2–4). Indeed, it is from his holy hill that he executes justice for his people (Ps 99:1–9).

Among God's dwelling places, *har* may sometimes refer to Sinai (e.g., Exod 3:1; Ps 78:54). In most cases, it alludes to the locale of the Jerusalem temple (e.g., Isa 2:2; 11:9; Ps 48:1, 2), and in a few instances it can even point to the heavenly Zion, Yahweh's heavenly abode (e.g., Ps 3:4).[26] This is significant because it is in the context of the Sinai revelation that Israel received God's justice on their behalf (Exod 15; Ps 77) and received their instructions for justice in the community.[27] Broadening the notion of justice, the psalmists proclaim the nature of God's judgment found in his person and acts in both a vertical and horizontal axis ("from his holy hill"; cf. Pss 20:6; 102:19).[28] This indicates a connection between the psalmists' appeal for divine adjudication on earth and God's action from his divine sanctum. In its poetic context, references to God's holy hill[29] may serve as a figure of speech (metonymy), which points to his cosmic sovereignty characterized by holiness and justice (Pss 43:3; 48:1; 87:1 ET).

24. Cf. Mount Zion (Pss 48:3, 12; 74:2; 78:68; 125:1).

25. See the parallel phraseology in Joel 4:17 HB where God is the subject, who "dwells" (*shakan*) in/on the "holy mountain."

26. Elias Brasil de Souza, "The Heavenly Sanctuary/Temple Motif in the Hebrew Bible: Function and Relationship to the Earthly Counterparts" (PhD diss., Andrews University, 2005), 144–45.

27. Elmer A. Martens, "How Is the Christian to Construe Old Testament Law?," *BBR* 12 (2002): 206–9.

28. W. A. VanGemeren, "Mountain Imagery," in *Dictionary of the Old Testament: Wisdom, Poetry, and Writings* (Downers Grove, IL: IVP Press Academic, 2008), 481–83.

29. Pss 99:5; 132:7; 1 Chr 28:2; Isa 66:1.

In the lament in Psalm 3, the cry for salvation from God in his holy hill comes from the experience of injustice.[30] *Har qodesh* expresses a certain dynamic of God's presence and the psalmist's desired deliverance. This gives perspective to David's initial cry for the divine judge to act according to his universal sovereignty. Further, the connection of Yahweh's divine sanctuary as protective residence filled with his glory provides the substance of David's imagery. Yahweh is a shield for him, his glory, and the one who lifts his head. He proclaims "you" (Yahweh) are "my glory." The correlation of Yahweh and glory by David has profound implications, because according to the historical superscription he was physically separated from the tent that housed the ark of God (Ps 3:1; 2 Sam 15:17–37). For David, Yahweh's glory is his presence and sustaining power. David is using the expression "holy hill" to point to God's abode as well as to how the expression of his glory results in deliverance and blessing (3:8–9). As divine judge, God's glory can thus be said to be a manifestation of his presence in maintaining justice. The parallel usage in Psalm 2:6 also addresses the issue of justice and connects it to messianic expectation.[31]

Qodesh

The next reference to the divine sanctuary is the word *qodesh*, "sanctuary," which is similar to the previous sanctum reference. As a dwelling place of God, its primary emphasis is the holiness of God. An extensive list of occurrences of this term for sanctum is found in Pentateuchal ritual texts that emphasize Yahweh's holiness, the people's holy calling, and the holiness of his dwelling place and its service (cf. Exod 25–Num 10). The same principle applies later in texts that deal with Israel's religious life in the temple precinct (1 Kgs 6–8). The psalmists pick up on this focus and with sanctum references often utilize the language of ritual and ethics to denote the environment of holiness.[32]

Qodesh first occurs in connection with Yahweh's glory in Psalm 24:3, which carries a parallel to the phrase "holy hill" addressed above. This processional text highlights the spatial scope of divine activity, which here seems to be a reference to an inaugural event. This festal processional act

30. Jerome Skinner, "The Historical Superscriptions of Davidic Psalms: An Exegetical, Intertextual and Methodological Analysis" (PhD diss., Andrews University, 2016), 30–40.

31. Pss 15:1; 24:3; 43:3; 48:2; 99:9. It is interesting that this phrase is used in another messianic passage (Isa 11:9).

32. Jackie A. Naudé, "קָדַשׁ," *NIDOTTE* 3:877–86. Cf. Pss 20:2–6; 63:3; 68:5, 17, 24–25; 74:1–8; 77:11–20; 102:15–23; 108:7; 134:2.

is analogous to Israel's journey in the wilderness as a holy camp, where God led the people by his glory cloud (Num 9:15–23; 10:11–36).[33] A similar notion of procession and entrance into the holy precincts is found in Psalms 15 and 24. Both psalms inquire about moral fitness (i.e., holiness) for access into God's presence and highlights divine residence as a holy environment in which God himself enters and leads the way by his righteous acts for his people. In harmony with the ancient Near Eastern practice of associating the earthly and heavenly sanctuary,[34] this liturgy of the entrance of Yahweh's holy presence as the King of Glory emphasizes a cosmic perspective. The psalm invites readers into this doxological extravaganza in verse 1 by focusing attention on the spatial arena of all creation ("the earth, and its fullness") as Yahweh's sovereign domain.

In Psalm 102, after recounting personal grief and lamenting Zion's inauspicious position, the psalmist points to an appointed time of judgment when nations will be humbled before Yahweh's glory. In what can be seen as a commentary on Psalm 2, here the glory of Yahweh is attached to his name (i.e., reputation), which is holy (Pss 29:2; 33:21; 103:1). The nations will fear his glory, for his holy residence (Zion) will be rebuilt and Yahweh's theophanic appearance in glory will bring judgment upon the whole earth, a cosmic judgment. The good news is that Yahweh looks down from his holy height, from heaven (Ps 33:13–14), and he acts on behalf of his people. What happens in the heavenly holy sanctuary has impact on what happens on earth in terms of deliverance for the holy people of God and judgment for the unholy, who reject his grace and are defiant to his reign.

Hekal

Another reference to God's sanctum that the psalmists expound upon is the noun *hekal*, "palace, temple."[35] This word indicates a royal palace. It is "a

---

33. Several commentators assess the text in Numbers as some type of battle hymn as the King, Yahweh, sets forth. R. Dennis Cole, *Numbers*, vol. 3B, NAC (Nashville: Broadman & Holman, 2000), 178–79; John T. Willis, "QÛMĀH YHWH," *JNSL* 16 (1990): 220. Cf. Pss 68:1–6; 132:8.

34. Crispin Fletcher-Louis, "Further Reflections on a Divine and Angelic Humanity in the Dead Sea Scrolls," in *New Perspectives on Old Texts: Proceedings of the 2005 Orion Dead Sea Scroll Conference*, ed. E. G. Chazon, B. Halpern-Amaru, and R. A. Clements (Leiden: Brill, 2010), 185–98. Joachim Kraus notes, "The cultic conceptions associated with 'King' YHWH cannot simply be identified with earthly dimensions." Kraus, *Psalms 1–59*, 315.

35. See 1 Sam 1:9; 3:3; 2 Sam 22:7; 1 Kgs 6:3, 5, 17, 33; 7:21, 50 of God's sanctuary/temple. *Hekal* is a loanword from Sumerian É.GAL, "big house" (i.e., palace or temple) and Akkadian *ekallu*, "palace/temple." Magnus Ottosson, "הֵיכָל," *TDOT* 3:382–83. The word has a long history of referring

residence and complex of a king and other royalty (1 Kgs 21:1; 2 Kgs 20:18; Ps 45:8)."[36] References to Yahweh's palace often highlight his sovereign presence. Moreover, his covenant faithfulness is the characteristic by which the psalmists plead for access to his throne. Yahweh is pictured as a reliable, powerful king, who is enthroned[37] in a holy palace.

In its use of this reference, Psalm 29 conveys Yahweh's kingly power as the focal point of worship (see also Ps 96). All the elements of tabernacle/temple worship are portrayed by the psalmist in majestic language, which builds the suspense-filled drama of doxology that is utilized elsewhere to highlight Yahweh's reign (see 1 Chr 16:28–29). The cosmic scope of Yahweh's reign is emphasized as the psalmist recalls one of the most significant demonstrations of it—the flood (Ps 29:10; Gen 6–8).[38] Ascribing to Yahweh glory and strength expresses the idea of recognizing, giving over, and acknowledging his cosmic sovereignty.[39] The mighty ones are to "show due honor to YHWH's 'glory and strength' and to his name." Adding further prestige to the King in residence, the psalmist writes that in Yahweh's palace all cry "glory." This type of repetitive praise is reminiscent of Isaiah 6, and the context of enthronement is also in view. In the bastion of God's beauty, the psalmist, like the seraphim, proclaims that Yahweh deserves recognition for his presence, mighty acts, and rulership from his heavenly palace. The impact of this doxology highlights the connection between who God is as King and the psalmist's requests. Robert Alter notes, "The psalm starts with a verb meaning 'to give' or 'to grant,' an act to be directed from the divine entourage to God, and concludes with the more common synonym for the act of giving, now directed from God to Israel."[40]

In Psalm 79, with the exile looming large in Israel's experience, its temple, the earthly locus of divine glory and activity has been besieged. Upon reflection on the defilement of the temple, the psalmist pleads with Yahweh

---

to either the palace of a human king or a temple, which is the palace of a deity. The word is especially appropriate for the sanctuary of Yahweh, who is Israel's Divine King.

36. James Swanson, "הֵיכָל," *Dictionary of Biblical Languages with Semantic Domains: Hebrew (Old Testament)*. This focus is affirmed in several synonyms including, citadel (*'armôn*, Ps 48:4, 14); military strongholds (*'almôn*, Isa 13:22); and fortified palace (*bîrâ*, perhaps a Persian loanword for palace, citadel, Esth 1:2). Leonard J. Coppes, "הֵיכָל," *TWOT* (electronic ed.), 214.

37. In the Psalter, the construction "YHWH sits" (YHWH + *yashab*) carries the connotation of divine enthronement (see Ps 9:7).

38. Allen Ross, *A Commentary on the Psalms: Volume 1 (1–41)* (Grand Rapids: Kregel, 2011), 661.

39. Harris, "יָהַב," *TWOT* 368.

40. Robert Alter, *The Book of Psalms: A Translation with Commentary* (New York: Norton, 2007), 101.

to show forth his salvation for the glory of his name. The unusual juxtaposition of the verb "defile" (*tame'*) with the object *hekal* brings into focus the idea that it is Yahweh's kingship that has been impinged upon; it is not simply a religious defamation.[41] The imagery of the temple defiled also conjures up thoughts of Yahweh's glory departing from among the people as their King because of defilement (Ezek 4–10). Furthermore, the psalmist's prayer for Yahweh to pour out his anger against kingdoms brings the issue of kingship into focus. The conflict is at the level of royal domains.[42] The nations assume that God is absent among his people because the temple in Jerusalem is laid waste. Yet, the psalmist's appeal for God to act is based on his sovereignty over the world and the nations. The Deuteronomic theme of covenant (*hasid*), Yahweh's name (*shem*), and the centrality of his royal kingship in his palace (*hekal*) is the framework for praying for the restoration of the people of God (Deut 12:5–11; cf. Pss 45:6; 93:2). As in Psalm 79, Psalm 138 also highlights the name (*shem*) of Yahweh, his covenantal love (*hesed*), and divine kingship (*hekal*; v. 2). Also, he is worthy of praise within a worldwide scope because of his glory (vv. 4–5). David will sing of the ways of Yahweh for his glory is elevated above all the rulers of the world. The language of the psalm highlights this notion of exaltation.[43] His covenant promises that are meted out in sovereign love and faithfulness set him above the pomp of earthly potentates.

Bet YHWH

The Psalter is filled with pictures of jubilation one attains when entering in the *bet YHWH*, "house of Yahweh." In Psalms 26:8 and 42:5 the psalmists affirm the earthly representation of God's habitation as a house of praise. This focus on God's house as a distinct dwelling heightens its centrality in Israel's life as a pilgrimage,[44] whose procession should end in worship (Ps 27:4; see also Ps 135). Psalm 66 ties together elements that depict this journey, including God's acts of creation, redemption, judgment, and kingship.

---

41. There are other references to the temple that are the object of the verb *tame'* in the piel stem: *bayit* (Jer 7:30; 32:34; Ezek 9:7; 2 Chr 36:14) and *miqdash* (Ezek 5:11; 23:38).

42. The nouns "nations" (*goyim*; Ps 79:1, 6, 10), "kingdoms" (*mamlakah*, 79:6), and "neighbors" (*shaken*, 79:4, 12) highlight this broad focus.

43. The descriptive language of Psalm 138 highlights the contrast between God and the arrogant. Of God, the psalmist states, "Your glory is great [*gadol*]," and "the Lord is exalted [*rum*]." Both words are often used in relation to God's high status as King (Ps 75:7; Isa 57:15). Of the arrogant, he states, "the haughty [proud] he knows," which is a play on another nuance of the root. H.-P. Stähli, "גבה *gbh* to be high," *TLOT* (digital edition), 296–99.

44. Pss 120–134; see also Exod 23:17; 34:18–26; Lev 23:4–38; Deut 16:1–16.

The focus of the psalm is the revelation of the mighty deeds of Yahweh in Israel's experience. A primary example is the reference to the judgment/vindication of the righteous as an experience that leads to praise (66:10–12).[45] The psalmist implores the people to sing Yahweh's praises in the midst of his judgments, as doxology in God's house is the climatic goal of his restorative activity.

Mishkan

The noun *mishkan*, "dwelling place, tabernacle,"[46] is another important term in the Psalter and Israel's formative descriptions of Yahweh's earthly abode (see Exod 25:9). The emphasis seems to be on the physical structure itself as a dwelling fit for Yahweh's glory (Exod 40:34, 35). In Psalm 26, the lament for vindication and justice are integrally connected with Yahweh's habitation, whose architecture served a functional purpose.[47] David refers to the altar, which was the place associated with forgiveness, atonement, fellowship, and moral purity (Ps 26:6; Exod 20:22–26). Only an ornate edifice befits the habitation of Yahweh's house as the place of the abode for his glory (see 2 Sam 7:1–17). David's quest was to beautify the place of God's choosing (i.e., Jerusalem), recognizing it would reflect Yahweh's real domain that is exalted above the heavens and manifests his glory (see 1 Chr 29:10–22).[48]

Khatser

The term *khatser*, "courtyard," refers to the semi-enclosed area of the temple complex and the temple court or courtyard. In the Psalter, when *khatser* appears, it is used in parallelism with some designation of the temple.[49] In a parallel expression to Psalm 29:1–3, Psalm 96:7–9 focuses on the majesty of Yahweh's presence with his people—their accessibility to such a gift (Ps 65:5; Lev 6:26 ET) and the spatial importance of his presence in terms of atonement (Pss 96:8; 116:17–19; see also 1 Kgs 8:64). In Psalm 96, the use of

---

45. Pss 7:10; 11:4–5; 17:3; 26:2; 66:10; 81:8; 139:23. Terry L. Brensinger, "בָּחַן," *NIDOTTE* 1:636–38.

46. This term refers in general to places of dwelling, "dwellings of both human and God. … There are several places in the Psalms where מִשְׁכָּן is used in the pl. referring to the temple complex (Ps 43:3; 46:4 [5]; 84:1 [2])." Richard E. Averbeck, "מִשְׁכָּן," *NIDOTTE* 2:1130.

47. In verse 8 many versions translate *mishkan* as if it is a verb: "dwells." However, the construct noun and familiar term *mishkan* used for the tabernacle/temple is used here and is better translated "the place of the dwelling place of your glory."

48. Pss 11:4; 14:2; 20:6; 33:13; 53:2; 57:3; 80:14; 102:19; 135:6; 136:26; 148:13.

49. "This illustrates the esteem the Israelites had for the courts as part of the temple structure, the most holy place in the Israelite religion." Mark F. Rooker, "חָצֵר," *NIDOTTE* 2:250.

the word *miqdash*, "sanctuary, holy place," sharpens the focus that the experience of access to Yahweh's glory via the altar (atonement) and entrance into the tabernacle/temple are in the realm of the holy.[50]

Ohel

A final term for Yahweh's sanctuary in the Psalter addressed here, *ohel*, "tent," is utilized in different ways throughout the Psalter. In one of its uses in connection to Yahweh's glory, the various references to the sacred tent carry overtones of the exodus motif in Scripture.[51] Exodus's strong emphasis on the presence of God dwelling with his people in his sanctuary leads to the high point of the manifestation of the glory of God in the tabernacle (Exod 40:34). It is significant that after Yahweh's glorious deliverance of his people from Egypt that this term designates the first architectural edifice where the glory of Yahweh is said to descend (Exod 40:34, 35). The doxological proclamation, "how lovely is your dwelling place," in Psalm 84:1 opens up this ode on the desire for fellowship in the tabernacle. The psalmist yearns to be in close proximity to Yahweh. This desire can be seen in the multitude of references to the sanctuary in this psalm.[52] Here it is Yahweh who bestows grace and glory from his presence.[53] It is in the tent of meeting where communion is held, where the pilgrim blesses and glorifies Yahweh. In return, Yahweh blesses and bestows his grace and glory on the worshiper which has a plethora of implications.

GOD'S GLORY IN HIS DIVINE SANCTUM

In the Psalter, out of the twenty passages that refer to some aspect of Yahweh's personal glory (see Fig. 16.1), fifteen passages contain temple references and some type of activity by God or about God. Contextually the thematic focus of Yahweh as Creator is seen once, the response of doxology

50. W. Kornfeld and Helmer Ringgren, "קדשׁ," *TDOT* 12:529.

51. Klaus Koch, "אֹהֶל," *TDOT* 1:118–130. It is significant that this is the first architectural edifice upon which the glory of Yahweh is said to descend (Exod 40:34, 35). Included in this reference is the nuance of Yahweh's abode particularly as it relates to the sacred confederacy of the holy worshiping covenant community (Exod 33:7–11; Lev 1–Num 10). It is usually referred to as the "tent of meeting," where divinity and humanity can commune together, and was associated with Yahweh's glory (Exod 29:42–43; see also 39:32; Lev 1:3). Another important focus is atonement and holiness (Exod 27:21; 28:43; 30:16). T. Desmond Alexander, *From Paradise to the Promised Land: An Introduction to the Pentateuch*, 2nd ed. (Grand Rapids: Baker Academic, 2002), 192–203.

52. *Mishkan* (Ps 84:2), *khatsor* (84:3, 11), *bayit* (84:4, 5, 11), and *tsion* (84:8).

53. J. L. Mays, *Psalms*, Interpretation (Louisville: Westminster John Knox, 1994), 274.

appears seven times, Yahweh's salvation appears four times, and judgment appears four times. The other passages in the Psalter associate God's glory with his work in the world, which encompasses several other important facets. Taken as a whole, the Psalter's picturesque quality vividly describes God's character, his exaltation, the world's relation to him, and the constant need for his glory to be proclaimed. His kingship is described in terms of the characteristic of glory. He is the glorious King (Ps 24:7–10), and the world is blessed through his glorious name (Ps 72:19). These references, seen in their literary contexts, bring an eschatological picture into focus, in which Yahweh is praised for his deeds and ultimately the response will be worldwide worship. While ritual texts usually point to a specific locale where Yahweh's glory appears, it is the whole earth as the domain where Yahweh's glory of his kingship will shine forth (see Pss 93–100).

The locus of Yahweh's glory extends beyond the Jerusalem temple. God's glory above the heavens (Ps 113:4) makes idol worship abhorrent because it limits the sphere of a deity's presence (Ps 106:20; see also 1 Sam 5:1–5). The nature of God's glory is expressed in how the world relates to its appearance; all creation is impacted in some way. The heavens declare God's glory (Pss 19:1; 97:6), and our glorious God thunders over creation (Ps 29:3). God's glory needs proclamation and expression through praise.[54] God's glory needs to be shown.[55] There is also a need for human beings to give God glory.[56]

CONCLUSION

After examining all the texts in the Psalter containing the noun *kabod*, "glory," conclusions can now be drawn about its meaning and implications for the focus of the Psalter. When referring to Yahweh, it carries a scope of meaning including, but not limited to, his presence, character, might, salvation, judgments, acts, essence, protection, providence, rulership, kingship, love, mercy, guidance, and care. It has been shown that his glory is integrally connected to his divine sanctuary and its earthly representation.

In the New Testament, the idea that Jesus came to reveal the glory of Yahweh (John 17:1–5) is consistent with the theological, historical, and eschatological hope set forth in the Psalter. The incarnation, crucifixion, and resurrection of Christ were the ultimate revelation of the glory of Yahweh

54. Pss 96:3; 138:5; 145:5, 11–12.

55. Pss 57:6, 11; 72:19; 79:9; 85:9; 102:15, 16; 104:31; 108:5; 115:1.

56. Pss 29:1, 2; 66:2; 96:7, 8.

(John 1:14; 2:11; Heb 1:1–3). The ritual language in the New Testament, with its references to Jesus's body being the temple (John 2:21), the sacrificial Lamb (John 1:29), the light (John 8:12), the bread (John 6:35), the door (John 10:7), and more, coincides with the close relationship between God's sanctuary and his glory in the book of Psalms. Ultimately, the books of Hebrews and Revelation take their audience's attention back to the divine sanctuary where Jesus ministers the same blessings and exhibits the same majestic reign of his glory that is amply described in the Psalter.[57]

57. Heb 4:14–16; 6:19–20; 8:1–2; 12:22–24; Rev 1; 4–5; 15; 21–22.

17

Perceptions of Divine Presence in the Levitical Psalms of Book II

THE PARADOX OF DISTANCE AND PROXIMITY

J. Nathan Clayton

This essay suggests that in the Levitical psalms of the Psalter's second book, the psalmists' perceptions of the divine presence are paradoxical in a derivational manner. This idea is first developed by showing how the function of the Levites in three Old Testament canonical stages (tribal foundation, tabernacle, and temple) can be seen as paradoxical. Second, some exegetical observations from Psalms 42–50 show that the interplay of three subthemes (perception of divine distance, perception of divine proximity, and holy space/Zion language) further illustrates this notion of paradox.

INTRODUCTION

Scholarly analysis of the Psalms continues to show the benefit of not only examining individual psalms according to their own genre and internal rhetorical development, but also considering the broader theological message present in the purposeful placement of various collections of psalms and the canonical shaping of the five books themselves.[1] These discussions

1. For a brief survey of the canonical approach to the study of the Psalms and the seminal influence of Gerald H. Wilson's *The Editing of the Hebrew Psalter* (SBLDS 76 [Chico, CA: Scholars Press, 1985]), see Nancy L. deClaissé-Walford, "The Canonical Approach to Scripture and *The Editing of the Hebrew Psalter*," in *The Shape and Shaping of the Book of Psalms: The Current State*

include the function of the Levitical psalms in Books II–III (Pss 42–72 and 73–89).[2]

In this essay, we propose to examine one avenue through which the Levitical psalms of Book II contribute canonically to the Psalter's perspective on a significant theme: that of the godly one perceiving Yahweh as both present and absent.[3] Our suggestion is that these psalms develop the pattern of a multifaced and, essentially, paradoxical perception of the divine presence. In support, we will briefly examine two broad areas of Old Testament tradition: (1) the paradoxical nature of the basic function of the Levites in the Old Testament canon more broadly, as a foundation for a richer understanding of (2) some illustrative paradoxical elements in the Levitical psalms of Book II.

The study of paradox in biblical literature is rooted in literary and rhetorical-critical interpretive approaches.[4] Here, we will proceed based on Narry Santos's helpful definition in his study of the Gospel of Mark. He suggests that "a [literary] paradox is a statement that departs from accepted opinion (the etymological nuance), or an apparently self-contradictory or absurd statement (the derivational nuance). Thus a 'paradox' is an unusual and apparently self-contradictory rhetorical statement or

---

of Scholarship, ed. by Nancy L. deClaissé-Walford (Atlanta: SBL Press, 2014), 1–11. For a broader analysis of Psalms study in recent decades, see David M. Howard Jr., "The Psalms and Current Study," in *Interpreting the Psalms: Issues and Approaches*, ed. David Firth and Philip S. Johnston (Downers Grove, IL: InterVarsity Press), 23–40. For a summary reflection on the broad theological message that can emerge from a canonical reading of the Psalter, see Nancy deClaissé-Walford, Rolf A. Jacobson, and Beth LaNeel Tanner, *The Book of Psalms*, NICOT (Grand Rapids: Eerdmans, 2014), 21–38.

2. For an analysis of the function of the Levitical psalm collections in the editing of the Psalter, see for instance Susan Gillingham, "The Levites and the Editorial Composition of the Psalms," in *The Oxford Handbook of the Psalms*, ed. William P. Brown (Oxford: Oxford University Press, 2014), 201–13.

3. In Old Testament theology, Samuel Terrien has especially developed this dual theme. See his *The Elusive Presence: Toward a New Biblical Theology*, Religious Perspectives 26 (San Francisco: Harper & Row, 1978), and his *The Psalms: Strophic Structure and Theological Commentary*, ECC (Grand Rapids: Eerdmans, 2003).

4. For representative studies, see Matthew R. Schlimm, "The Paradoxes of Fear in the Hebrew Bible," *SEÅ* 84 (2019): 25–50; David H. Wenkel, "The Paradox of High Christology in Hebrews 1," *Bib* 99 (2018): 431–46; Zoltán Schwáb, "I, the Fool: A 'Canonical' Reading of Proverbs 26:4–5," *Journal of Theological Interpretation* 10 (2016): 31–50; W. Domeris, "Meek or Oppressed? Reading Matthew 5:5 in Context," *AcT* 23 (2016): 131–49; Steven Dunn, *The Sanctuary in the Psalms: Exploring the Paradox of God's Transcendence and Immanence* (Lanham, MD: Lexington, 2016); P. W. Goodman, *Paradoxes of Paradise: Identity and Difference in the Song of Songs*, 2nd ed. (Sheffield: Sheffield Phoenix, 2011).

concept that departs dramatically from accepted opinion."[5] Santos also notes that the derivational meaning of a paradox, in particular, entails "an apparently self-contradictory statement or concept that can convey unified truth (i.e., the polaric aspect), despite existing contrariness of two opposing assertions (i.e., the antinomic aspect)."[6] We propose, then, the following question: to what extent may the perception of divine presence in the Levitical psalms of Book II be understood as evincing paradox, mostly in the derivational sense? That is, is a polaric and unified truth of Scripture—that God dwells with his people—communicated *antinomically* through two opposing claims: that the Levitical psalmists perceive God as both present and absent?

PARADOX IN THE OLD TESTAMENT FUNCTION OF THE LEVITES

The Old Testament data related to the Levites is complex. A number of scholarly theories related to the historical development of the Levites have been proposed. These include discussions of the relationship between the Levitical psalms and the presentation of the worship function of the Levites in Chronicles and Ezra-Nehemiah, especially.[7] In the following, we will highlight three aspects in the canonical presentation of the Levites in general support of the paradoxical nature of the ministry of the (non-Aaronite) Levites: their tribal foundation, their initial function with Moses at the tabernacle, and their expanded function with David in preparation for the Solomonic temple.

Tribal Foundation

The Pentateuch establishes the basic identity and purpose of the tribe of Levi. In Genesis 49, the patriarch Jacob gathers his twelve sons, so that, in

5. Narry F. Santos, "The Paradox of Authority and Servanthood in the Gospel of Mark," *BibSac* 154 (1997): 452–60.
6. Santos, "Paradox of Authority," 453.
7. On this, see further the first chapter of my study, J. Nathan Clayton, *Symbol, Service and Song: The Levites of 1 Chronicles 10–29 in Rhetorical, Historical and Theological Perspectives* (Eugene, OR: Pickwick/Wipf & Stock, 2021), 1–38. For instance, Yeong Seon Kim (*The Temple Administration and the Levites in Chronicles*, CBQMS 51 [Washington, DC: Catholic Biblical Association of America, 2014], 190–93) argues that the Chronicler's picture of Davidic Levitical temple preparations is merely reflective of a postexilic idealism, while Peter J. Leithart (*1 & 2 Chronicles*, Brazos Theological Commentary on the Bible [Grand Rapids: Brazos, 2019], 80–84) argues for strong historical and theological connections between Levitical psalmody/worship function and David's founding role.

his words, "I may tell you what shall happen to you in days to come" (Gen 49:1; ואגידה לכם את אשר־יקרא אתכם באחרית הימים).[8] In Genesis 49:5–7, Simeon and Levi receive their own word from Jacob. Simeon and Levi are steeped in "weapons of violence" (כלי חמס) in verse 5, and in "anger" (אף), as they killed men (v. 6). Their anger leads, then, to a "curse" (ארור) from Jacob in verse 7, as they will eventually be "divided" (verbal root חלק) and "scattered" (verbal root פוץ) in Israel. Most probably, Simeon and Levi's massacre of the men of Shechem in Genesis 34, because of the humiliation of their sister Dinah, stands at the root of this curse by Jacob.[9] Jacob's prophetic word is fulfilled in the subsequent life of ancient Israel, as the tribe of Simeon only inherits land within the broader land-area of the tribe of Judah (see Josh 19:1–9), and as the tribe of Levi inherits no tribal land, only the forty-eight Levitical cities (see Num 18:23–24; 35:1–8; Josh 21:1–45).

In this sense, the foundation of the tribe of Levi in the Pentateuch could be described as paradoxical in itself. It is rooted in two seemingly opposing realities: the tribal forefather, Levi, is cursed because of his fierce violence and anger, on the one hand; yet on the other hand, the tribe of Levi eventually inherits the special role of mediating the very presence of Yahweh himself for the whole community.[10]

Initial Tabernacle Function

In the context of further defining the duties of the priests and Levites in Numbers 18, Yahweh speaks directly to Aaron, as a representative of the whole tribe of Levi, and proclaims in verse 20: "You shall have no *inheritance* [verbal root נחל] in their land, neither shall you have any *portion* [the noun חלק] among them. I am your *portion* [noun חלק] and your *inheritance* [the verbal root נחל] among the people of Israel."[11]

Hence, from the time of Moses and the wilderness-Sinai period in the mid-second millennium BC, the tribe of Levi is established with a special religious and liturgical role in the life of ancient Israel, including the division between the Aaronite priestly Levites, who would be responsible for the core sacrificial ministries, and the non-Aaronite, nonpriestly Levites,

8. All Scripture citations are taken from the ESV unless otherwise noted.

9. So argues, for example, Kenneth A. Matthews, *Genesis 11:27–50:26*, NAC 1B (Nashville: Broadman & Holman, 2005), 887, 889.

10. On this point, Bruce K. Waltke and Cathi J. Fredricks concur in their *Genesis: A Commentary* (Grand Rapids: Zondervan, 2001), 603.

11. See also Deuteronomy 10:8–9 on the special inheritance language. Notice also the use of the root "divide" (חלק) in both the Genesis 49 and Numbers 18 passages.

who would be responsible for the assisting, nonsacrificial ministry roles at the tabernacle and, eventually, the temple. This Levitical division of labor is affirmed in Numbers 3–4, as the Israelites prepare to travel from Sinai. In Numbers 3:1–4, the sons of Aaron (בני־אהרן) are those who have been "anointed" (המשחים) and "ordained to serve as priests" (מלא ידם לכהן). In contrast, the Levitical clans of Gershon (גרשון), Kohath (קהת), and Merari (מררי) are set up for guard duty, which entails the care (Num 3:14–37; 4:1–46) and transportation of various parts of the tabernacle. The tabernacle represents a liturgical space that the glory of Yahweh had filled (כבד־יהוה, see Exod 40:34–38). It stands as a powerful and privileged external symbol of divine presence among the people. We find paradox here as well: the uncontainable, eternal, Creator God of the universe chooses to limit himself, at least symbolically, to this tabernacle space for redemptive purposes. The Levites are given a special role to play: helping the broader community of Israel engage this paradoxical divine presence at the tabernacle.[12]

Expanded Temple Function

This ministry role of the non-Aaronite Levites is significantly expanded at the time of David to include, most notably, music and worship leadership.[13] This expansion of the Levitical ministry under the kingship of David, in view of the Solomonic Temple, is a central rhetorical feature in 1 Chronicles 10–29.[14] In this way, the Chronicler helps readers establish a historical connection between the Levitical psalms and the key Levitical worship leaders David commissions for this new temple ministry. Indeed, in the context of having properly brought the ark of the covenant into Jerusalem in 1 Chronicles 16, David establishes some of the Levites "as ministers before the ark of the Lord to invoke (להזכיר), to thank (להודות), and to praise (להלל) the Lord, the God of Israel" and sets up Asaph as the chief Levite in this new group, whose focus is on singing thanksgiving to Yahweh (1 Chr 16:4–5).[15] Besides Asaph, 1 Chronicles 16 also notes the founding role of the Levites Heman and Jeduthun in this newly developed Davidic ministry "for

12. As Douglas K. Stuart (*Exodus*, NAC 2 [Nashville: Broadman & Holman, 2006], 791) also argues.

13. Peter J. Leithart (*From Silence to Song: The Davidic Liturgical Revolution* [Moscow, ID: Canon, 2003]) calls this the "Davidic liturgical revolution."

14. On this, see further Clayton, *Symbol, Service, and Song*, 90–139.

15. On these verbs describing the liturgical duties of the Levites see further Martin J. Selman, *1 Chronicles: An Introduction and Commentary*, TOTC Commentary 10a (Downers Grove, IL: InterVarsity Press, 1994]), 167.

the music and instruments for sacred song" (1 Chr 16:42; למשמיעים וכלי שיר האלהים). Further, 1 Chronicles 9:19 emphasizes the general connection of the Korahites (הקרחים) to the Levitical service. Asaph and Korah both figure prominently in the titles of the Levitical psalms of Books II and III of the Psalter.[16] With David, then, we find an expanded liturgical function of the non-Aaronite Levites to include music and song. This includes a prophetic overtone, as Asaph, Heman, and Jeduthun "prophesied (הנביאים) with lyres, with harps, and with cymbals" (1 Chr 25:1; see also 25:3).[17] Thus, the basic paradox of the Levites' function of assisting a sinful people in engaging with a holy God continues at the temple, with the added element of musical psalmody. In the language of Solomon's prayer of dedication in 2 Chronicles 6, the Levites support a temple ministry that, on the one hand, cannot contain God (6:18), whose "dwelling place" (מקום שבתך) is heaven (6:21), but that, on the other hand, becomes the "resting place" (נוח) of Yahweh (6:41).[18]

16. Heman the Ezrahite (a Korahite) appears in the title of Psalm 88 and Ethan the Ezrahite (also probably a Korahite) is noted in the title of Psalm 89. Both Heman and Ethan are connected to the musical Levites from the time of David (see 1 Chr 25:3–5). Jeduthun is also closely associated to the musical Levites in Chronicles (see 1 Chr 9:16; 16:38, 41–42; 25:1, 3, 6; 2 Chr 5:12; 29:14; 35:15). There is no biblical psalm with a title directly associated to Jeduthun, but one Davidic psalm is written "to Jeduthun" (לידיתון; Ps 39). Another Davidic psalm is written "according to Jeduthun" (על־ידותון; Ps 62); and per *BHS*, some medieval Hebrew manuscripts have harmonized to לידיתון, and one Asaphite psalm is also written "according to Jeduthun" (על־ידותון; Ps 77); this is the MT's *qere* reading, on which a number of ancient versions also agree; the *kethiv* also harmonizes to לידיתון and is mainly supported by the LXX.

17. The new musical function of the Levites is also emphasized in 1 Chronicles 25, in the context of the broader narrative unit in 1 Chronicles 21–29, focused on David's overall preparations for the transition to Solomon's reign, including temple preparations. For a helpful discussion of the prophetic aspect of Levitical song, see Mark J. Boda, *1–2 Chronicles*, Cornerstone Biblical Commentary 5a (Carol Stream, IL: Tyndale House, 2010), 193–96. Note as well, Gary N. Knoppers, "'To Him You Must Listen': The Prophetic Legislation in Deuteronomy and the Reformation of Classical Tradition in Chronicles," in *Chronicling the Chronicler: The Book of Chronicles and Early Second Temple Historiography*, ed. Paul S. Evans and Tyler F. Williams (Winona Lake, IN: Eisenbrauns, 2013), 187–91.

18. And note the parallel language between 2 Chronicles 6:41–42 and Psalm 132:8–10. Also, it is helpful to observe that 2 Chronicles 5:12 shows that Solomon has faithfully set up the Levitical singers, led by Asaph, Heman, and Jeduthun, to join the priests in leading the whole community in worship as the ark is brought into the temple and as Solomon prepares to deliver his prayer of dedication at the temple in 2 Chronicles 6.

PARADOXICAL ELEMENTS IN THE LEVITICAL PSALMS OF BOOK II

The broader Old Testament paradoxical worship function of the Levites is reflected in the Levitical psalms generally, and in the first Levitical collection of Psalms 42–50 in Book II of the Psalter specifically. These Levitical psalms contribute to the theme of the paradoxical perception of the presence of God with at least three supporting and interwoven themes.

Theme I: The presence of God is perceived as distant, and even absent, through the general language of human disorientation and also of divine judgment, which ultimately leads to either restoration or irrecoverable distance. Theme II: The presence of God is perceived as proximal, especially through the clarity of God's sovereign rule over all of creation, which includes Israel and the nations. Theme III: The presence of God is perceived as proximal, especially by means of the liturgical language of holy space (temple) and Zion. In the following, we will suggest some ways in which this may be observed exegetically.

Psalms 42–43

Psalms 42–43 introduce the Levitical collection. Psalm 42 is a Korahite psalm and, technically, Psalm 43 is anonymous. However, Psalm 43 has no superscription and Psalms 42 and 43 are connected by the identical refrain in 42:5, 11 and 43:5.[19] On this basis, both psalms are usually viewed as one rhetorical Korahite psalm with three strophes (42:1–5; 6b–11; 43:1–5) each concluded by the same refrain.[20]

Overall, Psalms 42–43 present a tension between the perception of God as distant (theme I) and the perception of Yahweh as proximal—here, through the language of holy space (theme III). First, this general tension is seen in the repeated refrain of 42:1–5, 6b–11, and 43:1–5. On the one hand, the psalmist expresses the scrambling of his inner person (נפש) through two parallel verbs of disorientation vis-à-vis the divine presence: "to be cast down" (שׂיח, in the *hithpolel*) and "to be in turmoil" (המה, in the *qal*).[21]

19. "Why are you cast down, O my soul, and why are you in turmoil within me? Hope in God; for I shall again praise him, my salvation and my God."

20. Terrien (*The Psalms*, 350), for example, highlights the relationship between these three strophes and the theme of pursuing the presence of God when he writes, "Only the quest for the divine presence seems to be a converging holiness, the altar of God."

21. A connection exists here between the sorrow experienced by the psalmist and the deep sorrow experienced by Christ in the garden of Gethsemane before the crucifixion. The phrase in the refrain of Psalms 42–43, such as in MT Psalm 42:6, מַה־תִּשְׁתּוֹחֲחִי נַפְשִׁי, translated as "why

On the other hand, "hope" in God (יחל, in the *hiphil*) and "praise" of God (ידה, in the *hiphil*) are both related to the proximal blessing of divine "salvation" (ישועה). This refrain, then, emphasizes the dual tension of realizing (1) that true salvation is only found in God's presence, but (2) that human experience often leads to a false perception regarding the ability to embrace such a salvation.[22]

Second, the rhetorical development of Psalms 42–43 as a whole sustains this incongruency.[23] In the first strophe (42:1–6a), intense language of yearning for a God who seems absent in verses 1–3 (panting/ערג, thirsting/צמא, pouring out/שפך) is further nurtured by Levitical remembrances of having led the people of God in joyful liturgical procession to the Jerusalem temple, the "house of God" (בית אלהים) in verse 4.[24] This strophe contains elements of both themes I and III. This paradoxical yearning is described in language rooted in the expanded musical worship function of the Levites at the temple. The second strophe in 42:6b further develops the concept of divine absence, as the poetry broadens with geographical memory (vv. 6b–7 especially), to conclude with a question lamenting the absence of God in verse 10, "where is your God" (איה אלהיך). In this meditation, the musical element also appears, as Yahweh's "song" (שיר) is part of the psalmist's nocturnal worship (v. 8).

The sense of distance from God is more acute in the third strophe of 43:1–5, as the poet employs singular imperatives (and one plural jussive) for the first time, in verses 1–3 (vindicate me/שפטני, defend me/ריבי, send out/שלח, let them bring me/יביאוני).[25] The psalmist is pleading for Yahweh

---

are you cast down, O my soul," is translated in the LXX as, ἵνα τί περίλυπος εἶ, ψυχή. This adjective, περίλυπος ("sorrowful, sad, deeply grieved," translating the *hithpolel* form of the Hebrew verb שיח [BDB reads the root as שָׁחַח and glosses the *hithpolel* occurrences in Pss 42–43 as "be cast down, despairing"]) is the same adjective used in the words of Christ with the Twelve, describing his own despair in Mark 14:34, περίλυπός ἐστιν ἡ ψυχή μου ἕως θανάτου· μείνατε ὧδε καὶ γρηγορεῖτε, translated as, "my soul is very sorrowful, even to death. Remain here and watch." Notice also the link between נפש and ψυχή in these two passages.

22. On this tension, see further Walter Brueggemann, *Spirituality of the Psalms*, Facets (Minneapolis: Fortress, 2002), 1–15.

23. For example, Gerald H. Wilson (*Psalms Volume 1*, NIV Application Commentary [Grand Rapids: 2002], 669) argued that in Psalms 42–43, which he viewed as one psalm, the two motifs of the psalmist's memory and the absence of God are at work.

24. C. S. Lewis (*Reflections on the Psalms* [New York: Harcourt & Brace, 1958], 50–51) described this as an "appetite for God." He also highlighted the paradoxical interplay in the psalms between God's presence at the temple structure and the worshiper's desire to be in God's very presence.

25. deClaissé-Walford posits that Psalm 43 should, in fact, be viewed as a *distinct* psalm from Psalm 42. She argues that in Psalm 42, the psalmist is speaking rhetorically to *himself* (to his

to make his presence known, even as the dichotomy in verse 2 between divine refuge (מעוז) and divine rejection (זנח) is experienced. Still, this tensive plea culminates with a commitment to enter into God's presence, the only source of true joy, in verse 4. This strophic conclusion (v. 4) also establishes the notion of the blessing of God's proximal presence through (1) the language of focused holy space, specified with the occurrence of the "altar of God" (מזבח אלהים), and through (2) a musical connotation, with the use of the term "lyre" (כנור). All in all, both the tone of the repeated refrain of Psalms 42–43, with its unresolved tension of knowing the benefit of, but not presently experiencing, the presence of God, as well as the overall strophic development of this poetic unit, support the notion that theme I (God's presence perceived as distant) is established here, with notable elements from theme III as well (the proximal presence of God mediated through holy-space liturgical language).[26]

Psalms 44–50

Korahite Psalm 44 mostly contributes to theme I, as it is a complaint to Yahweh, who has rejected the disgraced and lamenting community (see 44:9; זנחת ותכלימנו). Just as Yahweh has driven out the nations in judgment (44:2; גוים הורשת), so God's people experience scattering among the nations (44:11; בגוים זריתנו). The final strophe in 44:23–26 establishes an ambivalent conclusion: God is perceived as distant, his face is hidden, and the community's souls are crushed as, still, the call goes forth for the renewal of divine redemption, rooted in divine steadfast love (44:26; פדנו למען חסדך).[27]

So far, we have observed that Psalms 42–44 generally display perceptions of both divine distance and absence. Psalms 45–46, in turn, further modulate on themes II and III, where the perceptions of divine presence are more proximal. Royal psalm 45 is, at least originally, addressed to the Davidic king at the outset (vv. 1–5; v. 1: אמר אני מעשי למלך) and then shifts to proclaiming the eternal kingship of God himself, who provides the foundational authority for kingship.[28] In the final strophes (vv. 10–17), the people

---

soul), while in Psalm 43, the poet is addressing *God*. See further deClaissé-Walford, Jacobson, and Tanner, *The Book of Psalms*, 406.

26. Derek Kidner (*Psalms 1–72*, TOTC 14a [Downers Grove, IL: InterVarsity Press, 1973)], 165) also argues for a paradoxical sense in the psalmist's yearning in Psalms 42–43.

27. Peter C. Craigie (*Psalms 1–50*, WBC 19 [Waco, TX: Word, 1983], 335) has highlighted the problem of God's perceived distance here when he relates the overall tone of Psalm 44 to the problem of the book of Job, "namely the problem of God."

28. Psalm 45:7 MT reads כסאך אלהים עולם ועד שבט מישר שבט מלכותך, translated as "your throne, O God, is forever and ever. The scepter of your kingdom is a scepter of uprightness" (45:6 ET).

of God are likened to a bride who is called to commit herself to her husband, the king. Psalm 45 shows Yahweh as sovereign over creation and the psalmist is fully oriented to this perception (theme II).[29] Indeed, Psalm 46, a Korahite Zion hymn, also evinces a growing proximal orientation toward the blessing of God's presence.[30] The first major strophe (vv. 1–7), reflects a meditation on the blessing of the godly one being in the very presence of God. This is rooted in the liturgical language of holy space and Zion, such as the "city of God"/עיר־אלהים and the "holy habitation of the Most High"/קדש משכני עליון in verse 4 (theme III). The second strophe (vv. 8–11) reads as an invitation for the worshiper to engage in the presence of Yahweh, who stands sovereignly over all creation, including all nations (theme II; v. 10b, ארום בגוים ארום בארץ).[31]

Korahite Psalms 47–49 continue the collection's distinct emphases, with a similar blending of both themes II and III. Psalm 47 is rooted in theme II, as a hymn to God's kingship. Indeed, God is "the King over all the earth" (v. 7; כי מלך כל־הארץ), "reigns over the nations" (v. 8a; מלך אלהים על־גוים) and "sits on his holy throne" (v. 8b; ישב על־כסא קדשו). Psalm 48 moves to focus more precisely on theme III, since it represents a hymn in celebration of Zion, the special city of God. Zion becomes the paradoxical residence of God (vv. 1–3); it is the "holy mountain" (הר־קדשו) of God's presence spreading "joy" (משוש) to the whole earth. Holy space language is present, as the "temple" (v. 9, היכל) in Zion is affirmed as the location for reflecting on God's steadfast love. In the text, the Zion temple also serves as the source for God's salvific outreach to the whole earth. Psalm 49, a wisdom psalm, clarifies some of the implications of theme II: when the godly *engage* with the divine presence, they have an eternal hope of being "home" with God "forever."[32] In contrast,

In the New Testament, Hebrews 1:8–9 cites LXX Psalm 45:6–7 in support of the divine Son's superiority to the angels.

29. Wilson (*Psalms Volume 1*, 699–713) highlights the unique nature of Psalm 45. Initially a Davidic royal psalm, it calls for reinterpretation from the perspective of the final canonical form of the Psalter in the postexilic period, where a physical Davidic throne no longer exists.

30. For Psalm 46, Francis X. Kimmitt ("Psalm 46: Praise the Lord Our Help," in *The Psalms: Language for All Seasons of the Soul*, ed. Andrew J. Schmutzer and David M. Howard Jr. [Chicago: Moody, 2013], 63–74) emphasizes the blessing of the poet having discovered the trustworthiness of Yahweh in the face of crises.

31. James Limburg (*Psalms*, Westminster Bible Companion [Louisville: Westminster John Knox, 2000], 153), for example, emphasizes the orientation *toward* God's presence in Psalm 46, as he argues the psalm is a "song of Zion," whose "dominant theme is trust in God."

32. With contextual reference to the foolish and the stupid (Ps 49:10), Ps 49:12b MT reads קרבם בתימו לעולם משכנתם לדר ודר, and is translated as: "Their graves are their homes forever, their dwelling places to all generations" (Ps 49:11).

the wicked, who ultimately *reject* the blessing of the divine presence only have Sheol as their eternal home, where "death shall be their shepherd" (v. 14; מות ירעם), which then alludes to theme I as well.

Asaphite Psalm 50, the last Levitical psalm in Book II, contributes to themes II and III. God speaks as sovereign Lord from Zion (vv. 1–6), calls his covenant people to true worship (vv. 7–15), and rebukes the wicked ones (vv. 16–21). With a further allusion to theme I, Psalm 50 also concludes in verses 22–23 by noting that those who are far from God—those who "forget God" (v. 22; שכחי אלוה)—will suffer divine judgment. In contrast, those who remain near to God's good path and, hence, presence (v. 23; שם דרך), will be able to worship him faithfully.[33]

CONCLUSION

We have briefly explored the following question in relationship to the Levitical psalms in the Psalter's second book: Is the unified, polaric truth of Scripture—of God dwelling with his people—communicated antinomically through the opposing claims that the Levitical psalmists perceive God as both present and absent? We have suggested that an affirmative answer is plausible when considering some of the key features of the broader Old Testament worship function of the Levites, as well as some representative elements in the Levitical psalms of Book II. In fact, Santos posits that five elements make a literary paradox recognizable. The Old Testament worship function of the Levites and the sample of their psalmody in Psalms 42–50 appear to sustain all of these elements. Indeed, we see that: (1) a "both-and" proposition found in the perception of both divine presence and divine absence is at work, (2) a "tension" exists around the Levitical desire to engage the divine presence, but also to avoid final divine judgment, (3) an element of "awe, surprise, or amazement" is present, most notably in the Levitical joy of experiencing the blessed proximity of God, (4) an "intentional rhetorical" purpose seems present in the placement of these Levitical psalms toward engaging the reader in the tension of God's paradoxical self-revelation, and (5) these Levitical poems, as a part of canonical Scripture, call for a reading "audience" to "undergo a reversal of standards" consistent with biblical values—here, values specifically rooted in God's desire to dwell

33. As James L. Mays (*Psalms*, Interpretation [Louisville: Westminster John Knox, 1994], 194) notes of the overall tone of Psalm 50, "Here the Lord is presented as judge of the people of God, who holds them accountable for their worship and conduct."

among his people for a redemptive purpose.[34] As such, within the broader theological vistas of the Psalter, the Levitical psalms of Book II may be fruitfully read together, so as to better absorb the implications of their varying perceptions of the paradoxical presence of God.

34. See the discussion on "Method in the Study of Paradox" in Santos, "Paradox of Authority and Servanthood," 453–54.

18

Psalm 110, Jesus, and Melchizedek

David C. Mitchell

Jesus's interpretation of Psalm 110:1 (Matt 22:42–46) was the standard interpretation in the first century, as the Pharisees' response shows, and as other ancient texts attest. Jesus sees three people in verse 1: David (the speaking psalmist), Yahweh (who promises), and the Messiah (who is addressed). Further, Psalm 110:4 must be read with Melchizedek as a vocative. That gives three people in verse 4: David (the speaking psalmist), YHVH (who promises), and Melchizedek (who is addressed). I conclude that Jesus was telling the Pharisees that Melchizedek is the Messiah, and that it was as Melchizedek that Jesus was seen by Abraham (John 8:56–58).

I have pondered Psalm 110 for decades.[1] The New Testament cites it more than any other Hebrew Scripture—fourteen direct citations and many more allusions. It was important to Jesus. He cited it to the Pharisees and alluded to it at his trial. But, like the holy mountain, it is riddled with enigmas, terse, profound, and mysterious. I believe its implications are deeper than are commonly understood.

WHO'S WHO IN PSALM 110:1

In Psalm 110, the Holy One promises eternal priesthood and universal dominion to someone. The question is "To whom?" Any answer faces a host of

1. It is an honor to contribute a chapter to this new book. David Howard and Andrew Schmutzer are well-known for their work on the Psalms and this book will surely become widely treasured.

interpretational challenges, but the biggest ones are: "Who's who in Psalm 110:1?" and "Who's who in Psalm 110:4?" Let's begin with the first verse.

> A psalm of David.
>
> YHVH says to my lord,
> "Sit at my right hand until I make your enemies a footstool for your feet."[2]

The title—*A psalm of David*—is followed by an oath—*YHVH says* or *swears* to *my lord*. The questions are:

1. Who is recounting the words of the oath?
2. Who is *my lord* to whom YHVH delivers his promise?

Let's review the answers to these questions in chronological order.

1. The Old View

Jesus asks the Pharisees: "What do you think of the Messiah? Whose son is he?" (Matt 22:42). They say the Messiah is the son of David. Jesus replies, citing this psalm, that no one calls his own son "lord," and so the Messiah cannot be David's son. Thus Jesus assumes, from the title, that the psalm is spoken by David, that "my lord" is the Messiah, and that David is recounting an oath uttered by YHVH to the Messiah. Three people: David, Yahweh, Messiah. And it's fair to add that this looks like the plain reading of the psalm. There does seem to be three people in the opening verse.

Two things are implied in Jesus's interpretation. First, David knew or knew about the Messiah and about an oath made by the Holy One to the Messiah. Second, although Jesus leaves the question of the Messiah's paternity unanswered, since it is understood that no mortal can be greater than David, the implication is that the Messiah is a heavenly man.

The Antiquity of this Interpretation

Now Jesus did not invent this interpretation. It was ancient in his time. It is implied in Daniel 7:14, where a son of man comes into the presence of the Ancient of Days to receive universal dominion. His riding the clouds shows he is a divine figure.[3] The "thrones set in place" (7:9) imply that he is to sit enthroned at the hand of Yahweh. And he is to set up a righteous kingdom

---

2. Unless otherwise noted, citations are the author's own translation.
3. See J. A. Emerton, "The Origin of the Son of Man Imagery," *Journal of Theological Studies* 9 (1958): 225–42.

over the earth, just as in Psalm 110:5–6. The whole passage—heavenly man, seated at the right hand, ruling the earth—can only derive from Psalm 110. Daniel 7 foreshadows Jesus's interpretation of the psalm.

11QMelch, from the Dead Sea Scrolls, dates from about 100 BC, and features a heavenly hero called Melchizedek. Since Melchizedek appears in the Hebrew Scriptures only in Genesis 14 and Psalm 110, and since this heavenly conqueror looks much like the martial figure of the psalm, it is clear that the psalm is part of the unspoken background to 11QMelchizedek too. This Melchizedek comes to liberate Zion, reward the righteous, and destroy wickedness. He must be understood as the Messiah, for he is identified, in lines 15 to 20, with Isaiah's herald of peace to Zion (Isa 52:7), with Daniel's *mashiaḥ* prince (Dan 9:25), and with Isaiah's servant of YHVH anointed (*mashiaḥ*) by the Spirit to comfort the afflicted of Zion (Isa 61:1–3). Yet he is also the God who judges the gods in Psalm 82:1 (11QMelch ii.10). He is the Elohim of Psalm 7:8, who, in the psalm, is YHVH (11QMelch ii.10–11). The "year of the LORD's favor," spoken of in Isaiah 61:2, becomes the "year of Melchizedek's favor." This conquering Melchizedek is a divine Messiah.

The Similitudes of Enoch, dating perhaps from the turn of the era, take a similar line.[4] The Son of Man is the chosen one of the Ancient of Days (Similitudes of Enoch 46:2); he shall be summoned before the throne of the Ancient of Days (47:3; 48:2) and sit enthroned (45:3); he is eternally preexistent (48:5), he is the Messiah (48:11), with universal dominion to destroy the wicked and console the righteous (46–48). It is all built on Psalm 110 and Daniel 7.

These passages, from before Jesus's time, all derive from Psalm 110. They all interpret the psalm just as Jesus did—a divine Messiah comes from the presence of YHVH to rule the earth.

The Universality of This Interpretation

The antiquity of this view is confirmed by its universality in the time of Jesus. For the Pharisees also share it. After Jesus speaks, they do not reply, "We don't accept your interpretation because we do not believe David spoke about the Messiah." On the contrary, no one could answer him a word (Matt 22:46). Nor can anyone say this is just Matthew's spin on the debate. He wrote his Gospel for the Hebrew-speaking community who knew what the

4. Estimates on the date of the sections of the Enoch compendium vary widely. The Similitudes are generally said to date from the time of Herod the Great. See Leslie W. Walck, *The Son of Man in the Parables of Enoch and Matthew* (London: T&T Clark, 2011), 15–23.

Pharisees believed. His credibility depended on representing the Pharisees' view squarely.

The Persistence of This Interpretation

This view was not only ancient and universal in the time of Jesus; it persisted in Judaism right through the next millennium. In the midrash on Psalms we read:

> R. Yudan said in the name of R. Hama: In the time to come, the Holy One, blessed be he, seats the Lord Messiah at his right hand, as it is said, *HaShem says to my lord, "Sit at my right hand"* [Ps 110:1] (Midrash Tehillim 18.29).

Midrash Aleph Beth, from the fifth century, also gives a messianic interpretation.[5] Here "Ephraim" signifies Messiah ben Joseph while "Gog and Magog" sets the scenario in the great end-time conflict of Ezekiel 36–37.

> Ephraim my firstborn, come, sit at my right hand until I bring down the power of the horde of Gog and Magog, your enemies, beneath your footstool. As it is said, *HaShem says to my lord, Sit at my right hand, etc.* [Ps 110:1] (Midrash Aleph Beth §11b.1)

The midrash Otot Ha-Mashiaḥ, from the early seventh century, applies the same text to the Messiah.

> And Messiah ben David will go, and Elijah the prophet. ... And then the Holy One, blessed be he, needs nothing for the battle, but to say to him [Messiah ben David], *Sit at my right hand* [Ps 110:1].[6]

A little later, a similar interpretation is found in the midrash Tefillat Rav Shimon ben Yoḥai.

> The Holy One, blessed be he, will fight on behalf of Israel. He will say to the Messiah, *Sit at my right hand* [Ps 110:1].

As late as the thirteenth century, the Zohar makes the same interpretation, again of Messiah ben Joseph.

5. For the dating, see Deborah Sawyer, *Midrash Aleph Beth* (Atlanta: Scholars Press, 1993), 26–27.

6. §8. For the date of Otot Ha-Mashiaḥ and Tefillat Rav Shimon ben Yoḥai, see David C. Mitchell, *Messiah ben Joseph* (Newton Mearns: Campbell, 2016), 164, 265.

Jacob, changing his hands [Gen 48:14], placed ox [Ephraim] on the right and lion [Judah] on the left, for which reason *HaShem says to my lord: Sit at my right hand* [Ps 110:1]. This is the Tsadik Messiah ben Joseph (Zohar, Pinhas, §567).

Jesus's interpretation of the psalm was no novelty. It dated from at least the time of Daniel, it was widely accepted in his own day, and it persisted well into medieval times.

What Jesus Meant

Jesus, of course, claimed to be the Messiah. That was understood by everyone (Matt 12:23; 21:9), despite his reticence on the subject (e.g., Matt 16:20). But his particular claim in citing this psalm is that he is the Messiah whom David called "my lord," and he is therefore not David's son but a divine man. This agrees with what he says elsewhere about his own descent. For he never calls himself the son of David. Others do: Matthew the evangelist (Matt 1:1), the angel Gabriel (Luke 3:32), blind Bartimaeus (Matt 20:30–31; Mark 10:47), a Canaanite woman (Matt 15:22), the Palm Sunday crowds, and the children in the temple (Matt 21:9, 15; Mark 11:10). But Jesus never takes that name.

The preservation of this debate in all three Gospels suggests it became a *cause célèbre*. But following Jesus's explanation, the Pharisaic community would have found the old interpretation awkward. They found alternatives.

2. The Targum

One of these alternatives is preserved in the targum on Psalms, redacted in the mid-first millennium.[7] It exists in two variants.

> By the hand of David, a psalm. YY said in his decree [*b'memreh*] to make me lord of all Israel. But he said to me, "Wait yet for Saul of the tribe of Benjamin to die, for one reign must not encroach on another. And afterwards I will make your enemies a stool for your feet."
>
> [By the hand of David, a psalm.] YY said in his decree [*b'memreh*] to give me the dominion in exchange for sitting in study of Torah. "Wait at my right hand until I make your enemies a stool for your feet."

7. David M. Stec, *The Targum of Psalms* (London: T&T Clark, 2004) dates it from the fourth to sixth century, but notes that, like every targum, it is composed of older material.

The first one plays on "my right hand" (*y'mini*) and Saul the Benjamite (*ben-y'mini*). But both interpretations enshrine the same idea, namely that David is both the speaker and "my lord" who receives the promise. The three figures of the original psalm have become two: David the psalmist, YHVH the promiser, and David the promisee.

One might wonder how this happened. Of course, *b'memreh*, "in his decree," is common targum locution for divine speech. Perhaps it shouldn't arouse any speculation. Yet the change of just one letter—to *l'memreh*—would give a different sense altogether.

> By the hand of David, a psalm. YY said to his Memra [Logos], "Sit at my right hand," etc.

There is no surviving evidence for the existence of such a text.[8] But, if it ever existed, it would fully reflect the ancient three-person interpretation: David, Yahweh, and "my lord" the divine Memra.

But, however it happened, the fact is that the targum has lost someone from Psalm 110:1. David the speaker and David's "my lord" have melded together, something quite at odds with the psalm.

3. The Talmud Bavli

The Talmud Bavli, Nedarim 32b, presents another interpretation. It identifies Melchizedek with Shem ben Noah. The gist of it is that Melchizedek aka Shem was in line for the eternal priesthood or *k'hunah* spoken of in Psalm 110:4. But because he flouted blessing protocol—blessing Abram before El Elyon—the *k'hunah* went to Abram and his seed.

> R. Zechariah said in the name of R. Ishmael: The Holy One, blessed be He, wished to derive the *k'hunah* from Shem, as it is said: And he was *kohen* to El Elyon (Gen. 14.18). [But] since he [Shem/Melchizedek] prefaced the blessing of Avram to the blessing of ha-Maqom [the Omnipresent], he [God] derived it from Avram, as it is said: *And he blessed him and said, "Blessed be Avram by El Elyon possessor of the heavens and earth, and blessed be El Elyon"* (Gen 14.19–20).
>
> Avraham said to him, "And does one preface the blessing of the slave to the blessing of his master?"

8. Pietro Galatino (1460–1540) testified to having seen such a targum in the sixteenth century (so John Gill on Ps 110). But Galatino's polemical intent might lead to suspicion of his testimony.

> Immediately he [God] gave it [the *k'hunah*] to Avraham, as it is said, *HaShem said to my Lord, 'Sit at my right hand until I set your enemies as a stool for your feet'* (Ps. 110:1). And after this it is written, The Lord has sworn and will not repent. *You are a priest forever* 'al-dib̲rati *Malki-zedeq* (Gen. 110.4), that is, on account of that which Melchizedek had said [*l'divoro shel malki-tsedeq*]. This corresponds to what is written, *And he was kohen to El Elyon.* [Which means] he [Melchizedek] was a *kohen*, but his sons were not *kohanim* [i.e., Melchizedek lost the hereditary *k'hunah* to Avram]. (Nedarim 32b).[9]

Now, David is not even mentioned here. But the implication, in citing Psalm 110:1, is that while David could not call his son *lord*, he could call his ancestor Abraham *lord*. And so we get quite another three-person interpretation of verse 1: David the psalmist, Yahweh, and Abraham, who is "my lord." This view was endorsed by Rashi. But the problem with it, as Ibn Ezra rightly notes, is that Abraham never ruled from Zion.

4. Ibn Ezra

Ibn Ezra (1089–1167) developed a new version of the targum interpretation: the psalm was written not *by* David but *for* David by one of the temple singers. And so David was "my lord," but the speaker was one of the temple singers. So again, we have three people: Levite psalmist, Yahweh, and David ("my lord"). This view is followed by Radak (1160–1235), Yeshayahu Mitrani (d. 1260), and by most modern scholars. But it has two weaknesses. First, David did not become an eternal priest (Ps 110:4), and so the prophecy is false. Second, it assumes that *l'david* can be understood as *concerning David*. This assumption was accepted by no one in ancient times—neither Jesus nor the Pharisees nor the apostles nor the targum nor the Talmud. Nor could Ramban accept it.

---

9. See B. Sanhedrin 108b: R. Hana b. Liwai said: Shem Rabba [i.e., Melchizedek] said to Eliezer [Abraham's servant]: "When the kings of the east and the west attacked you, what did you do?" He replied, "The Holy One, blessed be he, took Abraham and set him at his right hand, and they threw dust which turned to swords, and chaff which turned to arrows, as it is said, *A Psalm of David. HaShem said to my lord, Sit at my right hand, until I make your enemies your footstool.* See also Midrash Psalm 110 §4.

5. Ramban

Ramban (1194–1270), at the Barcelona Disputation, offered an improvement of Ibn Ezra's theory. The psalm was written by David, as the title implies. But he wrote it for the singers to sing about him. Menachem Meiri (1249–1306) agreed, sagely adding that if David had written, "HaShem says to me," then it would have been untrue when sung by the Levite singers. So again, we have three people: Levite singer, Yahweh, and David (composer and "my lord"). But this interpretation has weaknesses too. As with Ibn Ezra's view, David was not a priest forever, and so the prophecy is false. Further, it paints a lonely picture of David writing praise songs and prophecies about himself, which isn't how it's supposed to be (Prov 27:2).

Summary

Jesus's interpretation of Psalm 110:1 was ancient and widespread in Jesus's own time. It was followed, naturally, by patristic writers. Yet Judaism, apparently in reaction to Christian use of the psalm, proposed a series of alternative interpretations. Strangely enough, modern scholarship—even conservative Christian scholarship—routinely ignores Jesus's interpretation in favor of Ibn Ezra's. Yet Ibn Ezra's view not only reduces the psalm to false prophecy and ignores the authorial sense of the title, but it leaves the psalm as only an ancient royal panegyric, legitimizing David's inheritance of a supposed line of Jebusite sacral kings—Melchizedek, Adonizedek (Josh 10:1–3)—which can be vaguely understood as pointing to the Messiah.[10]

If we ask why Jesus's view has been sidelined, the answer is surely that, while it is consistent enough, it is hard to swallow. For it implies that David is reporting an oath made by the Holy One to the Messiah. This implies, in turn, not only a preexistent Messiah—alive in David's time—but also David's insider knowledge of the promise made by the Holy One to the preexistent divine Messiah. That is a lot to take on board. But it is, I think, exactly what the psalm is saying. Let's turn to verse 4.

10. Examples could be numerous. From a generation ago, see Tomoo Ishida, *The Royal Dynasties in Ancient Israel*, BZAW 142 (Berlin: de Gruyter), 137–40; Leslie C. Allen, *Psalms 101–150* (Waco, TX: Word), 81; F. F. Bruce, *The Epistle to the Hebrews* (Grand Rapids: Eerdmans, 1990), 159–60; James Mays, *Psalms* (Louisville: Westminster John Knox, 1994), 351; John Goldingay, *Psalms 90–150* (Grand Rapids: Baker Academic, 2008), 291.

WHO'S WHO IN PSALM 110:4

Most translations of Psalm 110:4 run something like the NIV below.

> The LORD has sworn and will not change his mind:
> "You are a priest forever, in the order of ['al-dibrati] Melchizedek."

In other words, YHVH is appointing someone—perhaps "my lord" of verse 1—as an eternal priest. Yet all such translations have at their core an unbearable conundrum. Let's break it down into two puzzles.

Puzzle one: If YHVH makes someone a priest forever like Melchizedek, it implies that Melchizedek is a priest forever.

Someone might object: "No, this person is made an eternal priest *like* Melchizedek, but the original priesthood of Melchizedek was temporary, not eternal."

But that would be as if I, invested with high authority, said to someone, "I make you Archbishop of Canterbury forever and ever, in the order of Donald Coggan."

The recipient of my boon would reply, "Wow! Thank you. But hang on. Donald Coggan wasn't archbishop forever. He's dead!"

In the same way, it makes no sense to appoint someone an eternal priest in the image of a mortal.

Further, if Melchizedek's priesthood was not eternal, then who would want it? After all, the promise of verse 4 was made when the sons of Aaron had a functioning priesthood. That was worth something. But to bestow on someone the defunct priesthood of a defunct Canaanite was not better, but worse. All Canaanites were accursed (Gen 9:25). And even if Melchizedek's ancient priesthood was originally in some unknown way better than Aaron's, in what way, being extinct, is it now better? Better a live dog than a dead lion.

So, if Melchizedek is not a priest forever, then Psalm 110:4 is absurd. But if he is a priest forever, then he is an immortal. In that case, one must ask, "Where is Melchizedek and what is he doing now?"

Puzzle two: If Melchizedek is an eternal priest, and YHVH makes someone else an eternal priest, then there are now two eternal priests. How can this be? Either there are two rival priests eternally offering access to the one God, or there is something wrong with the translation.

In the "What" of Melchizedek?

The words "in the order of Melchizedek" represent the Hebrew *'al-diḇrati malki-tsedeq*. The word 'al means "upon" or "according to." And *malki-tsedeq* is self-explanatory. The key issue is what does *diḇrati* mean?

Diḇrati is a form of the feminine noun *diḇrah*. It's a rare word. But it comes from a common root—*dbr*—which gives rise to a constellation of related words meaning "word," "speak," "matter," "thing," "reason," or "promise." *Diḇrah* never appears in the Bible in its simple form, but only with its ending modified to *diḇrat* or *diḇrati*. These two forms look similar, but their meanings are different.

Diḇrat is in the Hebrew possessive or construct case.[11] It means "the *diḇrah* of [something]." This is how it appears in Daniel and Ecclesiastes, where it has roughly the sense "for the sake of" or "about the matter of."

> For the sake that [*'al-diḇrat*] the king may know the interpretation and that you may understand the thoughts of your heart. (Dan 2:30)

> I said in my heart about the matter of [*'al-diḇrat*] the sons of men. (Eccl 3:18)

> Consider that God has appointed this one as well as that, so that/for the sake that [*'al-diḇrat*] man may not find out anything that will be after him. (Eccl 7:14)

> Keep the king's command for the sake of [*'al-diḇrat*] your oath to God. (Eccl 8:2)

But *dibrati* has quite a different meaning. The final letter i is the first-person singular possessive suffix. So *dibrati* means "the *dibrah* of me" or "my *dibrah*." It appears only one other time in the Bible, in Job, where it means something like "my matter" or "case" or "cause."

> But I would seek God and to God would I commit my cause [*diḇrati*]. (Job 5:8)

Taking *diḇrati* as it stands, the natural reading of Psalm 110:4 should be:

11. In the English genitive, the possessor noun is modified: "The king's sons" (adding the genitive ending to king). But in Hebrew the end of the noun which is possessed is modified to the construct state: "sons-of the king" (*b'nei ha-melekh*).

You are a *kohen* forever, according to my *diḇrah* [*'al-diḇrat*].

There are no two ways about this. Those who translate *'al dibrati Malki-tsedeq* as "according to/in the order of Melchizedek" are ignoring the plain sense of the Hebrew. And we must ask how they justify it and why they do it.

They justify it by taking the i-vowel on the end of *dibrati* not as a possessive suffix, but as either a poetic flourish (a paragogic *yodh*) or as an archaic suffix to the simple construct.[12] Thus reckoned, *dibrati* means just *dibrat*: "the *dibrat* [of] Melchizedek."

Why they resort to this maneuver is another question altogether. It's not new. It is implied in the Vulgate of Jerome who endorsed the rabbinic idea that Melchizedek was Shem.[13] And it continues to this day because the implications of taking the i-vowel as a possessive are hard to swallow.

Yet the text makes perfect sense as plain classical Hebrew. One must simply take *'al-diḇrati* as it stands, as a first-person suffix, just as in Job. In that case, the Holy One is calling someone a *kohen* (priest) "for my sake" or "for my cause."[14]

But who? Well, if *diḇrati* is no longer in the construct case, then it is no longer joined to *malki-tsedeq*. There is no longer anything "of Melchizedek." The name Melchizedek has been cut free and must now be taken as a vocative, and the whole phrase becomes,

You are a *kohen* for ever for my sake, [O] Melchizedek.

And since nouns from the root *dbr* often carry the meaning of something said, we may take *dibrah* to mean "according to my promise" or "saying" or "decree":[15]

---

12. A parallel is seen in the name Melchizedek (*malki-tsedeq*) itself. The -i on the end of *malki* is indeed part of the ancient semitic construct, as the writer to the Hebrews understood when he translated it "king *of* righteousness" (Heb 7:2).

13. Jerome, Epistle 73. It is not implied in the LXX. For an extended discussion, see my forthcoming book, *Jesus: The Incarnation of the Word* (Newton Mearns: Campbell, 2021).

14. This is confirmed by the Masoretic cantillation: *'al-dibrati* is cantillated with *revia mugrash*, a pausal or disjunctive sign-pair. It is equivalent to a comma before Melchizedek, just as I have given it above: "for my sake, Melchizedek." But if *dibrati* were a construct form, with the sense "the order of Melchizedek," then a conjunctive sign would have been required. We see exactly this in the next psalm, where *yirat* and *yhvh* ("the fear of Yahweh") are joined with *illuy* over *yirat* (Ps 111:10); so too in Psalms 19:9 (ET) and 34:11 (ET), the same phrase is joined with conjunctives—*mahpakh* and *merkha* respectively.

15. Just as R. Zechariah, in Nedarim 32b, took *'al-dibrati* to mean "the saying of Melchizedek" (*l'divoro shel malki-tsedeq*).

> You are a *kohen* forever according to my decree, [O] Melchizedek.

Suddenly the light is switched on. The nameless figure in verse 4 is gone. With him is gone the intolerable conundrum of two eternal priests. There are not two priests, but one. And he is "my lord" of verse 1. It is Melchizedek alone who is promised eternal priesthood and universal dominion.

Lest anyone doubt such a translation, here's a passage from Zohar Ḥadash where *'al-diḇrati* can be understood only as a promise from the Holy One to Melchizedek.

> The Holy One, blessed be he, took Shem ben Noah and made him *kohen* of Elyon to serve him, and his *shekhinah* rested upon him. And he called his name Melchizedek, King of Salem. And his brother, Japheth, learned Torah from him in his school, until Abraham came and taught Torah in the school of Shem. And the Holy One, blessed be he, turned his attention to Abraham and forgot all the others. Abraham came and prayed before the Holy One, blessed be he, that his *shekhinah* should always dwell in the House of Shem, and he consented, as it is said: You are a kohen forever according to my promise (*al-diḇrati*), Melchizedek. (Noah §128)

In fact, the same interpretation can be detected in the passage from Bavli Nedarim 32b, cited above, where Melchizedek is ousted in favor of Abraham. For when R. Zechariah deflects the promise of *k'hunah* from Melchizedek-Shem to Abraham, the argument presumes that the promise was originally made to Melchizedek.

With this reading, Melchizedek is no longer a mysterious proto-Canaanite priest who met Abram a thousand years before David's time. He is someone David knew in his own time and called "my lord." David overheard words from the invisible God to Melchizedek. He heard the vow and recorded it. It may be mind-boggling. It may go against all current understanding of this and every psalm. But there it is. It is the plain sense of *'al-diḇrati*.

So Who Is Melchizedek?

This means that Melchizedek, who appeared to Abram, also appeared to David. Now I could argue from Genesis that Melchizedek was none other than the Angel of Yahweh, the divine Logos who appeared to Hagar, Abram, Jacob, Moses, and David. But space does not allow that. So let me cite others who have taken Melchizedek to be the Logos or a divine Messiah figure.

(1) 11QMelch makes Melchizedek the Messiah and Elohim of Israel. With my proposed reading of Psalm 110:4, the two texts now match up perfectly. For, in Psalm 110:5–7, it is now divine Melchizedek who conquers the world from Zion, while, in 11QMelch, it is divine Melchizedek who does the same thing.

(2) Philo Judaeus was much taken by the identity of the "second God," the Logos. The Logos is to God as sunlight to the sun (*On Dreams* 1.239). He is the one through whom all things were created and who sustains all things (*Planting* 10). He is "God's man, the Logos of the Eternal, who must be immortal" (*Tongues* 41). He is "the high priest, his firstborn, the Divine Logos" (*On Dreams* 1.215) and "the high priest and king" (*On Flight* 118). Moses saw the Logos on Sinai (*Confusion of Tongues* 97). The Angel of the Lord was the Logos (*Cherubim* 3, 35). The Logos is Melchizedek.

> Melchizedek shall bring forth wine instead of water, and shall give your souls to drink, and shall cheer them with unmixed wine, in order that they may be wholly possessed by divine intoxication, more sober than sobriety itself. For the Logos is a priest, having, as his inheritance the true God, and entertaining lofty and sublime and magnificent ideas about him, *For he is the priest of the most high God* (Gen. 14:18). (*Allegorical Interpretation* 3.82)

(3) The writer to the Hebrews says that Melchizedek is "without father or mother, without genealogy, without beginning of days or end of life, like the Son of God, he remains a priest forever" (Heb 7:3). If he meant what he said, then he believed Melchizedek is an unbegotten and immortal divinity.

Some object, saying, "like the Son of God" means Melchizedek is not the Son of God. But, in that case, we again have two eternal priests—Melchizedek and the Son of God. And that makes no more sense in Hebrews than it did in the psalm. So it cannot be correct. After all, if one asks, "Who is like the Son of God?," the answer must be, "Only the Son of God." I suggest that the author of Hebrews thought Melchizedek and the Son of God are one and the same.

(4) The Four Craftsmen *baraitha*, with its line-up of messianic heroes, appears throughout rabbinic literature. The oldest versions present Melchizedek as a priestly messiah to appear in the messianic time.

> The flowers appear on the earth (Song 2.12). R. Isaac said, "It is written: And the Lord showed me four craftsmen (Zech 2.3). These are

they: Elijah, the King Messiah, Melchizedek and the War Messiah." (Pesikta Rabbati §15.14–15).[16]

(5) Ambrose of Milan initially believed that Melchizedek was only a type of Christ.[17] But later he wrote:

> God is Melchisedech, that is, he is king of peace and justice, having neither the beginning of days nor end of life.[18]

CONCLUSION

My above reading of Psalm 110 sees three people in the psalm: David, Yahweh, and Melchizedek. Jesus, following ancient interpretation, also sees three people in the psalm: David, Yahweh, and the Messiah.

I suggest that Jesus and those who first coined this interpretation (a) were savvy enough to realize there could not be two eternal priests, (b) took *'al-dibrati* according to its plain sense, which makes Melchizedek inevitably a vocative, and (c) made the link between Melchizedek and the Messiah. In fact, according to any other reading, it is difficult to find the Messiah in the psalm at all. But with this reading, the Messiah is crystal clear.

Such a reading has implications for how we understand biblical prophecy. The contemporary view tends to see the prophets speaking of events in their own time and, unconsciously, uttering messianic pointers. Psalm 110 is viewed as an enthronement psalm that accidentally points to the Messiah. But, if my conclusions above are correct, there is no historical sacral kingship in this psalm. It was messianic prophecy *ab initio*. If that is so, we might find ourselves coming to similar conclusions about other psalms, particularly Psalm 2. This might influence how we read the Prophets as well.

But back to Jesus. If he believed Melchizedek is the Messiah, and if he believed himself to be the Messiah, then why did he not just say, "I am Melchizedek"? In John 8, he says,

> Your father Abraham rejoiced to see my day. He saw and was glad (8:56).[19]

---

16. The same text is in Pesikta de Rav Kahana 5.9 and Song Rabbah 2.13.4. For all the variants, and a discussion of the *baraitha* and its antecedents, see my *Messiah ben Joseph*, 140–43.

17. *On Faith* 3.11 (before AD 380); *On Abraham* 1.3 (AD 380). His view first changes in *On the Mysteries* 8.46 (AD 387).

18. *The Six Days of Creation* 1.3 (AD 389).

19. Ἀβραὰμ ὁ πατὴρ ὑμῶν ἠγαλλιάσατο ἵνα ἴδῃ τὴν ἡμέραν τὴν ἐμήν, καὶ εἶδεν καὶ ἐχάρη.

Some translations resort to paraphrase, implying that Jesus meant that Abraham foresaw the Messiah but did not actually see him. Others may imagine that Abraham, in the heavens, saw Jesus coming to earth. But Jesus's hearers understood his words perfectly well: "You are not yet fifty and you have seen Abraham!" (8:57). Nor does Jesus object. ("No, no. You've misunderstood. I meant that Abraham *fore*-saw me.") Not at all. He is happy with what they understand: Jesus saw Abraham, Abraham saw Jesus. In fact, he adds, he existed before Abraham: "Before Abraham was, I am" (8:58).

When did Abraham see Jesus? Was it when YHVH appeared to Abraham in human form in Genesis 18? Or when the divine angel spoke to him in Genesis 22? Perhaps. But these intermittent visits seem brief, whereas "Abraham rejoiced to see my day" implies a period of residence. I wonder if Jesus is not speaking of the time when Melchizedek, the angel of Yahweh, ruled in Salem and brought Abraham bread and wine at the defeat of the kings of the east.[20]

20. For those interested in other interpretational cruces of Psalm 110, the view I have given above supports the LXX reading of verse 3, which takes Hebrew ילדתיך as *y'lid'tikha*, "I have begotten you" [LXX: *exegennêsa se*] "from the womb, before the Morning Star," against the Masoretic Text's יַלְדֻתֶיךָ (*yaldutekha*) "your youth."

Contributors

C. Hassell Bullock is Franklin S. Dyrness professor emeritus of biblical studies at Wheaton College, Illinois. His PhD is from Hebrew Union College-Jewish Institute of Religion in Cincinnati, and he is the author of *Psalms 1–72* and *Psalms 73–150* in the Teach the Text series. His favorite psalm is Psalm 121.

J. Nathan Clayton is assistant professor of Old Testament at North Park Theological Seminary in Chicago, Illinois. His PhD is from Trinity Evangelical Divinity School. His writings on the Psalms include *Symbol, Service, and Song: The Levites of 1 Chronicles 10–29 in Rhetorical, Historical, and Theological Perspectives*, and a favorite psalm is Psalm 91.

Ryan J. Cook is associate professor of Old Testament and Hebrew at Moody Theological Seminary in Chicago, Illinois. His PhD is from Asbury Theological Seminary. His writings on the Psalms include *The Rhetoric of Praise: Prayer and Persuasion in the Psalms*, and a favorite psalm is Psalm 103.

Daniel J. Estes is distinguished professor of Old Testament at Cedarville University in Cedarville, Ohio. His PhD is from Cambridge University. His writings on the Psalms include the New American Commentary volume on Psalms 73–150 (with vol. 1 on Psalms 1–72 forthcoming), and his favorite psalm is Psalm 127.

Jill Firth is a lecturer in Hebrew and Old Testament at Ridley College in Melbourne, Australia. She holds a PhD from the Australian College of Theology. Her dissertation on "The Re-Presentation of David in Psalms 140–143" was summarized in *TynBul* 70 (2019): 149–52. A favorite psalm is Psalm 144.

Jamie Grant is vice-principal (academic) at Highland Theological College, University of the Highlands and Islands in Dingwall, Scotland. His PhD on the Psalms is from the University of Gloucestershire and published as *The King as Exemplar: The Function of Deuteronomy's Kingship Law in the Shaping of the Book of Psalms*. His favorite psalm changes almost as often as he reads the Psalter, but is—currently, at least—Psalm 130.

David "Gunner" Gundersen serves as lead pastor at BridgePoint Bible Church in Houston, Texas. His PhD is from The Southern Baptist Theological Seminary. He contributed the Psalms notes for *The Grace and Truth Study Bible*, and a favorite psalm is Psalm 90.

James M. Hamilton Jr. is professor of biblical theology at The Southern Baptist Theological Seminary and senior pastor of Kenwood Baptist Church in Louisville, Kentucky. His PhD is from Southern Seminary. He is author of a two-volume commentary on Psalms in the Evangelical Biblical Theology Commentary series, and a favorite psalm is Psalm 110.

Peter C. W. Ho is associate professor of Old Testament at Singapore Bible College in Singapore. His PhD is from the University of Gloucestershire. His writings on the Psalms include *The Design of the Psalter: A Macrostructural Analysis*, and a favorite psalm is Psalm 119.

David M. Howard Jr. is professor of Old Testament at Bethlehem College and Seminary in Minneapolis, Minnesota, and professor emeritus of Old Testament at Bethel Seminary in St. Paul, Minnesota. His PhD is from the University of Michigan. His writings on the Psalms include *The Structure of Psalms 93–100*, and a favorite psalm is Psalm 117.

Rolf A. Jacobson is professor of Old Testament and the Alvin N. Rogness chair of Scripture, theology, and ministry at Luther Seminary in St. Paul, Minnesota. His PhD is from Princeton Theological Seminary. His writings on the Psalms include *Invitation to the Psalms: A Reader's Guide for Discovery and Engagement*. A survivor of adolescent cancer, his favorite psalm is Psalm 30 ("you have turned my mourning into dancing").

Philip S. Johnston is an affiliated lecturer at the University of Cambridge (UK) and former senior tutor at one of its colleges. His PhD is from the University of Cambridge. His writings on the Psalms include contributing to and coediting *Interpreting the Psalms: Issues and Approaches*, and a favorite psalm is Psalm 90.

J. Clinton McCann Jr. is evangelical professor of biblical interpretation at Eden Theological Seminary in Webster Groves, Missouri. His PhD is from Duke University, and he is the author of the Psalms commentary in *The New Interpreter's Bible*. His favorite psalm changes regularly but is currently Psalm 82.

David C. Mitchell is director of music at Holy Trinity Pro-Cathedral in Brussels. His PhD is from New College Edinburgh. His writings on the Psalms include *The Message of the Psalter: An Eschatological Programme in the Books of Psalms*, and a favorite psalm is Psalm 150.

Seth D. Postell is academic dean and professor of biblical studies at Israel College of the Bibl in Netanya, Israel. His PhD is from Gateway Seminary in California. His writings on the Psalms include "Messianism in the Psalms" (in *The Moody Handbook of Messianic Prophecy*), and his favorite psalm is Psalm 45.

Andrew J. Schmutzer is professor of Bible at Moody Bible Institute in Chicago, Illinois. His PhD is from Trinity Evangelical Divinity School. His writings on the Psalms include contributing and coediting *The Psalms: Language for all Seasons of the Soul*. His current favorite psalm is Psalm 73.

Jerome L. Skinner is assistant professor of Old Testament exegesis and theology at Andrews University Seventh-day Adventist Theological Seminary in Berrien Springs, Michigan. His PhD is from Andrews University Seventh-day Adventist Theological Seminary. He is preparing to publish his dissertation on "The Historical Superscriptions of Davidic Psalms." A favorite psalm is Psalm 7.

Michael K. Snearly is scholar in residencee at Grace Church of Marin in Northern California. His PhD is from Gateway Seminary (formerly Golden Gate Baptist Theological Seminary). His writings on the Psalms include *The Return of the King: Messianic Expectation in Book V of the Psalter*, and a favorite psalm is Psalm 126.

May Young is associate professor of Old Testament and biblical Hebrew at Taylor University in Upland, Indiana. Her PhD is from Trinity International University. She is currently writing the Lamentations commentary for the Pillar Old Testament Commentary series. A favorite psalm is Psalm 27.

Bibliography

Ahearne-Kroll, Stephen P. "Psalms in the New Testament." Pages 269–80 in *The Oxford Handbook of the Psalms*. Edited by William P. Brown. Oxford: Oxford University Press, 2014.

Ahn, Kun. "I Salmi 146–150 come conclusione del Salterio." PhD diss., Pontifical Biblical Institute, 2008.

Alexander, Joseph A. *The Psalms Translated and Explained*. Grand Rapids: Baker Academic, 1975.

Alexander, T. Desmond, ed. *Dictionary of the Old Testament: Pentateuch*. 10 vols. Downers Grove, IL: InterVarsity, 2003–2014.

———. *From Paradise to the Promised Land: An Introduction to the Pentateuch*, 2nd ed. Grand Rapids: Baker Academic, 2002.

———. "The Psalms and the Afterlife." *IBS* 9 (1987): 2–17.

Allen, Leslie C. *Psalms 101–150*. WBC. Waco, TX: Word. 1983.

———. *Psalms 101–150*, Rev. ed. WBC. Nashville: Nelson, 2002.

Allen, Ronald B. "Psalm 87, A Song Rarely Sung." *Bibliotheca Sacra* 153 (1996): 131–40.

Alonso-Schökel, L. *A Manual of Hebrew Poetics*. SubBi 11. Rome: Editrice Pontificio Istituto Biblico, 1988.

———. "Motivos Sapienciales y de Alianza en Gn 2–3." *Bib* 43.3 (1962): 302–3.

Alter, Robert. *The Book of Psalms: A Translation with Commentary*. New York: Norton, 2007.

———. *The Five Books of Moses: A Translation with Commentary*. New York: Norton, 2004.

Anderson, Bernhard W. *Contours of Old Testament Theology*. Minneapolis: Fortress, 1999.

Arnold, Bill T., and John H. Choi. *A Guide to Biblical Hebrew Syntax*. Cambridge: Cambridge University, 2003.

Attard, Stefan M. *The Implications of Davidic Repentance: A Synchronic Analysis of Book 2 of the Psalter (Psalms 42–72) of Analecta Biblica Dissertationes*. Rome: Gregorian & Biblical, 2016.

Augustine. "Against Faustus the Manichee 12.27." Page vi in *Christ Meets me Everywhere: Augustine's Early Figurative Exegesis*. By Michael Camerson. Oxford Press: Oxford University, 2012.

Ayars, Matthew Ian. *The Shape of Hebrew Poetry: Exploring the Discourse Function of Linguistic Parallelism in the Egyptian Hallel*. Leiden: Brill, 2019.

Ballhorn, Egbert. "The Psalter as a Book: Genre as Key to Its Theology." Pages 155-69 in *The Psalter as Witness: Theology, Poetry, and Genre*. Edited by W. D. Tucker Jr. and W. H. Bellinger Jr. Waco, TX: Baylor University Press, 2017.

———. *Zum Telos des Psalters: Der Textzusammenhang des Vierten und Fünften Psalmenbuches (Ps 90–150)*. Bonner Biblische Beiträge 138. Berlin: Philo, 2004.

Barber, Michael. *Singing in the Reign: The Psalms and the Liturgy of God's Kingdom*. Steubenville, OH: Emmaus Road, 2001.

Barbiero, Gianni. *Das erste Psalmenbuch als Einheit: eine synchrone Analyse von Psalm 1–41*. ÖBS 16. Frankfurt am Main: Peter Lang, 1999.

———. *Il regno di JHWH e del suo Messia: Salmi scelti dal primo libro del Salterio. StudBib* 7. Rome: Città Nuova, 2009.

———. "Messianismus und Theokratie: Die Verbindung der Psalmen 144 und 145 und ihre Bedeutung für die Komposition des Psalters." *OTE* 27 (2014): 41–52.

———. *Perché, o Dio, ci hai rigettati? Salmi scelti dal secondo e terzo libro del Salteri. Analecta Biblica* 6. Rome: Gregorian & Biblical, 2016.

Barr, J. *The Garden of Eden and the Hope of Immortality*. London: SCM, 1992.

Barré, Michael L. "'Terminative' Terms in Hebrew Acrostics." Pages 207–15 in *Wisdom, You Are My Sister: Studies in Honor of Roland E. Murphy, O.Carm., on the Occasion of His Eightieth Birthday*. CBQ Monograph Series. Edited by Michael L. Barré. Washington, DC: Catholic Biblical Association of America, 1997.

Barth, C. F. *Die Errettung vom Tode in den individuellen Klage- und Dankliedern des Alten Testamentes*. Edited by B. Janowski. Stuttgart: Kohlhammer, 1997. First published 1947 Zollikon: Evangelischer.

Bauckham, Richard. "Biblical Theology and the Problems of Monotheism." Page 190 in *Out of Egypt: Biblical Theology and Biblical Interpretation*. Edited by Craig Bartholomew et al. Vol 5 of Scripture and Hermeneutics Series. Grand Rapids: Zondervan, 2004.

———. "The Power and the Glory: The Rendering of Psalm 110:1 in Mark 14:62." Pages 83–101 in *From Creation to New Creation: Biblical Theology and Exegesis*. Edited by Benjamin L. Gladd and Daniel M. Gurtner. Peabody, MA: Hendrickson, 2013.

Brown, Francis, S. R. Driver, and Charles A. Briggs. *A Hebrew and English Lexicon of the Old Testament*. Oxford: Clarendon, 1907.

Beckwith, Roger. "The Early History of the Psalter." *TynBul* 46 (1995): 1–28.

Belcher Jr., Richard P. *The Messiah and the Psalms: Preaching Christ from All the Psalms*. Fearn, Scotland: Christian Focus Publications, 2006.

Bellinger Jr., W. H. *Psalms as a Grammar for Faith*. Waco, TX: Baylor University Press, 2020.

———. "The Psalms as a Place to Begin for Old Testament Theology." Pages 28–29 in *Psalms and Practice: Worship, Virtue, and Authority*. Edited by Stephen Breck Reed. Collegeville, MN: Liturgical Press, 2001.

Berges, Ulrich. "Who Were the Servants? A Comparative Enquiry in the Book of Isaiah and the Psalms." Pages 1–18 in *Past, Present, Future: The Deuteronomic*

History and the Prophets. Edited by Johannes C. de Moor and Harry F. van Rooy. Leiden: Brill, 2000.

Berlin, Adele. *Lamentations: A Commentary*. OTL. Louisville: Westminster John Knox, 2002.

Biblia Hebraica Stuttgartensia. Edited by K. Elliger and W. Rudolph. Stuttagart: Deutsche Bibelstifting, 1977.

Birkeland, Harris. *The Evildoers in the Book of Psalms*. Oslo: Dybwad, 1955.

Blaising, Craig A., and Carmen S. Hardin. *Psalms 1–50*. ACCS 7. Downers Grove, IL: InterVarsity, 2004.

Blenkinsopp, Joseph. *Isaiah 40–55: A New Translation with Introduction and Commentary*. AB 19A. New York: Doubleday, 2002.

———. "The Servant and the Servants in Isaiah and the Formation of the Book." Pages 155–75 in *Writing and Reading the Scroll of Isaiah: Studies of an Interpretive Tradition*. Edited by Craig C. Broyles and Craig A. Evans. VTSup 70/1. Leiden: Brill, 1997.

Bloch-Smith, Elizabeth. "'Who Is the King of Glory?' Solomon's Temple and Its Symbolism." Pages 18–31 in *Scripture and Other Artifacts, Festschrift for Philip J. King*. Edited by Michael D. Coogan, J. Cheryl Exum, and Lawrence E. Stager. Louisville: Westminster John Knox, 1994.

Block, Daniel I. "Other Religions in Old Testament Theology." Pages 200–36 in *The Gospel According to Moses: Theological and Ethical Reflections on the Book of Deuteronomy*. Eugene, OR: Cascade Books, 2012.

———. *The Gods of the Nations: Studies in Ancient Near Eastern National Theology*. 2nd ed. Eugene, OR: Wipf & Stock, 1988.

Boda, Mark J. *1–2 Chronicles*. Cornerstone Biblical Commentary 5a. Carol Stream, IL: Tyndale House, 2010.

Boff, Leonardo. *Cry of the Earth, Cry of the Poor*. Translated by Phillip Berryman. Maryknoll, NY: Orbis Books, 1997.

Booij, Thijs. "Some Observations on Psalm 87." *VT* 37.1 (1987): 16–25.

Botterweck, G. Johannes, Helmer Ringgren, and Heinz-Josef Fabry, eds. *TDOT*. Translated by John T. Willis et al. 15 vols. Grand Rapids: Eerdmans, 1974–2006.

Boys, Thomas. *A Key to the Book of Psalms*. London: Seeley and Son, 1825.

Bridge, Edward J. "Loyalty, Dependency and Status with YHWH: The Use of *ʿbd* in the Psalms." *VT* 59 (2009): 360–78.

———. "Polite Language in the Lachish Letters." *VT* 60 (2010): 524–25.

———. "Self-Abasement as an Expression of Thanks in the Hebrew Bible." *Bib* 92 (2011): 255–73.

———. "The Metaphoric Use of Slave Terms in the Hebrew Bible." *BBR* 23 (2013): 14–27.

Briggs, C., and E. Briggs. *A Critical and Exegetical Commentary on the Book of Psalms*. 2 vols. ICC. Edinburgh: T&T Clark, 1906–1907.

Brodersen, Alma. "Quellen und Intertextualität. Methodische Überlegungen zum Psalterende," Pages 7–31 in *Intertextualität*. Edited by Brodersen, Neumann, and Willgren. BZAW 505. Berlin: Walter de Gruyter, 2017.

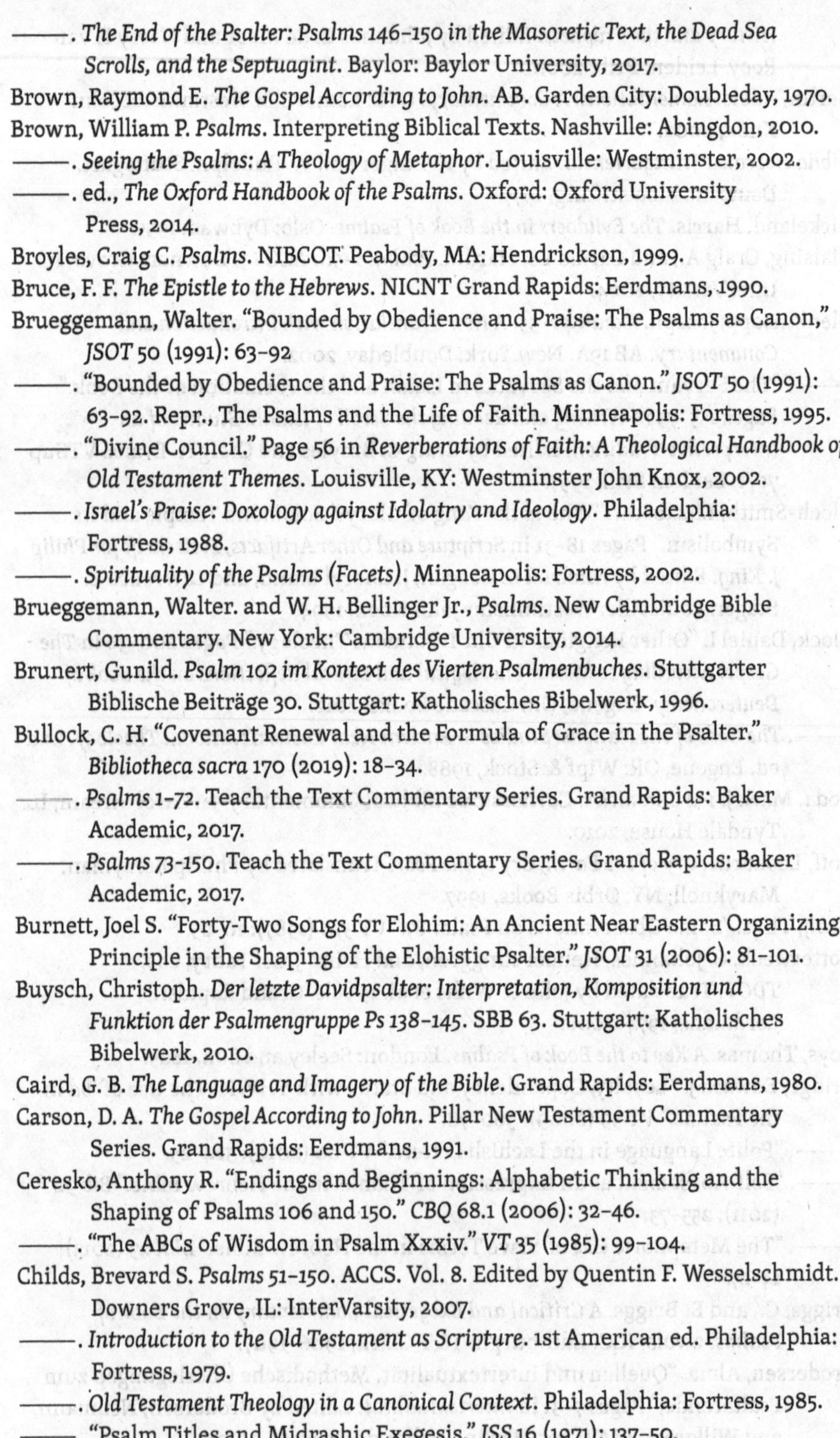

——. *The End of the Psalter: Psalms 146–150 in the Masoretic Text, the Dead Sea Scrolls, and the Septuagint*. Baylor: Baylor University, 2017.

Brown, Raymond E. *The Gospel According to John*. AB. Garden City: Doubleday, 1970.

Brown, William P. *Psalms*. Interpreting Biblical Texts. Nashville: Abingdon, 2010.

——. *Seeing the Psalms: A Theology of Metaphor*. Louisville: Westminster, 2002.

——. ed., *The Oxford Handbook of the Psalms*. Oxford: Oxford University Press, 2014.

Broyles, Craig C. *Psalms*. NIBCOT. Peabody, MA: Hendrickson, 1999.

Bruce, F. F. *The Epistle to the Hebrews*. NICNT Grand Rapids: Eerdmans, 1990.

Brueggemann, Walter. "Bounded by Obedience and Praise: The Psalms as Canon," *JSOT* 50 (1991): 63–92

——. "Bounded by Obedience and Praise: The Psalms as Canon." *JSOT* 50 (1991): 63–92. Repr., The Psalms and the Life of Faith. Minneapolis: Fortress, 1995.

——. "Divine Council." Page 56 in *Reverberations of Faith: A Theological Handbook of Old Testament Themes*. Louisville, KY: Westminster John Knox, 2002.

——. *Israel's Praise: Doxology against Idolatry and Ideology*. Philadelphia: Fortress, 1988.

——. *Spirituality of the Psalms (Facets)*. Minneapolis: Fortress, 2002.

Brueggemann, Walter. and W. H. Bellinger Jr., *Psalms*. New Cambridge Bible Commentary. New York: Cambridge University, 2014.

Brunert, Gunild. *Psalm 102 im Kontext des Vierten Psalmenbuches*. Stuttgarter Biblische Beiträge 30. Stuttgart: Katholisches Bibelwerk, 1996.

Bullock, C. H. "Covenant Renewal and the Formula of Grace in the Psalter." *Bibliotheca sacra* 170 (2019): 18–34.

——. *Psalms 1–72*. Teach the Text Commentary Series. Grand Rapids: Baker Academic, 2017.

——. *Psalms 73-150*. Teach the Text Commentary Series. Grand Rapids: Baker Academic, 2017.

Burnett, Joel S. "Forty-Two Songs for Elohim: An Ancient Near Eastern Organizing Principle in the Shaping of the Elohistic Psalter." *JSOT* 31 (2006): 81–101.

Buysch, Christoph. *Der letzte Davidpsalter: Interpretation, Komposition und Funktion der Psalmengruppe Ps 138–145*. SBB 63. Stuttgart: Katholisches Bibelwerk, 2010.

Caird, G. B. *The Language and Imagery of the Bible*. Grand Rapids: Eerdmans, 1980.

Carson, D. A. *The Gospel According to John*. Pillar New Testament Commentary Series. Grand Rapids: Eerdmans, 1991.

Ceresko, Anthony R. "Endings and Beginnings: Alphabetic Thinking and the Shaping of Psalms 106 and 150." *CBQ* 68.1 (2006): 32–46.

——. "The ABCs of Wisdom in Psalm Xxxiv." *VT* 35 (1985): 99–104.

Childs, Brevard S. *Psalms 51–150*. ACCS. Vol. 8. Edited by Quentin F. Wesselschmidt. Downers Grove, IL: InterVarsity, 2007.

——. *Introduction to the Old Testament as Scripture*. 1st American ed. Philadelphia: Fortress, 1979.

——. *Old Testament Theology in a Canonical Context*. Philadelphia: Fortress, 1985.

——. "Psalm Titles and Midrashic Exegesis." *JSS* 16 (1971): 137–50.

———. *The Book of Exodus: A Critical, Theological Commentary*. Louisville: Westminster John Knox, 1974.

Christensen, Duane. "Nations." *ABD*. 6:1037.

Clayton, J. Nathan. *Symbol, Service, and Song: The Levites of 1 Chronicles 10–29 in Rhetorical, Historical, and Theological Perspectives*. Eugene, OR: Pickwick/Wipf & Stock, 2021.

Clifford, Richard J. *Psalms 73–150*. AOTC. Nashville: Abingdon, 2003.

Cole, Robert L. "An Integrated Reading of Psalms 1 and 2." *JSOT* 26.4 (2002): 75–88.

———. "An Integrated Reading of Psalms 1 and 2." *JSOT* 98 (2002): 75–88.

———. "Compositional Unity in the Five Books of the Psalms: A Canonical Approach." Pages 451–56 in *The Moody Handbook of Messianic Prophecy: Studies and Expositions of the Messiah in the Old Testament*. Edited by Michael Rydelnik and Edwin Blum. Chicago: Moody, 2019.

———. *Numbers*. NAC 3B. Nashville: Broadman & Holman, 2000.

———. "Psalms 1–2: The Divine Son of God." Pages 477–91 in *The Moody Handbook of Messianic Prophecy: Studies and Expositions of the Messiah in the Old Testament*. Edited by Michael Rydelnik and Edwin Blum. Chicago: Moody, 2019.

———. *Psalms 1–2: A Gateway to the Psalter*. HBM 37. Sheffield: Sheffield Phoenix, 2013.

———. "Psalms 1 and 2: The Psalter's Introduction." Pages 183–95 in *The Psalms: Language for All Seasons of the Soul*. Edited by Andrew J. Schmutzer and David M. Howard Jr. Chicago: Moody, 2013.

———. *The Shape and Message of Book III (Psalms 73–89)*. JSOTSup 307. Sheffield: Sheffield Academic, 2000.

Cook, Ryan. "'They were Born There': The Nations in Psalmic Rhetoric." *HBT* 39 (2017): 16–30.

———. "Prayers that Form Us: Rhetoric and Psalms Interpretation." *JSOT* 39 (2015): 451–67.

Cottrill, Amy C. *Language, Power, and Identity in the Lament Psalms of the Individual*. LHBOTS 493. New York: T&T Clark, 2008.

Craigie, Peter C. *Psalms 1–50*. WBC 19. Waco, TX: Word, 1983.

Craigie, Peter, and Marvin Tate. *Psalms 1–50*. Rev. WBC 19. Nashville: Nelson, 2004.

Creach, Jerome F. *The Choice of Yahweh as Refuge in the Editing of the Psalter*. JSOTSup 217. Sheffield: Sheffield Academic, 1996.

———. "The Righteous and the Wicked." Pages 529–41 in *The Oxford Handbook of the Psalms*. Edited by W. P. Brown. Oxford: Oxford University Press, 2014.

———. "The Shape of Book Four of the Psalter and the Shape of Second Isaiah." *JSOT* 80 (1998): 63–76.

Crutchfield, John C. "The Redactional Agenda of the Book of Psalms." *HUCA* 74 (2003): 21–47.

Daly-Denton, Margaret. "Early Christian Writers as Jewish Readers: The New Testament Reception of the Psalms." *The Review of Rabbinic Judaism* 11 (2008): 181–99.

Daniélou, Jean. *From Shadows to Reality: Studies in the Biblical Typology of the Fathers*. Translated by Wulstan Hibberd. London: Burns and Oates, 1960.

Davila, James R. *Liturgical Works: Eerdmans Commentaries on the Dead Sea Scrolls*. Grand Rapids: Eerdmans, 2000.

De La Croix, Horst, Richard G. Tansey, and Diane Kirkpatrick. *Gardner's Art through the Ages: Renaissance and Modern Art*. 9th ed. Orlando, FL: Harcourt Brace Jovanovich, 1991.

de Souza, Elias Brasil. "The Heavenly Sanctuary/Temple Motif in the Hebrew Bible: Function and Relationship to the Earthly Counterparts." PhD diss., Andrews University, 2005.

deClaissé-Walford, Nancy L., ed. *The Shape and Shaping of the Book of Psalms: The Current State of Scholarship*. AIL 20. Atlanta: SBL, 2014.

———. *Reading from the Beginning: The Shaping of the Hebrew Psalter*. Macon, GA: Mercer University Press, 1997.

———. "The Canonical Approach to Scripture and The Editing of the Hebrew Psalter." Pages 1–11 in *The Shape and Shaping of the Book of Psalms: The Current State of Scholarship*. Edited by Nancy L. deClaissé-Walford. Atlanta: Society of Biblical Literature, 2014.

———. "The Meta-Narrative of the Psalter." Pages 363–76 in *The Oxford Handbook of the Psalms*. Edited by William P. Brown. Oxford: Oxford University Press, 2014.

deClaissé-Walford, Nancy L., Rolf A. Jacobson, and Beth LaNeel Tanner. *The Book of Psalms*. NICOT. Grand Rapids: Eerdmans, 2014.

Dempster, Stephen G. *Dominion and Dynasty: A Biblical Theology of the Hebrew Bible*. New Studies in Biblical Theology. Downers Grove, IL: InterVarsity, 2003.

Dobbs-Allsopp, F. W. "The Effects of Enjambment in Lamentations (Part 2)." *ZAW* 113 (2001): 370–85.

———. "The Enjambing Line in Lamentations: A Taxonomy (Part 1)." *ZAW* 113 (2001): 219–39.

Doble, Peter. "Luke 24.26,44—Songs of God's Servant: David and his Psalms in Luke-Acts." *JSNT* 28 (2006): 267–83.

Domeris, W. "Meek or Oppressed? Reading Matthew 5:5 in Context." *AcT* 23 (2016): 131–49.

Douglas McC. L. Judisch, "Propitiation in the Language and Typology of the Old Testament." *CTQ* 48 (1984): 233.

Dozeman, Thomas B. *Joshua 1–12: A New Translation with Introduction and Commentary*. The Anchor Yale Bible 6B. New Haven: Yale University Press, 2015.

Duhm, Bernard. *Die Psalmen eklärt*. KHC 14. Freiburg: Mohr Siebeck, 1899.

Dunn, Steven. *The Sanctuary in the Psalms: Exploring the Paradox of God's Transcendence and Immanence*. Lanham, MD: Lexington Books, 2016.

Eaton, John H. *Kingship and the Psalms*. 2nd ed. Sheffield: JSOT Press, 1986.

———. *The Psalms: A Historical and Spiritual Commentary with an Introduction and New Translation*. London: T&T Clark International, 2003.

Emadi, Samuel Cyrus. "Covenant, Typology, and the Story of Joseph: A Literary-Canonical Examination of Genesis 37–50." PhD Diss. The Southern Baptist Theological Seminary, 2016.

Emanuel, David "An Unrecognized Voice: Intra-Textual and Intertextual Perspectives on Psalm 81." *HS* 50 (2009): 85–120.

Emerton, J. A. "The Origin of the Son of Man Imagery." *Journal of Theological Studies* 9 (1958): 225–42.

Edwards, Jonathan. *The Works of Jonathan Edwards: Religious Affections*. Edited by John E. Smith. New Haven: Yale University Press, 2009.

Fabry, Heinz-Josef. "Der Psalter in Qumran." Pages 137–63 in *Der Psalter in Judentum und Christentum*. Edited by E. Zenger. Freiburg im Breisgau: Herder, 1998.

Ferris Jr., Paul W. "Lamentations." Page 624 in *Jeremiah-Ezekiel*. The Expositor's Bible Commentary 7. 2nd ed. Grand Rapids: Zondervan, 2010.

Fesko, J. V. Word. *Water, and Spirit: A Reformed Perspective on Baptism*. Grand Rapids: Reformation Heritage Books, 2010.

Firth, Gillian C. "The Re-Presentation of David in Psalms 140–143." PhD diss., Australian College of Theology, 2016.

Fleming, D. M. "The Divine Council as Type-Scene in the Hebrew Bible." PhD diss., The Southern Baptist Theological Seminary, 1989.

Fletcher-Louis, Crispin. "Further Reflections on a Divine and Angelic Humanity in the Dead Sea Scrolls." Pages 185–98 in *New Perspectives on Old Texts: Proceedings of the 2005 Orion Dead Sea Scroll Conference*. Edited by E. G. Chazon, B. Halpern-Amaru, and R. A. Clements. Leiden: Brill, 2010.

Flint, Peter W. *The Dead Sea Psalms Scrolls and the Book of Psalms*. STDJ 17. Leiden: Brill, 1997.

Flint, Peter W., and Patrick D. Miller Jr., eds. *The Book of Psalms: Composition and Reception*. VTSup 99. Leiden: Brill, 2005.

Forde, Gerhard. *On Being a Theologian of the Cross: Reflections on Luther's Heidelberg Disputation, 1518*. Grand Rapids: Eerdmans, 1997.

Freedman, D. N. et al. *TDOT*. Edited by G. J. Botterweck, H. Ringgren, and H.-J. Fabry. Translated by D. W. Stott. Grand Rapids: Eerdmans, 1999.

Fretheim, Terence E. *The Suffering of God: An Old Testament Perspective*. OBT. Philadelphia: Fortress, 1984.

Futato, Mark D. "Psalms 16, 23: Confidence in a Cup." Pages 231–36 in *The Psalms: Language for All Seasons of the Soul*. Edited by Andrew J. Schmutzer and David M. Howard Jr. Chicago: Moody, 2013.

———. *Interpreting the Psalms: An Exegetical Handbook*. Handbooks for Old Testament Exegesis. Grand Rapids: Kregel, 2007.

"Geniza Lab: Princeton University," https://genizalab.princeton.edu.

Gerstenberger, Erhard S. "Der Psalter als Buch und als Sammlung." Pages 3–13 in *Neue Wege der Psalmenforschung: Für Walter Beyerlin*. Edited by K. Seybold and E. Zenger. Herders Biblische Studien 1. Freiburg: Herder, 1994.

Gerstenberger, Erhard. *Review of The Formation of the 'Book' of Psalms: Reconsidering the Transmission and Canonization of Psalmody in Light of Material Culture and the Poetics of Anthologies by David Willgren*. *RBL* (January 2018), https://www.sblcentral.org/home/bookDetails/11966.

Giles, Terry, and William J. Doan. *Twice Used Songs: Performance Criticism of the Songs of Ancient Israel*. Peabody, MA: Hendrickson, 2009.

Gillingham, Susan. *A Journey of Two Psalms: The Reception of Psalms 1 and 2 in Jewish and Christian Tradition*. Oxford: Oxford University Press, 2013.

———. "The Levites and the Editorial Composition of the Psalms." Pages 201–13 in *The Oxford Handbook of the Psalms*. Edited by William P. Brown. Oxford: Oxford University Press, 2014.

———. "The Levitical Singers and the Compilation of the Psalter." Pages 35–39 in *Trägerkreise in den Psalmen*. F.-L. Hossfeld et al. BBB 178. Göttingen: Bonn University, 2017.

———. "The Messiah in the Psalms: A Question of Reception History and the Psalter." Pages 209–37 in *King and Messiah in Israel and the Ancient Near East*. Edited by. J. Day. JSOTSup 270. Sheffield: Sheffield Academic, 1998.

———. "The Zion Tradition and the Editing of the Hebrew Psalter." Pages 308–41 in *Temple and Worship in Biblical Israel*. Edited by John Day. Oxford Old Testament Seminar. London: T&T Clark, 2005.

Goldingay, John. "Death and Afterlife in the Psalms." Pages 61–85 in *Judaism in Late Antiquity*, Part 4. Edited by A. J. Avery-Peck and J. Neusner. Leiden: Brill, 2000.

———. *Old Testament Theology: Israel's Gospel*. Vol. 1. Downers Grove, IL: IVP Academic, 2003.

———. *Old Testament Theology: Israel's Faith*. Vol. 2. Downers Grove: IVP Academic, 2006.

———. *Psalms, Volume 1: Psalms 1–41*. BCOTWP. Grand Rapids: Baker Academic, 2006.

———. *Psalms, Volume 2: Psalms 42–89*. BCOTWP. Grand Rapids: Baker Academic, 2007.

———. *Psalms, Volume 3: Psalms 90–150*. BCOTWP. Grand Rapids: Baker Academic, 2008.

Goodman, P. W. *Paradoxes of Paradise: Identity and Difference in the Song of Songs*. 2nd ed. Sheffield: Sheffield Phoenix, 2011.

Gosse, Bernard. *L'espérance Messianique Davidique et la Structuration du Psautier*. Paris: Gabalda, 2015.

Goswell, Gregory. "The Non-Messianic Psalter of Gerald H. Wilson." *VT* 66 (2016): 524–41; Repr. in Andrew T. Abernethy and Gregory Goswell. *God's Messiah in the Old Testament: Expectations of a Coming King*. Grand Rapids: Baker Academic, 2020.

Goulder, M.D. *The Prayers of David (Psalms 51–72): Studies in the Psalter, II*. JSOTSup 102. Sheffield: JSOT Press, 1990.

———. "The Social Setting of Book II of the Psalter." Pages 349–67 in *The Book of Psalms: Composition and Reception*. Edited by Peter W. Flint and Patrick D. Miller. VTSup 99. Leiden: Brill, 2004.

Grant, Jamie A. "Creation and Kingship: Environment and Witness in the Yahweh Mālāk Psalms." Pages 92–106 in *As Long as Earth Endures: The Bible Creation and the Environment*. Edited by Jonathan Moo and Robin Routledge. Nottingham: Apollos, 2014.

———. "Editorial Criticism." Pages 149–56 in *Dictionary of the Old Testament: Wisdom, Poetry & Writings*. Edited by Tremper Longman and Peter Enns. Downers Grove, IL: InterVarsity, 2008.

———. *The King as Exemplar: The Function of Deuteronomy's Kingship Law in the Shaping of the Book of Psalms*. AcBib 17. Atlanta: Society of Biblical Literature, 2004.

Greidanus, Sidney. *Preaching Christ from Psalms: Foundations for Expository Sermons in the Christian Year*. Grand Rapids: Eerdmans, 2016.

Gressmann, Hugo. *Der Ursprung der israelitisch-jüdischen Eschatologie*. FRLANT 6. Göttingen: Vandenhoeck & Ruprecht, 1905.

Grogan, Geoffrey. *Prayer, Praise, and Prophecy: A Theology of the Psalms*. Rosshire: Christian Focus, 2001.

———. *Psalms*. The Two Horizons Old Testament Commentary. Grand Rapids: Eerdmans, 2008.

Gundersen, David Alexander. "Davidic Hope in Book IV of the Psalter." PhD diss., The Southern Baptist Theological Seminary, 2015.

Gunkel, Hermann. *Introduction to the Psalms: The Genres of the Religious Lyric of Israel*. Translated by James D. Nogalski. Macon, GA: Mercer University Press, 1998.

Hall, Douglas John. *Lighten Our Darkness: Toward an Indigenous Theology of the Cross*. Louisville: Westminster John Knox, 1971.

Hamilton, James. *God's Glory in Salvation through Judgment: A Biblical Theology*. Wheaton, IL: Crossway, 2010.

———. "John." Pages 19–308 in *John–Acts*. ESV Expository Commentary. Wheaton, IL: Crossway, 2019.

———. *Psalms*. 2 vols. Evangelical Biblical Theology Commentary. Bellingham, WA: Lexham Press, 2021.

———. "The Exodus in Biblical Theology." Pages 77–91 in *The Law, The Prophets, and the Writings: Studies in Evangelical Old Testament Hermeneutics in Honor of Duane A. Garrett*. Edited by Andrew M. King, William R. Osborne, and Joshua M. Philpot. Nashville: Broadman & Holman, 2021.

———. "The Seed of the Woman and the Blessing of Abraham." *TynBul* 58 (2007): 253–73.

———. "The Skull Crushing Seed of the Woman: Inner-Biblical Interpretation of Genesis 3:15." *The Southern Baptist Journal of Theology* 10. 2 (2006): 30–54.

———. "Was Joseph a Type of the Messiah? Tracing the Typological Identification between Joseph, David, and Jesus." *The Southern Baptist Journal of Theology* 12 (2008): 52–77.

———. *What Is Biblical Theology?* Wheaton, IL: Crossway, 2014.

Hamilton, Victor P. *Exodus: An Exegetical Commentary*. Grand Rapids: Baker Academic, 2011.

Hanson, A. T. *The Wrath of the Lamb*. London: SPCK, 1959.

Hanson, Kenneth C. "Alphabetic Acrostics: A Form Critical Study." PhD diss., Claremont Graduate School, 1984.

Haran, Menahem. "11QPs[a] and the Canonical Book of Psalms." Pages 193–201 in *Minhah le-Nahum*. Edited by M. Brettler, M. Fishbane, Nahum M., and Sarna Festschrift. JSOTSup 153. Sheffield: JSOT Press, 1993.

Harris, R . L. "The Meaning of the Word Sheol as Shown by Parallels in Poetic Texts." Pages 829–90 in *Theological Wordbook of the Old Testament*. Edited by R. Laird Harris, Gleason L. Archer Jr., and Bruce K. Waltke. Chicago: Moody, 1980.

———. "The Meaning of the Word Sheol as Shown by Parallels in Poetic Texts." *JETS* 4 (1961): 129–135.

Harris, R. Laird, Gleason L. Archer Jr., and Bruce K. Waltke, eds. *Theological Wordbook of the Old Testament*. 2 vols. Chicago: Moody, 1980.

Hassler, Andrew. "Ethnocentric Legalism and the Justification of the Individual: Rethinking Some New Perspective Assumptions." *JETS* 54 (2011): 327.

Hays, Richard B. *Echoes of Scripture in the Gospels*. Waco, TX: Baylor University Press, 2016.

———. *Echoes of Scripture in the Letters of Paul*. New Haven: Yale University Press, 1989.

———. *The Conversion of the Imagination: Paul as Interpreter of Israel's Scripture*. Grand Rapids: Eerdmans, 2005.

Heim, Knut M. "Personification of Jerusalem and the Drama of Her Bereavement in Lamentations." Pages 151–53 in *Zion, City of Our God*. Edited by Richard S. Hess and Gordon J. Wenham. Grand Rapids: Eerdmans, 1999.

Heller, Sheri. *A Clinician's Journey from Complex Trauma to Thriving: Reflections on Abuse, C-PTSD and Reclamation*. New York: Independently Published, 2017.

Hensley, Adam D. *Covenant Relationships and the Editing of the Hebrew Psalter*. LHBOTS 666. New York: T&T Clark, 2018.

Hilber, John W. "Psalms." Pages 344–98 in *Zondervan Illustrated Bible Backgrounds Commentary*. Vol 5. Edited by John H. Walton. Grand Rapids: Zondervan, 2009.

Hillers, Delbert R. *Lamentations*. AB 7A. Garden City, NY: Doubleday, 1972.

Ho, Peter C. W. "Can an Integrative Reading of the Masoretic Psalter Stand in the Presence of Variants Discovered around Qumran with a Different Canonical Order?" In *Holistic Readings on the Psalms and the Twelve*. Edited by Matthew Ayars and Peter C. W. Ho. Forthcoming.

———. *The Design of the Psalter: A Macrostructural Analysis*. Eugene, OR: Pickwick, 2019.

———. "The Shape of Davidic Psalms as Messianic." *JETS* 62 (2019): 515–31.

———. "Review of David Willgren, *Like a Garden of Flowers*." *Journal for the Evangelical Study of the Old Testament* 6 (2020): 73–76.

Høgenhaven, Jesper. "The Opening of the Psalter: A Study in Jewish Theology." *SJOT* 15.2 (2001): 169–80.

Holladay, William L. *A Concise Hebrew and Aramaic Lexicon of the Old Testament*. Grand Rapids: Eerdmans, 1988.

Hossfeld, Frank-Lothar, and Erich Zenger. *Psalms 2: A Commentary on Psalms 51–100*. Edited by Klaus Baltzer. Translated by L. M. Maloney. Hermeneia. Minneapolis: Fortress, 2005.

———. *Psalms 3: A Commentary on Psalms 101–150*. Edited by Klaus Baltzer. Translated by L.M. Maloney. Hermeneia. Minneapolis: Fortress, 2011.

———. "The So-Called Elohistic Psalter: A New Solution for an Old Problem." Pages 35–51 in *A God So Near: Essays on Old Testament Theology in Honor of Patrick D. Miller*. Edited by Brent A. Strawn and Nancy Bowen. Winona Lake, IN: Eisenbrauns, 2003.

Hossfeld, Frank-Lothar, and Till Magnus Steiner. "Problems and Prospects in Psalter Studies." Pages 240–58 in *Jewish and Christian Approaches to the Psalms: Conflict and Convergence*. Edited by Susan E. Gillingham. Oxford: Oxford University Press, 2013.

Howard Jr., David M. "Divine and Human Kingship as Organizing Motifs in the Psalter." Pages 197–207 in *The Psalms: Language for All Seasons of the Soul*. Edited by Andrew J. Schmutzer and David M. Howard Jr. Chicago: Moody, 2013.

———. "Introduction to Psalms." Pages in 868–76 in *NIV Biblical Theology Study Bible*. Edited by D. A. Carson. Grand Rapids: Zondervan, 2018.

———. *Joshua*. NAC 5. Nashville: Broadman & Holman, 1998.

———. "Recent Trends in Psalms Study." Pages 329–68 in *The Face of Old Testament Studies: A Survey of Contemporary Approaches*. Edited by D. W. Baker and B. T. Arnold. Grand Rapids: Baker Academic, 1999.

———. "Preaching the Darkest Psalm: Psalm 88." Pages 54–66 in *Text Message: The Centrality of Scripture in Preaching*. Edited by I. Stackhouse and O. Crisp. Eugene, OR: Wipf and Stock, 2014.

———. "Psalm 88 and the Rhetoric of Lament." Pages 132–46 in *"My Words Are Lovely": Studies in the Rhetoric of the Psalms*. Edited by R. Foster and D. Howard. LHBOTS 467. New York: T&T Clark, 2008.

———. "Psalm 94 among the Kingship of YHWH Psalms." *CBQ* 61 (1999): 667–85.

———. "The Case for Kingship in the Old Testament Narrative Books and the Psalms." *TJ* 9 (1988): 19–35.

———. "The Proto-MT Psalter, the King, and Psalms 1 and 2: A Response to Klaus Seybold." Pages 182–89 in *Jewish and Christian Approaches to the Psalter: Conflict and Convergence*. Edited by S. Gillingham. Oxford: Oxford University Press, 2012.

———. "The Psalms and Current Study." Pages 23–40 in *Interpreting the Psalms: Issues and Approaches*. Edited by David Firth and Philip S. Johnston. Downers Grove, IL: InterVarsity, 2005.

———. *The Structure of Psalms 93–100*. Biblical and Judaic Studies 5. Winona Lake, IN: Eisenbrauns, 1997.

———. "Wisdom and Royalist/Zion Traditions in the Psalter." *Structure*, 200–207.

Human, Dirk. "YHWH, the Israelite High God Bends Down to Uplift the Downtrodden: Perspectives on the Incomparability of YHWH in Psalm 113." *JNSL* 30. 1 (2004): 41–64.

Hunter, Alastair G. *An Introduction to the Psalms*. Pages 21–24 in Approaches to Biblical Studies. London: T&T Clark, 2008.

Hustad, Donald P. "Music and the Church's Outreach." *RevExp* 69 (1972): 178.

Ishida, Tomoo. *The Royal Dynasties in Ancient Israel*. BZAW 142. Berlin: de Gruyter, 1977.

Jacobs, Mignon R. "Toward an Old Testament Theology of Concern for the Underprivileged." Pages 205–29 in *Reading the Hebrew Bible for a New Millennium: Form, Concept, and Theological Perspective*. Vol. 1. Studies in Antiquity and Christianity. Edited by Wonil Kim et al. Harrisburg, PA: Trinity Press International, 2000.

Jacobson, Rolf A. "'The Faithfulness of the Lord Endures Forever': The Theological Witness of the Psalter." Page 121 in *Soundings of the Theology of the Psalms: Perspectives and Methods in Contemporary Scholarship*. Edited by Rolf A. Jacobson. Minneapolis: Fortress, 2011.

Jenkins, Steffen. "The Antiquity of Psalter Shape Efforts," *TynBul* 71 (2020): 161–80.

Jenni, Ernst, and Claus Westermann, eds. *Theological Lexicon of the Old Testament*. Translated by Mark E. Biddle. 3 vols. Peabody, MA: Hendrickson, 1997.

Jipp, Joshua W. "Luke's Scriptural Suffering Messiah: A Search for Precedent, a Search for Identity." *CBQ* 72 (2010): 255–74.

Johnston, P. S. "'Left in Hell'? Psalm 16, Sheol and the Holy One." Pages 213–22 in *The Lord's Anointed*. Edited by P. E. Satterthwaite et al. Carlisle: Paternoster, 1995.

———. "Death in Egypt and Israel: A Theological Reflection." Pages 94–116 in *The Old Testament in Its World*. Edited by R. P. Gordon and J. C. de Moor. OTS 52. Leiden: Brill, 2004.

———. "Psalm 49: A Personal Eschatology." Pages 73–84 in *"The Reader Must Understand."* Edited by K. E. Brewer and M. W. Elliott. Leicester: Apollos, 1997.

———. "Sheol." *NIDB* 5: 227.

———. *Shades of Sheol: Death and Afterlife in the Old Testament*. Downers Grove, IL: InterVarsity, 2002.

———. "Suffering Saints, Glorious Kings and Divine Deliverance: Context and Relecture in the Psalms." Pages 142–61 in *The Seed of Promise*. Edited by P. R. Williamson and R. F. Cefalu. GlossaHouse Festschrift Series 3. Wilmore, KY: GlossaHouse, 2020.

Jones, Christine. "The Message of the Asaphite Collection and Its Role in the Psalter." Pages 71–85 in *The Shape and Shaping of the Book of Psalms*. Edited by Nancy L. deClaissé-Walford. AIL 20. Atlanta: Society of Biblical Literature, 2014.

———. "The Psalms of Asaph: A Study of the Function of a Psalm Collection." PhD diss., Baylor University, 2009.

Jones, David Clyde. "The Multiracial City." *Presb* 21.2 (1995): 68.

Jüngel, Eberhard. *God as the Mystery of the World: On the Foundation of the Theology of the Crucified One in the Dispute between Theism and Atheism*. London: T&T Clark, 2014.

Kahle, Paul. *The Cairo Geniza*. 2nd ed. Oxford: Blackwell, 1959

Kaiser Jr., Walter. *Mission in the Old Testament: Israel as a Light to the Nations*. Grand Rapids: Baker Academic, 2000.

———. *The Uses of the Old Testament in the New*. Chicago: Moody, 1985.

Keel, Othmar. *The Symbolism of the Biblical World: Ancient Near Eastern Iconography and the Book of Psalms*. Translated by Timothy Hallett. Winona Lake, IN: Eisenbrauns, 1997.

Keil, Carl F., and Franz Delitzsch. *Old Testament Commentaries: Psalm 78 to Isaiah 14*. Vol. 4. Grand Rapids: Associated Publishers and Authors, 1960.

Kessler, John. *Old Testament Theology: Divine Call and Human Response*. Waco, TX: Baylor University Press, 2013.

Kidner, Derek. *Psalms 1–72*. TOTC 14a. Downers Grove, IL: InterVarsity, 1973.

———. *Psalms 73–150*. TOTC 14b. Downers Grove, IL: InterVarsity, 1975.

Kim, Daewoong. "Biblical Interpretation in the Book of Daniel: Literary Allusions in Daniel to Genesis and Ezekiel." PhD diss., Rice University, 2013.

Kimmitt, Francis X. "Psalm 46: Praise the Lord Our Help." Pages 63–74 in *The Psalms: Language for All Seasons of the Soul*. Edited by Andrew J. Schmutzer and David M. Howard Jr. Chicago: Moody, 2013.

Kirkpatrick, A. F. *The Book of Psalms*. Cambridge: Cambridge University Press, 1910.

Klingbeil, Martin. *YHWH Fighting from Heaven: God as Warrior and as God of Heaven in the Hebrew Psalter and Ancient Near Eastern Iconography*. OBO 169. Gottingen: Vandenhoeck & Ruprecht, 1999.

Knoppers, Gary N. "'To Him You Must Listen': The Prophetic Legislation in Deuteronomy and the Reformation of Classical Tradition in Chronicles." Pages 187–89 in *Chronicling the Chronicler: The Book of Chronicles and Early Second Temple Historiography*. Edited by Paul S. Evans and Tyler F. Williams. Winona Lake, IN: Eisenbrauns, 2013.

Koehler, Ludwig, Walter Baumgartner, and Johann J. Stamm. *The Hebrew and Aramaic Lexicon of the Old Testament*. Translated and edited under the supervision of Mervyn E. J. Richardson. 2 vols. Leiden: Brill, 2001.

Koenen, Klaus. *Jahwe wird kommen, zu herrschen über die Erde: Ps 90–110 als Komposition*. BBB 101. Weinheim: Beltz Athenäum, 1995.

Köstenberger, Andreas J. "John." Pages 464–67 in *Commentary on the New Testament Use of the Old Testament*. Edited by G. K. Beale and D. A. Carson. Grand Rapids: Baker Academic, 2007.

———. *John*. BECNT. Grand Rapids: Baker Academic, 2004.

Kraus, Hans-Joachim. *Psalms 1–59*. CC. Minneapolis: Fortress, 1993.

———. *Psalms 60–150*. CC. Translated by Hilton C. Oswald. Minneapolis: Fortress, 1983.

———. *Theology of Psalms*. CC. Minneapolis: Fortress, 1992.

Kugel, James L. *The Idea of Biblical Poetry: Parallelism and Its History*. Baltimore: Johns Hopkins University Press, 1981.

Kuntz, J. Kenneth. "Continuing the Engagement: Psalms Research Since the Early 1990s." *CurBR* 10 (2012): 321–78.

Kvalbein, Hans. "Poor/Poverty." Page 688 in *New Dictionary of Biblical Theology*. Edited by B. Rosner et al. Downers Grove, IL: IVP Academic, 2000.

Lanahan, William F. "The Speaking Voice in the Book of Lamentations." *JBL* 93 (1974): 41.

Leiman, Sid Z. *The Canonization of Hebrew Scripture: The Talmudic and Midrashic Evidence*. Transactions of the Connecticut Academy of Arts and Sciences 47. Hamden, CT: Archon, 1976.

Leithart, Peter J. *From Silence to Song: The Davidic Liturgical Revolution*. Moscow, ID: Canon, 2003.

———. *1 & 2 Chronicles*. Brazos Theological Commentary on the Bible. Grand Rapids: Brazos, 2019.

Leupold, H. C. *Exposition of the Psalms*. Columbus, OH: Wartburg, 1959.

Levenson, Jon D. *Creation and the Persistence of Evil: The Jewish Drama of Divine Omnipotence*. San Francisco: Harper & Row, 1988.

———. *Resurrection and the Restoration of Israel*. New Haven: Yale University Press, 2006.

Lewis, S., and M. Maslin. "Defining the Anthropocene." *Nature* 519 (2015): 171–80.

Limburg, James. *Psalms*. Westminster Bible Companion. Louisville: Westminster John Knox, 2000.

Loewenich, Walther von. *Luther's Theology of the Cross*. Minneapolis: Augsburg, 1976.

Lohfink, Norbert, and Erich Zenger. *The God of Israel and the Nations: Studies in Isaiah and the Psalms*. Translated by Everett Kalin. Collegeville, MN: Liturgical Press, 2000.

Longacre, Drew. "The 11Q5 Psalter as a Scribal Project: Standing at the Nexus of Textual Development, Editorial Processes, and Manuscript Production." ZAW 134 (2022): 1–27.

Longman III, Tremper. *Psalms*. TOTC. Downers Grove, IL: IVP Academic, 2014.

———. "The Messiah: Explorations in the Law and the Writings," Pages 23–24 in *The Messiah in the Old and New Testaments*. Edited by S. E. Porter. Grand Rapids: Eerdmans, 2007.

Longman III, Tremper, and Daniel Reid. *God Is a Warrior*. Grand Rapids: Zondervan, 1995.

Lowth, Robert, George Gregory, and Johann David Michaelis. *Lectures on the Sacred Poetry of the Hebrews*. London: Thomas Tegg, 1835.

Lowth, Robert. *Isaiah: A New Translation*. 1778; Repr., London: Routledge/ Thoemmes, 1995.

Lunn, Nicholas P. *Word-Order Variation in Biblical Hebrew Poetry: Differentiating Pragmatics and Poetics*. Paternoster Biblical Monographs. Eugene, OR: Wipf & Stock, 2006.

MacDonald, George. *Paul Faber, Surgeon*, ch. 7 (1900; repr., Project Gutenberg, 2004), https://www.gutenberg.org/ebooks/12387.

MacDonald, Nathan. *Not Bread Alone: The Uses of Food in the Old Testament*. Oxford: Oxford University Press, 2008.

———. *Deuteronomy and the Meaning of 'Monotheism'*. FAT 2/1. Tübingen: Mohr Siebeck, 2003.

Maier, Christl M. "Psalm 87 as a Reappraisal of the Zion Tradition and Its Reception in Galatians 4:26." *CBQ* 69.3 (2007): 473–86.

Mandolfo, Carleen. "Language of Lament in the Psalms." Page 114–30 in *The Oxford Handbook of the Psalms*. Edited by William P. Brown. Oxford: Oxford University Press, 2014.

Mann, Thomas W. *The Book of the Torah*. 2nd ed. Eugene, OR: Cascade Books, 2013.

Martens, Elmer A. "How Is the Christian to Construe Old Testament Law?" *BBR* 12 (2002): 206–9.

Marttila, Marko. *Collective Reinterpretation in the Psalms*. FAT 2/13. Tübingen: Mohr Siebeck, 2006.

Mathews, Josh. "Psalm 8: The Messianic Son of Adam." Page 508 in *The Moody Handbook of Messianic Prophecy*. Edited by Michael Rydelnik and Edwin Blum. Chicago: Moody, 2019.

Mathews, Kenneth A. *Genesis 11:27–50:26*. NAC 1B. Nashville: Broadman & Holman, 2005.

Mays, James L. *Psalms*. Interpretation. Louisville: Westminster John Knox, 1994.

———. *The Lord Reigns: A Theological Handbook to the Psalms*. Louisville: Westminster John Knox, 1994.

McCann Jr., J. Clinton. "Books I–III and the Editorial Purpose of the Psalter." Page 97 in *The Shape and Shaping of the Psalter*. Edited by J. C. McCann Jr., JSOTSup 159. Sheffield: JSOT Press, 1993.

———. ed., *The Shape and Shaping of the Psalter*. JSOTSup 159. Sheffield: JSOT Press, 1993.

———. "Reading from the Beginning (Again): The Shape of Book I of the Psalter." Pages 129–42 in *Diachronic and Synchronic*. Edited by Joel S. Burnett, W. H. Bellinger, and W. Dennis Tucker Jr. New York: T&T Clark, 2007.

———. "The Shape and Shaping of the Psalter: Psalms in their Literary Context." Pages 350–62 in *The Oxford Handbook of the Psalms*. Edited by William P. Brown. Oxford: Oxford University Press, 2014.

McClellan, Daniel. "The Gods-Complaint: Psalm 82 as a Psalm of Complaint." *JBL* 137 (2018): 833–51.

McConville, J. Gordon. *Being Human in God's World*. Grand Rapids: Baker Academic, 2016.

McKane, W. "Poison, Trial by Ordeal and the Cup of Wrath." *VT* 30 (1980): 474–92.

McKelvey, Michael G. *Moses, David and the High Kingship of Yahweh: A Canonical Study of Book IV of the Psalter*. Gorgias Biblical Studies 55. Piscataway, NJ: Gorgias, 2014.

———. "Review of David Willgren, *Like a Garden of Flowers*." *WTJ* 79 (2017): 161–63.

McKibben, Bill. *The Comforting Whirlwind: God, Job, and the Scale of Creation*. Cambridge, MA: Cowley Publications, 2005.

McKinion, Randall L. "Psalm 69: The Lament of the Messiah." Pages 591–603 in *The Moody Handbook of Messianic Prophecy: Studies and Expositions of the Messiah in the Old Testament*. Edited by Michael Rydelnik and Edwin Blum. Chicago: Moody, 2019.

Meynet, Roland. *Le Psautier. Cinquième Livre (Ps 107–150)*. Rhetorica Biblica et Semitica 12. Leuven: Peeters, 2017.

———. *Le Psautier. Premier Livre (Ps 1–41)*. Rhetorica Biblica et Semitica 16. Leuven: Peeters, 2018.

———. *Le Psautier. Quatrième Livre (Ps 90–106)*. Rhetorica Biblica et Semitica 23. Leuven: Peeters, 2020.

———. *Le Psautier. Troisième Livre (Ps 73–89)*. Rhetorica Biblica et Semitica 19. Leuven: Peeters, 2019.

———. *Treatise on Biblical Rhetoric*. International Studies in the History of Rhetoric 3. Leiden: Brill, 2012.

Milgrom, Jacob. "The Cultic שגגה and Its Influence in Psalms and Job." *JQR* 58 (1967): 115–125.

Millard, Matthias. *Die Komposition des Psalters. Ein formgeschichtlicher Ansatz*. FAT 9. Tübingen: Mohr Siebeck, 1994.

Miller, Charles William. "Poetry and Personae: The Use and Function of Changing Speaking Voices in the Book of Lamentations." PhD diss., University of Denver Iliff School of Theology, 1996.

Miller, Patrick D. "The Beginning of the Psalter." Pages 83–92 in *Shape and Shaping of the Psalter*. Edited by J. C. McCann Jr. JSOTSup 159. Sheffield: Sheffield Academic, 1993.

———. "The Psalter as a Book of Theology." Pages 87–98 in *Psalms in Community: Jewish and Christian Textual, Liturgical, and Artistic Traditions*. Edited by Harold Attridge and Margot Fassler Atlanta: Society of Biblical Literature, 2003.

———. "The Psalms as a Meditation on the First Commandment." Page 101 in *The Way of the Lord: Essays in Old Testament Theology*. Grand Rapids: Eerdmans, 2004.

———. "The Ruler of Zion and the Hope of the Poor: Psalms 9–10 in the Context of the Psalter." Pages 170–71 in *The Way Of The Lord: Essays In Old Testament Theology*. Tübingen: Mohr Siebeck, 2004.

Mitchell, David C. "Lord, Remember David: G. H. Wilson and the Message of the Psalter." *VT* 56.4 (2006): 526–48.

———. *Messiah ben Joseph*. Newton Mearns: Campbell, 2016.

———. *The Message of the Psalter: An Eschatological Programme in the Books of Psalms*. JSOTSup 252. Sheffield, England: Sheffield Academic, 1997.

Moberly, R. W. L. *Old Testament Theology: Reading the Hebrew Bible as Christian Scripture*. Grand Rapids: Baker Academic, 2013.

Moltmann, Jürgen. *The Crucified God*. 4th ed. Minneapolis: Fortress, 2015

Mowinckel, Sigmund. *The Psalms in Israel's Worship*. Vol. 1. Translated by D. R. Ap-Thomas. Nashville: Abingdon, 1962.

Mroczek, Eva. *The Literary Imagination in Jewish Antiquity*. Oxford: Oxford University Press, 2016.

Mullen Jr., E. T. *The Assembly of the Gods: The Divine Council in Canaanite and Early Hebrew Literature*. HSM 24. Chico, CA: Scholars, 1980.

Murphy, Roland E. "Reflections on Canonical Interpretation of the Psalms." Pages 21–28 in *Shape and Shaping of the Psalter*. Edited by J. C. McCann Jr., JSOTSup 159. Sheffield: JSOT Press, 1993

Nasuti, Harry P. *Defining the Sacred Songs: Genre, Tradition and the Post-Critical Interpretation of the Psalms*. Sheffield: Sheffield Academic, 1999.

Nicole, Emile. "בחר," *NIDOTTE* 1:638–42.

Noonan, Benjamin J. "Review of David Willgren, *Like a Garden of Flowers*," *BBR* 27 (2017): 253–55.

O'Connor, Kathleen M. *Lamentations and the Tears of the World*. Maryknoll, NY: Orbis, 2002.

O'Connor, Michael. *Hebrew Verse Structure*. Winona Lake, IN: Eisenbrauns, 1980.

Pajunen, Mika. "Perspectives on the Existence of a Particular Authoritative Book of Psalms in the Late Second Temple Period." *JSOT* 39 (2014): 139-63.

———. "Textual Plurality of Scripture in the Dead Sea Scrolls and Theories of Textual Transmission." *Biblische Notizen* 186 (2020): 7–28.

———. "Glocal, Local, or Group Specific? Origins of Some Particular Scribal and Interpretive Practices in the Qumran Scrolls," *Scriptures in the Making: Texts and Their Transmission in Late Second Temple Judaism*. Edited by Raimo Hakola, Jessi Orpana, Paavo Huotari. Contributions to Biblical Exegesis & Theology 109 (2022): 33–56.

Parker, Simon B. "Sons of (the) God(s)." Pages 794–800 in *DDD*. Edited by Karel van der Toorn, Bob Becking, and Pieter W. van der Horst. 2nd ed. Grand Rapids: Eerdmans, 1999.

Pavan, Marco. "Review of David Willgren, *Like a Garden of Flowers*." *Biblica* 99 (2018), 124–27.

———. The Psalter as a Book? A Critical Evaluation of the Recent Research on the Psalter." Pages 11–82 in *The Formation of the Hebrew Psalter: The Book of Psalms between Ancient Versions, Material Transmission and Canonical Exegesis*. Edited by Marco Pavan, Gianni Barbiero, and Johannes Schnocks. FAT I 151. Tübingen, Germany: Mohr Siebeck, 2021.

Pedersen, J. *Israel: Its Life and Culture I-II*. London: Oxford University Press, 1926.

Pietersma, Albert. *A New English Translation of the Septuagint*. Oxford: Oxford University Press, 2000.

Pope Francis. *Laudato Si': On Care for Our Common Home*. Vatican City: Libreria Editrice Vaticana, 2015.

Postell, Seth D. *Adam as Israel: Genesis 1–3 as the Introduction to the Torah and the Tanakh*. Eugene, OR: Pickwick, 2011.

———. "A Literary, Compositional, and Intertextual Analysis of Psalm 45." *Bibliotheca Sacra* 176 (2019): 146–64.

———. "Messianism in the Psalms." Pages 457–75 in *The Moody Handbook of Messianic Prophecy: Studies of the Messiah in the Old Testament*. Edited by Michael Rydelnik and Edwin Blum. Chicago: Moody, 2019.

———. "Psalm 16: The Resurrected Messiah." Pages 513–27 in *The Moody Handbook of Messianic Prophecy: Studies of the Messiah in the Old Testament*. Edited by Michael Rydelnik and Edwin Blum. Chicago: Moody, 2019.

Prinsloo, Gert T. M. "Reading the Masoretic Psalter as a Book: Editorial Trends and Redactional Trajectories." *CurBR* 19 (2021): 145–77.

Prinsloo, W. S. "Psalm 82: Once Again, Gods or Men?" *Biblica* 76 (1995): 219–28.

———. "Psalm 88: The Gloomiest Psalm?" *OTE* 5 (1992): 322–45.
Provan, Iain W. "Past, Present and Future in Lamentations III 52–66: The Case for a Precative Perfect Re-Examined." *VT* 41, 2 (1991): 164–75.
Quinn Richards, Carissa M. "The King and the Kingdom: The Message of Psalms 15–24." PhD diss., Golden Gate Baptist Theological Seminary, 2015. Forthcoming, Lexham Academic.
Rendtorff, Rolf. "The Psalms of David: David in the Psalms." Pages 53–64 in *The Book of Psalms: Composition and Reception*. Edited by Peter W. Flint and Patrick D. Miller Jr. Leiden: Brill, 2005.
Renkema, Johan. *Lamentations*. Historical Commentary on the Old Testament. Leuven: Peeters, 1998.
Richards, E. "Voice." Pages 1525–27 in *The Princeton Encyclopedia of Poetry and Poetics*. Edited by Roland Greene. 4th ed. Princeton: Princeton University, 2012.
Ridderbos, Herman. *The Gospel of John: A Theological Commentary*. Grand Rapids: Eerdmans, 1997.
Roberts, Alexander, James Donaldson, and A. Cleveland Coxe. eds., *ANF* Vol. 5. New York: Scribner's Sons, 1919.
Robertson, O. Palmer. *The Flow of the Psalms: Discovering Their Structure and Theology*. Phillipsburg, NJ: P&R, 2015.
Rogers, Carl R. *On Becoming a Person: A Therapist's View of Psychotherapy*. Boston: Houghton Mifflin, 1961.
Rohde, Michael. "Observations on the Songs of Ascents: A Discussion about the So-Called Zion-Theology of Psalms 120–134." *Baptistic Theologies* 1.2 (2009): 24–42.
Root, Andrew. *Christopraxis: A Practical Theology of the Cross*. Minneapolis: Fortress, 2014.
Rosner, Brian S. "Biblical Theology." Pages 3–11 in *New Dictionary of Biblical Theology*. Downers Grove, IL: IVP Academic, 2000.
Ross, Allen P. *A Commentary on the Psalms: Volume 1 (1–41)*. Kregel Exegetical Library. Grand Rapids: Kregel Academic & Professional, 2011.
———. *A Commentary on the Psalms: Volume 2 (42–89)*. Kregel Exegetical Library. Grand Rapids: Kregel Academic, 2013.
———. *A Commentary on the Psalms: Volume 3 (90–150)*. Kregel Exegetical Library. Grand Rapids: Kregel Academic, 2016.
Routledge, Robin. *Old Testament Theology: A Thematic Approach*. Downers Grove, IL: IVP Academic, 2008.
Rydelnik, Michael A. "Psalm 110: The Messiah as Eternal King Priest." Page 678 in *The Moody Handbook of Messianic Prophecy: Studies and Expositions of the Messiah in the Old Testament*. Edited by Michael Rydelnik and Edwim Blum. Chicago: Moody, 2019.
Rydelnik, Michael and Edwin Blum, eds., *The Moody Handbook of Messianic Prophecy: Studies and Expositions of the Messiah in the Old Testament*. Chicago: Moody, 2019.

Ryken, Leland. "Metaphor in the Psalms." *ChrLit* 31 (1983): 9–30.
Sanders, James A. *The Dead Sea Psalms Scroll*. Ithaca. NY: Cornell University Press, 1967.
Santos, Narry F. "The Paradox of Authority and Servanthood in the Gospel of Mark." *Bibliotheca Sacra* 154 (1997): 452–60.
Santrac, Dragoslava. *Sanctuary Cult in Relation to Religious Piety in the Book of Psalms*. Lambert Academic Publishing, 2013.
———. "The Psalmists' Journey and the Sanctuary: A Study in the Sanctuary and the Shape of the Book of Psalms." *Journal of the Adventist Theologic* 25/1 (2014): 23–42.
Sarna, Nahum M. *The JPS Torah Commentary: Exodus*. Philadelphia: Jewish Publication Society of America, 1991.
Sawyer, D. *Midrash Aleph Beth*. Atlanta: Scholars Press, 1993.
Sawyer, J. F. A. "Hebrew Words for the Resurrection of the Dead." *VT* 23 (1973): 232.
Schaefer, Konrad. *Psalms*. Berit Olam. Collegeville, MN: Liturgical Press, 2001.
Schaper, Joachim. *Eschatology in the Greek Psalter*. WUNT 2. Tübingen: Mohr Siebeck, 1994.
Schlimm, Matthew R. "The Paradoxes of Fear in the Hebrew Bible." *SEÅ* 84 (2019): 25–50.
Schnabel, Eckhard. "Israel, the People of God, and the Nations." *JETS* 45 (2002): 35–57.
Schreiner, Thomas R. *Paul, Apostle of God's Glory in Christ: A Pauline Theology*. 2nd ed. Downers Grove, IL: InterVarsity, 2020.
Schwáb, Zoltán. "I, the Fool: A 'Canonical' Reading of Proverbs 26:4–5." *Journal of Theological Interpretation* 10 (2016): 31–50.
Scobie, Charles "Israel and the Nations: An Essay in Biblical Theology." *TynBul* 43 (1992): 283–305.
Selman, Martin J. *1 Chronicles: An Introduction and Commentary*. TOTC 10a. Downers Grove, IL: InterVarsity, 1994.
Seybold, Klaus. "The Psalter as a Book." Pages 168–81 in *Jewish and Christian Approaches to the Psalms: Conflict and Convergence*. Edited by Susan Gillingham. Oxford: Oxford University Press, 2013.
Shepherd, Jerry Eugene. "The Book of Psalms as the Book of Christ: The Application of the Christo-Canonical Method to the Book of Psalms." PhD diss., Westminster Theological Seminary, 1995.
Skinner, Jerome L. "The Historical Superscriptions of Davidic Psalms: An Exegetical, Intertextual, and Methodological Analysis." PhD diss., Andrews University Seventh-Day Adventist Theological Seminary, 2016.
Smith, J. *Dust or Dew*. Cambridge: James Clarke and Co, 2012.
Smith, Mark S. "The Structure of Psalm LXXXVII." *VT* 38.3 (1988): 357–58.
Stephen J. Smith, *The Conflict between Faith and Experience, and the Shape of Psalms 73–83*, LHBOTS 723 (London: T&T Clark, 2022).
———. "The Shape and Message of Psalms 73–78." *CBQ* 83 (2021): 20–39.
Snearly, Michael K. "The Return of the King: An Editorial-Critical Analysis of Psalms 107–150." PhD diss., Golden Gate Baptist Theological Seminary, 2012.

——. "The Return of the King: Book V as a Witness to Messianic Hope in the Psalter." Pages 209–17 in *The Psalms: Language for All Seasons of the Soul*. Edited by Andrew J. Schmutzer and David M. Howard Jr. Chicago: Moody, 2013.

——. *The Return of the King: Messianic Expectation in Book V of the Psalter*. LHBOTS 624. New York: T&T Clark, 2016.

Soll, Will. *Psalm 119: Matrix, Form, and Setting*. CBQ Monograph 23. Washington: Catholic Bible Association of America, 1991.

Stadelmann, Andreas. "Psalm 87(86): Theologischer Gehalt und gesellschaftliche Wirkung." Pages 333–56 in *Ein Gott, eine Offenbarung: Beiträge zur biblischen Exegese, Theologie und Spiritualität*. Edited by Friedrich V. Reiterer. Würzburg: Echter Verlag, 1991.

Stead, Michael R. "Suffering Servant, Suffering David, and Stricken Shepherd." Pages 59–79 in *Christ Died for our Sins: Essays on the Atonement*. Edited by Michael R. Stead. Barton, ACT: Barton Books, 2013.

Stec, D. M. *The Targum of Psalms*. London: T&T Clark, 2004.

Stendahl, Krister. "The Apostle Paul and the Introspective Conscience of the West." *HTR* 56 (1963): 199–215.

Stuart, Douglas K. *Exodus*. NAC 2. Nashville: Broadman & Holman, 2006.

Swanson, James A. *Dictionary of Biblical Languages with Semantic Domains: Hebrew (Old Testament Dictionary of Classical Hebrew)*. Oak Harbor, WA: Faithlife, 1997.

Sweeney, Marvin A. *Tanak: A Theological and Critical Introduction to the Jewish Bible*. Minneapolis: Fortress, 2012.

——. "Form and Eschatology in the Book of the Twelve Prophets." Page 160 in *The Book of Twelve & The New Form Criticism*. Edited by Mark J. Boda et al., ANEM 10. Atlanta: Society of Biblical Literature, 2015.

Tanner, Beth. "Preaching the Penitential Psalms." *Word & World* 27 (2007): 88–98.

Tate Marvin E. *Psalms 51–100*. WBC 20. Dallas: Word, 1990.

——. "Rethinking the Nature of the Psalter." Pages 438–72 in P. C. Craigie, *Psalms 1-50*. WBC 19. Revised edition. Nashville: Nelson, 2004.

Terrien, Samuel. *The Elusive Presence: Toward a New Biblical Theology*. Religious Perspectives 26. San Francisco: Harper & Row, 1978.

——. *The Psalms: Strophic Structure and Theological Commentary*. ECC. Grand Rapids: Eerdmans, 2003.

Thompson, Deanna. *Crossing the Divide: Luther, Feminism, and the Cross*. Minneapolis: Fortress, 2004.

Todd III, James M. *Remember, O Yahweh: The Poetry and Context of Psalms 135–137*. Eugene, OR: Wipf & Stock, 2015.

Tomes, Roger. *"I Have Written to the King, My Lord": Secular Analogies for the Psalms*. HBM 1. Sheffield: Sheffield Phoenix, 2006.

Tromp, N. J. *Primitive Conceptions of Death and the Nether World in the Old Testament*. Rome: Pontifical Biblical Institute, 1969.

Tsevat, Matitiahu. "God and the Gods in Assembly." *HUCA* 40 (1969): 123–37.

Tucker Jr, W. Dennis. *Constructing and Deconstructing Power in Psalms 107–150*. Atlanta: Society of Biblical Literature, 2014.

Tucker Jr., W. Dennis, and Jamie A. Grant. *Psalms, Volume 2*. NIVAC. Grand Rapids: Zondervan, 2018.

Ulrich, Eugene. *The Dead Sea Scrolls and the Developmental Composition of the Bible*. VTSup 169. Leiden: Brill, 2015.

Vaillancourt, Ian J. "Formed in the Crucible of Messianic Angst: The Eschatological Shape of the Hebrew Psalter's Final Form." *Scottish Bulletin of Evangelical Theology* 31 (2013): 127–44.

———. *The Multifaceted Saviour of Psalms 110 and 118: A Canonical Exegesis*. HBM 86. Sheffield: Sheffield Phoenix, 2019.

VanGemeren, Willem A., ed. *NIDOTTE*. 5 vols. Grand Rapids: Zondervan, 1997.

———. "Mountain Imagery." Pages 481–83 in *Dictionary of the Old Testament Wisdom, Poetry, and Writings*. Edited by Tremper Longman III and Peter Enns. Downers Grove, IL: IVP Academic, 2008.

———. "Psalms." *The Expositor's Bible Commmentary*. Edited by Frank E. Gaebelein. Grand Rapids: Zondervan, 1991.

Villanueva, Federico. *Psalms 1–72: A Pastoral and Contextual Commentary*. Asia Bible Commentary Series. Carlisle: Langham Global Library, 2016.

Volf, Miroslav. *Exclusion and Embrace: A Theological Exploration of Identity, Otherness, and Reconciliation*. Nashville: Abingdon, 1996.

Von Rad, Gerhard. *Old Testament Theology, Vol. 2*. Translated by D. M. G. Stalker. New York: Oliver & Boyd, 1965.

Vos, Geerhardus. *Biblical Theology: Old and New Testaments*. London: Banner of Truth, 1975.

Walck, L. W. *The Son of Man in the Parables of Enoch and Matthew*. London: T&T Clark, 2011.

Walker, Alice. *In Search of Our Mothers' Gardens: Womanist Prose*. London: Phoenix, 2000.

Wallace, Howard N. *Psalms*. Readings: A New Biblical Commentary. Sheffield: Sheffield Phoenix, 2009.

Wallace, Robert E. "Gerald Wilson and the Characterization of David in Book 5 of the Psalter." Pages 193–208 in *The Shape and Shaping of the Book of Psalms: The Current State of Scholarship*. Edited by Nancy deClaisse-Walford. Atlanta: Society of Biblical Literature, 2014.

———. *The Narrative Effect of Book IV of the Hebrew Psalter*. StBibLit 112. New York: Lang, 2007.

———. "The Psalms as a Place to Begin for Old Testament Theology." *PRSt* 44 (2017), 239–48.

Waltke, Bruce K. "A Canonical Process Approach to the Psalms." Pages 3–18 in *Tradition and Testament*. Edited by. J. S. and P. D. Feinberg. Chicago: Moody, 1981.

———. "Atonement in Psalm 51." Pages 51–60 in *The Glory of the Atonement: Biblical, Theological & Practical Perspectives: Essays in Honor of Roger Cole*. Edited by Charles E. Hill and Frank A. James III. Downers Grove, IL: IVP Academic, 2004.

———. *Old Testament Theology: An Exegetical, Canonical, and Thematic Approach*. Grand Rapids: Zondervan, 2007.

Waltke, Bruce K, and Cathi J. Fredricks. *Genesis: A Commentary*. Grand Rapids: Zondervan, 2001.

Walton, John. *Old Testament Theology for Christians: From Ancient Context to Enduring Belief*. Downers Grove, IL: IVP Academic, 2017.

———. "Psalms: A Cantata about the Davidic Covenant." *JETS* 34 (1991): 21–23.

Watson, Wilfred G. E. *Classical Hebrew Poetry: A Guide to Its Techniques*. JSOTSup 26. Sheffield: JSOT Press, 1984.

Watts, James W. "Psalm 2 in the Context of Biblical Theology." *HBT* 12 (1990): 73.

Weber, Beat. "BiblioPss1990ff.: Bibliography of Psalms and the Psalter since 1990," Update 57 (II.2021): 272, https://www.academia.edu/5910732/BiblioPss1990ff_Bibliography_of_Psalms_and_the_Psalter_since_1990.

Weiser, Artur. *The Psalms: A Commentary*. OTL. 3rd. ed. Translated by H. Hartwell. Philadelphia: Westminster, 1962.

Wendland, Ernst R. *Discourse Perspectives on Hebrew Poetry in the Scriptures*. New York: United Bible Societies, 1994.

Wenham, Gordon J. *Psalms as Torah: Reading Biblical Song Ethically*. Grand Rapids: Baker Academic, 2012.

———. "Sanctuary Symbolism in the Garden of Eden Story." *WCJS* 9A (1985): 19–25.

———. *The Psalter Reclaimed: Praying and Praising with the Psalms*. Wheaton, IL: Crossway, 2012.

Wenkel, David H. "The Paradox of High Christology in Hebrews 1." *Bib* 99 (2018): 431–46.

Westermann, Claus. *Handbook to the Old Testament*. Translated by Robert H. Boyd. Minneapolis: Augsburg, 1967.

———. *Lamentations: Issues and Interpretation*. Minneapolis: Fortress, 1994.

———. *Praise and Lament in the Psalms*. Translated by Keith R. Crim and Richard N. Soulen. Atlanta: John Knox, 1981.

Wevers, John W. *Notes on the Greek Text of Deuteronomy*. SCS 39. Atlanta, GA: Scholars Press, 1995.

Whybray, Norman. *Reading the Psalms as a Book*. JSOTSup 223. Sheffield: Sheffield Academic, 1996.

Wifall, Walter. "Gen 3:15—A Protevangelium?" *CBQ* 36 (1974): 361–65.

Wilks, John G. F. "The Suffering Servant and Personhood." *The Evangelical Quarterly* 77 (2005): 195–210.

Willgren, David. *Like a Garden of Flowers: A Study of the Formation of the "Book" of Psalms*. Lund: Lund University, 2016.

———. *The Formation of the "Book" of Psalms: Reconsidering the Transmission and Canonization of Psalmody in Light of Material Culture and the Poetics of Anthologies*. FAT 88. Tübingen: Mohr Siebeck, 2016.

———. "A Teleological Fallacy in Psalms Studies? Decentralizing the 'Masoretic' Psalms Sequence in the Formation of the 'Book' of Psalms." Pages 330–50 in *Quellen und Intertextualität. Methodische Überlegungen zum Psalterende*. Edited by A. Brodersen, F. Neumann, and D. Willgren. Vol. 10 of *Intertextualität und die Entstehung des Psalters*. Edited by A. Brodersen, N. Friederike, and D. Willgren. FAT II/114. Tübingen: Mohr Siebeck, 2020.

Williams, Ronald J. *Williams' Hebrew Syntax*. 3rd ed. Revised and Expanded by John C. Beckman. Toronto: University of Toronto, 2007.

Williamson, H. G. M. "Reading the Lament Psalms Backwards." Pages in *A God So Near*. Edited by B. A. Strawn and N. R. Bowen. Winona Lake, IN: Eisenbrauns, 2003.

Willis, John T. "Psalm 1—An Entity." *ZAW* 91 (1979): 381–401.

———. "QÛMĀH YHWH." *JNSL* 16 (1990): 220.

Wilson, E. O. *The Creation, An Appeal to Save Life on Earth*. New York: Norton, 2006.

Wilson, Gerald H. "King, Messiah, and the Reign of God: Revisiting the Royal Psalms and the Shape of the Psalter." Pages 391–406 in *The Book of Psalms: Composition and Reception*. Edited by Peter Flint and Patrick Miller. VTSup 99. Leiden: Brill, 2005.

———. *Psalms Volume* 1. NIVAC. Grand Rapids: Zondervan Academic, 2002.

———. "Shaping the Psalter: A Consideration of Editorial Linkage in the Book of Psalms." Pages 72–92 in *Shape and Shaping of the Psalter*. Edited by J. C. McCann Jr., JSOTSup159. Sheffield: Sheffield Academic, 1993.

———. *The Editing of the Hebrew Psalter*. SBLDS 76. Chico, CA: Scholars Press, 1985.

———. "Qumran Psalms Scroll (11QPs[a]) and the Canonical Psalter: Comparison of Editorial Shaping." *CBQ* 59 (1997): 448–64.

———. "The Structure of the Psalter." Pages 229–46 in *Interpreting the Psalms*. Edited by David Firth and Philip Johnston. Downers Grove, IL: InterVarsity, 2005.

———. "The Use of Royal Psalms at the 'Seams' of the Hebrew Psalter." *JSOT* 35 (1986): 85–94.

Witt, Andrew Carl. *A Voice without End: The Role of David in Psalms 3–14*. Journal of Theological Interpretation Supplements 20. University Park, PA: Eisenbrauns, 2021.

Wittman, Derek E. "Let Us Cast Off Their Ropes from Us: The Editorial Significance of the Portrayal of Foreign Nations in Psalms 2 and 149." Page 56 in *The Shape and Shaping of the Book of Psalms: The Current State of Scholarship*. Edited by Nancy L. deClaissé-Walford. Atlanta: Society of Biblical Literature, 2014.

Wright, Christopher J. H. *The Mission of God: Unlocking the Bible's Grand Narrative*. Nottingham: Apollos, 2006.

Wu, Dan. "The Role of Lament in the Shape of the Psalter." Pages 133–47 in *Finding Lost Words: The Church's Right to Lament*. Edited by G. Geoffrey Harper and Kit Barker. Australian College of Theology Monograph Series. Eugene, OR: Wipf and Stock, 2017.

Yarchin, William. "Is There an Authoritative Shape for the Hebrew Book of Psalms? Profiling the Manuscripts of the Hebrew Psalter." *RB* 122 (2015): 355–70.

———. "Were the Psalms Collections at Qumran True Psalters?" *JBL* 134.4 (2015): 775–89.

———. "Why the Future of Canonical Hebrew Psalter Exegesis Includes Abandoning Its Own Premise." Pages 119–38 in *The Formation of the Hebrew Psalter. The Book of Psalms between Ancient Versions, Material Transmission and Canonical Exegesis*. Edited by Gianni Barbiero, Marco Pavan, and Johannes Schnocks. FAT. Tübingen: Mohr Siebeck, Mohr Siebeck, 2021.

Yeong Seon Kim. *The Temple Administration and the Levites in Chronicles*. CBQMS 51. Washington, DC: Catholic Biblical Association of America, 2014.

Zenger, Erich, "Der Psalter als Buch: Beobachtungen zu seiner Enstehung, Komposition und Funktion." Pages 1–57 in *Der Psalter in Judentum und Christentum*. Edited by Erich Zenger. Herders Biblische Studien 18. Freiburg: Herder, 1998.

———. "New Approaches to the Study of the Psalter." *Proceedings of the Irish Biblical Association* 17 (1994): 37–54.

———. "The Composition and Theology of the Fifth Book of Psalms 107–145." *JSOT* 80 (1998): 77–102.

———, ed. "Psalmenexegese und Psalterexegese: Eine Forschungsskizze." Pages 17–65 in *The Composition of the Book of Psalms*. Bibliotheca, Ephemeridum Theologicarum Louvaniensium 238. Leuven: Peeters, 2010.

———. *The Composition of the Book of Psalms*. Bibliotheca, Ephemeridum Theologicarum Louvaniensium 238. Leuven: Peeters, 2010.

Zernecke, Anna Elise. "Mesopotamian Parallels to the Psalms." Pages 27–42 in *The Oxford Handbook of the Psalms*. Edited by William Brown. New York: Oxford University Press, 2014.

Index of Subjects and Authors

Index of Scripture & Other Ancient Literature

Old Testament

Genesis

Ancient Jewish Literature